and

Passing Frenzies

Also by Francis Wheen

Karl Marx
Tom Driberg: His Life and Indiscretions

Hoo-Hahs
and
Passing Frenzies

COLLECTED JOURNALISM
1991–2001

FRANCIS WHEEN

ATLANTIC BOOKS
LONDON

First published in 2002 by Atlantic Books, on behalf of Guardian Newspapers Ltd.
Atlantic Books is an imprint of Grove Atlantic Ltd.

10 9 8 7 6 5 4 3 2 1

A CIP catalogue record for this book is available from the British Library

ISBN 1 903809 42 8

Printed in Great Britain by CPD, Ebbw Vale, Wales
Design by Geoff Green Book Design

Grove Atlantic Ltd
29 Adam & Eve Mews
London W8 6UG

To Michael Foot, with affection and gratitude

Contents

Introduction

MY CAREER IN FLEET STREET began inauspiciously: the very first feature I wrote for the *Guardian*, more than a quarter of a century ago, elicited a libel writ. A blizzard of writs, in fact, and all from the same person. By reporting that he had a dozen ballpoint pens in his breast pocket, I had allegedly implied that he was some kind of nutter. After many months of legal arm-wrestling we had him struck off as a 'wilful and vexatious litigant' – or, in plain English, a nutter.

Rather to my surprise, a couple of million words later, I have still not been taken to court for any of my articles in the national press. There have been threats, of course, including a hilariously angry letter from a Cabinet minister in John Major's government who warned that if I didn't apologize by noon the same day there would be a full-scale legal bombardment. The *Guardian* told him to shove the letter up his bum (or politer words to that effect), and he duly did. On another occasion the late Robert Maxwell went on a TV chat show to announce, 'My lawyers have told me that I would win a million pounds in damages from Mr Wheen for what he has said about me – but I don't need a million pounds.' True, up to a point; he needed far more than that, as the world learned soon after his death.

One reason for my success in seeing off potential litigants is that I don't like to go into print without checking my facts. This isn't meant as a boast; I'm sure minor errors creep in occasionally. It is merely a reflection of my old-fashioned belief that journalism involves telling people things they couldn't have found out for themselves – and that readers should be able to trust the essential accuracy of what I report. In the words of the nineteenth-century *Times* editor John Thaddeus Delane: 'The business of the press is disclosure.'

This is not the attitude of the man who now owns Delane's old paper, Rupert Murdoch. When *The Sunday Times* published Adolf Hitler's 'secret diaries' without bothering to ascertain if they were genuine or not, Murdoch appeared sublimely untroubled by this dereliction of journalistic duty. All that mattered to him was that the sales of the paper had gone up. 'After all,' he said, 'we are in the entertainment business.'

He certainly is, as the man who brought us *Home Alone* and presides over the Fox TV network. And, thanks in part to Rupert's corrupting influence, the getting and giving of information now seem to be a minor function of the press, as newspapers become 'lifestyle packages' stuffed with It girls and solipsists who witter on profitably about their love lives or their shopping habits. For many decades, thoughtful hacks have argued about whether journalism is a profession or a trade; in normal parlance, however, the opposite of 'professional' is 'amateur', and this is more in line with what is happening today – the notion that anyone can 'do' journalism. It's a revival, in some ways, of the old credo of the Victorian ruling class. Just as a degree in Greats at Oxford used to be thought more than adequate as a qualification for running Whitehall or a large corporation, so now there is a growing belief that anyone who can surf the Internet is a 'journalist' since the information is all out there and freely available. When the latest proprietor of the *Daily Express*, Richard Desmond, was told that he needed to hire somebody to replace the departing health correspondent, he replied dismissively: 'Can't we get all that stuff off the Web?'

No we can't. Long before the Internet had been invented, the legendary muckraking reporter Claud Cockburn explained why. To hear people talking about facts, he said, you would think that they lay about like pieces of gold ore in the Yukon days waiting to be picked up – arduously, it is true, but still definitely and visibly – by strenuous prospectors whose subsequent problem was only to get them to market.

> Such a view is evidently and dangerously naive. There are no such facts. Or if there are, they are meaningless and entirely ineffective; they might, in fact, just as well not be lying about at all until the prospector – the journalist – puts them into relation with other facts: presents them in other words. Then they become as much a part of a pattern created by him as if he were writing a novel. In that sense all stories are written backwards – they are supposed to begin with the facts and develop from there, but in reality they begin with a journalist's point of view, a conception...All this is difficult and even rather unwholesome to explain to the layman, because he gets the impression that you are saying that truth does not matter and that you are publicly admitting what he long ago suspected, that journalism is a way of 'cooking' the facts. Really cunning journalists, realising this, and anxious to raise the status of journalism in the esteem of the general public, positively encourage the layman in his mistaken views. They like him to have the picture of these nuggety facts lying about on maybe frozen ground, and a lot of noble and utterly unprejudiced journalists with no idea

whatever of what they are looking for scrabbling in the iron-bound earth and presently bringing home the pure gold of Truth.

Unimprovably put; and it may explain the curious paradox that, although we live in 'the Information Age', the status of the reporter – as against the lifestyle gusher, or the sad sap who rewrites PR handouts about minor pop stars for a showbiz column – has been dangerously downgraded. In the words of Ian Jack, a distinguished former editor of the *Independent on Sunday*, 'Britain has developed a singular sort of media culture which places a high premium on excitement, controversy and sentimentality, in which information takes second place to the opinions it arouses.' Nothing wrong with opinions, of course; you'll find plenty of them in these pages. But they need some sort of anchorage in fact.

The Week magazine, a useful news digest, has a regular column headed: 'Boring but Important'. Although I admire the spirit, I do also recognize an imperative to make journalism readable – and, if possible, entertaining. However important the story, if it is presented in an indigestibly boring fashion, then the newspaper has failed in its duty. But a far greater dereliction of duty is the lack of any sense of history, and the swiftness with which newspapers lose interest in Last Week's Thing. During one of the early scandals to hit his government, Tony Blair dismissed all the fuss as 'a bit of a hoo-hah'. A couple of years later, still riding high in the opinion polls despite scandals galore, he observed, 'The daily headlines, the passing frenzies – and I have lost count of the number of times this or that week was supposed to be our toughest since taking over – all that comes and goes.'

Too true, alas. And politicians should be extremely grateful for it, since amnesia is the handmaiden of hypocrisy. When Margaret Thatcher raged indignantly against the Argentine invasion of the Falklands, scarcely anybody remembered – at least until the fighting was over – that two years earlier one of her favourite ministers, Nicholas Ridley, had proposed transferring sovereignty over the islands to Argentina. During her equally bellicose fulminations about Iraq's invasion of Kuwait, no one mentioned that her government had thitherto been arming and abetting Saddam Hussein; it was only six years later that the Scott Report pointed out what should have been noticed at the time.

'The more newspapers people read, the shorter grows their historical memory; yet most people read little else.' Thus began *The Long Weekend*, an account by Robert Graves and Alan Hodge of 'what took place, of a forgettable sort', between 1918 and 1939. Any 'sudden overwhelming public event', they argued, acts as a kind of sponge for all the events that preceded it, absorbing and concealing them. Without wishing to do down my own profession, I have to say that this seems even truer today than when it was published, in 1940. As we race down the fast lane of the information superhighway, events hurtle past at such a rate that we seldom glance at their bald tyres or stolen numberplates. Lacking historical perspective, we are in danger of knowing everything but learning nothing. Thanks to twenty-four-hour rolling news, some correspondents now deliver so many 'live updates' that they are too busy to get out and investigate what is actually happening, let alone provide any context or background.

A week is not only a long time in politics: it is the maximum attention span of sensation-hungry editors, which is why so many news items burn as brightly but as briefly as a catherine wheel on Guy Fawkes night. A typical 'passing frenzy' begins when a minister appears on David Frost's Sunday morning show and says something slightly out of sync with official policy. This duly gets splashed all over Monday's front pages, whereupon opposition MPs scamper round TV and radio studios making a hullabaloo, which in turn provides another day's headlines. By Tuesday, the Downing Street spin doctors are letting it be known that what was a pledge two days earlier is now nothing more than a vague aspiration. On Wednesday, the Tory and Labour leaders exchange pointless insults on the subject at Prime Minister's Questions, thus keeping the story alive for another day. At the weekend, Sunday papers weigh in with full-page 'news features' analysing the affair, under portentous headlines such as 'Crisis? What Crisis?' or 'Seven Days that Shook the Government'. Later that morning, another politician makes an unguarded comment on television and the whole merry-go-round starts again. What was the previous week's fuss about? No one knows or cares.

In the autumn of 1997, for instance, the media were in a state of hyperventilating excitement about an undeclared £1 million donation to the Labour Party from Bernie Ecclestone, the boss of Formula One motor-racing. Asked if Tony Blair had 'done the right thing' in returning Ecclestone's gift, William Hague answered with a simple 'yes'. No journalist thought to ask him why, in that case, he had still not repaid the £365,000 given to the Tories by a fugitive from justice, Asil Nadir. When I reminded one hack of this festering scandal at the time, he was disarmingly honest: 'Oh, I'd forgotten about that. But the Nadir story is pretty old potatoes now.'

So is the Ecclestone story, now. Before long, the hot potatoes of the last week or so will also have gone into the pigswill. Tony Blair, who poses as an agent of 'progress', suggests that only the 'forces of conservatism' care about these things, or even recall them, for more than a few days. But he is wrong. As George Santayana pointed out a century ago: 'Progress, far from consisting in change, depends on retentiveness. Those who cannot remember the past are condemned to fulfil it.' And what could be more conservative than that?

***

ONE OF THE PLEASURES of publishing this selection of essays and articles is that it gives me a chance to thank the editors who have been kind enough to publish my work over the years – particularly Bruce Page, Mark Boxer, Andreas Whittam Smith, Stephen Glover, Alexander Chancellor, Rebecca Nicolson, Auberon Waugh, Ian Hislop, Roger Alton, Ian Katz and Alan Rusbridger. Thanks, too, to Toby Mundy of Atlantic Books, who suggested the book, and to my literary agent Pat Kavanagh.

HAPPY, SHINY PEOPLE

The unspeakable in
pursuit of the unthinkable

I N J U N E 1990, the Governor of Minnesota hosted a lunch for President
Gorbachev. Also present was Robert Maxwell. Unwilling to miss any
opportunity to hog the limelight, Maxwell stood up at the end of the meal
and announced that he was donating $50 million of his own money to endow
a new think-tank in the city, the Gorbachev–Maxwell Institute for Technology. The institute would 'unleash an incredible volume of brainpower for the
benefit of mankind', thereby solving 'problems ranging from food and health
to global warming and communication'. It worked. The next day's headlines
were full of Maxwell, while poor Gorby was hardly mentioned.

After the captains and the kings had departed, the Governor of Minnesota
was left with the task of turning Maxwell's ambitious dream into reality. Visiting scientists were begged for suggestions as to what the institute should do.
Find a cure for Aids? Fill the hole in the ozone layer? A couple of months later
I asked one of the governor's staff, Tor Aasheim, how he was getting on. 'We
have something, but we're not releasing it yet,' he told me. 'There's a lot of
things happening but it's difficult to put my hands on it...environment, communications...' Still, he added, some progress had been made. After many
hours of 'brain-storming sessions' with academics from Britain and America,
Aasheim had decided that the title Gorbachev–Maxwell Institute for Technology did not reflect the 'thrust' and 'synergies' of the enterprise. He had conse-
quently proposed that it should be renamed the Gorbachev–Maxwell
Institute for Technological Change.

As it turned out, this was the institute's one and only contribution to
mankind. Maxwell fell off his yacht shortly afterwards, the promised $50 mil-
lion never arrived and the 'incredible volume of brainpower' remained firmly
leashed in its kennel.

It seemed a fitting end to the era of think-tanks. During the 1980s, self -
important institutes and centres and foundations had proliferated like
bindweed, fertilized by the enthusiasm with which Margaret Thatcher and

Ronald Reagan greeted their crackpot schemes. 'We propose things which people regard as on the edge of lunacy,' Dr Madsen Pirie of the Adam Smith Institute boasted in 1987. 'The next thing you know, they're on the edge of policy.' Once Thatcher and Reagan had retired, I assumed – or at least hoped – that the think-tanks would soon join them on the compost heap.

Not so. The convolvulus is flourishing and its suffocating tendrils are now spreading leftwards. A few years ago some of Neil Kinnock's supporters set up the Institute for Public Policy Research to act as an 'intellectual powerhouse' for the Labour Party. More recently, Messrs Martin Jacques and Geoff Mulgan founded an outfit called Demos, 'to encourage radical and iconoclastic thinking about the long-term problems facing modern societies'. Jacques, the former editor of *Marxism Today*, is one of Tony Blair's favourite gurus; Mulgan used to work for Gordon Brown. When Demos speaks, the leader of the Labour Party listens.

Whether he can actually understand what is being said is another matter. Demos's latest pamphlet, *No Turning Back: Generations and the Genderquake*, is littered with incomprehensible diagrams provided by a company called Synergy Brand Values Ltd, in which words such as 'connectedness', 'risk', 'sexuality', 'technophobia', 'balance', 'empathy', 'health', 'familism', 'accept' and 'rigidity' float randomly across the page – thereby proving, apparently, that among young people between the ages of eighteen and thirty-four there has been a swing away from 'sustenance-driven needs' to 'outer-directed values'. If Blair is to win the support of these people, it argues, he needs to 'develop a political language and agenda which resonates with [their] core values'.

As if that weren't enough for the new leader to chew on, Demos has also published a 3,000-word 'open letter to Tony Blair' which purports to explain 'what sort of government Britain needs in the second half of the 1990s'. It is a masterpiece of vacuous flannel. 'We should build on our strengths'; 'you could help people regain a sense of control over their locality by enabling them to forge new communities'; 'at all times your government should be on the side of the people against the elites'. Finally, Blair must 'bring different expertises into policy formulation and implementation, and to test new ideas'. Such as, we must assume, the 'ideas' pouring out of Demos.

'Get your tanks off my lawn, Hughie!' Harold Wilson shouted at the engineering union leader Hugh Scanlon in 1969. A quarter of a century on, Blair ought to issue a similar warning to his well-wishers: 'Get your think-tanks off my lawn!' They are an unmitigated menace, the unspeakable in pursuit of the unthinkable, bringing grief and disaster to any politician foolish enough to listen to their wild warblings. Not a single good idea has ever emerged from their ruminations.

Or have I missed something? Last week I rang round some of the older institutions engaged in the racket and asked them to list their successes. At the Social Affairs Unit, there was nothing but a recorded message; perhaps the director, Digby Anderson, was so deep in thought that he didn't want to be interrupted by piffling inquiries from the likes of me. At the Centre for Policy Studies, founded twenty years ago by Margaret Thatcher and Sir Keith Joseph, I was informed that the present director, Gerald Frost, had 'left the office after lunch' and could not be traced. Dr Eamonn Butler, director of the Adam Smith Institute, told me that he was unable to think straight because 'I've only just stepped off a plane from France where I've been at a conference.' He passed me on to the institute's president, Dr Madsen 'Mad' Pirie, the man who spent the Thatcher years living at the edge of lunacy.

So, Dr Mad, what twenty-four-carat brainwaves can think-tanks claim the credit for? He rattled through a list of Greatest Hits: NHS reforms ('internal markets, fund-holding doctors, hospital trusts'), privatization of the railways, privatization of the Post Office... Oh, and it was an Adam Smith Institute pamphlet which first proposed that other great triumph of the Thatcher years, the community charge – 'Although,' he added proudly, 'we actually called it the poll tax.' Unless Blair wishes to come to as sticky an end as Thatcher or Maxwell, he must tell Demos, politely but firmly, to keep its synergies to itself.

(*Observer*, 9 October 1994)

Sleeping with the enemy

ACCORDING TO SOURCES close to Tony Blair, Margaret Thatcher 'is someone worth listening to. She has a mind worth picking and he wants to see her again'. When I first read this, I assumed there must be a misprint: 'She has a mind worth pickling' would make rather better sense, though some might say that her brain cells are pretty well

pickled already. But no; it turns out that the PM is indeed planning to have
regular chats with the Batty Baroness.

'Readers should not fall for the facile insult that the Prime Minister is a
closet Thatcherite himself,' a *Guardian* editorial has advised. The trouble is
that those who make the comparison usually intend it as a compliment, not
an insult. Listen to Paul Johnson, now basking in his new status as First Friend
to the Blairs: 'I often say to Blair: "Don't forget that useful Victorian word,
improvement. That's what the country needs, not revolution, but improvement." But I'm preaching to the converted, for he, too, believes in Victorian
values.' Or hearken unto Lord Rothermere, the new Labour peer: 'This government, like the first Thatcher government, seems to me set to do great
things.' Or Irwin Stelzer, the right-wing economic consultant: 'I know Tony
Blair...Blair is one of Thatcher's children. And I think he knows it.' I fear he
does. Since becoming leader of the Labour Party, has he ever criticized anything the old girl did? There was nearly an embarrassing slip on a phone-in
during the election, when he denounced the Tory record 'over the past...' It
sounded as if he was about to say 'eighteen years' but in the nick of time he
corrected himself; 'over the past...few years'. Thus all the blame was heaped
on the luckless Major.

By their friends shall ye know them, and Tony Blair has some very odd
friends indeed. Like Thatcher, he is absurdly impressed by City financiers and
captains of industry. She sought advice from Lord Rayner, Sir John Hoskyns,
Lord Sterling and Lord Young; Blair prefers the chairman of BP, the chief
executive of Barclays Bank and the chairman of Pearl Assurance. He has even
found room in his government for Lord Donoughue, who as vice-chairman of
Robert Maxwell's London and Bishopsgate Investments failed to prevent the
fat fraudster from misappropriating £400 million of pension-fund shares.
Nor should we overlook Lord Hollick, who has spent the past couple of years
sacking hundreds of staff from Anglia TV and Express Newspapers; amazingly enough, he is now a special adviser to the Industry Secretary, Margaret
Beckett.

'Would it be unfair,' David Winnick MP asked during the Queen's Speech
debate last week, 'to say that, by and large, bankers have not been particularly
sympathetic to what the Labour movement and the Labour Party have stood
for?' Answer came there none. Money talks, and for bankers and tycoons it is
the only language they understand. Blair may be in love with Rupert Murdoch, the billionaire liar and tax-dodger, but the *tendresse* will be reciprocated
only for so long as it serves the commercial interests of News Corporation.
Multinational companies have never allowed moral or political scruples to

come between them and their profits; many of them, including ITT and Esso, maintained friendly relations with both the Nazis and the Allies during the Second World War. More recently, Murdoch happily ditched BBC news programmes from his Star satellite channels in Asia in order to ingratiate himself with the late Deng Xiaoping.

How can the new Prime Minister hope to control the power of these corporations if he is dishing out official jobs to their bosses? He has clearly learned nothing from the Scott Report, which revealed in exhaustive detail what happens when relations between Whitehall and big business become too cosy. And if he thinks that the arms-to-Iraq affair was an exclusively Tory scandal, let me remind him that something very similar tainted the last Labour administration. Although Harold Wilson had insisted that economic pressure would end Rhodesia's UDI in 'weeks rather than months', Ian Smith's illegal regime survived for fourteen long years thanks to the sanctions-busting enterprise of British oil companies – including BP – to which Labour ministers turned a blind eye.

It was also firms such as BP that kept apartheid alive after the Arab countries introduced an oil embargo in 1973. 'There can be no greater blessing for South Africa,' the *Johannesburg Financial Mail* observed gleefully at the time, 'than that the oil business is still in the hands of international companies with no discernible leanings of excessive patriotism.' Soon after Labour's election victory in 1974, the then chairman of BP boasted that he had 'intentionally set out to thwart...embargoes on countries like South Africa'.

Now, more than two decades later, the latest chairman of BP is a Labour minister. The proprietor of the *Daily Mail* – the paper which brought us the Zinoviev letter – is sitting on the Labour benches in the House of Lords. The chief executive of Barclays Bank – who has thrown thousands of his staff on to the dole in the past three years – is advising the government on how to end 'welfare dependency'. And the chairman of Whitbread, who was paid £1 million last year, has been mentioned as a possible chairman of the government's Low Pay Commission.

As Tony Blair's favourite Prime Minister once said: funny old world, isn't it?

(*Guardian*, 28 May 1997)

Tales from the nursery

———————————

CCORDING TO HIS new biography, the young Gordon Brown
'was enthralled by the adventures of Thomas the Tank Engine' and
could recite all the stories from memory by the age of four. This
explains a lot. As fellow devotees of the Rev. W. Awdry will recall, Gordon was
a 'very big and very proud' engine who liked to show off 'how fast he could
go'. (Echoes here of Brown's pre-election promise to 'hit the ground running'.)
He thought himself vastly superior to the lightweight Thomas, but after an
unfortunate accident at a mineshaft he decided they should form an alliance –
rather like the alleged pact under which Brown agreed to support Blair's leadership ambitions.

'An Ally – what – was – it?' the junior partner asked.

'An Alliance, Thomas. "United we stand, together we fall",' said Gordon
grandly. 'You help me and I help you. How about it?' Thomas agreed – only to
go back on his word. 'Wake up lazybones,' he whistled at the somnolent
Gordon one day, 'do some hard work for a change – you can't catch me!'
Gordon avenged himself by dragging Thomas on a breakneck journey
through the countryside. 'Well, little Thomas,' he chuckled, 'now you know
what hard work means, don't you?' Poor Tony – sorry, Thomas – was so out
of breath that he couldn't reply. As the Rev. Awdry records, 'He went home
very slowly and was careful afterwards never to be cheeky to Gordon again.'

(*Guardian*, 14 January 1998)

When Brucie backed Britain

'COOL BRITANNIA is not a term I have ever used,' Tony Blair claimed last Friday – forgetting that he had used the dread phrase only five days earlier in an article for *The Sunday Times*. Blair now says that his preferred slogan is Best of British. 'Modern Britain is good for business...Let's be patriotic about this, let's shout about it. Britain is blessed with creativity, innovation, humour and imagination.' Hence his oddly named exhibition, *powerhouse: uk*, which 'demonstrates that we have a dynamic future' (and that we have a fashionable disregard for upper-case letters). Hence, too, his creation of Panel 2000, whose members are the Best of British personified – the chairman of British Airways, the executive producer of *Big Breakfast*, Nightshade from ITV's *Gladiators*, Peter Mandelson and, er, Lady Chalker. Now the government's New Millennium Experience wants to commission a Best of British theme tune – something 'inspirational to sum up Britain's inheritance'.

Why not revive the Bonzo Dog Band's 'Cool Britannia'? It was written more than thirty years ago during the last epidemic of Swinging London nonsense, and it has a rousingly patriotic chorus: 'Britons never never never shall be hip.' Better still, why not exhume Bruce Forsyth's 'I'm Backing Britain', released on the Pye label in 1968? But I suspect Blair doesn't want us to be reminded of the 'I'm Backing Britain' crusade. It began on New Year's Day 1968 when five typists in Surbiton announced that they would work an extra half-hour a day free of charge. Edmund Dell, a minister for economic affairs, was dispatched to Surbiton on a fact-finding visit. The Labour Party issued a 'Back Britain with Labour' poster. As with Blair's 'Best of British', a committee of TV stars, impresarios, captains of industry and advertising agents was set up to promote the 'energy and talent' of British business. And a bright young Labour politician who was said to have a genius for 'marketing' and 'communication' was put in charge.

Robert Maxwell (for it was he) took out full-page newspaper adverts listing

'100 uncranky suggestions of ways to help your country – and yourself'. The most memorable suggestions were that children should forgo their free school milk and that patriotic adults should start drinking British mead. 'I'm Backing Britain' became a national joke overnight, and that was the end of that. Despite all the razzmatazz, the campaign did absolutely nothing to improve our national reputation – or our productivity figures.

'It was a big terrifying fuss,' the Surbiton typists said afterwards. 'We got mixed up when asked horrid questions about trade unions. Thanks to all the interviewing and things we just didn't get any typing done. Going to lunch at the House of Commons was lovely, but we saw all those MPs with their legs up. That George Brown with his flesh-coloured socks!' I trust the members of Panel 2000 will learn the lessons of this debacle. Don't trust Labour politicians who claim to have 'communication skills'; don't give up the day job; don't answer horrid questions about trade unions; and, above all, have nothing to do with men in flesh-coloured socks.

(*Guardian*, 8 April 1998)

A prince among men

IT IS EXACTLY 500 years since a ministerial reshuffle brought Niccolò Machiavelli into the government of the Florentine republic. To mark this slightly obscure anniversary, Contessa Beatrice Machiavelli visited Manchester this week for a conference celebrating her ancestor's enduring influence.

He hasn't always enjoyed such an exalted status. The Roman authorities placed *The Prince* on their List of Prohibited Books in 1559, and the Inquisition ordered all his works to be destroyed. In our own century, his reputation was scarcely improved by the behaviour of three of his keenest devotees – Stalin, Hitler and Mussolini. (Il Duce wrote a doctoral thesis on Machiavelli, and the Führer always kept his books on the bedside table.) As recently as 1972, Henry Kissinger became quite indignant when asked if he had been influenced by Machiavelli to even the slightest degree. 'No, not at all,' he spluttered. 'To none whatever.' Since then, however, there has been a thorough rehabilitation – not least because anyone disliked by Dr Kissinger can't be all bad. In 1993 the political commentator Edward Pearce published *Machiavelli's Children*, which cited the careers of General de Gaulle, George Bush and Margaret Thatcher as proof that 'most of Machiavelli's assumptions hold true'. A year earlier the Tory grandee Lord McAlpine went so far as to write *The Servant*, a sequel to *The Prince*, which he dedicated 'to the most magnificent Baroness Thatcher of Kesteven'.

We can all see what the most magnificent Baroness Thatcher of Kesteven owed to the Florentine rogue. But what of that nice Mr Blair? A glance at a computer database reveals that the adjective 'Machiavellian' has appeared 358 times in the national press during the twelve months since the general election – mostly with reference to Peter Mandelson, Alastair Campbell and the Prime Minister, the three crisis-jockeys of the Apocalypse.

This is an age in which irony has superseded ideology: highbrows boast of their enthusiasm for naff 1970s pop groups, socialists go gooey-eyed about market forces. No surprise, then, that 'modernizing' politicians should find those old Machiavellian tricks so alluring. For all his earnest babble about the Third Way, I suspect that Tony Blair still prefers to consult his well-thumbed copy of *The Prince* in times of trouble: he has certainly heeded its suggestion that a prince ('and especially a new prince') can camouflage any embarrassing misdemeanours by boasting loudly of his 'faith, integrity, humanity and religion' – or, one might add, by going on TV to assure us that he's 'a pretty straight kind of guy' whenever his actions suggest otherwise.

Interviewed on the *Today* programme this week, the Contessa Beatrice Machiavelli tried to rescue her forebear from his cynical disciples. 'He was a moral person,' she insisted. 'He never said that "the end justifies the means".' Her loyalty does her credit, but she is wrong. 'In the actions of men, and especially of princes, from which there is no appeal, the end justifies the means,' Machiavelli wrote in Chapter 18 of *The Prince*. 'Let a prince therefore aim at conquering and maintaining the state, and the means will always be judged honourable and praised by everyone, for the vulgar is always taken by appearances and the issue of the event; and the world consists only of the vulgar, and the few who are not vulgar are isolated when the many have a rallying point in the prince.' Sounds familiar? Machiavelli would have admired the nimble footwork with which Blair escaped from the arms-to-Africa scandal: allow an unpopular colleague to take the flak for a while, then descend like a deus ex machina to point out that it all ended happily anyway. And he would have loved the lordly insouciance with which the PM dismissed the fuss about officially sanctioned lawbreaking as 'a bit of a hoo-hah'. The only

unMachiavellian element in the story is the involvement of Sandline's merce-
naries; he thought freelance warriors 'useless and dangerous', arguing that 'a
wise prince, therefore, always avoids these forces and has recourse to his own'.
But then Florentine foreign ministers of the early sixteenth century didn't
have to deal with such tiresome inconveniences as UN resolutions and arms
embargoes.

In every other respect, however, the new government is keeping faith with
Old Nick. Advising rulers on how to confuse their rivals and allies, Machiavelli noted that 'a talent for addling men's brains is part of the armoury of
any successful prince'. Or, as he might have put it today: when hosting a G8
summit in Birmingham, be sure to make your fellow leaders sit through a
'gala concert' by Mick Hucknall.

(*Guardian*, 20 May 1998)

The gospel according to Tony

'*Yes, we are a democratic socialist party. It says so in the new Clause Four ... but it
stands in a tradition bigger than European social democracy, bigger than any 'ism',
bigger than any of us. It was there when the ancient prophets of the Old Testament
first pleaded the cause of the marginal, the powerless, the disenfranchised...* ' – Tony
Blair, Labour Party conference speech, September 1996.

IN THE BEGINNING was the Word, and the Word was Tony. In him
was life; and the life was the light of men. And the light shineth in the
darkness; and the darkness comprehended it not.

And the Word was made flesh, and dwelt among us, full of grace and truth.
He came unto his own, and his own received him not. But as many as received
him, to them he gave power; and to Peter, son of Mandel, he gave a portfolio.
Thou art Peter, he said, and upon this rock will I build my Dome; and the
gates of hell shall not prevail against it.

There was a man sent from Hull whose name was John, of the tribe of
Prescott. He had his raiment of camel's hair, and a girdle of skin about his

loins; and he did eat locusts and wild honey. The same came for a witness, to bear witness of the Light, that all men through him might believe in Tony. For in 1991 John had belonged to the Supper Club, a group of 'soft Left' MPs who opposed the Gulf War, together with Michael Meacher, Margaret Beckett, Chris Smith, Joan Ruddock, Dick Caborn and Clare Short – who resigned as shadow minister for social security over the bombing of Baghdad, which is in the land of Mesopotamia where milk and anthrax flow.

And John spake unto them, saying, sod this sterile purist posturing; wouldst thou live on locusts all thy days, when he who is to come hast promised us loaves and fishes – yea, even ciabatta and chargrilled sardines? And he taketh them up into an exceedingly high place and sheweth them all the departments of Whitehall and the glories of them, not to mention the chauffeur-driven Rovers, and saith unto them: All these things will be given unto thee if thou wilt fall down and worship Tony and minister unto him. And they did so, with remarkably little wailing or gnashing of teeth.

There was rejoicing in the land, for Tony hath filled the hungry with good things, and the rich he hath sent empty away. But men such as Lord Sainsbury, Bernie Ecclestone and Rupert Murdoch went away sorrowful for they had great possessions. And he said unto them, It is easier for a camel to pass through the eye of a needle than for a rich man to benefit from a Labour government – unless thou becometh a 'significant donor', of course, in which case thou shalt be welcomed into thy Master's house at Downing Street, where there are many mansions, and fed upon the fatted calf.

It came to pass in those days that a decree went out that all the world should be taxed, or at least move towards fiscal harmonization. And there was great tribulation and lamentation, as the people asked, Must we render unto Oskar Lafontaine that which is Caesar's? And the scribes and pharisees that dwell in Wapping waxed wrathful, saying that Tony hath betrayed them and sold his birthright for a mess of pottage. What profit hath a man of all his Labour, if he loseth the *Sun*? And while Tony wrestled with his conscience, as Jacob hath wrestled with an angel, there came a new sorrow. For the scribes and pharisees brought unto him a president taken in adultery, and they said, Moses in the law commended us that such should be stoned but what sayest thou? This they said, tempting him, that they might have to accuse him. But the Prime Minister said unto them, He that is without sin among you, let him first cast a stone. Master, they cried, thou alone among us art without sin. Why not cast a stone – or, better still, a few laser-guided missiles – at Baghdad? And Tony pondered the idea in his heart, and saw that it was good. For he hath recalled the book of Leviticus in which the Lord saith that a scapegoat shall bear upon him all the iniquities and transgressions of the congregation, carrying their sins into the wilderness.

Now there were in the wilderness of Mesopotamia, that is also known as Iraq, shepherds abiding in the field, keeping watch over their flocks by night. And, lo, there was a bright light in the heavens like unto a furnace of fire; and they were sore afraid, recognizing the arrival of Stand-Off Land Attack Missiles, Joint Direct Attack Munitions, Smart Penetrating Bombs, Joint Stand-Off Weapons and Tomahawk Cruise Missiles, as it had been foretold by the defence correspondents.

And Tony said unto those who dwelt in Mesopotamia, Be of good cheer; it is my Christmas present to the people of Baghdad. O ye of little faith, can ye not understand that we're blitzing you for your own good? Ye shall hear of wars and rumours of wars: see that ye be not troubled, for all these things must come to pass, but the end is not yet. The wind bloweth where it listeth, and thou hearest the sound thereof but canst not tell whence it cometh, and whither it goeth; for it is so much hot air. Watch therefore, for ye know not when I shall start smiting again; and there shall be famines and pestilences, plagues and earthquakes, all transmitted live on CNN.

And the people that had laboured under the yoke of Saddam were dismayed and confounded, asking, Wilt thou deliver us from the oppressor? But Tony heeded them not. Verily, he said, it is written in the rules of the United Nations that thou shalt not topple a head of state; and we must obey international laws, except for those we choose to ignore. Thus I shall smite the lintel of Saddam's door that the posts may shake, yea and I shall bring ruin to his palaces and dominions; but into his bedchamber I shall not venture, for not an hair of his head shall be touched. Our war aim is only to keep the lion in his cage, so that we may poke him with a stick from time to time. But woe unto them that are with child, and to them that give suck, in those days! For they too shall be trapped in the cage with him, and they will surely perish.

And Tony's disciples came, and said unto him, Why speakest thou to them in parables and gibberish? He answered, saying, Because it is given unto you to know the mysteries of Anglo-American strategy, but to them it is not given. Or, as the Prime Minister's spokesman hath said last weekend, explaining why the *Sun* had news of the air strikes before they had even begun, 'It is important in situations such as this that key messages are communicated to prime audiences.' And the same spokesman warned the scribes and pharisees to shun the bearers of false witness. As it is reported in the *Sunday Telegraph*, 'Downing Street has chastised broadcasters for failing to point out that access to sites in Iraq is tightly controlled by the authorities – who have a record of fabricating destruction. "The truth is that you can't believe a word these people say," said one Downing Street official. "We've all heard how teams of builders would remove roof tiles from houses before reporters were brought to the area to see the damage."' Unlike the forces of righteousness, of course. Yet in the selfsame edition of the *Sunday Telegraph* the moving finger of Sir Charles Powell, former foreign affairs adviser to Margaret Thatcher and John Major, hath written as follows: 'One gets the impression that American pictures of the performance of Cruise missiles and laser-guided bombs are genuine this time, rather than the manufacturers' videos used in Pentagon briefings in 1991.' As Pontius Pilate himself said, What is truth? Verily, it is the first casualty on both sides.

And for three nights there was a sound from heaven as of a rushing mighty wind; there appeared in the sky cloven tongues like fire. After the third day Tony declared that his mission was accomplished, and the *News of the World* carried a huge headline: 'RAF HEROES CHEER VICTORY IN DESERT'. Behold, Tony saith, I bring you tidings of great joy for there is now peace on earth, just in time for Christmas.

But the growing multitude of doubting Thomases, from Lord Healey to General Sir Peter de la Billière, looked upon this 'victory'. They saw that the wounds of the Iraqi people were not healed nor mollified with ointment, and that the 'weapons of mass destruction' were not extinguished, and that no UNSCOM inspector would be allowed into the country for a long time to come – and that Saddam himself was still smiling like a locust in a garden of cucumbers. Truly, they said, this is indeed the peace that passeth all understanding.

(*Guardian*, 23 December 1998)

Spoiled goods

A T FIRST SIGHT, a Tesco superstore seems to offer all that the shopper could desire; and yet I often trudge along aisles of this capitalist cathedral – past countless shelves stacked with pre-packaged, pre-processed gunk – without seeing anything to tickle the palate. How fitting, then, that Tesco should be the outlet chosen to distribute the government's annual report. At first glance, you are awestruck by the variety of Blairite sweetmeats on offer; it's only when you try to digest them that the ninety-page booklet turns out to be as blandly unsatisfying as one of Tesco's perfectly formed tomatoes.

'We will try to deliver every one of our 177 manifesto commitments,' the Prime Minister announces in his preface. 'If there are any commitments we fail to meet, we will have the honesty to say so. Today the total kept or done stands at 90, with 85 on course to deliver and only two which have still to be timetabled.' Phew! With 175 already 'sorted' and only two to go, one wonders how on earth the government will fill the time between now and the next general election.

Only the most dedicated cavillers or malcontents will bother to read the small print in the appendix, which explains how Labour has fulfilled each one of those 177 promises. Number 172, for instance: 'Leadership in the Commonwealth. Kept. The UK hosted a successful meeting of Commonwealth heads of government in Edinburgh in October 1997...' Little did the Commonwealth leaders guess, as they gathered for this routine chinwag, that they were in fact helping Tony Blair to deliver a manifesto commitment. Number 162 is even more bizarre: 'Hold referendum on any EMU decision. Kept.' Can one really keep a promise merely by repeating it?

Between the idea and the reality, between the motion and the act, falls the Shadow. But although Tony Blair promises us an honest picture in full chiaroscuro, the shadows are invisible. Beside promises 150 and 151 ('Streamline the system of appeals; ensure swift and fair asylum decisions'), there is a two-sentence progress report: 'On course. The Immigration and Asylum Bill is now before Parliament.' And, er, that's it. No mention of the thousands of refugees who have been stranded in official limbo by the computer cock-ups at Lunar House; no hint that the Immigration and Asylum Bill, far from introducing a fairer system, has been denounced by the UN High Commission for Refugees as 'a violation of international rights'.

Still, mustn't grumble. As Tony Blair says in the report, his achievements prove that 'it is possible to combine a successful economy and support for business with fairness and reward'. And we can all share in the rewards: for every copy you buy you'll be given two points on your Tesco Clubcard, worth a lip-smacking 2p towards the cost of your next purchase.

(*Guardian*, 28 July 1999)

Boomerang politics

L AMONT SLAMS MAJOR. Major Lashes Thatcher. It is a most enjoyable bloodsport, but Blairites who are tempted to gloat should bear in mind that, within a decade or so, members of the present government may well be publishing their memoirs. Will they be any more complimentary about their own Dear Leader?

'In public, her certainties were off-putting,' John Major writes of Margaret Thatcher. 'In private, she was capable of changing her mind with bewildering speed until she had worked out her public position.' Alter the pronouns and you have a fair description of Tony Blair and his cronies – except that most of their volte-faces are conducted in the full glare of the spotlight. A few delegates in Bournemouth last week may have been old enough to recall the 1996 party conference, at which the shadow transport minister, Andrew Smith, went into full rhetorical overdrive: 'The Tories have dreamed up a crazy new scheme to privatize the air!' he yelled. 'They want to flog off the air-traffic control service! Let me warn the Transport Secretary: Labour will do everything to block this sell-off. Our air is not for sale!' Cometh the crazy scheme, cometh the crazy guy: John Prescott is now preparing to force the privatization through Parliament on a three-line whip.

Only a few months ago, the transport select committee advised that the sell-off should be postponed for at least three years because of a computer fiasco at the new air-traffic control centre in Swanwick, Hampshire, which was due to open in 1996 but won't be working until 2002 at the earliest. The committee warned that safety might be 'compromised for the sake of profit' if the sale went ahead. 'I understand the concern about proposed changes to air-traffic control,' Prescott told his party conference last week, 'and of course we will continue to consult all the interested parties, including the unions...' He may consult them, but he is unlikely to heed their objections. 'This is a question of priorities,' he explained. 'Our priority is not rigid dogma.'

True enough. But what exactly are Labour's priorities? Before the election,

Jack Straw may have seemed pretty rigid in his opposition to Michael Howard's plan to curtail trial by jury; now he has taken up the idea himself, saying that only 'eccentrics' still believe in the ancient right to a verdict of one's peers. As he told a BBC interviewer recently, 'It must be possible to change one's mind. I don't change my mind on many things, as most people famously know.' Well, perhaps one or two things. As shadow home secretary, Straw promised a full-blooded Freedom of Information Bill, in which 'the balance of presumption must be reversed so that in most cases information will be made public unless there is a good case for secrecy'. Now he has decided that perhaps it would be better after all to keep us in the dark about our rulers' ruminations. In opposition, he declared that privatized prisons were 'morally repugnant...it is not appropriate for people to profit out of incarceration'. Since he arrived at the Home Office, the number of private jails has trebled. It was Jack Straw who led the attack on Michael Howard's 'three strikes and you're out' policy; now he supports it. Before the election, he argued that whistleblowers from MI5 or MI6 should be allowed a 'public interest' defence; now he takes out draconian injunctions against the MI5 whistleblower David Shayler. In the spring of 1997, he declared unequivocally that 'the denial of social security benefits to asylum seekers is inhumane'; two years later, this inhumanity was incorporated into his Immigration and Asylum Bill.

Tony Blair has often reminded his MPs that 'we must say what we mean and mean what we say'. Until 1996, he said that he deplored the Prevention of Terrorism Act, and particularly its powers of detention without trial ('Contrary to the principles of British justice...serious and fundamental departures from the normal process of British law'). Even when barracked by Tories for his libertarian scruples, he stood his ground: 'If we cravenly accept that any act introduced by the government and entitled "Prevention of Terrorism Act" must be supported in its entirety without question, we do not strengthen the fight against terrorism; we weaken it...I hope that no Honourable Member will say that we do not have the right to challenge powers to make sure that they are in accordance with the civil liberties of our country.' You can guess the sequel. During the summer of 1998 this same Tony Blair recalled Parliament to force through an even more draconian Criminal Justice (Terrorism and Conspiracy) Bill in about five seconds flat; and last week he jeered at the 'libertarian nonsense' spouted by people who, er, care about the civil liberties of our country.

According to the Prime Minister, the only people who disagree with him are 'the forces of conservatism, the cynics, the elites, the establishment'. Yet it is noticeable that each of his many U-turns has left him facing in the same direction as those forces of conservatism which he affects to despise. Who is the real cynic – a party leader who declares war on elites and establishments only hours before hosting a £350-a-head dinner for corporate donors and VIPs, or the disgruntled bystander who raises a weary eyebrow at this charade?

(*Guardian*, 6 October 1999)

Let me count the ways...

W HAT IS THE THIRD WAY? Does it occupy the vacant space between the Fourth Dimension and the Second Coming? Is it a Fifth Column of Seventh-Day Adventists? And, as Isobel Barnet used to ask on *Twenty Questions*: can you eat it? Tony Blair is doing his best to feed our curiosity. On Monday he published a Fabian pamphlet, *The Third Way: New Politics for the New Century*. Then he jetted off to New York on Concorde – the only acceptable method of transport for Tertiary Voyagers – to participate in a multilateral wonkfest on this fashionable but enigmatic catchphrase.

Hillary Clinton, who hosted Monday's seminar, has been coquetting with the idea for years. As long ago as 1993 she told the *New York Times* that she was seeking a 'unified field theory of life', no less, which 'would marry conservatism and liberalism, capitalism and statism, and tie together practically everything: the way we are, the way we were, the faults of man and the word of God, the end of communism and the beginning of the third millennium, crime in the streets and on Wall Street, teenage mothers and foul-mouthed children and frightening drunks in the parks, the cynicism of the press and the corrupting role of television, the breakdown of civility and the loss of community'. And she succeeded. As her husband announced proudly in his last State of the Union address: 'My fellow Americans, we have found a Third Way.'

If the Holy Grail has indeed been located, why is Blair still searching for it? In his Fabian pamphlet he insists that 'our work is at an early stage'. This may explain a certain vagueness in some of his preliminary findings. 'The arts and the creative industries should be part of our common culture.' Most original, I'm sure. 'Education is not enough.' Fancy! 'We support the efforts of peace-makers and peacekeepers abroad as an extension of our mission at home.' Who would have guessed it? Blair can also reveal that the Third Way is 'vibrant' and 'passionate', rather like Bill Clinton's libido, but also 'flexible' and 'innovative', like Clinton's definition of sexual relations. It rejects 'selfishness' and 'inefficiency'. It prefers nice things to nasty things. It takes its holidays at a prince's palazzo in Tuscany, but will happily sink a tankard of best bitter at the Trimdon Workingmen's Club. It is tender but tough, firm but fair, sour but sweet – in short, a lemon-meringue pie.

'There are even claims that it is unprincipled,' Blair admits. 'But I believe that a critical dimension of the Third Way is that policies flow from values, not vice versa. With the right policies, market mechanisms are critical to meeting social objectives, entrepreneurial zeal can promote social justice.' Are entrepreneurs and corporate chieftains really so benign? Apparently so. 'Companies will devise ways to share with their staff the wealth their know-how creates,' he assures us. In the very next paragraph, however, we are told that 'government intervention is necessary to protect the weak and ensure that all gain some of the benefits of economic progress. That is why we insist on minimum standards for pay and conditions at work.' If companies will naturally share out the spoils fairly, why does government need to intervene at all? This, we soon learn, is how the Third Way works – reconciling contradictions by pretending that they don't exist. 'Governments in the course of this century have proved themselves well equipped to cut or raise interest rates...That is why we have given operational independence in the setting of interest rate policy to the Bank of England.' Admittedly the first of those sentences appears on page seven and the second on page eight, but they still make for a pretty weird dialectic.

Or try this. 'Dynamic markets and international competition are vital spurs to economic growth and innovation. That is one reason we have introduced in our first year one of Europe's toughest competition policy regimes.' And yet the Prime Minister's favourite tycoon, Rupert Murdoch, is one of the most determined monopolists in the world. Blair says that there must be no return to the old politics of 'tax and spend'; but he praises previous Labour governments for producing 'a fairer sharing of taxation and growth, and great improvements in working conditions and in welfare, health and educational services'. How does he think this was achieved if not through progressive taxation and spending? As Clinton's former colleague Robert Reich pointed out this week, 'The better-off have to pony up.'

Talking of ponies, I wonder if Blair has studied the fate of an earlier experiment in political innovation. Just over a century ago, when the French proto-fascist General Georges Boulanger stood for election against a wet Radical, the socialist leader Jules Guesde urged disaffected electors to support a 'Third Way' candidate – Boulanger's horse. Though the nag won only a few hundred votes, it was still a more substantial alternative than the vapid, vacuous musings of our PM. After reading his Fabian pamphlet, with its ceaseless appeals to 'duty' and 'prudence', I found myself reciting Roy Campbell's old verse on certain South African novelists:

> You praise the firm restraint with which they write –
> I'm with you there, of course:
> They use the snaffle and the curb all right,
> But where's the bloody horse?

(*Guardian*, 23 September 1998)

Liar, liar, pants on fire

JOHN MAJOR LIKES to joke that even if he stood unopposed in an election, he'd still come second. Frank Dobson has an equally rare but more useful talent. When he stands in a contested election and wins a mere 25,000 votes against 80,000 for his main rival, wily old Dobbo is still declared the winner.

'Stop whining,' John Prescott instructs those of us who have the temerity to raise an eyebrow at this extraordinary feat of ballot-rigging, which would make the late Mayor Daley sigh with admiration. But who are the noisiest whiners? Frank Dobson was belly-aching even after his victory, grumpily assuring us yet again that he was wholeheartedly opposed to Tony Blair's 'electoral college' (which is not so much a college as one of those grand-sounding but bogus universities that will sell you a degree certificate for $10). What he wanted, he said, was the verdict of Labour members, as delivered through one member, one vote.

Though he affects to be unaware of it, that verdict was duly delivered; and he lost. It's just as well he doesn't have to face himself in the shaving mirror every morning; if he means what he says, how can Dobson pretend that he is the legitimate Labour candidate? I put this point to the Home Office minister Barbara Roche on a Radio 5 phone-in sometime after midnight on Sunday. 'Good question,' she replied. In my experience, politicians use this compliment only when they have no intention of answering the question, and so it proved. 'Ken Livingstone's campaign,' Roche hissed indignantly, 'attracted people who are not friends of the Labour Party, including some Conservatives!' Has Roche already forgotten that this was precisely how she, Tony and the rest of their unlovely gang came to power in 1997? In other circumstances, and with a different set of dramatis personae, Ken's pluralistic appeal would be hailed by Blairites as a vindication of the Dear Leader's 'big tent' strategy.

And what of the selection process? Although Dobbo himself can't defend it, Roche is willing to have a go. 'The electoral college isn't a new thing...We used this electoral college for the election of Tony Blair and John Prescott.' Not true, of course. When Tony Blair first made this claim last year, he was swiftly reminded that there were no block votes in the college which elected him, since John Smith had pushed through a rule change forcing unions to ballot their members. And yet automatons such as Roche still repeat it, hoping that mere repetition will make it true.

In this, as in everything, they are simply following their leader. Political power does strange things to the brain: by the time Margaret Thatcher was evicted from Downing Street, she was as nutty as a pecan pie; within weeks of his resignation, Harold Wilson announced that he was a big, fat spider in the corner of the room, and ordered two BBC journalists to go and kick a blind man in the Charing Cross Road; the late Sir William Armstrong, Ted Heath's omnipotent Cabinet Secretary, was effectively running the country in 1973 while labouring under the delusion that he was a poached egg. The only difference in Tony Blair's case is how quickly the derangement has set in.

The first sound of bats flapping in his belfry was heard even before the election, in December 1996, when he told Des O'Connor that as a fourteen-year-old he had run away to Newcastle airport and boarded a plane for the Bahamas: 'I snuck onto the plane, and we were literally about to take off when the stewardess came up to me...' Quite how he managed this without a boarding card or passport was not explained. It certainly came as a surprise to his father ('The Bahamas? Who said that? Tony? Never'), and an even greater surprise to staff at the airport, who pointed out that there has never been a flight from Newcastle to the Bahamas.

A couple of years later, he told an interviewer that his 'teenage hero' was the footballer Jackie Milburn, whom he would watch from the seats behind the goal at St James's Park. In fact, Milburn played his last game for Newcastle United when Blair was just four years old, and there were no seats behind the goal at the time.

Harmless enough, you may think: many of us romanticize or reinvent our childhoods. Even Blair's friend Robert Harris – a writer of fiction, fittingly enough – admits that the PM has a penchant for 'reinterpreting reality...re-tailoring himself and his history to suit the moment'. But Tony's more recent fantasies go beyond boyish daydreams. On *Question Time* last summer, he informed the audience that he had voted for Mike Foster's Anti-Hunting Bill, which had then been blocked by the wicked old hereditary peers. As I pointed out at the time, Blair did not vote for Foster's bill and it never reached the House of Lords – not because of the hereditaries, but because Blair's own government refused to give it parliamentary time. Nevertheless, he has repeated this self-serving nonsense several times since. Does Blair know that he's telling falsehoods? Or does he genuinely think that whatever he says must be correct? Mendacious politicians are common enough, and easily dealt with. Sincere fantasists, who can persuade their disciples to believe six impossible things before breakfast, are a more dangerous breed. Some become the leaders of chiliastic cults; others become fascists. Now we appear to have one as Prime Minister.

In July 1995, on the fiftieth anniversary of the election of the Attlee government, Blair gave a speech to the Fabian Society describing the damage done by the block vote. 'The party lost contact with the electorate, and in the name of internal party democracy gave away its ultimate source of accountability: the people at large. That is why the change to one member, one vote and the changes in the organization of party conference are so important.' Five years on, the man who once promised 'a politics of trust' has no trust whatever in his own members, which is why he finds himself maintaining that gerrymandered ballots are the noblest and most modern form of democracy. It would be comforting to think that he is lying. The more likely and more alarming possibility is that he means it.

(*Guardian*, 23 February 2000)

Small riot: no one dead

T HE ENGLISH, on the whole, dislike young people. At my local pub, parents with children are banished to the far end of the garden and scowled at by the landlord. The manager of my nearest teashop takes great pleasure in evicting anyone who arrives with a child, snarling: 'Can't you bloody read? No kids!'

The hatred becomes particularly intense whenever youthful political dissent manifests itself. Young people are routinely denounced in the right-wing media as idle good-for-nothings and couch potatoes; but they are even more severely vilified if they actually show some spirit. It happened with the Anti-Nazi League in the seventies, and with the peace camps at nuclear bases in the eighties. Now the targets are the predominantly youthful supporters of Reclaim the Streets. 'On Monday, a crowd of ugly, scruffy social deviants are planning yet another "anti-capitalist" march,' the *Daily Mail* reported last Saturday. On the morning of May Day itself, the *Telegraph* decided that the threat was grave enough to merit a lengthy editorial. In tones of spluttering incredulity, it noted that the Green candidate for London mayor, Darren Johnson, was proposing a 20mph speed limit in the capital, a ban on cars in the centre and a £10 charge for motorists who drive into London. 'There is,' it observed, 'an alarming degree of support for this sort of nonsense' – not least from the 'anarchist hooligans' who were intending to plant flowers and vegetables in Parliament Square. According to the *Telegraph*, now visibly foaming at the mouth, all criticisms of globalization and turbo-capitalism 'amount to a direct assault on the most basic human freedoms, on the prosperity and additional freedoms which trade generates for all'. Luckily, however, 'occasional demonstrations against capitalism, such as today's, are a fleck of dust on the vast landscape of capitalist demonstrations'.

Well, quite. Every day, in countless hideous ways, triumphalist capitalism demonstrates its globe-girdling dominance. Monday's protest, which was largely peaceful and good-humoured, seems pretty mild by comparison. It

was not a 'full-scale riot' or a 'mob frenzy'. Even the small number of guerrillas
bent on violence did little damage; the Lords of the Golden Arches are
unlikely to lose much sleep over the trashing of one branch of McDonald's.
SMALL RIOT NEAR TRAFALGAR SQUARE: NO ONE DEAD. Why, then, do Tony
Blair and the *Telegraph* feel so threatened by a mere fleck of dust? Shouldn't a
few thousand Greens be able to bring rhubarb and apple trees to Parliament
Square on one day a year without finding themselves branded as 'idiots' who
are 'beneath contempt'?

There are ironies galore here. On the same day that Blair denounced the
anti-capitalists, he expressed a fervent hope that Rover could be rescued from
the malign capitalist grasp of BMW. And, while our motor industry may be
terminally ill, there is still one British enterprise that has a powerful presence
in the international market: street protests. The *Nation* magazine in New York
pointed out last week that recent American demonstrations against the
World Trade Organization and the International Monetary Fund took their
cue from our very own Reclaim the Streets, which began life as a campaign
against the M11 extension in east London. 'RTS's global impact has been as
formidable as it was unexpected,' it reported admiringly.

There are also some ancient but resonant echoes. As the *Nation* remarked,
RTS uses 'the strength of sheer absurdity and spectacle to bring traffic to a
halt...Typically, this is achieved by the speedy erection of a "tripod scaffold
structure" – a giant, three-pronged contraption spanning the street from the
top of which one lucky RTSer is dangled for the admiration of bystanders.'
Turn now to *The Golden Bough*, that great study of folklore and ritual, where
Sir James Frazer describes the English figure Jack-in-the-Green: a leaf-clad
mummer 'who walks encased in a pyramidal framework of wickerwork, which
is covered with holly and ivy, and surmounted by a crown of flowers and rib-
bons. Thus arrayed he dances on May Day...' The tree-planters of Parliament
Square are, in other words, guardians of a very old tradition – as they emphasized through their slogan, 'Resistance is Fertile'. May is named after Maia,
the Roman goddess of growth, and its arrival has always been marked by fertility celebrations. 'It would be needless,' Frazer writes, 'to illustrate at length
the custom which has prevailed in various parts of Europe, such as England,
France and Germany, of setting up a village May-tree or May-pole on
May Day.'

In the sixth century, St Augustine – the first Archbishop of Canterbury,
rather than the author of *City of God* – complained to the Pope that Kentish
youngsters had put up floral branches from a may tree outside his cathedral;
in 772, a maypole in north Germany was destroyed on the orders of Charle-

magne. Eight hundred years later, that puritanical old misery guts Philip Stubbes published his *Anatomie of Abuses* to draw attention to the excesses of Merrie England: 'Against May, Whitsonday, or other time, all the yung men and maides, olde men and wives, run gadding over night to the woods, groves, hils, and mountains, where they spend all the night in plesant pastimes...' Oliver Cromwell outlawed maypoles altogether.

With his hyperbolic reaction to Monday's events, Blair places himself squarely in the tradition of Stubbes and Cromwell. For centuries, 1 May has been a day for upturning the established order through anarchic stunts; a day when official potentates are overthrown by Robin Hood, the Lord of Misrule and the Queen of the May. Could this be why control-freaks fear it so?

(*Guardian*, 3 May 2000)

No huddled masses, please

DOES ANYONE REMEMBER 'joined-up government'? It might have been a silly phrase, but it was one of the Blairites' better ideas: that Whitehall's various fiefdoms should compare notes occasionally, to check that the efforts of one department weren't being sabotaged by the policies of another. Between the idea and the reality, however, there is an apparently unbridgeable gulf. I learned this week of a woman from Mauritius who has been working as a nurse in the NHS for the past six years but was recently told by the Home Office that she would be kicked out of the country as an 'overstayer'. When she contacted her family back home to say that she might be returning, she discovered that the newspapers in Mauritius were full of adverts from the British Department of Health – pleading for nurses to come over here and work in the NHS.

It is one of the ripest ironies of 'globalization' that those rich Western countries which are pushing most forcefully for the free international movement of capital and goods are also reinforcing their borders to ensure that the principle isn't extended to human beings. To see how this contradiction militates against joined-up thinking, one need look no further than the hopelessly

scrambled brain of Barbara Roche, the immigration minister at the Home
Office.

For much of this year, Roche has been trying to outdo Ann Widdecombe
with regular tirades against 'bogus asylum seekers' and 'economic migrants';
in one famous outburst, she described them as 'vile'. At the end of July, however, she suddenly started fretting about Britain's dearth of skilled workers,
and delivered a speech in Paris calling for an 'imaginative rethink' of attitudes
to economic migration. 'It is clear throughout the centuries that immigrants
have had a very positive impact on the societies they join. I welcome the
debate and want to play a full part in it.' As well she might: if Roche's forebears hadn't migrated from eastern Russia shortly before the First World
War, she wouldn't now be sitting in judgment on other members of the hud-
dled masses who yearn for the privilege of living in Tony Blair's New Britain.
A couple of days after her speech, she revealed that foreign 'business innova-
tors' would be encouraged to settle here by a relaxation in the rules which had
hitherto required such people to invest £1 million in the country or buy a
British company worth at least £200,000.

But Mr Hyde soon regained control of Roche's synapses. Since 1986,
asylum seekers have been banned from doing any paid work for their first six
months here; after that, they can ask for an 'employment concession' which
allows them to take a job while awaiting the Home Office's decision on their
status. It isn't much of a concession: if a husband and wife who are both qualified doctors flee to Britain, for instance, only one of them may apply for permission to practise their profession. Nevertheless, in the first week of August,
Roche announced that even this small sop would be snatched away, because it
attracted economic rather than political migrants. 'We're determined to end
it,' a Home Office spokesperson explained. 'It's an anomaly that acts like a
magnet for bogus claimants.'

Now, barely a month later, we learn that Roche is about to give another
speech, in which she will propose that immigration controls should be loosened so that thousands of qualified teachers, doctors, engineers and information technologists can come to Britain. According to the *Guardian*, she
intends to 'emphasize the historic role economic migrants [have] played in
Britain'. Quite so; was it not her own government which dealt with the
crisis at the Millennium Dome by importing a Frenchman, Monsieur P.-Y.
Gerbeau? Economic migration has been a motive force of history since *Homo
sapiens* first started walking upright and wondering if the grass might be
greener elsewhere. For the past thirty years, British politicians have believed
that mere legislation can thwart the ancient human urge to travel huge

distances in search of a better life. The discovery of fifty-eight dead Chinese people in a truck at Dover proved what folly this is.

Even so, Roche's belated apostasy deserves only a small cheer. Nelson Mandela has already complained that Britain is wooing away many of South Africa's best social workers and doctors. By inciting a new exodus of trained professionals from countries such as India and the Philippines, the Labour government will actually widen the gap between rich and poor nations. A simpler and better solution to Britain's 'skills shortage' would be to recruit the talent that is already here, among the thousands of applicants for refugee status who are stuck in hostels and detention centres. In the London area alone, according to the British Medical Association, there are several hundred asylum-seeking foreign doctors who could be requalified to work in the NHS without too much trouble or expense. As Hernan Rosenkranz of the World University Service points out: 'Refugee professionals are a gift, not a burden.' So why not accept the gift? Someone who specializes in training refugees gave me the answer: 'The Home Office thinks that if you do anything that seems at all favourable to asylum seekers, it'll be seen as a "pull factor" for others.' And so, while Dr Jekyll wails about our lack of nurses and maths teachers, Mr Hyde does his utmost to prevent asylum seekers who happen to be nurses or maths teachers from finding employment.

The government will never achieve joined-up thinking on this issue so long as it continues to insist on a strict separation between asylum and immigration. If Barbara Roche were a persecuted Tamil from Sri Lanka who came to Britain in search of the job opportunities which were denied her at home by Sinhala chauvinism, would she be a political refugee or an economic migrant? Or, to put it in language that even the most moronic minister might understand: if there's no overlap between politics and economics, should we infer that the Chancellor of the Exchequer isn't a politician?

(*Guardian*, 6 September 2000)

Having to think a bit

L AUNCHING LABOUR'S election manifesto in April 1997, Tony
Blair described it proudly as 'the final nail in the coffin of the old tax-
and-spend agenda'. Now, however, there are ghostly noises from the
crypt. What rough beast, its hour come round at last, slouches towards
Brighton to be reborn? It looks eerily like the two-headed monster that was
buried three and a half years ago. According to advance briefings, 'the central
theme of Blair's keynote speech on Tuesday will be to challenge the Tories
over the "tax and spend" issue. Blair will insist that Britain has to spend more
on under-invested services such as education and health.' He confirmed as
much in his pre-conference interview with the *Independent on Sunday*. 'People
don't want to pay tax,' he observed, 'but they do want the spending on public
services. Now at some point you've got to have a serious debate with people
about this. I am not against tax cuts, but it shouldn't be at the expense of
investment in the future.'

And why has there been no 'serious debate' on the subject in recent years?
Because Messrs Blair and Brown have suppressed it. Back in March 1987, as a
young shadow Treasury spokesman, Blair told the House of Commons that
'income tax cuts are the worst thing that can be done for the economy and the
least effective way to provide jobs'. Within a few years, however, taxing and
spending had become dirty words which must be expunged from the party's
vocabulary. Labour frontbenchers believed they lost the 1992 election because
of John Smith's 'shadow budget', which proposed a new 50p rate of income
tax for very high earners. As it happens, most reputable analysis of the result
shows that the election was already lost well before the announcement. However, Tory propaganda about 'Labour's double whammy' had a profound
effect on Smith and his colleagues.

Not everyone was happy with their new timidity. In April 1994, Alastair
Campbell wrote an article lamenting the 'obsessive caution' of Smith and his
shadow team. 'There are few, if any, circumstances I could envisage that

would lead me not to vote Labour,' he revealed, 'but if I thought Labour wouldn't spend more on health and schools, or that they wouldn't adopt a more interventionist approach to the economy, or that they wouldn't raise my taxes, then I'd have to think a bit. This is not an "irresponsible shopping list". It is the absolute minimum, surely, that the public will expect of Labour.' A few months after issuing this radical ultimatum, Campbell left Fleet Street to work for Blair – who quickly proved himself to be far more obsessively cautious than Smith. In January 1997 Labour gave a solemn pledge that it would stick to the Tories' spending targets for at least two years, and that it wouldn't put up Campbell's income tax (or anyone else's) within the lifetime of the next Parliament.

Contrary to Blairite mythology, tax and spend was not some madcap notion dreamed up by the 'loony Left'. It was also the credo of Croslandite social democrats such as Roy Hattersley, who believed there was no point in having a Labour Party at all unless it attempted to create a more equal society through public education, health and welfare, financed by direct taxation based on ability to pay. Rather belatedly, Blair seems to have got the point about spending. But he is still in a hopeless muddle over tax. During the fuel blockades, he could plausibly have said that high petrol taxes were necessary for environmental reasons. Instead, however, he claimed that the duties couldn't be reduced without jeopardizing his glorious plans for 'schools and hospitals' (as public spending is invariably called these days).

Disingenuous nonsense, of course; with the biggest budget surplus in living memory, Gordon Brown does not rely on recent windfall gains from high oil prices for the fulfilment of his comprehensive spending review. But even if he did, would this be the most virtuous way of raising the money? When buying a litre of petrol or a pint of beer, the duke and the dock worker pay exactly the same amount of tax. Labour ministers have been so brainwashed by Blairo-Thatcherite economics that they seem to have forgotten a principle which was accepted by their party for most of its 100-year history: that progressive taxation is better than regressive taxation.

During the 1997 election, the Liberal Democrats were the only party brave enough to say, unapologetically, that there should be a 50 per cent rate of income tax for people earning more than £100,000, as well as a 1p rise in the basic rate. 'Electoral suicide!' the New Labourites sneered. In fact, the Lib Dems emerged with more parliamentary seats than at any time since the war. Over the past three years they have continued to make the case for direct taxation, while also being far bolder and more progressive than Labour on issues such as asylum seekers, trial by jury and an elected upper house. And where has it got them? The latest NOP poll shows Lib Dem support at 22 per cent, only ten points behind Labour itself. More than three years after its forcible interment, 'the old tax-and-spend agenda' is suddenly looking rather healthier and more alluring than the man who hammered the nails into its coffin.

'I don't deny there has been a battle over tax and spend, but that battle has been won,' Blair boasted at a Newspaper Society lunch in March 1997. 'We can now go to party conferences and win applause for vowing to keep spending down, for vowing to keep taxes down and, if possible, to lower them.' Can this be the same Tony Blair who now seeks applause from the party conference for vowing to increase spending, and who berates the electorate for not understanding that this has to be paid for through taxation?

(*Guardian*, 27 September 2000)

Running on empty

MORE THAN A thousand petrol stations are closed; flying pickets lay siege to oil refineries; an OPEC meeting is front-page news. As the *Observer*'s headline put it: 'Welcome back to the 1970s.' As if sensing the national mood, my telephone went dead on Monday morning and a magnificently surly woman at BT informed me that nothing could be done until Thursday at the earliest. 'I can confirm that the civil contingency committee met today,' John Reid MP announced gravely on Monday's *Newsnight*. Can a three-day week be far behind?

Yes, against all expectations, the seventies are returning to haunt us. According to those who know about such things, the next trend in male fashion will be chunky gold medallions, loud shirts and bouffant hair. Meanwhile, one of the big new movies in America is Cameron Crowe's *Almost Famous*, a coming-of-age story about a teenage boy who 'glimpses the future while listening to the Who's rock opera *Tommy*'. The soundtrack also features Rod Stewart, Black Sabbath and Yes. (What, no Emerson, Lake and Palmer?) A film of *Charlie's Angels* is in production, and *Crossroads* is returning to British TV – where it will compete with the almost incessant re-runs of *Fawlty Towers*, *The*

Sweeney and *Whatever Happened to the Likely Lads?* on digital channels. I assume that dedicated viewers splash themselves with the great smell of Brut and crack open a Watney's party seven before settling down to watch.

During the power workers' dispute of Christmas 1970, a letter to *The Times* began: 'Sir: May I, writing by candlelight, express my full support for the government...' It inspired a brilliant essay by E. P. Thompson on the 'flaring-up of the British spirit' in times of adversity or emergency. 'Only then,' he suggested, 'do those proper guardians of the conscience of the community – the retiring middle classes – shed their usual reticence and openly articulate their values and commitments.'

But here's the difference. If Disgusted of Dorking contacted *The Times* today – writing, as ever, on behalf of the 'silent majority' – he or she would be more likely to begin: 'Sir: May I, with an empty petrol tank, express my full support for the splendid pickets...' When miners or power workers blockade fuel depots, they can expect to be denounced as 'wreckers' and 'bully boys' by tabloids and Tory frontbenchers. In the present crisis, however, criticism from this quarter has been all but inaudible, possibly because the 'Dump the Pump' campaign was incited by the *Sun*, the *Mail* and the Tories in the first place. I even heard one Conservative spokesman mutter that it would be wrong to condemn people who felt impelled to take direct action: will this reticence, I wonder, extend to the next anti-capitalist demo in the City?

The right of gas guzzlers to buy cheaper petrol is one of the least noble causes ever to bring the country to a standstill, and it would be easy to mock. Nevertheless, I think there are two good reasons for celebrating the protest. First, it may have a wholly unintended consequence. People with a dwindling supply of petrol in their tank, forced to ask themselves 'Is this journey really necessary?', may belatedly notice the existence of public transport – and continue to use it after the crisis is over. Even those of us who live in the sticks, far from the nearest bus or train, may reconsider our habit of leaping into the car and driving many miles merely to buy a loaf of bread.

More importantly, it challenges the idea that politics is the exclusive preserve of ministers, and that a citizen's only legitimate involvement in the process is to turn out and vote every five years. The consequences of that deadening doctrine were foreseen as long ago as 1968 by the authors of the *May Day Manifesto*:

> In separating itself from continuing popular pressure, [Parliament] becomes empty of the urgent and substantial popular content which would enable it to resist or control the administrative machine...The government is then not the people in power but a broker, a coordinator, a part of the machine. What can

then be achieved – the process is of course not complete – is the final expropria-
tion of the people's active political presence.

And, of course, their alienation from the system – which is why fewer and
fewer people bother to vote.

Tony Blair seems blithely untroubled by this democratic deficit, to judge
by his insistence that governments must never be influenced by civil unrest or
disobedience. 'That's not the way to make policy in Britain,' he declares, 'and,
as far as I'm concerned, it never will be.' Perhaps the PM has never heard of
the suffragettes, but even he must remember the huge demonstration against
the poll tax in the spring of 1990 which helped to speed the abolition of the
'community charge' and the downfall of its only begetter.

The hauliers and farmers may be latter-day Poujadists; I daresay many of
them vote Tory. But they are at least defying the modern orthodoxies of technocratic, managerial 'consensus politics' – and, like many protesters before
them, discovering the exhilaration and strength of comradeship in a cause.
An Essex farmer admitted this week that only now did he understand (and
sympathize with) the reasons for the miners' strike in the 1980s. As E. P.
Thompson noted at the end of his essay on writing by candlelight, it is only
when dustbins linger in the street, unsorted post piles up or petrol pumps run
dry that people 'know suddenly the great unspoken fact about our society:
their own daily power'.

(Guardian, 13 September 2000)

The national cock-up syndrome

MANY YEARS AGO, my first editor in London taught me an
essential trick of the trade: when reporting disasters, one should
always use the headline 'We name the guilty men' and a graphic
captioned 'Arrow points to defective part'. Last Thursday night my ex-editor
sent me an e-mail. 'Just saw *Channel 4 News.* Was I the only person who felt
that when we moved from the UK and BSE to Russia and the submarine admi-
rals there was no real change? If we go on trying to run a high-tech society

with the sort of liars we have in charge now, it won't be too long before we go the same way as the Russkies.'

Lord Phillips, despite being a high court judge, does not presume to pass judgment on the officials who deceived their ministers, who in turn misled MPs, who then offered false reassurance about BSE to their constituents. Like Lord Justice Scott a few years ago, however, he does provide enough detail to let us find the defective parts of a system corroded by secrecy and negligence.

The symptoms of our National Cock-Up Syndrome are unignorable – BSE, Railtrack, the Millennium Dome, the National Lottery Commission, the national stadium, the army radio farce, plus medical scandals and educational disasters too numerous to mention. 'Last week with railways, this week with BSE,' Stephen Glover observed mournfully in the *Daily Mail*, 'we are reminded how oddly incompetent is the British state.' But the state has nothing to do with it. Can Glover recall what happened to Lloyd's of London a few years ago? Does he imagine that the London stock exchange, which has just shot itself twice in the bum, is a nationalized industry? And has he already forgotten the magnificent blunder perpetrated last year by the Bank of Scotland, which had to abandon its furtive joint venture with the Rev. Pat Robertson, a right-wing American evangelist? The cock-up syndrome pays no attention to ideology, nor to the private/public distinction; it is a deep-vein infection caused by information-deficiency disease, which is as common in large corporations as in the Min of Ag and Fish. When, for example, the Bank of Scotland and Robertson Financial Services applied for a national charter for their bank, much of the application was blacked out because of 'commercial confidentiality'; even the signatories to the agreement remained anonymous.

Although we are said to live in the Information Age, crucial information is still severely rationed. David Shayler's allegation that MI5 suppressed an advance warning of a terrorist attack on the Israeli embassy, which was widely ridiculed as another of his 'fantasies', now turns out to have been true. When Judith Ward's wrongful conviction for the M62 bombing was finally overturned, in 1992, the appeal court admonished the prosecution for not disclosing 'vital evidence' that would have acquitted her in the first place; four years later, the Tories pushed through the Criminal Procedure and Investigations Act, which gave Inspector Knacker and the Crown Prosecution Service a statutory power to withhold material from defence lawyers. Needless to say, the new Labour government happily accepted the law, maintaining that police and prosecutors would never conspire to convict an innocent person by hiding relevant facts. But as Malcolm Fowler of the Law Society pointed out in *The Times* last year: 'Whether it's the cock-up theory or the conspiracy theory, it doesn't make any difference to the victim of a miscarriage of justice.'

Or, one might add, to the victims of BSE and the Hatfield rail crash – or to the thousands of service personnel who have been used as guinea pigs at Porton Down, the government's chemical and biological weapons research centre. 'I was aware that testing on soldiers was ongoing at Porton Down – but I did not know the details,' the former defence minister Lord Healey told the *Sunday Telegraph* last weekend, commenting on a new police inquiry into the affair. 'Even I as minister did not want to know all secrets at the MoD and only wished to be told on a "need to know" basis. The great problem with this is that I was only given information that civil servants wanted to tell me.'

Beautifully put, Denis. Arrow points to another defective part: the 'need to know' principle. (Even this is something of a misnomer. Since privatization, every railway station in Britain has gone ex-directory, to deter inquisitive passengers who 'need to know' whether the trains are running. Is there any other nation on earth which has such a policy?) Perhaps the most alarming lesson of Lord Phillips's inquiry into the BSE fiasco is that Jack Straw's feeble little Freedom of Information Bill would have made no difference whatever. If something similar happens again – and, be assured, it will – ministers can still conceal the truth from the public.

Awestruck profile writers often refer to the 'Rolls-Royce minds' of Whitehall mandarins and corporate chieftains. But it seems to me more likely that we have the most incompetent business and administration class in the Western world. Besides, even a Rolls-Royce won't get far if it is driven with the handbrake on and the fuel tank empty. Kipling, as so often, had the right phrase. It comes from 'The Secret of the Machines':

> But remember, please, the Law by which we live,
> We are not built to comprehend a lie,
> We can neither love nor pity nor forgive.
> If you make a slip in handling us you die!

(*Guardian*, 1 November 2000)

The whole truth about Peter's friends

F LAYED BY THE MEDIA and excoriated by his Cabinet colleagues, Peter Mandelson is entitled to feel puzzled. Can it be true, as they say, that he only ever had one friend, who happened to be the Prime Minister? In the words of Sir Thomas Wyatt, 'I have seen them gentle, tame and meek,/That now are wild, and do not once remember...'

The *Sun* dismisses him as 'a lying, manipulative, oily, two-faced, nasty piece of work who should never have been allowed near the government in the first place', yet in 1997 the newspaper praised Mandelson as a formidable politician who should be promoted to the Cabinet forthwith. Ditto the *Mirror*; and ditto ditto our old friend Paul Johnson of the *Daily Mail*. Johnson now denounces the 'corrupt' and 'wretched' Mandelson as 'the fastest and most determined social climber I have ever come across' (a title which many of us thought Johnson himself had won outright), and chides the PM for making 'the crass mistake of restoring Mandelson to office after the most perfunctory interval – an act of folly strongly criticized at the time by his own colleagues and backbenchers'.

Is this the same Paul Johnson who in November 1997 wrote that 'Mandelson is tall, dark, handsome and...probably the most hard-working man in British politics today'? And who in April 1998 advised Blair to make Mandelson Foreign Secretary, 'a job for which his discretion and astonishing industry make him well suited'? And who, a few months later, deplored 'the recent vicious campaign against Peter Mandelson', advising Blair to show his confidence in this 'faithful lieutenant' by 'giving him a prominent place in the Cabinet'? Even at the time of Mandelson's first resignation, two years ago, Johnson's enthusiasm was undimmed: 'I know Mandelson well and like him. I also admire his skill and dedication in the public service, his devotion to the Prime Minister and his aims, and the guts with which he has faced more than his fair share of often grotesquely ill-informed criticism...My own view, as one who wishes to remain his friend, is clear. His political career can still be salvaged.'

They flee from Peter that sometime did him seek, and all is turned into 'a strange fashion of forsaking'. Yet he emerges from this with rather more credit and integrity than those who feel emboldened to kick him only now that he's down. Whatever one's opinions of New Labour, he was at least a true believer – with the emphasis on the word true. This made the supposedly devious Mandelson a more honest character than his colleagues who privately wince and snigger at the Third Way but nevertheless spout unadulterated Blairite jargon in public and in Cabinet.

A week after his downfall, it is still difficult to see what uniquely vile offence Mandelson committed. If being chummy with the Hindujas is grounds for resignation, the front benches of both major parties would be almost empty. Ah yes, say the tinpot Torquemadas of Westminster, but he told a lie to the *Observer* – or, at the very least, gave a misleading answer. As Clare Short put it: 'He went because he has got problems telling the truth.'

If that were the real reason, many other ministers would have preceded him to the gallows. When Gordon Brown appeared on the *Today* programme just as the Bernie Ecclestone scandal broke, he was asked point-blank if Ecclestone had given money to Labour. 'You'll have to wait and see, like I'll have to wait and see when the list is published,' he replied. 'I've not been told.' This was a lie: Blair had told Brown about the donation the previous week.

Blair himself then submitted to a TV interrogation by John Humphrys. He claimed that Ecclestone's second donation was refused 'before any journalist had been in touch', and that 'the question then arose which was uppermost in my mind, what about the original donation? We decided to seek the advice of Sir Patrick Neill.' Both these statements were lies: the letter to Neill was written only after journalists began sniffing around; and it asked for advice only about the second donation, not the first. (Lest we forget, this was the same interview in which the PM boasted of being a pretty straight kinda guy.)

What of Jack Straw, the sea-green incorruptible who shopped Mandelson to Downing Street because ministers have a sacred duty 'to give the whole truth'? At the Labour conference in 1999 the Home Secretary declared, 'We will be giving the police the money they need to recruit 5,000 more officers. That's 5,000 more officers over and above the police service's recruiting plans. That's not the sort of hollow promise the Conservatives used to make.' But it was. Alan Milburn, then Chief Secretary to the Treasury, had sent Straw a warning letter three days before the speech. 'I must stress that, as has been discussed at length and agreed with your officials and contrary to your letter of 23 September to Derry Irvine, the package does not provide for 5,000 "additional" officers,' he wrote. 'There should therefore be no references to this package being one for 5,000 additional officers.'

Milburn became Health Secretary soon after the party conference – and promptly revealed his own talent for creative accountancy by announcing that he intended to recruit an 'extra' 410 consultants in heart disease by the year 2005. All these new doctors turned out to be people who were already working as senior heart specialists in the NHS; all he meant was that they would have qualified as consultants by 2005. In the very same week, an all-party committee of MPs condemned Stephen Byers for his 'regrettable habit' of giving 'potentially misleading' information. One example was his claim that financial support for research and development in small firms would increase to almost £100 million. The true figure was £35 million. 'Much of the funding described in March as "new money" has been subject to multiple announcements,' the committee observed.

There have been dozens of these multiple announcements – and straightforwardly bogus announcements – since May 1997. Many ministers, it seems, have 'problems telling the truth'. Messrs Blair, Brown, Straw, Byers and Milburn have not resigned yet; nor has anyone seriously suggested that they should. Why, then, is Mandelson cast into the outer darkness with many a shout of 'good riddance'?

The answer can be found in *The World of the Favourite*, a recent book of scholarly essays edited by the historians Sir John Elliott and Laurence Brockliss. Although commentators have often described Mandelson's position at the Court of Tony as 'unprecedented' and 'extraordinary', the minister-favourite is in fact a familiar historical type. Edward II had Piers Gaveston, Catherine the Great had Potemkin, Louis XIV had Fouquet, Henry VIII had Wolsey, James I had Somerset and then Buckingham. Strong rulers as well as weak ones have found it useful to share their burdens with a single trusted and efficient minister. But the favourite's power and influence provoke intense ill-feeling among other courtiers, who regard him as a sinister usurping parvenu with ideas above his station, or perhaps even a sorcerer. (When the Earl of Somerset fell from favour in 1616, he was charged with witchcraft.) As Brockliss points out, it was the favourites who 'took the flak' for unpopular decisions, allowing the monarch to remain unscathed. Which is why their downfall is almost inevitable, and has been so ever since the execution of Sejanus, the supposedly untouchable chief minister of the Emperor Tiberius. Piers Gaveston was killed, as was the seventeenth century's most famous Mandelsonian figure, the Duke of Buckingham.

Now that Mandelson has more leisure time, he may find some consolation

from reading about his predecessors. Things look pretty bleak, but at least
he won't be disembowelled: the worst fate that he can expect is a company
directorship.

(Guardian, 31 January 2001)

Only trying to help

A N U R G E N T 'product recall' announcement appears in the latest
issue of *Private Eye*. 'Millions of complaints have been received
regarding the constituent parts of Britain – none of which appears to
work. Furthermore, some of them are extremely dangerous and can cause
serious injury. The manufacturers regret that Britain no longer conforms to
acceptable safety standards and have therefore decided to withdraw the product from the market.' At a time when half the British population is swabbing
down its gumboots with disinfectant and the other half is trapped in trains
that go nowhere, it might indeed seem that the slogan of UK plc should be
Disasters R Us. All the more reason, then, to celebrate the one component of
the British state that continues to operate smoothly amid the chaos.

In Sir Anthony Hammond's report on the Hinduja affair, there are only
two moments when the reader fears that Whitehall's famous Rolls-Royce
engine may need some fine-tuning. The first occurs when Peter Mandelson
explains why he was unlikely to have rung Mike O'Brien, the immigration
minister at the Home Office. 'Mr Mandelson...told me that he did not have a
ministerial telephone directory in his office, so would not have known how to
contact Mr O'Brien.' Fear not, however: there's a back-up system. As Sir
Anthony notes: 'Mr Mandelson could have used the Number 10 Downing
Street switchboard, which would have connected him to Mr O'Brien's office.'

The other tiny malfunction is the failure of Andrew Walmsley, head of the
immigration and nationality directorate, to write a formal report on his decision to speed up and then grant S. P. Hinduja's application for citizenship.
Though this was contrary to 'good practice', managers in the directorate said,
'Mr Walmsley was an expert on nationality policy and tended to keep a lot of
the reasons for his decision-making in his head. As such, they suggested, the

lack of minuting did not suggest that Mr Walmsley was being evasive or trying to hide the reasons for his decisions.'

Although requests for citizenship would normally be handled by more junior officials, Walmsley chose to deal with the 'high-profile' case of S. P. Hinduja himself. Hammond finds this a plausible reason for the astonishing speed with which Hinduja was waved through. As a senior civil servant, 'Mr Walmsley did not have the same volume of casework to deal with and Mr S. P. Hinduja's application did not need to join the queue of cases waiting to be processed...In line with his general philosophy, Mr Walmsley had wanted to be helpful.' Hinduja didn't even have to bother with fresh paperwork; he merely dug out an old application form he had first submitted (unsuccessfully) under the Tory government. When Hammond queried this departure from normal procedure, Walmsley replied that it 'should be seen in the context of the nationality directorate wanting to offer applicants a swift and helpful service, saving them the effort of having to fill in a new form'.

Less exalted immigrants who have had dealings with the Home Office may be surprised to learn it, but 'helpfulness' is the department's motto. And the Home Secretary leads by example, as he proved last May when Peter Mandelson forwarded a letter from G. P. Hinduja, asking if yet another brother, Prakash, could have a British passport, even though he lived in Switzerland. Jack Straw scribbled a note to his private secretary: 'Mara – Mr Mandelson raised this matter with me. Please have a word first then get some advice. ?Zola Budd.' Straw told Hammond he 'could not recall' why he mentioned the South African athlete. Suspicious observers might guess he was trying to be very helpful indeed by citing a previous case in which someone who did not meet the residency requirements had been given British citizenship. Fortunately, Sir Anthony is not a suspicious observer: 'I do not regard this as significant.'

What of the letter Straw's private secretary then sent to Andrew Walmsley, asking him to look at Prakash Hinduja's request 'as soon as possible', and the subsequent phone call in which she revealed that 'the Home Secretary would like the case to be dealt with "helpfully" '? Straw informed Hammond that 'in his view, the word "helpfully" meant he wanted the matter dealt with properly, as was his approach to all cases'. Sir Anthony agrees: 'I am satisfied that the use of the word "helpfully" did not have any suspicious connotations, nor did it suggest that the Home Secretary wished to give Mr Prakash Hinduja any preferential treatment.'

From which we can only conclude that all applicants receive the same Rolls-Royce service, complete with a uniformed chauffeur. The former immigration minister Mike O'Brien confirmed as much, telling Hammond that in 1999, when S. P. Hinduja's naturalization was approved, he was encouraging immigration officials to take 'a more positive attitude' to citizenship applications. Can this be the Mike O'Brien who pushed through the draconian Immigration and Asylum Bill that year? The minister who cocked up the introduction of a new computer system in the immigration and nationality department, creating a backlog of 80,000 cases and misery galore?

Presumably not, since Sir Anthony neglects to mention it. The phrase 'I am satisfied' is repeated no fewer than eighteen times in his report; he believes that everyone has behaved 'perfectly properly'. Who could fail to be inspired by such excellence? If we all try a little bit harder to imitate the Whitehall elite, poor old Britain may yet be saved from the scrapheap.

(*Guardian*, 14 March 2001)

Let them drink cappuccino

LAST SUNDAY I heard the unmistakable sound of the first cuckoo, traditional harbinger of a spring election. Neal Lawson, described as a former aide to Gordon Brown and a prominent member of Labour's 'modernizing tendency', was being interviewed on *The World This Weekend*. 'Labour got to the stage in the early 1990s where we'd give up virtually anything to get elected,' he said, 'and that was right to do so. But now I think we need to look a bit more at the issues of principle and what the party stands for.' One such issue, he suggested, could be 'social justice'.

This daring proposal – that after four years in office Labour might at last be permitted to mention one of its founding ambitions – seemed oddly familiar. Shortly before the general election of 1970 *The Sunday Times* published an interview with David Kingsley, the advertising executive who had created the slogan 'Let's Go with Labour' in 1964. Speaking in the excitable language of his trade, Kingsley declared: 'Ideals are coming back. They're the now thing. This is an interesting thought that has only just occurred to me – we could really sell the Labour Party on ideals in the present climate of opinion. I don't think, in practical terms, we could have talked about them in '64 or '66.'

Tempting though it is to blame Tony Blair and his teenage tacticians for the wholesale slaughter of long-cherished principles, we shouldn't forget those earlier 'modernizers' who supplied the weapons. Take Neil Kinnock, who was asked in 1993 why, as a lifelong CND man, he had forced Labour to abandon its support for unilateral nuclear disarmament. 'We still had policies that were a source of disadvantage to us,' he replied. 'However much the policy as it existed commended itself to us . . . it simply was not accepted or acceptable to the great majority of our fellow citizens, and anybody who's serious about their politics has got to heed that basic fact of life.'

Pause to disentangle the reasoning. Unilateralism commended itself to Kinnock and his party; but, since it was disliked by other voters, the policy had to be turned on its head. Using exactly the same logic, he could have announced that Labour was now committed to bringing back the death penalty. For Kingsley and Kinnock, principles were apparently no more than a gimmick, like a free Disney CD in a packet of frosted Shreddies, which could be added – or, more importantly, omitted – according to consumer demand and the state of the market. To judge by Neal Lawson's remarks, and by the number of promises which Labour has jettisoned since 1997 (on child benefit, privatization, asylum seekers, nuclear weapons, trial by jury et bloody cetera), this remains the case.

Lawson is a figure of some consequence: he runs Nexus, the Blairite 'ideas network', and edits its quarterly journal, *Renewal*. He is also a founder-director of Lawson Lucas Mendelsohn (LLM), a political consultancy whose inaugural brochure in 1997 promised to bring an 'ethical' fragrance to the niffy business of parliamentary lobbying. 'We are in touch and in tune with the new government,' it boasted, 'but more importantly we are in touch and in tune with the times.' An accompanying glossary contrasted the language of 'the passing world' with the buzzwords of 'the emerging world': out went 'ideology', to be replaced by 'pragmatism'; boring old 'conviction' had been supplanted by 'consumers'.

What this meant in practice was revealed by the *Observer*'s 'Lobbygate' investigation in 1998. Posing as an American businessman, undercover reporter Greg Palast asked what he could expect if he handed over a monthly retainer. Trumping a rival firm, which had promised tea with Geoffrey Robinson, Lawson offered to 'reach anyone. We can go to Gordon Brown if we have to.' He explained that in an era of 'politics without leadership' and 'non-ideologically poisoned decision-making', where lack of firm convictions was regarded as a virtue, ministers were always susceptible to influence. 'The Labour government is always of two minds: it operates in a kind of

schizophrenia. On big issues especially, they don't know what they are thinking. Blair himself doesn't always know what he's thinking.'

It's an infallible rule that anyone gittish enough to think that schizophrenia means nothing more than 'of two minds' is himself quite capable of believ-
ing in several contradictory ideas simultaneously. In public, Lawson presents
himself as a progressive social democrat committed to 'the traditional values
of the Left'. As early as March 1998, in a lengthy screed for the *New Statesman*,
he declared that 'the strategic objective of government is to enhance freedom
through greater equality' and attacked other Labour modernizers 'who have
failed to escape from the influence of neo-liberalism'. Privately, however, he
seems happy enough to lend the neo-liberals a hand. In July 1998 LLM
was reported to have saved Tesco £40 million by persuading ministers to
abandon plans for a supermarket car park tax. Later that year trade unions
threatened to boycott Lawson's company after learning that it was advising
Rupert Murdoch's News International on how to undermine the government's Fairness at Work proposals. Yet in the pages of *Renewal*, Lawson has
continued to chide Labour for not challenging the power of right-wing newspapers and corporate chieftains. 'Too many members and activists feel
despised and alienated from "their government",' he warned in an editorial
last May. 'The well of reasonable excuses for lack of radical progress has run
dry.'

If I seem to harp on about Lawson – a man of whose existence you were
probably and happily unaware – it is because he exemplifies the contradictions at the heart of New Labour. The Blairites are forever announcing 'initia-
tives' that imply purposeful action; yet they also parade their own impotence,
insisting that government can no more hinder the tsunami of deregulated
globalization than Canute could turn back the tide. They mock the crude, discredited determinism of old-style communists who spoke of capitalism's
inevitable crisis; yet they recite the equally deterministic shibboleth that the
New Economy and New World Order are, er, inevitable.

In his *New Statesman* article of March 1998, Lawson warned that 'if the gap
between the poorest and the average, never mind between the poorest and the
richest, were wider after ten years of Labour government, it would be a significant failure'. This echoed a remark by Blair one month after he moved into
Downing Street: 'I don't want any forgotten people in the Britain we're trying
to build.'

Well, the half-time scores are now in: the latest Wealth of the Nation
report, published a fortnight ago, showed that the gap between rich and poor
households has actually widened since Labour's election victory. Blair reacted

to the news by having himself chauffeured to the East End of London for a photo opportunity with a few poor people. 'You know better than anyone that we have still not succeeded in giving everyone a share in Britain's economic success,' he simpered. 'For many people on estates like this, life remains a real struggle. There are still whole areas, not just individual people, that remain outside the nation's prosperity.' And what did he have to offer? A grand total of £130 million would be allocated to eighty-eight deprived areas; but it was 'a deal, not a handout', tied to performance targets for exam results, burglary rates 'and other key indicators'. People in these communities can expect to see results 'within ten to twenty years' – if they aren't already dead by then.

Still, never mind. At least Labour has chosen a great song for the election campaign: 'What have you done today to make you feel proud?/It's never too late to try...' Oh, and visitors to the official party website can order souvenirs embellished with the stylish new 'squiggle' logo, which is said by a party spokesman to 'stand for our enduring belief in fairness and equality'. The natty golfing umbrella is £19.99, while the cappuccino cup (perhaps an ironic reference to Blair's distaste for 'froth') will cost you just £12.99. With such treats available to all, one would have to be inexcusably greedy to ask for social justice as well.

(*Guardian*, 7 February 2001)

Orders of merit

THE MOST INFLUENTIAL books are always those that are not read. So says Michael Young, and he should know. His classic *The Rise of the Meritocracy*, published in 1958, endowed the language with a word which has been misinterpreted ever since. As he pointed out recently, hardly anyone seems to realize that the book is a satire, and that the society it envisaged is a doomed dystopia. 'I wanted to show how overweening a meritocracy could be,' Young explained, 'and indeed the people generally who thought they belonged to it, including the author to whom the book was attributed.' Silly old sausage: didn't he realise that irony and satire will always be taken literally by at least half the people who read it, and by a far higher percentage of those blithering bratwursts who haven't read it at all but base their inferences on the title alone?

One such, I suspect, is our own Prime Minister. But this hasn't inhibited him from holding forth on the subject: 'We are light years from being a true meritocracy' (July 1995); 'I want a society based on meritocracy' (April 1997); 'The Britain of the elite is over. The new Britain is a meritocracy' (October 1997); 'The old establishment is being replaced by a new, larger, more merito-cratic middle class' (January 1999); 'The meritocracy is built on the potential of the many, not the few' (October 1999); 'The meritocratic society is the only one that can exploit its economic potential to the full for all its people' (June 2000).

Despite the obvious and comical contradictions – how could something that was 'light years away' in 1995 have arrived a mere two years later? – Blair is at least consistent in never using the M-word pejoratively. Last week, how-ever, a small caveat appeared for the first time. 'In the past, the idea of meri-tocracy has been attacked,' he declared in his Enfield speech. 'But creating a society that is meritocratic is not wrong, it is just insufficient.' But the qualifi-cation seems to be largely rhetorical: even if meritocracy is not enough, according to Blair, it is still 'an indispensable part of building a decent and prosperous society' by 'breaking down the barriers to success'.

To Tony Blair, meritocracy is synonymous with equality of opportunity – and who could object to that? Well, Michael Young, to name but one. 'I thought equality of opportunity, the way it was thought of and the way it is still thought of, was a baneful thing,' he said a few years ago, in a radio inter-view marking the fortieth anniversary of *The Rise of the Meritocracy*. 'I saw the meritocracy as becoming less and less concerned with the main body of people, establishing a sort of culture of their own, an elite culture with a good deal of arrogance in it. These things have largely happened...' Or, as he put it in his book, equality of opportunity tends to mean, in practice, equality of opportunity to be unequal. As if to prove the point, the Prime Minister used the phrase again on Monday when presenting his plan to reintroduce a two-tier system of secondary schools. Far from 'breaking down the barriers to suc-cess', meritocracy erects daunting new hurdles. Anyone who doubts this should read *The Big Test: The Secret History of the American Meritocracy*, in which Nicholas Lemann reveals how the Scholastic Aptitude Test (SAT) was used to select the ruling class of post-war America.

In the days of aristocratic dominance, there were at least some in the upper class who felt insecure in their hereditary power, and many in the lower classes who refused to accept the legitimacy of their rule. But when merit alone reigns, and is almost universally accepted as the fairest arbiter, those in the elite entertain no doubts at all: they are there because they bloody well deserve to be. Those who lose out are condemned to helpless despair, stigmatized by their own alleged inadequacy. And the new order soon becomes as stratified as the old. As T. S. Eliot, who was not exactly a loony lefty, wrote in his *Notes Towards the Definition of Culture*: 'An elite, if it is a governing elite, so far as the natural impulse to pass on to one's offspring both power and prestige is not artificially checked, will tend to establish itself as a class.' One obvious way of introducing an 'artificial check' would be to challenge the influence of the public schools, but this Labour government – like all its predecessors – has no intention of doing so.

In Young's book, the British meritocracy eventually provokes an uprising of 'populist' democrats opposed to a system which evaluates people only according to their intelligence, education, occupation and power, with little account given to qualities such as imagination, courage or generosity. Could there be a similar backlash against Blair's New Jerusalem? Surely not. Young's satirical fantasy imagined a meritocratic society of huge and widening inequalities, with a technocratic superclass at the top and a sullen underclass below. It suggested that the new British elite would be not only unrepresentative but also more interested in consolidating its own power than in improving the common weal. It also predicted that by the twenty-first century the Labour Party would have rebranded itself with a more 'modern' name, and would set about abolishing comprehensive education. ('To us the failure of comprehensive schools does not seem to require explanation. We can hardly conceive of a society built upon consideration for the individual regardless of his merit, regardless of the needs of society as a whole.') Even more absurdly, it envisaged a 'progressive' government which stripped hereditary peers of their parliamentary privileges – only to replace them with life peers chosen from among the most eminent members of the new privileged class. 'Skipping all the intermediate stages of democracy (as some countries have jumped straight from railways to rockets), an instrument of the aristocracy was by one brilliant stroke made an instrument of the meritocracy.'

Pure fiction, thank God.

(*Guardian*, 14 February 2001)

DISPATCHES FROM THE CLASS WAR

Baying for broken glass

‘ THE CLASS WAR IS OBSOLETE,’ Harold Macmillan announced
after winning the 1959 general election. He then formed a government whose members included a Duke, three Earls and a Marquess.
Thirty years on, another Conservative politician inspected this body-strewn
battlefield. During the Tory leadership contest of 1990, John Major caught the
headlines with a pledge that was, as one would expect, both clumsily phrased
and rash: 'In the next ten years, we will have to continue to make changes that
make the whole of this country a genuinely classless society.' Has he been any
more successful than Harold Macmillan? I visited my newsagent last week to
see how the classless society is shaping up. Here is what I found:

Item. The April issue of *Tatler*. One of its cover stories accuses the Princess
of Wales of becoming an Essex girl; it observes with a shudder that she looks
'dead common'. Elsewhere in the mag, there is a far more enthusiastic profile
of one Tiggy Legge-Bourke, the new secretary to the Prince of Wales's private
secretary. It summarizes her qualifications for the job thus: 'Born on April
Fool's Day, 1965, elder daughter of William and the Hon. Shan Legge-
Bourke – lady-in-waiting to the Princess Royal and granddaughter of Peggy
Viscountess De L'Isle – Tiggy has always been on the periphery of royal circles
and has, in fact, known the Prince for some time. Her brother, Harry, was a
page-of-honour to the Queen and is now in the Welsh Guards, and both she
and her sister Zara, who is married to Richard Grosvenor Plunkett-Ernle-
Erle-Drax, were debs.'

Item. The London *Evening Standard*. The main story in its Londoner's
Diary informs us that 'twenty lissome debutantes, including Minky Sloane
and Bianca Job-Tyoran (who has embarked on the Season with the fearless
declaration that she hopes to "run a stud farm"), gamely disported themselves
at the forty-first Berkeley Dress Show last night.' The newspaper is so thrilled
by the news that, further down the page, it runs a second article about the
implausibly named Minky Sloane and 'her nineteen other dewy friends'.

Item. A glossy new magazine, *Voila!*, which was launched in March this year under the editorship of Dai Llewellyn, son of Sir Harry 'Foxhunter' Llewellyn. Its recruitment policy is all too apparent from the staff list. Sports editor: the Earl of Westmorland. Social editor: Prince Mangal Kapoor. Charity correspondent: Lady Bernard. Motoring correspondent: the Marquess of Blandford. Antiques correspondent: Jonathan Bolton Dignam of Triermaine. Aviation correspondent: Lord Valentine Cecil. Other contributors include Lady Kate Douglas (who has written a profile of her dad, the Marquess of Queensberry), Viscount Pollington and Amanda, Lady Phillimore. The contents are equally wide-ranging: 'Handles and Gongs: Who Outranks Whom?'; 'The Prince of Wales: Did He Go to the Wrong School?'; 'Profile: Lady Elizabeth Anson'; 'Eaton Square: Playground of the Rich'.

Surveying this unappetizing bundle of posh-porn one might conclude that John Major will have to get a move on if he is to achieve his ambition of a classless society by the year 2000. But lo, what is this discordant noise from the servants' quarters? It is Professor David Cannadine, who has followed his monumental study *The Decline and Fall of the British Aristocracy* with a new collection of essays, *Aspects of Aristocracy: Grandeur and Decline in Modern Britain*. The gist of these fascinating and entertaining books is that the upper classes have had their day and are slouching towards extinction. He is even now sharpening his scalpel for the post-mortem.

Alas, he may have a long wait. Because aristocrats have no more brain cells than the dinosaurs, it's easy to assume that they are a doomed species: to judge by their reaction to Professor Cannadine, however, they're fierce little fighters when cornered. As Evelyn Waugh wrote in *Decline and Fall*, just before Paul Pennyfeather was debagged by a gang of upper-class hearties: 'Any who have heard that sound will shrink at the recollection of it; it is the sound of English county families baying for broken glass.' When Cannadine's own *Decline and Fall* appeared, four years ago, he was roughed up almost as badly as poor Pennyfeather. Hugh Montgomery-Massingberd was given a full page of the *Daily Telegraph* in which to mock 'our Dave' as a lower-middle-class counter-jumper who knew nothing about the resilience of top people. 'The truth remains,' Montgomery-Massingberd declared, 'that the aristocracy is more than capable of renewing itself...the power and influence of the territorial magnates is by no means extinct.'

This time round, the fury of the toffs and their courtiers has, if anything, been even greater, particularly at Cannadine's suggestion that Harold Nicolson and Vita Sackville-West were snobs. The former *New Statesman* editor Paul Johnson, a genuflecting worshipper of the aristocracy, has denounced

Cannadine as 'a mighty silly fellow' who 'ought to write about the rise and fall of the proles'. Nigel Nicolson, son of Harold and Vita, says it is 'monstrously unfair' of Cannadine to accuse his parents of snobbery. 'I suspect he is from a poor family,' he sneers. Better still is a letter in *The Times* from James Lees-Milne, who was a friend of Harold and Vita. They were not snobs, he insists, since 'they paid no heed whatever to the social standing of their friends as long as they subscribed to the civilized code of manners in which they had been brought up'. Oblivious to any non sequitur, he adds: 'To them the vulgarity and stupidity of low-born and ill-bred persons were anathema.' Which is, of course, precisely what David Cannadine has been alleging.

Although my sympathies are entirely with the professor, I fear that on the main issue he is too optimistic by half. Karl Marx, like Cannadine, was continually reporting the imminent demise of the British upper class – and was continually wrong. In March 1855, he wrote that 'the aristocracy...has now been obliged to sign its own death warrant'. After a mass demonstration against the ruling class in June that year, he was ecstatic: 'We do not think we are exaggerating in saying that *the English revolution began yesterday in Hyde Park.*' (His italics.) In the New York *Daily Tribune* three years earlier, he had predicted this outcome: 'It is clear that from the moment when the landed aristocracy is no longer able to maintain its position as an independent power, to fight, as an independent party, for the government position, in short, from that moment when the Tories are definitively overthrown, British history no longer has any room for the Whigs.' The Whigs turned up their toes long ago, but the Tories – and the aristocracy – are still with us.

In *1066 and All That* the Cavaliers were Wrong but Wromantic, while the Roundheads were Right but Repulsive. Now the roles are reversed. Paul Johnson, Hugh Montgomery-Massingberd and their braying Cavalier chums are repulsive but right; and it will take more than a few bland words from John Major to see them off. Tiggy Legge-Bourke and Minky Sloane can sleep easily in their beds for many, many years to come.

(*Observer*, 24 April 1994)

Semi-detached

'THE LONDON BOROUGH OF BROMLEY has emerged from suburban obscurity to play a strategic role in British foreign policy.' This startling news was hidden away on an inside page of the *Guardian* the other day. After seven years of trilateral negotiations between the Foreign Office, the Treasury and the civil service trade unions, the government has decided that overseas allowances for British diplomats are to be based on the cost of living in the south London suburb. Once a year, a team of 'special investigators' will descend on the town, armed with clipboards and calculators, to check on the price of haircuts, dry-cleaning and baked beans.

So it's official: the borough where I was born, and where I spent much of my childhood, is the most typical, the most representative, the most utterly average place in the land. Now that the secret is out, there may be visitors from further afield than Whitehall, curious to see for themselves the quintessence of modern Britain. Is Bromley ready for the coach parties and the camera crews? Last week I set off on my own fact-finding expedition.

I asked a woman at the reception desk in the Civic Centre if she could direct me to the tourist office. 'Er, we don't have one,' she confessed. Well, could she point out a few of Bromley's more noteworthy landmarks and attractions? 'We don't actually have very many. We're not really a tourist area.' Any interesting buildings, perhaps? 'No, not really.' But then, as a native son, I knew that. What Bromley does have is shops; and shops; and more shops. 'People here shop like maniacs,' a woman in the High Street told me. There's a new Habitat store built on the scale of the *QE2*; there are two huge malls, one of them implausibly named The Glades. Thanks to the Foreign Office, the din of Bromley's cash registers can now be heard from Toronto to Tirana.

The only sanctuary from this consumerist frenzy is the Churchill Theatre halfway up the street, currently staging a revival of Noel Coward's *This Happy Breed*. The title and indeed the plot of the play might well have been chosen by the non-existent Bromley Tourist Board to market the town. To quote from the synopsis provided by the drama critic of the *Bromley and Beckenham Times*: 'Frank and Ethel Gibbons are the worthy parents at the head of a hard-working, God-fearing, working-class suburban London family...' Alarmingly, however, even the local paper can hardly stifle a yawn: 'In 1994 a contemporary audience is more likely to sympathize with the rebellious daughter Queenie, who runs away from the suffocating atmosphere of the home to find more excitement on the Continent.' The contemporary audience will find itself in good company. H. G. Wells, who was born at 47 High Street (now the site of an Allders department store), left town at the age of thirteen. Hanif Kureishi, who grew up in Bromley during the 1960s, also scarpered as soon as he could – later taking his revenge in *The Buddha of Suburbia*, where he describes Bromley as 'a dreary suburb of London of which it was said that when people drowned they saw not their lives but their double-glazing flashing before them'.

Suburbia has been enduring similar insults for as long as it has existed. 'A suburb,' the *Builder* magazine remarked in 1848, 'is the most melancholy thing in existence.' 'I must confess honestly,' Dorothy Peel wrote in *The New Home*, a book of domestic advice published in 1898, 'that the suburbs of any large town appear to me detestable.' Nastier still was Le Corbusier, who in 1933 persuaded the International Congress on Modern Architecture to approve the following declaration: 'The suburb...is a kind of scum churning against the walls of the city...It constitutes one of the greatest evils of the century.' (This at a time when Hitler had already come to power, and when the more obvious evils of the First World War were still fresh in the memory.)

Urban tower blocks were the preferred alternative of Le Corbusier and his modernist disciples. After the war, many of them were duly built – and equally duly demolished. But even though Mon Repos and Dunroamin had proved rather more successful as 'machines for living' than any of Le Corbusier's schemes, the sneering at suburbia continued regardless. Remember Manfred Mann's 'Semi-Detached Suburban Mr James', which reached number two in the hit parade in 1966? Or, come to that, the Pet Shop Boys' 'Suburbia' ('Lost in the high street, where the dogs run/Roaming suburban boys.../Stood by the bus stop with a felt pen in this suburban hell')? Only last month, on Channel 4, the architectural writer Jonathan Glancey unleashed a torrent of abuse against Bromley's neighbouring suburb, Chislehurst. 'Here, in not-quite-London, not-quite-Kent,' he complained, 'it is as if the neutron bomb has dropped: the people have been vaporized, but the houses and their coordinated fabrics and furniture remain standing.' A couple of days later, one Elizabeth Brooke (described as a 'white witch') told a newspaper: 'I grew up in the suburbs and had a long-standing fantasy of detonating Bromley High Street.'

It is easy to mock suburbia, and even easier to be bored there. But why should it provoke such violent rage? The answer, I suspect, is political. To quote one of the few sympathetic studies of this subject, *Dunroamin: The Suburban Semi and its Enemies* (1981): 'At the root of the attack on suburban living there is the strong presupposition that a collective expression of housing (for example a Georgian terrace, or apartments by Le Corbusier) is somehow preferable to the individualistic expression of a single house.' For although critics often accuse suburbia of being monotonous, what they really object to is that it is just the opposite – a cacophony of discordant individuality. Suburbanites are forever embellishing their houses with little differentiating touches: carriage lamps, new porches, wrought-iron gates, leaded lights – something, anything, to prove that their home is indeed their castle, and that within the privet-hedged boundaries they can do with it whatever they jolly well like. It is a Thatcherite dream, the living proof of Lady T's claim that 'there is no such thing as society; there are individual men and women and there are families'. No wonder it irritates metropolitan leftists, who are convinced that anyone moving to the suburbs will immediately fall into a trance of atomized, self-contained, Pooterish contentment. And, of course, they aren't entirely wrong. Here is 'Our Suburb', a turn-of-the-century poem by Ernest Radford:

> He leaned upon the narrow wall
> That set the limit to his ground,
> And marvelled, thinking of it all,
> That he such happiness had found.
> He had no word for it but bliss;
> He smoked his pipe; he thanked his stars...

But there is more to suburbia than that. Look again at those garden gnomes, or those ridiculous suburban house names, or those hedges topiarized into the shape of battleships. Are they merely expressions of terminal tastelessness – or might they be gestures of subversive nonconformity? After all, the Russian anarchist Peter Kropotkin lived at 6 Crescent Road, Bromley, for some years, and suburban submersion certainly didn't turn him into a complacent Tory; he returned to Moscow in 1917 bursting with revolutionary ardour. True, he later became disillusioned; but that was the fault of Bolshevism, not Bromley.

Suburbia has outlived Soviet communism, just as it outlived the modern movement. Jeer and scoff as we may, the garden gnomes will always have the last laugh.

(*Observer*, 21 May 1994)

Angst on Acacia Avenue

T HE MIDDLE CLASSES are in a sulk. According to a MORI poll, 'They feel forsaken by the government, fearful about the future and threatened by a disintegrating social fabric of the nation.' Meanwhile, the ex-Thatcherite Oxford don John Gray has published a widely noticed pamphlet arguing that the middle classes have suddenly become subject to 'insecurities'.

The only surprise about this is that it should be turned into front-page news, as it was on Sunday. The middle classes have been making similar complaints for as long as I can remember. Back in the mid-1950s, the residents of a private housing estate in Oxford erected a wall across a road to prevent council tenants from walking past their houses on the way to the shops. What was that if not a sign that they already felt 'threatened by a disintegrating social fabric'?

The great heyday of middle-class grumbling was the early 1970s. One survey published at the time, *Voices from the Middle Class*, was a rich treasury of all the same anxious mutterings that turned up in last weekend's MORI poll. 'We struggle to buy our own homes and send our children to good schools,' one couple griped, 'while the poorer people live in council estates and have everything done for them.' It was also in the 1970s that Patrick Hutber, a City writer on the *Sunday Telegraph*, asked his middle-class readers to write to him with their grievances. He had so much mail that he managed to fill a whole book with it. A typical reader described himself as being 'up against the wall' because he could no longer afford a gardener: 'It amounts to a social revolution.' The Tory MP John Gorst was so shocked by this deprivation that he founded a pressure group, the Middle Class Association, whose admirably vague objective was 'to take whatever action may be deemed necessary to further the interests of their members'.

It's true that middle-class belly-aching did subside slightly during the Thatcher era – as well it might, since she represented what even Sir Peregrine Worsthorne was once moved to criticize as 'bourgeois triumphalism'. But the wringing of hands and gnashing of teeth were bound to start again in earnest before long. Anyone who has ever attended a meeting of a suburban residents' association will know that the middle classes can always find something to complain about, even if it's only the noise of their neighbour's electric hedge-trimmer.

And so the familiar litany of woe which has been recited at dinner-parties from Orpington to Petersfield for decades – school fees, the state of the property market, difficulties with au pairs – is taken up once again. It may be distressing to some, but it's nothing we haven't heard before. If the middle classes ever quit moaning for good, on the other hand, that really would be newsworthy.

(*Guardian*, 29 June 1994)

The heart of the country

W E W E R E D U E F O R another sociological stereotype. During the past fifteen years we've had Sloane Rangers, Wallies, Young Fogeys, Essex Men and Essex Girls, all of which served their purpose of making a fast buck for entrepreneurial hacks. (Remember all those copies of *The Official Sloane Ranger Handbook* that were dished out as Christmas presents? And *The Essex Girl Joke Book* – which, I can now reveal, was co-authored by the right-wing pundit Richard Littlejohn under the pseudonym of Ray Leigh?) Islington Person looked briefly promising when it was unveiled a couple of weeks ago, but the poor creature was dead within a couple of days, before a single publisher had managed to commission an instant *Country Diary of an Islington Person* or *Toujours Islington*.

Never mind. Islington Person's arch-enemy – commonly if vaguely described as 'Middle England' – is still going strong, and anyone who wants to earn a few quid would be well advised to start writing *101 Uses for Middle England* forthwith. A database trawl reveals that the phrase has been used no fewer than 319 times in the national press during the last year. In the past couple of weeks alone, it has been cited by Liz Forgan, the head of BBC Radio (who boasted that *Anderson Country* had 'upset parts of Middle England'), and by Kenneth Clarke, the Chancellor of the Exchequer. Clarke has long regarded himself as Middle England's champion. More than two years ago, as Home Secretary, he issued a warning to the Association of Chief Police Officers: 'My gut feeling is that Middle England, which supports the police, wants to be reassured.' He returned to the subject last month. 'It is idle,' he told the Social Market Foundation, 'to think that Middle England does not sometimes feel worried.' Poor Middle England: even its defenders seem to think of it as joyless, fragile and fretful. True, a reviewer of Michael Barrymore's seaside variety show noted that the audience was 'Middle England out for an escapist night – to see a traditional dancing-girls routine, a female singer and then a top of the bill who will have them rolling in the aisles'. But I can find no other recorded instance of Middle England allowing itself a laugh. It is, if the media are to be believed, a very serious-minded place indeed. 'That group of people known as Middle England,' a *Sunday Times* editorial commented, 'are [*sic*] insecure, uncertain and angry.' In the *Independent*, Andrew Marr wrote of 'the cautious, pragmatic, furrow-browed, often-disappointed people of Middle England', a point echoed by the former Labour MP David Marquand in the *Guardian*. 'Middle England has realized,' Marquand reported, 'that the values it prizes most – the decency, tolerance, civility and mutual trust – are in danger.' The *Daily Mail* published a full-page hymn of praise to the 'fortitude and bravery of Middle Englanders', with their 'sensible' and 'un-trendy' values. 'Middle England,' it concluded, 'is where most of us live.' Another commentator has suggested that Middle England is also where the 'next election will be fought'.

But where is it? The *Oxford English Dictionary* is of no assistance. It offers Middle English and Middle-lander ('an inhabitant of the Midlands'), but clearly the next election is not going to be decided by Brummies who speak in Chaucerian dialect. Perhaps Middle England is too recent a coinage to merit inclusion – though my own burrowings have turned up a reference as early as 1982, when a former chairman of the Supplementary Benefits Commission launched a tirade against 'the complacent people of Middle England'. Still, the *OED* does provide a useful history of the analogous phrase 'Middle America', which for many years defined the area that includes Mexico, the West Indies and (of course) Central America. In 1968 the American journalist Joseph Kraft tried to give it a new twist by describing the ethnically diverse municipal employees of New York City – Jewish schoolteachers, Irish policemen, Italian sanitation workers – as 'Middle American'. Soon afterwards, however, Richard Nixon issued his appeal to 'the forgotten Americans' of 'the great silent majority', and the epithet was transferred to them. By 1969, *Collier's Encyclopaedia Year Book* was already noting that 'Mrs Nixon's looks and taste are classic Middle American, even as her husband's are.' It was not implying that the Nixons looked like New York police officers. It meant that they were middle-aged, middle-class middlebrows – perfect specimens of what D. H. Lawrence once denounced as 'the bourgeois middlingness'.

This is also true of Middle Englanders. It is no coincidence that the person mentioned by Kenneth Clarke as the archetypal denizen of Middle England is a 'middle-manager'. When Middle Englanders play cricket, they always take their guard on middle stump. They will happily drive the full length of the M4 in the middle lane, while listening to Andrew Lloyd Webber's *Requiem* on the car stereo. They are neither high church nor low church, neither rich nor poor, neither left-wing nor right-wing.

But, so we are told, they are in a sulk. 'They feel betrayed,' *The Sunday Times* announced recently. 'They no longer even believe that a university education will guarantee their children a better future.' On that, at least, I can alleviate their worries. They should send their children to a little-known seat of learning, which I have been running for some years at a secret address in the heart of this sceptr'd isle. Formerly the Central English Poly, it now rejoices in the title of the University of Middle England.

Our curriculum is small and carefully designed. Physics lessons stop well short of chaos theory (far too upsetting a concept for our sensitive undergraduates). In History, the only set books are those of Sir Arthur Bryant, though we do sometimes allow students to refer to Winston Churchill's *History of the English-Speaking Peoples*. The Philosophy course is built around the works of Patience Strong. No foreign languages are studied. To those who ask 'What should they know of England that only England know?' we reply: 'Quite enough, thank you.' Our core subject, as you would expect, is English – freed of the continental 'theory' that so disfigures the discipline in other universities. The syllabus includes all the immortals of our native literature, with special papers on Sir Henry Newbolt ('Drake he's in his hammock till the great Armadas come/Capten, art tha sleepin' there below?') and Sir John Betjeman. Our flourishing Dramatic Society performs one Shakespeare play and one Savoy Opera every term. We award only second-class degrees, since our motto is 'Moderation in All Things'.

Contrary to what you may read in other papers, we are not unduly angry or insecure at the moment. We approve of the present government, and we take a certain parental pride in John Major's reassuring policy of doing neither one thing nor the other. Being a modest man, he pretends that his academic achievements were limited to a couple of O levels, but we know better. He was, in fact, one of our first graduates.

Why don't you follow his example? The University of Middle England still has places available for the course that starts this October. Our facilities are second to none: the campus is green and pleasant, set in a silver sea, under an English heaven; the communal dining hall serves the roast beef of England for lunch every day. And, yes, there is honey still for tea.

(*Observer*, 7 August 1994) This article elicited a letter from the journalist Robert Chesshyre, who claimed the earliest recorded use of the dread phrase. As an *Observer* reporter, covering the 1975 Common Market referendum, he had written of a pro-EC audience: 'Sometimes dubbed "the silent majority", they are, in fact, "middle England", who support good causes (in this case the market), go to the theatre and garden fêtes, and believe that heckling is vulgar intrusion.' Chesshyre told me that he was 'rather proud of the coinage'.

Dining with danger

O F ALL THE DISEASES afflicting this country, none is more painful than the decline of good old-fashioned manners. A generation ago, it would have been unthinkable to pass the port anti-clockwise after dinner, or to eat peas with a spoon. Now, these solecisms are commonplace. Some people, I am told, even have 'settees' in their 'lounges'. But rescue is at hand: Digby Anderson, director of the right-wing Social Affairs Unit, has edited a handy volume of essays to remind us of the importance of 'keeping up appearances', 'speaking properly', 'knowing your place' and 'being a gentleman' (or, as the case may be, a lady).

The prescriptions and proscriptions in his book are impressively severe. One contributor, the sociologist Athena S. Leoussi, is almost incoherent with rage at the ubiquity of blue denim. 'Men and women in jeans,' she argues, 'offer other men and women the violent, cold and limited life of dire necessity, not humanity.' Leoussi also believes that the fashion for displaying 'animal motifs' on clothes is 'the logical culmination of this so-called pluralist culture, namely the dissolution of all culture into barbarity. They are the motifs of the culture of militant self-assertion, infinite and arbitrary rights and zero obligations.' Now that she has pointed this out, I can see that my baby son's militant self-assertion is almost certainly provoked by his Pingu the penguin T-shirts and Winnie the Pooh pyjamas.

The rules of etiquette may seem trivial, but according to Anderson they are essential to prevent 'the destruction of shared civic values'. His mission is to restore politeness and tolerance to a society that is drowning in 'lack of consideration, petty selfishness, forgetfulness of others, and boorishness'. For more than ten years this same Digby Anderson has written a cookery column for the *Spectator*. A very good column it is too: he loves his grub, and conveys his enthusiasm with gusto. But his *Spectator* pieces are not exactly brimming over with civility and courtesy. Whether writing about university students ('lazy and ignorant'), British housewives ('spineless, ignorant'), young people in general ('ghastly'), left-wing journalists ('bleating'), shopkeepers ('morose ignoramuses'), or vegetarians ('absurd and ungrateful wretches'), he is often tremendously rude. Even his hosts and guests don't escape: after dining with two friends, Nigel and Susan, he penned a devastating post-mortem on their soggy rice, even soggier gammon and 'boring' cheese. For good measure, he drew attention to Susan's 'unpleasant smell', apparently caused by 'a particularly repugnant talcum powder'.

His worst *bêtes noires* are people who say that they 'can't' eat such delicacies as eels, aspic or kidneys. 'If you have one of the whining "can't" brigade at your table,' he advised *Spectator* readers a few years ago, 'persist, push the inquiry. "Come, Stephen, you're a grown man, time you got over this nonsense..." On no account must his whining be indulged. It is not a kindness to permit these morally flaccid persons to continue in their craven condition. All the force of ridicule, social stigma, emotional blackmail and even physical force must be used to crush them.' Having consulted all the relevant authorities – from Lady Troubridge's *Book of Etiquette* to Drusilla Beyfus's *Guide to Modern Manners* – I can find no support for the contention that physical violence is acceptable in the dining room, especially when there may be ladies present. How, then, can Anderson presume to set himself up as an expert on 'gentility'?

It was ever thus. Nancy Mitford's famous list of 'U' and 'Non-U' phrases reduced an entire generation of social climbers to nervous wrecks, terrified that they might disgrace themselves by calling a napkin a serviette. And yet, as Evelyn Waugh pointed out, while ambitious middle-class families were hastily hiding their fish-knives (an irredeemably Non-U form of cutlery), 'at many of the really august stately homes fish-knives have been in continuous use for nearly a hundred years'. Chiding Mitford for her arbitrary distinctions between U and Non-U, Waugh noted that 'few well-bred people are aware, still less observant, of more than a small fraction of this code.' To judge by his own boorish advice, Digby Anderson must be very well bred indeed. I wonder if he owns a pair of jeans?

(Guardian, 5 June 1996)

Kitty litter

M Y FRIEND KITTY KELLEY has taken quite a pasting from the *Daily Mail*, that ever-vigilant guardian of taste and ethics. Its attitude to her can be summarized thus: how dare an American presume to write a book about our royal family? Kitty has asked herself the same question many times. During her visits to London, she often seemed utterly mystified by the unfamiliar territory on which she was trespassing. When I introduced her to a braying, drunken aristocrat, it was as if I'd taken a Martian to the FA Cup final. Even now, she cannot understand why 'Jeffrey Archer' and 'Lord Archer' are both correct forms of address, whereas 'Lord Jeffrey Archer' is a shocking solecism.

She was equally puzzled when the Queen's press secretary, Charles Anson, sent a letter to Kitty and her publishers warning them not to suggest that she had received any 'special cooperation' or 'approval' from the Palace: 'If the limited help we have given you is misrepresented in any way in future, we will consider taking appropriate action.' As an American unaccustomed to our quaint British way of doing things, Kitty was taken aback by Anson's apparent belief that the Queen of England still has absolute jurisdiction over citizens of the United States. 'Dear Francis,' she wrote to me. 'You speak the Queen's English, so please translate "appropriate action".' I was unable to assist; but she managed pretty well herself, firing off a splendidly insolent reply in which she pointed out that her reputation as the queen of unauthorized biographies could be gravely damaged by any hint that she had the approval of the royal family. If Anson repeated this false allegation, she would 'consider taking appropriate action'. Her New York publishers, Warner Books, entered into the spirit of *lèse-majesté* by framing the royal message and hanging it in their corporate loo.

Now, alas, the Warner bosses have decreed that her book will not be available in Britain, because of their exaggerated fear of libel suits. Last Friday she rang to say that she would send me a copy by special courier, but on Sunday I learned that Warner had vetoed the idea. She isn't allowed to give interviews to British journalists, and American bookshops have been told not to fulfil any transatlantic mail-orders.

Some liberals – even some republicans – may think it is no bad thing to protect the British public from Kitty's disclosures. Since the death of Princess Diana, it seems to have become the received wisdom on both Left and Right that all 'intrusions into royal privacy' must cease. Where, however, does this privacy end? If the Labour government were to raise income tax, newspapers would feel entitled to point out that it had broken an election promise. The royals, who have never been elected, derive their power and glory entirely from the premise of the hereditary principle, which gives constitutional weight to the most intimate details of their lives – the marriages and adulteries, conceptions and deaths. Hence the necessity of confirming Lady Diana Spencer's virginity before she could marry Prince Charles. Hence the fact that it is still a treasonous offence to have an affair with the heir's wife. Hence, too, the old tradition – which continued well into this century – that a member of the government must be present at every royal birth.

Writing in the *Daily Mail* yesterday, the author Philip Ziegler deplored Kitty's interest in 'who went to bed with whom' and 'who is illegitimate'. As the official biographer of Edward VIII, he should know better than most that in a royal family the question of 'who went to bed with whom' can have great political significance. At least one historian has argued that the Norman Conquest in 1066 'was a direct result of irregular sexual habits' since the chaste Edward the Confessor produced no heir, leaving Harold of Wessex and William of Normandy to fight over the succession. Had a sixteenth-century Kitty Kelley written about Henry VIII's marital shenanigans, she would have been denounced by the leader-writers of *Ye Daily Maile*; but no one today would deny that his polygamy had serious consequences for the nation. In these circumstances, why shouldn't a biographer investigate the Queen's lineage? It is, after all, Her Majesty's only qualification for the job.

Kitty's greatest crime, to judge by the insults hurled at her by the London press, is that she has no instinctive respect for the monarchy. In my view, this makes her the ideal person to write a genuinely independent book about it. Our home-grown royal-watchers – even those who fancy themselves as fear-less gumshoes – can never quite escape the treacly deference that smothers all discussion of the Windsors.

> O wad some Pow'r the giftie gie us
> To see oursels as others see us!
> It wad frae mony a blunder free us,
> And foolish notion.

It is all too typical of the British that, when a feisty foreign democrat at last offers an unillusioned outsider's view of our foolish notions, none of us is per-mitted to see it.

(*Guardian*, 17 September 1997)

Mind-forg'd manacles

Now here's a rum do. Elton John's new version of 'Candle in the Wind', which sold 600,000 copies last Saturday alone, was issued as a tribute to the Princess of Wales; but its lyrics are partly inspired by William Blake, a radical and republican. 'And your footsteps will always fall here/Along England's greenest hills...' Or, as Blake put it nearly 200 years ago: 'And did those feet in ancient time/Walk upon England's mountains green?' I was surprised that no commentator at the funeral saw fit to mention this obvious echo – especially since the sixteen-year-old William Blake began his artistic apprenticeship by drawing pictures of the royal tombs in Westminster Abbey, and the Princess's friend Dodi Fayed was an assistant producer on *Chariots of Fire*. Perhaps they feared accusations of blasphemy, since the feet in Blake's poem were those of 'the holy Lamb of God': even in the beatifying atmosphere of her funeral, the equation of the saintly Diana with Jesus Christ might have been too much for some worshippers.

No matter. Now that Elton John's record can be heard in almost every household in the land, I hope it will do for Blake what *Four Weddings and a Funeral* achieved for W. H. Auden, or *The English Patient* for Herodotus. Those who buy his collected works in search of 'Jerusalem' will find much to ponder.

'Blake was himself an ardent member of the New School,' his first biographer recorded, 'a vehement republican and sympathiser with the Revolution, hater and contemner of kings and king-craft.' A neat if ill-punctuated précis of his opinions can be found in a marginal scribble in one of his notebooks: 'Princes appear to me to be Fools Houses of Commons & Houses of Lords appear to me to be fools they seem to me to be something Else besides Human Life.' No Blairite he.

In the first draft of his famous poem on London, Blake wrote:

> In every cry of every man
> In every voice of every child
> In every voice in every ban
> The German forged links I hear.

The Germans in questions were, of course, the Hanoverians who had taken over the English throne. But then he changed 'German forged links' to 'mind-forg'd manacles', an inspired description of the British people's wilful self-imprisonment in royal fantasyland. An NOP poll last weekend found that 53 per cent of us want the Queen to abdicate within the next three years, and that 60 per cent think she should be succeeded by Prince William – a schoolboy who hasn't even taken his GCSEs yet. Our minds may be securely manacled, but our brains have apparently gone AWOL. Nurse! The screens!

(Guardian, 17 September 1997)

The pinkos and the purple

I T I S , I F I N D , a pretty safe rule in life that any idea supported by Tony Blair, Rupert Murdoch and Jeffrey Archer must be a dud. The campaign by this gruesome threesome to 'modernize' the House of Windsor is no exception. A modern monarchy is possible, of course – just as it's possible to buy alcohol-free lager or vegetarian sausages that look and smell vaguely like pork. But what's the point? Lord Archer claims that the royal rules of succession, under which male heirs take precedence over females, are an unfair anachronism. Hasn't he noticed that the same can be said of any hereditary sovereign, regardless of gender? Similarly, Tony Blair is putting pressure on

Buckingham Palace to do away with 'outdated pomp and ceremony' at the state opening of Parliament. Hasn't he noticed that the Queen will still have all her antique powers and prerogatives, regardless of whether she arrives by Rolls-Royce or horse-drawn carriage?

If Her Majesty had an ounce of gumption, she would tell Blair and his accomplices to bugger off. But, according to the *Mail on Sunday*, she is torn between two conflicting views. 'On one side, she is being advised by her deeply conservative husband, Prince Philip, that Britain's first family is too ancient and steeped in history to be changed.' Quite so: the monarchy cannot be meaningfully reformed – only abolished. Nevertheless, to appease the modernizers she is considering 'a raft of dramatic reforms which would have been unthinkable only a few years ago. They include a radical suggestion that the title "Royal Highness" – now held by eighteen family members – should be restricted to the heir to the throne and his (or her) immediate successor.'

Radical, dramatic, unthinkable. If that is really how Her Majesty sees these trifling adjustments, she must lead a very cloistered life indeed. But then so do her subjects. 'There was another welcome sign of the times yesterday – the Union flag flew proudly over Buckingham Palace,' the *Sun* declared in a triumphant editorial last Saturday. 'The change was not announced, but *Sun* readers quickly noticed, and rejoiced...Now a flag will always flutter. The Queen is, as she promised, learning to listen to her people, with wise guidance from Premier Tony Blair.' More fool her, if she listens to the sort of people who rejoice at such things. And before heeding any more 'wise guidance' from the Dear Leader, she should look up what Blair said about the deficiencies of the British constitution in his John Smith Memorial Lecture two years ago: 'The case for reform is simple and obvious. It is in principle wrong and absurd that people should wield power on the basis of birth, not merit or election...There are no conceivable grounds for maintaining this system.' He was, of course, talking about hereditary peers. When it comes to the hereditary absurdity at the very apex of our constitution, the great modernizer is either too timid or too opportunistic to follow his own logic.

In this, if nothing else, he is very Old Labour indeed. More than a century ago, during Queen Victoria's diamond jubilee, Keir Hardie said that arguments about the monarchy were a waste of breath: 'Until the system of wealth production be changed, it is not worth exchanging a queen for a president. The robbery of the poor would go on equally under the one as the other.' Incredibly enough, the issue has only once been debated at a Labour conference. In 1923, a motion from the Stockton and Thornaby Labour Party daringly proposed 'that the Royal Family is no longer necessary as part of the

British Constitution, and that the Labour Party is therefore asked to state definitively its view of this matter'. George Lansbury, as left-wing a leader as the party has ever had, replied on behalf of the National Executive. Why, he asked, fool about with an issue that had no real importance? 'What is the use of bothering about that just now?' To clinch the argument, Lansbury revealed that he had once 'sat behind two princes at a football match' and, he could assure delegates, 'they were just ordinary common people like themselves'. The resolution was defeated by a large majority, and that was that. Even Tony Benn, who as Postmaster-General in the 1960s ran a quixotic campaign to remove the Queen's head from postage stamps, was eventually forced to conclude that republicanism was a distraction from more urgent tasks. 'It's much more important to keep in with Harold,' he noted glumly in his diary, 'and it would be silly to run any risk of a row politically.'

And so the strange love affair between the People's Party and the folks at the Palace has continued. After attending the wedding of Prince Andrew and Sarah Ferguson, Neil Kinnock emerged from Westminster Abbey to inform the press, in best George Lansbury fashion, that Fergie had smiled just like an 'ordinary' person. 'That smile was worth all the rest of it!' he gushed.

The man who deserves most credit for keeping Labour untainted by republicanism is that wily old devil Lord Mountbatten, who realized long ago that it would be a useful precaution for the royal family to woo and beguile influential figures on the Left. During the abdication crisis of 1936, it was he who persuaded Edward VIII that the best outlet for pro-royal stories was *The Week*, a muckraking rag edited by the communist journalist Claud Cockburn. 'So we're King's men now, are we?' a puzzled colleague of Cockburn's inquired. 'King's men my foot!' Cockburn said. 'If the King has got around to supporting us against Baldwin, I wish him all the best of British luck.'

Another of his lordship's regular 'conduits' was the left-wing MP and columnist Tom Driberg. In 1946, when Princess Elizabeth was preparing to announce her engagement, Mountbatten asked Driberg to invite a posse of Tribunite backbenchers to lunch with Prince Philip. 'Thank you for being so kind to my nephew Philip,' he wrote afterwards. 'It is most kind of you to say that you will help to give the right line in the press when news of his naturalization is announced.' Hilariously, Mountbatten even managed to convince Driberg that Philip was himself a bit of a pinko. 'I was agreeably surprised,' he wrote in 1947, 'to find that only the *Daily Worker* appeared to condemn my nephew's engagement on political grounds. Even if they knew the truth about him [i.e., about his socialist sympathies], I feel it would be too good a propaganda point for them to pass up altogether. I am so grateful to you for telling people the truth about him. As you know, I am an ardent believer in constitutional monarchy as a means of producing rapid evolution without actual revolution.'

The picture of the royals as a Trojan horse within the establishment may seem preposterous but plenty of liberals and socialists have fallen for it – as Prince Charles, Mountbatten's favourite great-nephew, can testify. A left-wing acquaintance of mine who was recruited by the Prince as an informal adviser in the 1980s used to boast that the heir to the throne had done far more than the Labour front bench to discredit the Tories. I suspect that Blair, too, sees Charles as a potentially helpful ally. It is hard to think of any other reason why his antipathy to the 'hereditary principle' doesn't extend to the principle's most senior beneficiary.

'We know in our hearts that the monarchy is a historical absurdity,' the playwright David Hare argued at a Charter 88 conference five years ago, 'but because we lack the courage to abolish it (as indeed we lack the courage for any radical undertaking), instead we are taking out our anger at our own bad faith by torturing the individuals involved. Newspapers, led by the Murdoch group, have begun the project of putting the royal family in such a state of tension that their lives will become unliveable.' I see no harm in torturing a few royals now and again, *pour encourager les autres*. But there's nothing to be gained from persecuting the Windsors if those issues so carefully avoided by Labour leaders from Keir Hardie to Tony Blair – the need for a head of state, the purpose of the royal prerogative, the status of the Church of England, the concept of 'the nation' – remain submerged beneath a lot of twaddle about the correct method of addressing Princess Beatrice, or the necessity of curtseying to Princess Michael of Kent. The Duke of Edinburgh may be 'deeply conservative', but he is absolutely right to resist New Labour's blandishments. If he's prepared to take on the combined might of Downing Street and Wapping, I wish him all the best of British luck.

(*Guardian*, 11 March 1998)

Enough to make you weep

PROFESSOR ANTHONY O'HEAR has been accused of presenting 'a grotesque caricature' of the Princess of Wales and those who mourned her. But his own critics have caricatured the professor's argument no less grotesquely. Contrary to what you may have heard or seen, his notorious essay – which appears in a book published by the right-wing Social Affairs Unit – is not a simple hatchet job. 'There is no doubt that she did quite a lot of good both for individuals and for the causes with which she was associated,' he acknowledges. 'There was something touching in her reaching out to the socially excluded...' What of the crowds who grieved? O'Hear denies that they were hysterical or deranged. 'They were, in fact, quiet, orderly and in demeanour dignified.' All he says is that the reaction to Princess Diana lacked a sense of proportion.

This point is amply confirmed by the reaction to his own modest heresy. O'Hear has been vilified in the *Mirror* as a 'rat-faced little loser', described as a 'desiccated calculating machine' by the lovely Lord St John of Fawsley and dismissed as an 'old-fashioned snob' by Tony Blair. Why, I wonder, does a British Prime Minister feel obliged to interrupt crucial diplomatic business in the Middle East to attack an eight-page essay written by an obscure academic for a little known think-tank? The pillorying of O'Hear is like the rage of Caliban seeing his own face in the glass: it suggests that he has come dangerously close to the truth.

The *Guardian*'s editorial last Saturday argued that the lads and lasses of the Social Affairs Unit 'emerge as a slightly fogeyish bunch'. Conservative think-tanks jolly well ought to be fogeyish: the alternative is far worse. When I last met the Thatcherite president of the Adam Smith Institute, Dr Madsen Pirie, I mentioned an amazing poll which showed that 93 per cent of Britons supported the new government. 'Yes, it's incredible,' he agreed. 'How can there be as many as seven people in a hundred who don't approve of Tony Blair? We're all Blairites now, aren't we?' As if to prove his Cool Britannia credentials, he revealed that he had lately taken up rollerblading. The grumpy old curmudgeons of the Social Affairs Unit have many faults, but at least they preserve some sense of decorum.

And yet, perversely, the other criticism made of O'Hear and his colleagues is that they're not fogeyish enough. 'The professor is right, of course, in his wider point that there is a powerful streak of sentimentality in the British character,' writes Dominic Lawson, one of the Princess's friends. 'But he is startlingly wrong in thinking that there is anything new in it. The British have been this way before, and at a time of greatness rather than of decadence.' According to this interpretation, sentimentality is a grand old national tradition that should be cherished by true conservatives.

Readers of Dickens won't need reminding that there was indeed plenty of mawkishness in nineteenth-century England. As the historian G. M. Young recorded in his classic *Portrait of an Age*, it was a period when ministers often wept at the dinner table and 'the sight of an infant school could reduce a civil servant to a passion of tears'. But these lachrymose performances were often little more than a pose: some Victorians deliberately smudged the ink on letters of condolence, sprinkling water over the page to simulate the tears they could not summon.

The 'language of feeling' first entered British discourse in the mid-eighteenth century through the novels of Laurence Sterne and Samuel Richardson, and the moral philosophy of David Hume. Sterne played it strictly for laughs, fearing that if he ever took anything seriously he'd sink into a quicksand of melancholy. Richardson, who enjoyed a good blub, preferred to explore the 'feminine sensibility' of sighing and swooning. Hume's purpose was to establish the supremacy of passion over reason. But in spite of their differences, all these authors regarded sentimentality as a cure for solitude – hence the title of John Mullan's excellent book on the subject, *Sentiment and Sociability*. 'The passions are so contagious,' Hume wrote in his *Treatise of Human Nature*, 'that they pass with the greatest facility from one person to another, and produce correspondent movement in all human breasts.'

Which is, of course, precisely what happened last summer. The periodic swellings of emotion in England over the past couple of centuries aren't signs of 'greatness', as Lawson claims. They are the anguished pleas of a lonely and atomized populace, desperate for company. What fascinated my foreign friends at the time of the Princess's funeral was the obvious yearning for an excuse – any excuse – to talk to complete strangers without embarrassment. 'We have Independence Day and Thanksgiving,' one said, 'but I suppose you don't have many occasions when you can get together as a nation.' It is absurd and pathetic, in the last years of the twentieth century, that our only opportunity should be the death of a rich aristocrat – whom we are then forced to canonize, in defiance of all reason, simply to justify our own rational desires.

'When they go on about fake sentimentality in relation to Princess Diana, people really felt that,' Blair complains. 'Why is it fake?' But O'Hear hasn't said it was. He emphasizes that the emotion was spontaneous and genuine – 'misdirected maybe, as in the case of the man who said that Diana's death meant more to him than that of his parents, and, in that sense, irrational, but it was not insincere or superficial. Whatever it was people felt, they really felt it.' In his study of eighteenth-century feelings, Mullan argues that sentimental passion and sympathy offered 'a more inclusive vocabulary of social coherence' than politics could provide. They still do. During the 1980s politics was dominated by somebody who insisted that 'there is no such thing as society, only individual men and women and their families'. Now we have a Prime Minister who regards comradeship and collective association as anachronisms that should be excluded from the political lexicon. Is it any wonder that so many people cling to the memory of Princess Diana, just as an earlier generation tried to revive the spirit of the Blitz or Dunkirk? If a large throng of demonstrators stopped the traffic to express their solidarity with a victimized trade unionist whom they had never met, Blair would be the first to denounce it as 'unlawful secondary action'. To take to the streets on behalf of a victimized princess is, however, quite permissible – not least because it distracts us from the inadequacies of politics. 'Grief is a vital safety valve,' the *Sun* commented this week, accidentally giving the game away.

It is difficult if not impossible to weep and think at the same time. And so, as the *Sun* cheerfully exhorted its readers: 'Keep grieving.'

(Guardian, 22 April 1998)

Voting with dinosaurs

L ORD ALLI'S DISCLOSURE that he has detected some racism and homophobia among his fellow peers is astonishing indeed, and well worth the front-page billing it was given in the *Independent on Sunday*. I haven't been so shocked since Woodrow Wyatt revealed in his diaries that the Queen Mother isn't entirely sympathetic to the aims and objects of the Socialist Workers' Party.

Baron Tebbit of Chingford finds Lord Alli's complaint incredible. 'It is all in the mind,' he says. 'There is certainly no racist environment.' Can this be the same Lord Tebbit who, in a speech earlier this year, taunted Lord Alli for being a gay Asian and therefore in a minority of a minority?

The bad news is that milord Tebbit will survive Tony Blair's reform of the Lords. The good news is that his hereditary colleagues have been forced to justify their existence by issuing brief statements explaining why they should survive the cull. These documents, which can be inspected at the House of Lords record office, will be a priceless resource to future historians; indeed, the pathetic, hilarious spectacle of these lumbering beasts sleepwalking towards extinction would make a perfect sequel to *Walking with Dinosaurs*.

After reading all their manifestos, I can see why the hereditaries are so reluctant to offer themselves to the voters: they haven't quite got the hang of this electioneering lark. 'I may have a contribution to make,' the 6th Earl Cairns proposes shyly. 'I shortly expect to have more time.' The Earl of Glasgow, a Liberal Democrat, admits that he has been 'only able to attend the House approximately three days a month but expects to become more available in the future'. Jolly Liberal of him, I'm sure. The election address of the Tory peer Lord Morris, who hopes to become a deputy speaker, runs to just one sentence: 'It is hardly for me to attempt to proselytize my candidature; it is a matter for my peers.' This is not a technique one would recommend to parliamentary hopefuls on the hustings, but it seems to appeal to their lordships. 'It would be as vainglorious to proclaim a personal manifesto,' the Earl of Onslow writes, 'as it would be arrogant to list any achievement.' Lord Pender's sales pitch consists of the single word 'duty'.

Other lords, however, are willing to confront the big issues. Lord Rathcavan promises 'to represent the Union, the countryside and the hospitality industry'. Lord Sudeley, a veteran far-right activist and Monday Clubber, 'would like to keep an eye on all measures from the Synod affecting the prayer book'. Viscount Monckton of Brenchley has more ambitious policies: 'I support the Queen and all the royal family...All cats to be muzzled outside to stop the agonizing torture of mice and small birds...LEVEL UP not level down. God willing.'

In an election address, candidates are usually expected to give some idea of their qualifications for the job. Here is Lord Napier and Ettrick: 'Having retired after twenty-five years as private secretary to Princess Margaret, I am now available.' The Viscount Massereene and Ferrard notes with pride that he is president of the Monday Club and an 'active member' of the UK Offshore Operators' Group. Lord Beaverbrook draws attention to his financial expertise, having been treasurer of the Conservative Party from 1990 to 1992, but omits to add that he had to resign on being declared bankrupt. He looks forward to 'contributing to debate on the Party Funding Bill expected in the next session'.

The great virtue of the lords, of course, is that they are wholly disinterested – or 'indifferent', as one charmingly puts it. 'It is because I am neither elected nor receive a salary that I only have the good of the country at heart,' Viscount Mountgarret observes. 'I do not have to curry favour with constituents.' Just as well, really. Only three weeks ago, an employment tribunal in Leeds ordered him to pay £20,000 to a gamekeeper, Michael Rushby, who had endured eight years of Mountgarret's 'unpredictable, irrational and intolerable rages'. In 1982, the public-spirited peer was fined £1,000 for peppering with birdshot a hot-air balloon which flew over his estate.

It is solely because of their ancestry that these boobies are eligible to stand in next week's election. And yet, with only a couple of exceptions (milords Alanbrooke and Alexander of Tunis, both of whom rely on their fathers' achievements), they are curiously coy about their forebears. The Duke of Montrose, for instance, claims: 'My family has a long history of service to our monarchy and the Union of Great Britain.' You would hardly guess from this that his father, the 7th Duke, was a minister in the illegal Rhodesian regime led by Ian Smith, and couldn't attend his son's wedding for fear that he would be charged with treason as soon as he set foot on British soil.

Lord Moynihan, the former Tory MP Colin Moynihan, tells us of his Oxford scholarship and his Olympic rowing record but forgets to say how he became a hereditary peer. After losing his Commons seat in 1992, he spent five years establishing that he was the true heir of his half-brother, the 3rd Baron, a bongo-playing brothel-keeper and drug-dealer who had fled to the Philippines while awaiting trial on no fewer than fifty-seven charges of fraud. (I still cherish the opening sentence of the *Daily Telegraph*'s obituary: 'The 3rd Lord Moynihan, who has died in Manila, aged fifty-five, provided, through his character and career, ample ammunition for critics of the hereditary principle.') Colin Moynihan's rival for the title was a seven-year-old Filipino, Andrew Moynihan, and the case hinged on whether the third baron could have fathered a child in spite of his 'very low sperm count'. As the Attorney-General commented afterwards, with no hint of irony: 'It is essential that no one be admitted to the Lords who is not properly qualified to sit.'

This sentiment would be heartily endorsed by Geoffrey Russell, the 4th Baron Ampthill, who in the past year or two has emerged as the strongest defender of hereditary privileges. He joined the Upper House in 1976 after a two-year battle with his younger half-brother – who pointed out that the marriage of Geoffrey's parents was unconsummated, as the Baroness had revealed at the time of her divorce. She spent only one night in bed with her husband, during which he engaged in 'Hunnish practices', otherwise known as masturbation. However, the Hon. Geoffrey Russell persuaded the House of Lords privileges committee that a few drops of baronial sperm had somehow entered Lady Ampthill, thus making him the rightful heir. In his manifesto, the current Lord Ampthill boasts of having chaired the refreshment subcommittee for twelve years. 'Living nearby, can undertake late Woolsack duties,' he adds helpfully. But there is not a dickybird about the Hunnish practices.

I fear that he has missed a Unique Selling Point here. Of all the candidates in next week's election, Ampthill is the only one who can justly claim to have earned his seat in parliament by proving that his father was a wanker.

(*Guardian*, 27 October 1999)

The price of honour

‘I SUPPOSE THAT PEERAGE cost the old devil the deuce of a sum,’ Bingo Little tells Bertie Wooster in *The Inimitable Jeeves* after Bingo's Uncle Mortimer, who made his pile from Little's Liniment ('It Limbers up the Legs'), has become the noble Lord Bittlesham. 'Even baronetcies have gone up frightfully nowadays, I'm told.'

The Inimitable Jeeves was published in 1924. A year later, on 7 August 1925, King George V gave his royal assent to the Honours (Prevention of Abuses) Act. And eight years after that, the notorious honours broker Maundy Gregory became the first person to be convicted under the new law, having tried to wheedle £10,000 out of a naval commander in return for procuring a knighthood. The commander, who was quite happy with his Distinguished Service Order, had gone straight to the police. 'In my opinion, the maximum fine of £50 would be wholly inadequate to meet the facts of this case,' said the chief magistrate at Bow Street, Sir Rollo Frederick Graham-Campbell, who had himself been knighted only a month earlier. 'But as this is the first case under the Act I do not propose to impose the maximum penalty allowed by the law to a court of summary jurisdiction.' He sentenced Gregory to two months' imprisonment as well as the £50 fine.

After completing his sentence Gregory moved to France, where he lived off a handsome pension of £2,000 a year. Some historians have claimed that it was a stipend from the Conservative Party, but this is not quite correct. As Tom Cullen noted in his excellent biography of Gregory, Conservative Central Office 'merely acted as an "honest broker", if one may use the term in this context, in bringing together a group of noble lords and knights who had been Maundy Gregory's clients in the past, and who were prepared to underwrite Gregory's future in return for his silence'.

The trial of Maundy Gregory took place in February 1933. Nearly seventy years on, although the law is still on the statute book, he remains the only person ever to be prosecuted under the Honours (Prevention of Abuses) Act. A visiting Martian might reasonably infer that no other 'abuse' has occurred.

Anyone with a GCSE in modern history could swiftly put the Martian right. A few years ago the diligent sleuths at the Labour Research Department calculated that although only 6.2 per cent of British companies gave money to the Tories between 1979 and 1992, more than 50 per cent of peerages for 'services to industry' during this period went to executives of firms which had donated to the party. (The chance of this being coincidence was 1 in 10 to the power of 133.) Labour's record is no better: reciting the list of crooks and spivs honoured by Harold Wilson – Lord Kagan, Lord Plurenden, Sir Eric Miller, old uncle Lord Brayley and all – is still enough to give me a migraine.

No wonder the law has not been enforced: all the major parties have a vested interest in keeping the system corrupt. 'You and I know that the sale of honours is the cleanest way of raising money for a political party,' Lloyd George confided to the Tory politician J. C. C. Davidson. 'The worst of it is that you cannot defend it in public.' If Labour invited the police to consider milord Ashcroft of Belize's donations, William Hague would probably ask them to take a look at some of Tony Blair's 200 new peers as well. It may have been the Liberal Lloyd George who made Maundy Gregory rich, but it was the Tories who bought his silence – and a Labour Prime Minister, Ramsay MacDonald, who gave a knighthood to Julien Cahn, the Conservative fixer responsible for arranging his French exile. 'Maundy Gregory's papers and Maundy Gregory's presence here would stir up such a filthy sewer as would poison public life,' MacDonald wrote in his diary, after learning from Stanley Baldwin that several Labour figures were also implicated in the racket. 'Mr Baldwin involves me in a scandal by forcing me to give an honour because a man has paid £30,000 to get Tory headquarters and some Tories living and dead out of a mess.'

So it has continued ever since. In the early 1990s, a roguish friend of mine, who makes his living advising right-wing tycoons and politicians, was approached by a businessman with a blunt request: 'I want you to get me a knighthood. I'm prepared to pay up to £50,000.' My friend replied that this wasn't nearly enough, pointing out that Maundy Gregory used to charge almost as much for a baronetcy just after the First World War. Half a million quid would be the minimum necessary outlay these days, he said. The businessman then lowered his sights, asking if £50,000 might at least buy him an OBE. My friend thought that should be possible.

But why shell out fifty grand for a piffling little OBE, which will impress hardly anyone, when you can have a far grander honour free of charge? Five years ago, the then Lord Chancellor revealed in a written answer that 'there is nothing to prohibit any individual from describing himself [sic] as a peer of the realm, for any purpose not unlawful'. In short, we can all follow the examples of Duke Ellington and the Duchess of Duke Street. True, we shan't be able to sit in the House of Lords – but after reading Lord Hattersley's article on Monday most of us will feel rather grateful for that. The main purpose of a title is to inflate one's self-importance, impress bank managers, win admiring glances from American hotel receptionists and get tables in fashionable restaurants. An extra benefit, if we all start calling ourselves Lord This and Lady That, is that Lord Ashcroft will feel very common indeed. As A. J. P. Taylor wrote of Lloyd George: 'He detested titles. This, no doubt, is why he distributed them so lavishly.'

I can see, however, that this isn't a Blairite, market-minded solution. So here's the alternative: repeal the 1925 Act, which is manifestly useless anyway, and announce that titles will be sold off rather as the DVLA sells personalized number plates, with all revenues from this 'vanity tax' going directly to the education service and the NHS. Some may fear that such a scheme would degrade and demean Parliament; but the PM has already done that by filling the 'modernized' Upper House with his cronies and benefactors. If preening, stupid tycoons yearn for ermine, let's force the old devils to pay us the deuce of a sum for the privilege.

(*Guardian*, 5 April 2000)

One hundred years of platitudes

T HE QUEEN MOTHER'S longevity is impressive, but not half so impressive as the Stakhanovite work rate of her hagiographers. Last weekend's output alone included a twelve-page supplement in the *Sunday Times*, a 'definitive' sixteen-page pull-out in the *Sunday Telegraph*, and a *Mail on Sunday* partwork running to more than 50 pages. Seldom in the history of hackery have so many column inches been filled with so little information.

According to Walter Bagehot, the monarchy has two distinct parts to play in the tragicomedy of British life – a 'dignified' role and an 'efficient' role. In the former – which can be summarized as smiling, waving and wearing extravagant hats – the Queen Mum is clearly an Oscar-winner, but this doesn't make the task of her word-churning idolaters any easier. Once you've used up every synonym in the thesaurus for 'serene' and 'diaphanous', what more can be said? The prolific Paul Johnson lists her finest achievements thus: 'Opening things and saying a few well-chosen words, fishing, remembering faces, singing in church'. Perhaps sensing that these humdrum accomplishments scarcely justify his claims for her historical significance, he adds that the Queen Mum 'benefits from a deep-rooted veneration the British have – it is more manly than deference, akin rather to admiration – for the landed aristocracy'. Speak for yourself, matey. Nevertheless, let's accept that she is indeed a serene and diaphanous figure whose presence would enhance any church fête. What of her political or 'efficient' duties? The birthday tributes are astonishingly coy on this subject. 'Not giving interviews – it's a brilliant ploy,' Lord Bell of Belgravia writes in *The Sunday Times*. 'Absolutely nobody knows what she thinks about anything.'

What codswallop. Thanks to the recently published diaries of her friend Woodrow Wyatt, we know many of the Queen Mother's opinions. In March 1986, for instance, she tells Wyatt that when the royal family are alone together they 'often drink a toast at the end of dinner to Mrs Thatcher. She adores Mrs Thatcher.' She also adores President P. W. Botha of South Africa, and 'thinks it is awful how the BBC and media misrepresent everything that Botha is trying to do'. That summer, while lunching at Clarence House with Wyatt and Douglas Fairbanks Jr, Her Majesty delivers an unprompted rant against black Commonwealth countries which have been pressing for sanctions against South Africa. Would she mind, Wyatt wonders, if some black countries resigned from the Commonwealth in protest against Thatcher's line? 'Not at all, if that's what they want to do,' the Queen Mother replies, briskly denouncing President Kenneth Kaunda of Zambia as 'an idiot'.

A few months before the 1987 election, a nervous Queen Mum asks Wyatt for reassurance that the Tories will stay in power. As he writes, 'she is much more pro-Conservative than the Queen or the Prince of Wales'. She is also opposed to female ordination, since 'the women who wanted to be priests all seem so aggressive'. After a discussion on the War Crimes Bill, Wyatt records, 'We talked about Jews for a bit and she said she liked them very much but they were a separate people and a strange people, keeping to themselves and their own ways. She clearly has some reservations about Jews in her old-fashioned English way.' Other 'reservations' surface in these chats with her confidant. 'Actually, she doesn't really like the French very much at all,' Wyatt writes in March 1991. Later in the year they talk about the European Community. 'She is terrified of the Germans, and said, "Never trust them, never trust them. They can't be trusted." I thought that quite amusing as the Royal Family is of German origin.'

In revealing the Queen Mother as a right-wing xenophobe, Lord Wyatt's diaries merely confirm what we always suspected. Still, it is rather surprising that this useful corroborative source hasn't been mentioned in any of the 'special supplements' and 'souvenir magazines' that purport to tell us what she is really like.

There is an even more striking omission. Right up until the start of the Second World War, the then Queen was an enthusiastic appeaser of Hitler. Yet the word appeasement has appeared in none of the lengthy articles by supposedly serious historians over the past few days. Writing in the *Sunday Telegraph*, Andrew Roberts maintains that she, along with Winston Churchill, came 'to symbolize Britain's determination to withstand Hitler and eventually to conquer him'. Roberts should reread his own book *Eminent Churchillians*, published in 1994. In a most instructive chapter titled 'The House of Windsor and the Politics of Appeasement', he observed that the Queen and King 'failed to make the mental leap necessary to appreciate that feeding the Nazi beast whetted its appetite, and that only a firm stance early on could have averted war. They represented the most unprepossessing aspects of conventional wisdom, at precisely the time when it was proving dangerously mistaken.' Nor was she 'noticeably concerned by the plight of the Nazis' victims, considering a country's internal political arrangements to be her own affair'.

In his gawd-bless-yer-ma'am essay last weekend, Roberts cited a state visit to France in July 1938 as an example of her high diplomatic skills. 'With the deteriorating international situation of the late 1930s it was vital for Britain's allies and potential allies to be as well disposed towards her as possible in the event of war. She performed superbly.' Er, not quite. As Roberts pointed out in *Eminent Churchillians*, the Queen's behaviour in Paris led the French Prime Minister, Edouard Daladier, to conclude that she was 'an excessively ambitious young woman who would be ready to sacrifice every other country in the world so that she may remain Queen'. This seemed to be borne out by her subsequent intrigues. When Neville Chamberlain returned from Munich on 30 September 1938, he was driven straight from Heston aerodrome to Buckingham Palace – where, by royal invitation, he stood alongside the King and Queen on the balcony to acknowledge the cheers of the crowd. John Grigg once described this photo opportunity, which took place before Parliament could debate or vote on the Munich agreement, as 'the most unconstitutional act by a British sovereign in the present century'. In December 1938, the pro-appeasement *Times* produced Christmas cards bearing an 'exclusive souvenir photo' of the balcony scene in which the King and Queen endorsed the PM's abandonment of Czechoslovakia. The same photograph is, however, conspicuously absent from all the lavishly illustrated brochures marking the Queen Mother's '100 Glorious Years'.

Is it unfair to blame her for the actions of her husband? Not at all. It was she who led the royal campaign in favour of Neville Chamberlain and against Winston Churchill, whom she loathed. At a Buckingham Palace dinner in the summer of 1939, Chamberlain was seated between the Queen and the Duchess of Kent, both of whom spent the evening urging him forcefully not to bring Churchill into the government. Anyone who doubted the wisdom or morality of appeasement – including the King's private secretary, Sir Alexander Hardinge – was regarded as an enemy. Following Hardinge's eventual resignation, the diplomat Oliver Harvey wrote in his diary that 'there has been friction for some time (beginning from Munich and NC), largely caused by the Queen, who was determined to get him out. The King is fundamentally a weak character and certainly a rather stupid one. The Queen is a strong one out of a rather reactionary stable.'

When Churchill took charge in May 1940, she was appalled. In a handwritten letter of condolence to Chamberlain, she revealed 'how deeply I regretted your ceasing to be our prime minister. I can never tell you in words how much we owe you. We felt so safe with the knowledge that your wisdom and high purpose were there at our hand.' Referring to the war, she added: 'You did all in your power to stave off such agony and you were right.' As Roberts admitted in his book, 'she clearly felt little need to maintain even the fiction of royal impartiality in politics'. Which is more than can be said for the household cavalry of constitutional historians and political leaders who are now peddling that same feeble fiction all over again. When Her Majesty 'says a few words' later today, I trust she will put them right.

(*Guardian*, 19 July 2000)

FORWARD INTO THE PAST

The first hippies

A NGUS MCBEAN is famous for his flattering, 'surrealized' photographs of stage people, mostly from the 1940s and 1950s: Ivor Novello inside an hourglass, Hermione Gingold flying through the clouds in an old hip-bath, Ralph Richardson on the stage of a toy theatre. As a young man in the 1920s he took some equally surreal photographs. These, however, needed no trickery or retouching, since they were quite weird enough already: a man squatting, naked, at the root of the penis on the Cerne Abbas giant, intent on absorbing its phallic energy; another naked man silhouetted on a hillside, his arms splayed so that his body formed the letter K; two men in shorts facing each other, one holding a flag and the other wearing a hood, their arms raised in salute.

This phase is not recorded in the official story of his life. Adrian Woodhouse's biography of 1982 mentions in passing that the young McBean 'joined one of the numerous "Healthy Life" Societies of the time', but tells us no more. The sect he joined was in fact the Kindred of the Kibbo Kift, founded in 1920 as a breakaway movement from Baden-Powell's Boy Scouts. Unlike the Scouts, it was open to any age and either sex – though all members were called Kinsmen. Kibbo Kift, meaning 'proof of great strength', was said to be an ancient dialect phrase from Kent, or Cheshire, or perhaps even Old Norse: the leaders never quite synchronized their story on this point.

'The kindred is strongly heterosexual and dislikes any blurring of the edges of male and female qualities,' declared *The Confession of the Kibbo Kift*, its manifesto. The movement wanted 'healthy, attractive and graceful women, and well setup and vital men in sound sexual contrast'; ugly people were 'immoral'. Nevertheless, the homosexual Angus McBean – or Angus Og, to use the name he adopted for his KK antics – was appointed 'kin fool' and official photographer. As his pictures suggest, the cult of the body became entangled with a hungry sexuality. The kin's leader, John Hargrave, tellingly described the KK as 'a Positive Upright Fertilising Principle [whose] creative climax of Lingam in Yoni is reached when it has penetrated inertia and given form to formlessness'.

These were hippies half a century ahead of their time. A collection of Kibbo Kift memorabilia, now stored at the Museum of London, includes banners emblazoned with such slogans as 'Glastonbury', 'Life or Death' and 'War Won't Work'. Their costumes were mostly in shades of green, 'the healing hue'; red was shunned as the colour of 'violence, blood and war'. The kin numbered no more than a few hundred members, but there were some notable sponsors besides McBean. The advisory council included Havelock Ellis, Julian Huxley, Rabindranath Tagore and H. G. Wells (though none of them, as far as one can discover, ever donned the tunics, tabards, jerkins and cloaks favoured by Kibbo Kift zealots). What enticed them to the movement was the magnetic character of its founder and 'Headman', John Hargrave – or White Fox, as he preferred to be known. Hargrave's death in November 1982, at the age of eighty-eight, went largely unremarked. But he was eulogized as 'a remarkable Englishman' by Michael Wharton in the *Daily Telegraph*'s Peter Simple column. 'A time may come,' Wharton wrote, 'when this extraordinary man will have the fame and esteem he deserves.'

John Hargrave was born in Midhurst, Sussex, in 1894, the son of impecunious Quakers. Although he had almost no formal education, he was something of a child prodigy as an artist and draughtsman. By the age of fifteen he was earning his living as an illustrator of books, including the novels of John Buchan; at seventeen he was appointed chief cartoonist of the London *Evening Times*. During his childhood – as his parents moved from Sussex to the Lake District, and then to Buckinghamshire – young Hargrave nourished his passion for the great outdoors, tracking and tree-spotting and learning to survive in the wild. He admired the American author Ernest Thompson Seton, whose book *The Birch-Bark Roll of the Woodcraft Indians* urged boys to model themselves on Red Indian braves. And in 1908 he joined Robert Baden-Powell's fledgling Boy Scout movement, where his skills as an outdoorsman soon brought him to the founder's attention.

Hargrave and Baden-Powell had a wary respect for each other. But the youngster's unwillingness to take orders guaranteed that he would sooner or later fall out with his Chief. The first public signs of dissent appeared in Hargrave's book *Lonecraft*, published in 1913, which addressed itself to those scouts who preferred not to belong to any particular troop. At the same time he wrote a series of articles for the *Scout* magazine proposing a new category of 'Woodcraft Scouts' who would wear a uniform of buckskin-fringed tunic and moccasins. Before Baden-Powell could do anything about his young lieutenant's waywardness, the First World War intervened. As a pacifist Quaker, Hargrave enlisted in the Royal Army Medical Corps and, after flatly refusing to work in a VD clinic, found himself sent to the Dardanelles as a stretcher-bearer. He was invalided out in 1916.

On Hargrave's return to England, Baden-Powell appointed him Commissioner for Woodcraft and Camping, and he was seen by some scouts as the heir apparent. But confrontation was inevitable. While Hargrave's pacifism had been strengthened by his harrowing experiences at Gallipoli and Suvla Bay, Baden-Powell seemed to be driving the scouts towards militarism. In 1919, under his pseudonym 'White Fox', Hargrave began to attack B-P through the pages of *The Trail*, official organ of the London Scout Council. He and his disciples also created several underground groups – including 'Ndembo, the Chapter of Seven Eremites' and the Scalp Hunters' Club, which met for lunch at a restaurant in St Martin's Lane every Wednesday 'to cultivate the interest of people interested in woodcraft and camping and anti-military propaganda'.

Baden-Powell was increasingly alarmed by his commissioner's 'ultra views, and the possibility of his going off at a wrong tangent'. Anticipating their expulsion, Hargrave and some fellow 'ultras' convened a meeting on 18 August 1920, at which, according to the minutes, 'the following decisions were arrived at: That the Kibbo Kift be formed. That the covenant drafted by White Fox be adopted. That White Fox be Headman.' The record adds wryly that one member's 'prolonged attempt to secure the appointment of a council to control the Headman was unsuccessful'.

By the time Hargrave and the other anti-war scoutmasters were in fact excommunicated from the Boy Scouts, in January 1921, he thus had a ready-made movement of which he was the unchallenged – indeed, unchallengeable – leader. He set about forming its rules and customs with relish. There was to be an annual council, known as Althing; the membership roll was called Kinlog. Each Kinsman was given a 'woodcraft name' (Little Elk, Seonee Wolf, Wap-o, Lone Owl), usually Red Indian in inspiration though Celticisms such as McBean's Angus Og were acceptable. Office-holders bore the titles of Ritemaster, Campswarden or Tallykeeper. Everyday costume, in shades of green and brown, consisted of shorts, jerkin, cloak and a Saxon cowl; for ceremonial occasions, bright silk robes were worn.

Although it never had more than a few hundred members, the Kibbo Kift was surprisingly well known. D. H. Lawrence wrote that Hargrave was 'overweening and he's cold. But, for all that, on the whole, *he's right*, and I respect him for it. I respect his courage and aloneness. If it weren't for his ambition

and his lack of warmth, I'd go and Kibbo Kift along with him.' Other sympa-
thizers had similar reservations. In 1924 the south-east London tribe resigned
from the Kindred en masse in protest at Hargrave's autocratic style. Their
splinter group, the Woodcraft Folk, outlived the Kibbo Kift and continues to
this day as a left-wing rival to the Scouts and Guides. Since Hargrave saw the
Kin as an elite, he was not unduly troubled by defections: the very act of
defecting proved that those people were unworthy to belong to his gang.
What did begin to unsettle him was the Kibbo Kift's evident lack of any grand
purpose beyond the elevation of camping and hiking into a religion. Where
was the One Big Idea? In the mid-1920s, without any warning, the Kibbo Kift
journal *Nomad* suddenly ordered the faithful to read the works of Major C. H.
Douglas, the Scottish engineer who had devised the theory of Social Credit.

Today, Major Douglas is almost as forgotten a figure as John Hargrave –
except in Canada, where there is a flourishing Social Credit Party. But
between the wars his doctrine was astonishingly popular, especially among
the unemployed, who more than once filled Trafalgar Square to chant the
peculiar slogan, 'Declare the National Dividend Now!'

It is easy to see the allure of Social Credit. Douglas argued that all citizens
should be given a regular handout – the National Dividend – which would be
enough to live on. This would encourage them to buy more goods. As a further incentive, prices would be 'scientifically adjusted at the retail end' –
reduced, in a word. A few spoilsports wondered if this lotus-eating vision
wasn't too good to be true. When Hargrave later wrote a pamphlet called
Social Credit Explained: 101 Questions Answered, one of the questions was: 'Isn't
Social Credit a "something for nothing" scheme?' His reply was characteristically brisk: 'What makes you think a "something for nothing" scheme is
wrong? When the Sun shines upon the Earth there is no charge for the stream
of Solar Energy we receive. It comes to us free of charge. *It is something for
nothing.* Yet without this stream of Solar Energy there would be no life of any
kind on this planet – not so much as a blade of grass! Solar Energy is God's gift
to man. Social Credit is a method for allowing God's gift to man to be used –
in the form of goods and services – by everyone.'

Some of his followers were still unconvinced, not least because Hargrave's
sudden enthusiasm for Social Credit changed the whole character of the Kin.
The need for the National Dividend was so urgent, he now believed, that the
Kibbo Kift must be transformed from a small band of middle-class ruralists
into a mass urban movement. Hiking across the Chilterns gave way to marching in city centres. The old cloaks and jerkins were replaced by a simpler uniform of green military shirts and shorts. (The Kibbo Kift outfit cost about £4 a

time, which was beyond the pocket of Hargrave's new working-class supporters; the Greenshirt look could be bought for 10 shillings.) He started recruiting in the East End of London, a place he had hitherto despised. Many old-timers departed, including Angus McBean. But other famous names took their place. The 'Green Shirt Movement for Social Credit', as it was eventually called, was endorsed by Compton Mackenzie, Augustus John ('One voice alone is heard to ring out with the accent of authority. It is the voice of John Hargrave') and the Archbishop of Canterbury, William Temple.

Given their apparent similarity to Mosley's Blackshirts, another movement of the 1930s with a charismatic leader and silly uniforms, one might assume that the Greenshirts were anti-Semitic – especially as their supporters included Ezra Pound and Henry Williamson, author of *Tarka the Otter*, who certainly were fascists. Yet Hargrave went out of his way to praise Jewish achievements. 'For centuries the Jews have been a convenient scapegoat,' he wrote. 'But in fact the socio-economic troubles of this country and the world today have nothing to do with any particular race.' (He even became a feminist of sorts: the Greenshirts offered 'equal pay for equal work', insofar as anyone would actually do any work in their utopia, and promised that the National Dividend would save Womankind from being 'bound to some man who ill-treats her'.) However, the nice distinction between Hargrave's crusade and that of the Mosleyites was lost on the government, which was alarmed by the fascist violence in London. In 1937 it rushed through the Public Order Act, outlawing political uniforms. The Greenshirts tried, ingeniously, to circumvent the ban by carrying their shirts on coat hangers in front of them as they marched through London. But it was a forlorn gesture. Support was falling away, and as war with Germany came to seem inevitable Hargrave exhorted his remaining tribe to join the forces. In a typically futile but eye-catching gesture, a green-clad archer fired a green arrow through the open door of 10 Downing Street.

And that was the end of the Greenshirts. After the war, Hargrave revived his campaign briefly through the Social Credit Party of Great Britain, standing as a parliamentary candidate in Stoke Newington at the 1950 election. He lost his deposit. Later that year he dissolved the party. The few loyal survivors of the original Kibbo Kift, obedient as ever to their Headman, retreated to their lairs and burrows with a sigh.

White Fox himself did not disappear from view entirely. He had never been paid a salary by the Kin or the Greenshirts, and throughout the 1930s had earned his living by drawing and writing. There were several books on woodcraft, which sold well, but his most ambitious project was an 877-page novel, *Summer Time Ends*, published in 1935. It was a 'panorama of contemporary life', with no punctuation or capital letters. 'No, no!' wrote Cyril Connolly, reviewing it in the *New Statesman*. 'I found this literally unreadable.' The *Observer* sent it to A. G. MacDonnell (author of *England Their England*), who wailed that 'there are moments when a conscientious reviewer feels like bursting into tears...I must confess that my main feeling about it was that whereas summer might end, this book never would.' Hargrave consoled himself with the letter of commiseration he received from John Steinbeck: 'I have just finished reading *Summer Time Ends* for the third time. It is still a fine thing...Either you and I are crazy, or you struck a blind spot in the critical mind.' There were also tributes from William Carlos Williams ('this book fascinates me') and the inevitable Ezra Pound.

In the decades after the war, Hargrave continued to earn a fragile living from his pen, cartooning for the *Daily Sketch* and writing books about subjects as incongruous as Paracelsus, education and the First World War. But he scented a nest-egg when he read in 1967 that the new supersonic aeroplane, Concorde, would use a 'moving map' to navigate. He had invented a similar navigation system before the war, and although he had let the patent lapse he believed that he was morally entitled to an ex gratia payment of £1,800,000 from the government. After being bombarded with correspondence from him for nine years, in 1976 the civil service department wearily commissioned a tribunal to investigate his claims. (It was chaired by Thomas Bingham, later to become Master of the Rolls.) The 81-year-old Hargrave made the most of his day in court – 'I only ask for justice and fair play,' he pleaded – and melodramatically collapsed from exhaustion just before he was due to give his closing address. To no avail: Bingham concluded that even if Hargrave's invention had been copied, he wasn't entitled to any money.

Penniless and dejected, Hargrave nevertheless perked up shortly afterwards when a rock musical about his pre-war antics – *The Kibbo Kift* – was performed at the Edinburgh Festival. It had been written by Chris Judge Smith, a founder of the seventies rock group Van der Graaf Generator. 'I came to it initially in a spirit of mockery, because there are very comic aspects,' Smith says. But after some research he became a convert: the Kibbo Kift was 'a more hard-edged, interesting, grown-up affair' than he had anticipated, and he was impressed by John Hargrave. 'He wasn't a charlatan.'

'Well,' he adds, 'only the charlatanry that every leader gets up to.'

Even a touch of charlatanry wasn't enough to save John Hargrave, a.k.a. White Fox, from the slide into oblivion. Like so many self-styled Men of Destiny, from Oswald Mosley to Dr David Owen, he was a 'born leader' who

eventually noticed – with anguished surprise – that his only remaining follower was his own shadow.

(Independent Magazine, August 1991)

Breakfast in America

T HERE'S AN OLD CLICHÉ that often comes to the rescue of foreign correspondents who are witnessing some historic event and
aren't quite sure what to make of it. 'One thing is certain,' they conclude gravely. 'Nothing will ever be the same again.' This familiar refrain has
been echoing round Washington ever since Newt Gingrich and his chums
won control of Congress last November. The word 'revolution' has also been
working overtime, and I'm told that even 'end of an era' has come out of
retirement for the occasion. The message is inescapable: all is changed,
changed utterly; a terrible Newty is born.

Or is it? On closer inspection, one finds that some things will indeed be the
same again. The latest issue of the *American Spectator*, one of the Newt-
fanciers' parish magazines, carries a large picture of Ronald Reagan on the
front page, under the ecstatic headline: 'He's Back!' Meanwhile, the right-
wingers' other favourite journal, the *National Review*, is tempting subscribers
with a 'special offer': for a mere $100 you can buy *Remembering Reagan*, a col-
lection of 220 colour photographs comprising 'the highlights of the remarkable Reagan Years'. You will, apparently, be 'deeply moved by the
behind-the-scenes glimpses of the public and the private life of our beloved
fortieth President'.

To judge by the reverential sales pitch, this 'beautiful new book' may not
include all the highlights some of us would want. Are there any behind-the-
scenes glimpses of Nancy's astrologer? Or Oliver North? Do we get to see the
meetings at which the beloved leader agreed to sell TOW missiles to Iran in
return for the release of American hostages? Will there be space in the 'intimate pictorial history' for that memorable moment in 1983 when Reagan
boasted to the Israeli Prime Minister, with shameless mendacity, that he knew
all about the Holocaust because he had been present at the liberation of the

Nazi death camps? I doubt it. Nor, I suspect, will it draw attention to the fact that Reagan – who, like the Gingrichites of today, was forever holding forth about the moral necessity of balancing the budget – in fact created the biggest federal budget deficit in American history. The photo in the advertisement shows us what we can expect – a smiling, sun-dappled Reagan on horseback, cantering towards a brighter tomorrow. 'It's morning in America again!' the caption announces.

Not being much of a morning person myself, I've never been able to understand the appeal of this Reaganite catchphrase. When I hear the word 'morning', I think of a screeching alarm clock, an interrupted dream, a search for a clean shirt, a somnambulant queue outside the bathroom, a missed breakfast, a car that won't start, a cancelled train. Who needs it? Who'd vote for it? Ah yes, you may say, but Reagan never expected or solicited support from the likes of me. His vision of a dewy dawn, where the lark's on the wing and the snail's on the thorn, was deeply inspiring to those well-scrubbed citizens who tuck themselves into bed promptly at 10 p.m. and never wake up with a brain-battering hangover – the sort of conservatives described by Norman Mailer as 'people who went to their piano lessons when they were kids'.

True enough. But I wonder if this constituency can ever be 'the same again'. As a recent article by James Atlas in the *New York Times* pointed out, the architects of last November's Republican triumph aren't the dweebs and goody-goodies we usually associate with the phrase 'young conservative'. They drink, they smoke, they adore *Pulp Fiction*. At a pro-Newt dinner in Washington, Atlas observed with surprise that 'no one seemed to be going home, even though it was after eleven'. The musical accompaniment to their riotous parties comes from Smashing Pumpkins; their favourite author is P. J. O'Rourke of *Rolling Stone* magazine, the Republican Party's very own rock'n'roll animal. As James Atlas reported, 'these young men and women are, in effect, a new conservative opinion elite, a counter-counterculture.'

Newt Gingrich has described Bill and Hillary Clinton as 'counterculture McGoverniks', by which he means that they are dissolute relics of that much-reviled decade, the 1960s. But the champions of the counter-counterculture are products of the permissive society, too – more so, if anything, than the ageing hippies in the White House. Like Bill Clinton, Gingrich opposed the Vietnam War and managed to avoid the draft. Unlike Clinton, who puffed on a joint but never inhaled, Gingrich inhaled like billy-o in his pot-smoking youth. Whereas Bill and Hillary at least pay lip service to the concept of 'family values', gamely sticking together in sickness and in health, Gingrich ditched his first wife when she was stricken with cancer. Some of his most prominent supporters, according to the *New York Times*, are 'openly gay'. The new conservative courtiers are 'hip to a pop culture many liberals think of as something wholly their own'.

Odd, then, that they should be trying to kick-start a Reagan revival. Have they forgotten that, while he was Governor of California, their hero argued that homosexuals should be 'barred from the Department of Beaches and Parks'? And that, when he was President, his secretary of the interior tried to stop the Beach Boys performing at a Fourth of July concert because of their 'unwholesome' demeanour? Of course it's rather touching, now that Reagan is suffering from Alzheimer's disease, to see these eager wannabes striving to win one for the Gipper. But they are doomed to fail. If the young conservatives of America are as culturally 'hip' as we are led to believe, they are unlikely to be impressed by a fuddy-duddy whose idea of a good time was to curl up in front of a video of *Mr Smith Goes to Washington* or *It's a Wonderful Life*. Instead of retrieving old 1980s images of 'morning in America', the Republican Party needs to come up with something truer to the fun-loving spirit of the time – a slogan which will grab the imagination of right-wing baby-boomers who have heard the chimes of midnight. I offer my own suggestion to Newt Gingrich free of charge: 'It's cocktail hour in America! And the drinks are on me!'

(*Observer*, 26 February 1995)

Strange days indeed

T O   T H O S E   O F   U S who lived through that dismal era of polyester and platform shoes, one thing seemed certain: there would never, *ever* be a seventies revival. As Christopher Booker wrote in his end-of-term report, published in 1980, it was 'a decade of unending hard slog through the quicksands...hardly a time which in years to come is likely to inspire us with an overpowering sense of nostalgia.'

He – and we – reckoned without the transforming powers of amnesia and false perspective. All of a sudden, the most hideous paraphernalia of a hideous age (lava-lamps, glam-rock, loon pants, Burt Reynolds's toupée, Roger Moore's lapels) have been fished out of time's sewer and treated as objects of wonderment and adoration – so bad they're good, so naff they're cool, even if they do pong a bit. Disco dervishes do their John Travolta strut; All Saints have disinterred 'Voulez-Vous Coucher avec Moi'; the style sultans fondly recall a lost age of innocence and simple pleasures. I hardly dare turn on the TV these days for fear of discovering that *Jeux sans Frontières* or *Bless This House* have come back to haunt us, and not only on UK Gold. Fleetwood Mac's new best-seller, *The Dance*, is billed as 'seventeen of their greatest tracks recorded to celebrate the twentieth anniversary of *Rumours*'. Celebrate? *Celebrate?* Anyone young and lucky enough to have missed it the first time round should be warned that *Rumours* is Bill Clinton's fave-rave album of all time. I suspect that Tony Blair also has a copy somewhere in his Downing Street den, filed between the Electric Light Orchestra and Genesis.

The seventies certainly had naffness in abundance – Kevin Keegan's hair, the Bay City Rollers' trousers – but those who think it cute or clever to exhume these relics should hang on a minute. NAFF, lest we forgot, was also the acronym of the National Association for Freedom, an exceedingly right-wing pressure group supported by senior figures from MI5 and the Conservative Party. You want to celebrate the seventies? OK, let's do a roll-call: power-cuts, food shortages, petrol rationing, prices and incomes policies, National Front marches, the Lib-Lab pact, the winter of discontent. Fun, fun, fun, eh? The surly nihilism of punk may still be remembered, but the cultural and political stagnation which provoked it seems to have been written out of the script.

Don't believe the calendar: decades have no fixed duration. The fifties, for instance, held sway from 1956 to 1963, until the combined forces of Harold Wilson and the Beatles sent them packing. The seventies materialized like a thick fog in the winter of 1973 with the overthrow of Allende, the oil-price hike and the three-day week, dispersing only when Thatcher strode into Number 10 in May 1979. More like five years than ten, I agree, but it seemed an eternity. If the sixties were a wild weekend and the eighties were a hectic day at the office, the seventies were one long Sunday evening, heavy with gloom and torpor.

Harold Wilson, who only a few years earlier had been the cheeky chappie, returned to office in 1974 looking whey-faced and weary. There were no more of his babblings about a new society forged in the white heat of the technological revolution; no more jokes about how we only ever win the World Cup under Labour. All he could offer was a grimly monolithic corporate state, a pay freeze and a ceaseless succession of crises. New rumours about the PM surfaced almost daily, thanks to his enemies in high places. Peter Wright and a posse of fellow spooks planned to confront Wilson with his MI5 file (which, as you would expect, was a steaming ragout of forgeries and fantasies), and tell him 'that we wanted him to resign. That there would be no publicity if he just quietly went.' According to Wright, this deranged idea was 'deadly serious'. Even Sir Michael Hanley, the head of MI5 in the mid-1970s, was later obliged to admit to Wilson that some members of the security service had been 'behaving oddly'.

Who wasn't? David Bowie and Eric Clapton begged their audiences to give white supremacy a chance. Retired generals and SAS men started recruiting private armies to 'restore order'. Captains of industry demanded a 'national government' led by capable patriotic tycoons such as themselves. Two Fleet Street journalists of my acquaintance, Bruce Page of *The Sunday Times* and Mike Molloy of the *Mirror*, were invited to dinner in May 1975 by Sir Val Duncan, chairman of Rio Tinto Zinc, to hear his plans for taking over the country. 'When anarchy comes,' Sir Val explained, 'we are going to provide a lot of essential generators to keep electricity going, and we invited you, the editors, to tell us if you can maintain communications to people. Then the army will play its proper role.' Like so many conspirators of the time who spoke of the need for 'efficient administration', Sir Val was hopelessly inefficient: Page and Molloy, his chosen propagandists, were both paid-up members of the Labour Party. But the really astonishing thing about this story is that neither of them bothered to report it in his newspaper. An attempted putsch by rich reactionaries was, apparently, too humdrum to merit a paragraph. The only mention was a tiny item in the *Daily Telegraph* a few days later, which commented cryptically that Rio Tinto Zinc was 'in a position to furnish a coalition government should one be required'.

Actually, a coalition was not required. What these schemers wanted was a right-wing junta on the South American model. The managing director of Cunard, John Mitchell, was approached by 'army and secret service people' who were preparing a military coup; they asked if he would lend them the QE2 as a 'floating prison for the Cabinet'. The demented former press baron Cecil King toddled down to Sandhurst and urged the top brass to march on Downing Street. 'I had no doubt,' said one of those present, the military historian John Keegan, 'that I was listening to a treasonable attempt to suborn the loyalty of the Queen's officers.' Tony Benn learned from the Commander of the National Defence College, Major-General Bate, that 'there was a movement called PFP – [Prince] Philip for President. The paras were supposed to be involved, and some movement of troops in Northern Ireland was contemplated.' Brian Crozier, a British right-winger financed by the CIA, revealed in his memoirs that 'during this critical period of 1975–8, I was invited several times, by different Army establishments, to lecture on current problems. These invitations were not, to my knowledge, concerted. But the fact that they came from different places during that period did suggest some kind of malaise within our armed forces.' And, of course, he was only too glad to spread the virus. After a lecture to the Army Staff College at Camberley, in which he discussed the possibility of military intervention against 'the enemy' – meaning the government – Crozier had an eye-opening letter from the Commandant, General Sir Hugh Beach. 'Action which armed forces might be justified in taking, in certain circumstances, is in the forefront of my mind at the moment,' Beach confessed, 'and I do hope we may have the chance of carrying the debate a stage further.'

No wonder Harold Wilson toppled into the abyss of paranoia. In 1976, only weeks after resigning as Prime Minister, he summoned two young BBC journalists whom he scarcely knew to his house in Lord North Street and asked them to investigate MI5's machinations. 'I see myself as a big fat spider in the corner of the room,' the eminent statesman announced. 'Sometimes I speak when I'm asleep. You should both listen. Occasionally when we meet I might tell you to go to the Charing Cross Road and kick a blind man standing on the corner. That blind man may tell you something, lead you somewhere.'

Strange days indeed. But it got worse. After the surrealism and absurdity of Wilson, we had to endure three years under bluff, banal Jim Callaghan. Even Nature itself felt obliged to protest, by inflicting on us the most parched and drought-stricken summer of the century – an ironic welcome, perhaps, for the man who liked to be known as Sunny Jim.

If you want proof that the seventies revival depends on acute memory loss and a complete suspension of critical faculties, you need look no further than the recent rehabilitation of Callaghan. How the reviewers loved his official 800-page biography, published last September! And how reliably they all pointed out that he is still the only person to have held all four major offices of state, while neglecting to add that in every job – Chancellor, Home Secretary, Foreign Secretary and Prime Minister – he was a disastrous failure. Instead they took their cue from the book's reverential author, Professor Kenneth O. Morgan, whose chapter on the 1976–9 period is headed 'A Successful Government'. What successes? Morgan argues that 1977, in particular, was 'an annus mirabilis, with Callaghan's presidency of the European Community and successful chairing of the Commonwealth Prime Ministers' and NATO meetings, and the economic summit in London, along with ample photo opportunities during the royal jubilee...Labour showed real signs of being not just in office but in power.' And yet the fickle British voters booted him out at their first chance. How ungrateful can you get – especially to a man who had enjoyed 'ample photo opportunities' with Her Majesty?

Canvassing for Labour in the 1979 general election was a wretched experience. 'Why,' I was asked on every doorstep, 'should we support your lot again?' And, for the life of me, I couldn't think of an answer. A few months earlier the government had done its utmost to imprison a *New Statesman* colleague of mine, Duncan Campbell, for the crime of publishing a few nuggets of information that were already in the public domain anyway. If that was how Labour treated its friends, why should I lie to save Jimbo's skin? 'Er, well,' I'd mutter, 'things will be even worse if Thatcher gets in.' Understandably enough, no one believed me. How *could* things be any worse? The word that appeared in front-page headlines almost daily – 'stoppage' – was all too apt. After a while it became hard to remember a time when there *weren't* blank television screens, electricity shortages or train cancellations. We were blocked, choked, paralysed, as we had been ever since September 1976, when the government of this sceptr'd isle was forced to beg for alms from the International Monetary Fund. The conditions on which the IMF insisted – spending cuts, pay cuts and all the other bright ideas they teach you at Harvard Business School – had consequences that any fool could have predicted; any fool, that is, except Jim Callaghan.

'The press is just full of crises, anarchy, chaos, disruption,' Tony Benn noted on 22 January 1979. 'I have never seen anything like it in my life.' His diary entry a month later is even more evocative: 'The Terrorism Committee met at 9.15. Just beforehand, Merlyn Rees told me that as chairman of the committee of the Contingencies Unit he was considering whether we could have steam trains running up and down the country for emergency purposes, in the event that we ran out of electricity or diesel fuel.' Labour's defeat in the May election came as a merciful release; if the voters hadn't put Callaghan out of his misery, he'd probably have started sending small boys up chimneys 'for emergency purposes'.

Rather carelessly, the Callaghan revisionists and seventies revivalists haven't quite synchronized their alibis for the 1979 débâcle. 'Some evangelists for New Labour in the 1990s, who wrote off the late 1970s as the death-pangs of an old corporatist order, failed to acknowledge that it was then that many of their party's social and economic policies were modernised and refined,' writes Professor Morgan on page 558 of his recent biography. By page 673, however, he admits that 'Britain, in the last phase of Labour corporatism, seemed close to being ungovernable.'

That's more like it. If Callaghan deserves to be remembered at all, it is as the seventies version of John Major – a blundering buffoon who led his once-mighty party into the wilderness. I don't give a toss about the Tories, but I do bear a grudge against the man who reduced Labour to such a pitiful state of enfeeblement and exhaustion that it was ripe for takeover by vacuous but energetic 'modernizers'. Like Major, he was chippy about his lack of a university education. As with Major, even his enemies were prepared to allow that he was personally a decent and straightforward chap – though all the evidence suggested otherwise.

Joan Lestor, his under-secretary at the Foreign Office, was one victim. 'Callaghan claimed to regard her as his conscience,' Kenneth Morgan writes, forgetting to mention his sneering comment to a group of civil servants when she was appointed: 'Miss Lestor's to be our conscience in this department. And we all know what we do with our consciences, don't we?' After sacking her shortly afterwards, Jim explained with a merry twinkle: 'You see, my dear, the trouble is that I like to have people around me who are *friends* of mine.'

And what a gruesome crew the friends of Jim Callaghan turned out to be. There was Sir Julian Hodge, a Welsh financier known to *Private Eye* readers as 'the usurer of the valleys', whose loans propped up a notorious pyramid-selling operation; in the early 1970s Callaghan joined the board of Hodge's fringe bank, the Commercial Bank of Wales. He also became a director of the Italian International Bank, an outfit specializing in currency speculation. After resigning as party leader, he chummed up with the founder of the Bank of Credit and Commerce, Agha Hassan Abedi – later exposed as one of the biggest fraudsters of all time.

Morgan skips lightly over these embarrassments. For we are now in the final chapter, which concludes with a magnificently meaningless tribute to this dull, depressing politician and the dull, depressing decade he personified. Callaghan's career is 'a parable of and commentary on his country's recent history. It tells us in human terms precisely how, why and when England arose. It illustrates the schizoid quality of *fin de siècle* Britain, its commitment to the past and its capacity to renew. It shows how both have been reconciled in an ageless Burkean continuity.'

Come again? Or, rather, please don't. If a 'commitment to the past' means having to renew one's acquaintance with the Bee Gees and the ABC trial, the National Enterprise Board and the National Front, I'll stick with the present day, thanks all the same. The most enduring image of the seventies, from the winter of discontent, is a mountain of uncollected rubbish piled high in Leicester Square. Let it rot.

(*Modern Review*, April 1998)

Wibley Wob and magic lanterns

JOHN PRESCOTT will publish his transport white paper next month. If early leaks are to be believed, our modernizing government has adopted one of the most ancient and ineffective transport policies ever devised – putting the cart before the horse, and then slamming the stable door long after the incredulous nag has scarpered.

Of course there are too many cars on the roads, not least the sleek Jaguars favoured by the Deputy Prime Minister. But what does he hope to achieve by imposing a 'congestion tax' on drivers in city centres during the rush hour? Commuter carriages are already quite crowded enough without extra passengers clamouring to get on. Only this week, privatized railway companies in London were fined £4 million by the Office of Passenger Rail Franchising for running trains that were too short and too late. Prescott admits that he is 'powerless' to compel firms such as Great Western or the aptly named Connex to provide a decent service; and they have clearly calculated that it's cheaper to keep paying the fines than to invest in new rolling stock and more staff.

There is one obvious solution to the failure of private transport: it's called public transport. 'The public sector can be enterprising and we can encourage innovation and change,' John Prescott told *Tribune* ten years ago. 'But what we must be wary of is appearing to tolerate or even encourage private shareholdings in what should be public utilities. It feeds the idea, which is quite wrong, that owning shares is a way of encouraging accountability of the enterprise and can be seen as compatible with social ownership. I don't think it can.' In a 1989 policy document, *Moving Britain into the 1990s*, he set out a plan to allow British Rail to use private finance while remaining a public utility. 'It is essential,' he said as recently as 1993, 'that the Labour Party has always believed that public ownership is part of our philosophy. Public ownership is a distinguishing feature between a left-of-centre party and a right-of-centre party.' Since then, of course, Prescott has become the deputy leader of a very right-of-centre party indeed, committed to a mystical Third Way which can't even make the trains run on time. So he has decided to blame the victims. Not content with punishing motorists who have been forced off the trains by villainous private operators, he intends to levy a tax on people who take their cars to supermarkets. According to one Whitehall source: 'Charging shoppers directly would be more effective than taxing supermarkets, whose huge profits would enable them to absorb much of the cost.'

More effective for whom? Not for the customers who will have to pay the impost; nor for the government, which will incur much unpopularity. The winners will be the supermarkets, who won't have to contribute a penny. Once again, Tony Blair's 'hard choices' turn out to favour the rich and powerful at the expense of the ordinary citizen. It is, I'm sure, the merest coincidence that the decision to leave those huge profits untouched was taken just as Lord Sainsbury announced his intention of becoming a full-time Labour politician. If anyone is responsible for the proliferation of traffic, it is not the shopper but Lord Sainsbury and his fellow retailers. I witnessed their malign powers four years ago when Tesco opened a vast superstore a few miles from my house in rural Essex. Within three months, our village shop and sub-post office had gone out of business; within another six months, many of the best shops in the small town nearby – a fishmonger, a greengrocer, a baker, a delicatessen – had closed as well. So, if I want a fresh haddock, I am now obliged to drive to the out-of-town Tesco.

I don't enjoy it, of course. The aisles of this capitalist cathedral never fail to confirm Wheen's Law of Modern Shopping: that the range and attractiveness of goods stocked in an emporium are in inverse proportion to the amount of floor space. But what's the alternative? According to one report, Prescott's aim is to persuade shoppers to 'switch to public transport' (impossible in my case, since there's no bus) or to use 'home delivery services where they order their supplies by phone, fax or through the Internet'.

Here, for once, the government may be on to something. These days we associate the phrase 'home shopping' with tiresome gadgets from the Innovations catalogue or tat from the television shopping channel QVC, on which Stepford salespersons peddle carpet shampoo as if their very lives depended on it. But a century ago things were very different. Once the Victorians had established their own version of the information superhighway – the railways, the postal service and the telephone – all the great London stores created mail-order departments, catering for every imaginable material want. I have a couple of massive Army & Navy catalogues, which were sent annually to customers throughout the British Empire in the Victorian and Edwardian eras. Their comprehensiveness puts today's megastores and hypermarkets to shame: double-barrelled shotguns, magic lanterns, suitcases, hat-stands, Wibley Wob table football, Orilux Morse Code signalling lamps, Ottoman foot-warmers, bound volumes of Dickens, hair tonic, cigars, vintage port. There are forty varieties of briar pipe, and even loo paper comes in thirteen different types – including Mazella ('crepe paper, perforated'), Mikado ('Japanese crepe paper, not perforated') and, for the fastidious, Manahan's Japanese Tar ('highly medicated').

Some of the bigger branches of Tesco and Sainsbury's have recently announced, with a great fanfare, that they will take orders over the Internet for delivery the following day. Big deal: as long ago as 1902, the Army & Navy offered its mail-order customers such delights as the Luncheon Hamper for twelve persons, 'containing linen, plate, glass, cutlery, &c.', which was packed with lobster, salmon, pigeon pie, roast fowls, roast lamb and mint sauce, galantine of veal, cut ham, rolled tongue, salad and dressing, mayonnaise, bread, rolls, butter, cheese, condiments, cake and pastries – plus a dozen bottles of champagne, two of sherry, four of claret, a bottle of whisky, and two dozen bottles of seltzer and mineral water. It cost just over £8. 'Orders by post should arrive on the morning of the day before their despatch is required,' the catalogue advised.

So we beat on, boats against the current, borne back ceaselessly into the past. A good thing too, if some cyber-entrepreneur is willing to match the variety of products and quality of service which Army and Navy customers took for granted at the beginning of this century. Until then it is pointless to penalize motorists for crimes committed by huge corporations. Anyone who spends an hour or two in the sanitized hell that is Tesco has surely been punished enough for one lifetime.

(*Guardian*, 13 May 1998)

Paradise regained?

PETER HITCHENS' NEW BOOK, *The Abolition of Britain: From Lady Chatterley to Tony Blair*, is a plangent lament for the old England, the land of warm beer and lengthening shades on the village cricket pitch; but it can also be read as an obituary for the old *Daily Express*. When

Hitchens joined the paper, in 1977, it was still the voice of grumpy suburban reactionaries. Now it is edited by a founder of *Spare Rib* magazine and owned by a Blairite. Even the word *Daily* has been dropped from the title.

No wonder he feels that the country is going to the dogs. And he knows who or what is responsible for this sorry state of affairs: the Bloomsbury Group, Wallis Simpson, council estates, Dutch elm disease, Elvis Presley, *Lady Chatterley's Lover*, working women, *Beyond the Fringe*, *That Was the Week That Was*, the Beatles, John Mortimer, *Oz*, bolshie students, trendy vicars, decimalization, Reith lecturers, *Coronation Street*, *The Archers*, Roy Jenkins, the Teletubbies, Ben Elton, Harry Enfield, Princess Diana, Tony Blair. Wherever he looks, Hitchens espies yet more culprits. Central heating and double-glazing are blamed for allowing families 'to avoid each other's company in well-warmed houses, rather than huddling round a single hearth'. Even duvets incur his disapproval.

As an undergraduate Peter Hitchens was a member of the International Socialists, whose slogan was 'neither Washington nor Moscow', and although he has long since lurched rightwards this plague-on-both-your-houses attitude lingers on. The very thought of Europe makes him furious; unlike many other Europhobes, however, he hates America too, with its 'high-octane American ways of speaking and behaving'. He remembers with a shudder the constant industrial strife of the 1970s, but then chides Mrs Thatcher for breaking the trade unions. 'The unions and their block votes may have forced Labour to adopt dreary and impractical economic policies, but they had also given it a sort of working-class, monarchist patriotism...For the most part, they were even more mistrustful of foreign nations than the Tories.' Like the old *Express*, in other words. And, like the old *Express* readers, they disappeared without trace: 'Margaret Thatcher's carelessness with traditions and institutions...helped to weaken the foundations of everything that had seemed permanent before.'

Not that there were many foundations left by then, if the author is to be believed. Though the general direction of his argument is clear enough, his chronology is sometimes puzzling. 'Few now recall,' he writes, 'that the immediate post-war years were a time when many were alarmed by a rapid increase in crime, an atmosphere of purposeless rebellion among the young and a great deal of family breakdown.' It seems that the few who recall all this do not include Hitchens himself, who has told us only a few pages earlier that violent crime, youthful rebellion and family breakdown scarcely existed before the 1960s – and were caused by, respectively, the abolition of hanging, the advent of pop music and the rise in the female workforce.

By the end of this elegantly written 350-page jeremiad, many readers will probably feel like killing themselves in despair – especially since, as Hitchens complains, attempted suicide is no longer a criminal offence. But in the final pages there is a flicker of hope. The referendum on the single currency will be 'a last unrepeatable moment at which we can halt our extinction as a culture and a nation', provoking a tremendous debate on all the other reforms and upheavals of recent decades. This opportunity must be seized by 'those many millions who feel that they have become foreigners in their own land and wish with each succeeding day that they could turn the clock back'.

Back to what, however? To show us what we have lost but may yet regain Hitchens compares the Britain of 1965, the year of Churchill's funeral, with the Britain which revealed itself in the days after Princess Diana's death. Imagine, he says, that a young woman is transported back to the streets of London in 1965. 'She would be pleased to find the walls clear of the scribblings of graffiti artists...There would be less litter, less dog-muck and much less chewing gum stuck to the pavement.' So far so good. But as the time-traveller continues her exploration, Hitchens' Paradise Lost seems rather less appealing:

> She would search long and hard for a public telephone...London itself would seem extraordinarily dark and dirty even by daylight...The colour brown, in fact, would seem to crop up in almost every aspect of urban life, from food to furniture...She would rapidly notice that the past was smellier than the present, the air often reeking of breweries, cattlemarkets, cabbage and hot grease...At her hotel, she would be struck by the way the staff had never heard of credit cards, by the fact that her room lacked its own bathroom...Perhaps moving on to a café, she would gag at the thick gravy, push aside the watery murdered vegetables, refuse the stodgy pudding and reject the washy unrecognisable coffee...

All most evocative. But would anyone, other than the splendid Peter Hitchens, vote for this Elysium of brown armchairs and boiled cabbage?

(*Literary Review*, January 2000)

KILLJOY WAS HERE

The thing that people do

———————————

WHAT IS THE government's policy on sex? Ever since the Back to Basics crusade turned into an ignominious retreat, overwhelmed by a raggle-taggle army of ministerial mistresses, rent boys and 'love children', we have been in the dark on this one. Ministers are certainly not averse to thinking about sex, if Alan Clark's diaries are any guide, but most of them now keep their thoughts to themselves, having learned that the beast with two backs has a habit of biting any opportunistic politician who tries to saddle it up for a quick canter. To quote from an old ditty by James Fenton and John Fuller:

> Oh the thing that people do,
> The thing that people do!
> It's deep and wet and dangerous,
> With more than a whiff of glue.
> But you're in it up to your shoulder-blades
> And you wish you'd brought a canoe.
> It'll come to a sticky end all right,
> The thing that people do.

Official guidance is now at hand, however. It comes from Mr Ian McLachlan, an officer in Directorate Division 3, Branch C, of HM Customs and Excise, who has written to an American businesswoman to explain why his colleagues seized a parcel of erotica which she had tried to send to Britain.

'Dear Madam,' he writes.

I have today received a copy of your letter...in which you are seeking information on the law as it applies to the seizure of indecent and obscene material on importation to the United Kingdom. The prohibition is contained in Section 42 of the Customs Consolidation Act 1876. Although the legislation was set out over 100 years ago, the guidelines to which we adhere are subject to the changing standards of society...The object of the control is to prevent the importation of material which could not be lawfully offered for sale in this country. The material consigned by you to your client in the UK contained explicit scenes of fellatio, ejaculation, masturbation and fisting, sufficient, in my experience, to bring the goods well within the scope of the prohibition. Other portrayals considered to be obscene are analingus, bestiality, bondage, buggery, coprophilia, cunnilingus, insertion of an object, intercourse, necrophilia, paedophilia, sado-masochism, scatophagy and urolagnia.

Phew! Woody Allen once said that sex is the most fun you can have without laughing, but you need to be a most dedicated public servant – as Mr McLachlan undoubtedly is – to keep an entirely straight face as you study the bizarre juxtapositions on that list. I particularly like the otiose mention of 'intercourse': wouldn't it be covered by the ban on 'insertion of an object'? And how impressive that HM Customs and Excise observes the nice distinction between coprophilia and scatophagy.

But Mr McLachlan, helpful though he is, raises more questions than he answers. Why doesn't the ban on public displays of coprophilia apply to picture-books about the habits of dung beetles? And if bestiality refers to sex with animals, oughtn't it (in all logic) to include sex between animals? For it isn't only humans who do this thing that people do: birds do it, bees do it, even educated fleas do it. The mink does it but once a year; the dragonfly does it in mid-air; the male praying mantis gets his head bitten off – literally – when he does it. Sea-slugs do it in groups; some Indian pythons do it for six months without a break. The barnacle, being a hermaphrodite, is capable of a full DIY job but prefers to seek out other barnacles with its penis – which, when fully extended, is forty times as long as its body.

None of these rough cavortings disturbs the sleep of Mr McLachlan; show him a photograph of humans doing it, however, and he swoops. We are allowed to see explicit sex on early-evening television – but only as long as the participants are hummingbirds, hyenas or hedgehogs, with a *sotto voce* running commentary from David Attenborough. You never hear a whimper of complaint from Mary Whitehouse about all this prime-time rutting. Why are the sexual habits of *Homo sapiens* so uniquely threatening?

By way of reply, all Mr McLachlan can say is that 'the guidelines to which we adhere are subject to the changing standards of society...' If you watch a Carry On movie after reading *The Canterbury Tales*, you might wonder what these 'changing standards' are. When I went into a large London bookshop last week and asked for books about sex, I was immediately directed to the humour department – where there was a big bookcase packed with nudge-nudge titles such as *The Complete Dick, Well Hung, Phallic Thimbles: The*

Illustrated Book of Sexual Trivia, How to Have Sex in Public without Being Noticed, Keeping It Up!, Have You Got It on Yet?, Everybody's Doing It, 69 Things to Do When You're Not Doing It, 101 Things Not to Say During Sex and, inevitably, *101 Uses for a Condom.* 'Haven't you got anything more serious?' I asked. The assistant then led me to the 'Health' section, where I found a large display of copies of a new American book – *203 Ways to Drive a Man Wild in Bed*, by Olivia St Claire.

This is a very serious work indeed. 'Use veils, feathers, gloves, garter belts, whatever you can think of...Costume yourself as a maid, soldier, waitress, nurse, torch singer, another man, circus performer, dairy maid or whatever...Write him a lewd note and slip it secretly into his jacket or pants pocket, or tuck it into his *Wall Street Journal.*' Ms St Claire has useful tips on everything from feathers ('have a wide assortment at the ready: a feather duster, a boa, a quill, a peacock feather') to fruit ('mash the banana first'). The male praying mantis doesn't know what he's missing. Although there is intercourse galore in between the advice about boas and bananas, none of it falls foul of the Customs and Excise. Why? Because it isn't illustrated. In this country, we are allowed to see pictures of sexual acts only if they purport to be 'educational': one can buy *Lovers' Guide* videos in high-street newsagents, but erotic continental films are consigned to the Whitehall incinerator.

It is now more than thirty years since *Time* magazine's famous 'Swinging London' issue, which reported that 'on the island where the subject has long been taboo in polite society, sex has exploded into the national consciousness and national headlines...Britain is being bombarded with a barrage of frankness about sex.' The explosion still continues, every day. Here are a few headlines from last Sunday's *News of the World*: 'He Lusted for Sex with Mum-in-Law'; 'Look Who Derek's Bedding Now'; 'Court with Pants Down!'; 'Wicket Past of Tufnell's Maiden'; 'Winner's Porn Pain'; 'Soccer Ace Shacks up with New Girl'; 'Caravan Love-Nest'; 'Sex-Hungry Doc Liked to Have Me for Lunch'; 'Porn Star in Love Triangle with Mad Cow Man'. How can a country with such a one-track mind also maintain the most draconian obscenity laws in the free world, policed by the ever-vigilant Mr McLachlan? Why are we simultaneously so frank and yet so frigid? Every member of the present Cabinet is the product of sexual intimacy (even though some of them would prefer to imagine that they arrived by immaculate conception); yet the government apparently thinks that the sky will fall in if adult British citizens are permitted to witness 'intercourse'.

The real English vice is a mixture of salacity and shame, prurience and prudery. Sex is like the fake hare in a greyhound race: constantly dangled in front of us, yet forever kept tantalizingly out of reach. The *News of the World* articles, while wallowing in the lasciviousness they reveal, are all written in a sternly disapproving tone of voice; the voice of a porn-reading clergyman who expiates his guilt with a fire-and-brimstone sermon once a week. In this they accurately reflect the official attitude. Ministers – and their army of censors and suppressors – seem to believe that we inhabit a latter-day Garden of Eden, where the tree of sexual knowledge is heavy with ripe and alluring fruit which we must, for our own good, be prevented from tasting. We must continue tut-tutting primly at love-hungry docs and caravan love-nests, and give thanks in our prayers for Mr McLachlan's brave efforts to protect us from 'insertion of an object'. As James Fenton and John Fuller remind us:

> When God created Paradise,
> As every child can tell,
> He placed old Adam gardener
> With woman there as well.
> Said God: 'Enjoy yourself, me lad,
> And enjoy your woman, too
> But never let me catch you at
> The thing that people do.'

Quite right too. For if we did sample the fruit of the forbidden tree, we might discover that sex is indeed deep and wet and dangerous – and, horror of horrors, we might get to enjoy it.

(Observer, 12 June 1994)

Effing magic

ROM BEYOND THE GRAVE, Dennis Potter continues to make mischief. We are informed that his television drama *Karaoke*, to be shown on BBC1 later this month, includes 'more than thirty uses of the F-word'. What is so surprising about this news is not the swearing – we would expect nothing less – but the fact that some diligent scrutineer actually kept a tally.

Unless you are a hermit or a babe-in-arms, you will know the word in question. It was uttered on a late-night chat show more than thirty years ago by Kenneth Tynan. In the early seventies no less a figure than Sir Peregrine Worsthorne blurted it out on *Nationwide*, an early-evening news programme. It appears more than 4,000 times in James Kelman's Booker Prize-winning novel, *How Late It Was, How Late*. Only last month, a Tory MP was heard repeating it on a Channel 4 comedy programme. The most successful British film of modern times, *Four Weddings and a Funeral*, which was praised for its innocent, old-fashioned comedy, begins with a positive blizzard of effing.

Can anyone still be shocked by it? Although the prudish editors of the *Oxford English Dictionary* kept out the dread monosyllable until 1912, it has a long and impressive literary history. The earliest *OED* reference comes from a poem of 1503, and the list of subsequent F-fanciers includes Florio, Rochester, Burns, Rossetti, Joyce and, of course, D. H. Lawrence.

Knowledge is power, which is why Mervyn Griffith-Jones QC posed his famous question to the jury at the *Lady Chatterley* trial: 'Is it a book that you would even wish your wife or your servants to read?' There was no suggestion that anyone in court would be depraved or corrupted by the novel; what alarmed the prosecutor was the idea that wives, servants and the great mass of the British public might get their hands on this awesome weapon.

Nearly forty years on, our moral invigilators are still fighting the same old battle. Armed with the shield of righteousness, they do not fear the word's effect on themselves; their only concern is to protect children and other impressionable souls. Perhaps they would worry less if they spent a few minutes in any playground, where the Lawrentian expletive can be heard in all its forms – verb, noun, prefix, and much else besides. What was once defined as barrack-room language is now ubiquitous: the F-word appeared 328 times last year in the *Guardian* and the *Independent*. You will even find it in this article, if you look closely enough.

How can a nation that slavers over the *News of the World* every Sunday also maintain the most draconian obscenity laws in the free world? Why are we simultaneously so prurient and so prudish? Kelvin MacKenzie, the former editor of the *Sun*, reported the *Independent* to the Press Council a few years ago when it quoted a four-letter eruption in a cricket report; yet this selfsame MacKenzie made his reputation (and Rupert Murdoch's fortune) by treating his readers to a daily feast of titillating tales about 'bonking' – an exact synonym for you-know-what-ing.

What the censors have failed to notice is that the word retains its shock value only because of their tireless attempts to suppress it. If it could be used as easily on radio and television as it already is in books and films, custom would soon stale its all-too-finite variety, and we should turn to the lexicon in search of more startling slang. The word might linger on as a meaningless linguistic tic, like 'sort of' or 'y'know', but the accompanying frisson would be gone – and, with it, the allegedly terrifying potency of those four little letters.

There are plenty of precedents. In 1939 American cinemas showing *Gone with the Wind* were picketed by citizens who were outraged at Rhett Butler's 'Frankly my dear, I don't give a damn'; nowadays, the film is shown on Sunday afternoon television without a murmur of protest. The British Prime Minister, John Major, is happy to describe Cabinet colleagues as 'bastards'. At some point in the next century, more likely than not, the F-word will go the same way. For those who believe that there ought to be at least one taboo in the vocabulary, a simple remedy is available. Once a year, Parliament should pick a word – any word – and outlaw it for the next twelve months, with dire penalties for transgressors. Vernacular English includes thousands of suitable candidates: 'ninny-hammer', for instance, or 'jobbernowl', or 'dickey-dido', or the evocative 'tootledumpattick'. Or how about the epithet uttered last week by the outgoing chairman of the BBC, Duke Hussey, when he jokingly referred to himself as an 'Olympian nincompoop'? According to *A Dictionary of the Vulgar-Tongue* (published in 1811), a nincompoop is a man who has never seen his wife's pudenda. While such dangerous obscenities are still on the menu, Dennis Potter's F-plan diet seems harmless indeed. Who gives a fig?

(*Sunday Telegraph*, 7 April 1996)

Married to the mob

T HOSE JADED CITIZENS who complain that Parliament is incapable of sustaining intelligent life are often advised to come along and watch a debate on an issue of 'conscience', where no three-line whips apply and MPs are able to discuss an issue purely on its merits. Then, we are told, you will see the House of Commons at its best.

There was just such an occasion last week, on backbench amendments to Lord Mackay's Family Law Bill. Having studied a Hansard transcript of the entire six-hour debate, I have only one conclusion: if this is really the best the House can offer, God preserve us from its worst. Swarms of non sequiturs flapped and buzzed through the chamber as self-righteous politicians boasted of their unswerving commitment to the sanctity of marriage. At the end of the evening, they voted to extend the 'cooling-off period' for parting couples from twelve months to eighteen months, and more than a hundred of them supported an unsuccessful amendment challenging the main point of the bill – the 'no fault' divorce. The *Daily Mail*, which has run a ceaseless and increasingly deranged campaign on this subject in recent months, was delighted. 'The very concept of "no fault" divorce devalues marriage,' it thundered, 'reducing it to the status of a temporary arrangement, breakable on a whim. The pity is that the Lord Chancellor seems uncritically to have swallowed the liberal arguments peddled by that unelected and unrepresentative quango, the Law Commission.' Unlike the heroic Tory dissidents, of course, who swallowed the arguments of the unelected and unrepresentative *Daily Mail*.

The ghastliness of last week's debate was, however, relieved by occasional flashes of sanity and common sense. Interestingly enough, almost all of them came from MPs who have worked as divorce lawyers and have seen for themselves how much misery is caused by the quest for 'blame' in broken marriages. 'My experience is that in very few marriages is the fault wholly on one side,' the Labour MP Donald Anderson observed. 'In connection with one or two well-publicized difficulties of some of the senior members of the royal family, it is certain that both the parties could, if they were so minded, rely on various faults in a divorce petition.' Even the *Mail* seems to admit as much: one day it denounces Prince Charles for his adultery; the next it damns Princess Diana for the same offence. No human being is faultless – not even, dare I say, the editor of the *Mail* – yet we are asked to believe that either a husband or a wife must always be the sole culprit.

The Tory MP Patrick Nicholls was magnificently incredulous at the idea that 'by encouraging bitterness and mud-throwing we shall protect the institution of marriage'. Having dealt with countless divorce cases during his career as a solicitor, Nicholls demolished the *Mail*'s moralistic blatherings with one well-chosen example: 'What about the situation in which a wife deserts her husband and commits an act of adultery? That is a bad enough fault, but wait a moment. She may claim that she was driven out by a hard and domineering husband, so perhaps the fault was his. But hold on another moment – the husband may claim that he had to control and direct his wife because she was a rotten housekeeper, was getting the finances wrong and the children were suffering. Then the wife might say, "Come off it, I married at

eighteen. I didn't know enough, so obviously I was going to get it wrong."
What is the answer?' Answer came there none.

The sabotaging of the bill was greeted in the *Mail* as a victory for the moral
majority. 'A study of the 171 Tory rebels reveals it was the night when the
family men from "Middle England" came out in force,' it reported. 'The rebels
represent a class who believe that marriage is for life.' Oh really? Here are a
few of them: Vivian Bendall, Stephen Day, David Faber, Sir Peter Fry, Roger
Gale, Sir George Gardiner, John Horam, Toby Jessel, Michael Mates, Sir
Nicholas Scott, Richard Spring, Sir Malcolm Thornton, Nigel Waterson, John
Wilkinson. What do these men have in common, apart from finding themselves in the same division lobby last week? They have all been divorced at
least once, and in some cases more than once: Roger Gale is currently on wife
number three.

True, some of the rebels have stayed clear of the divorce courts. Tim Yeo is
still married to his first wife in spite of having fathered a child by another
woman. Tony Marlow was so keen on the family that he maintained two of
them: a wife and five children in his constituency; a lover and four children in
London. Another uxorious Tory, Hartley Booth, sent drippy love letters and
poems to a female student. Yet another, Robert Hughes, resigned as a minister when his jilted 'mistress', Janet Oates, revealed all to the *News of the World*
('My Great Sex with Tory Who Wanted All-Night Sessions).

It is unpleasant to exhume all these foibles and infidelities – but not half as
unpleasant as the sight of a posse of maritally challenged Conservative MPs
leading a crusade against divorce. How do they explain the contradiction?
Most were unwilling to try. 'I don't have anything to do with the *Guardian*,'
Roger Gale informed me. 'When you've settled your case against my colleague
Jonathan Aitken I might consider talking to the *Guardian* again. Until then,
forget it.' (Actually, the *Guardian* has no lawsuits outstanding against
Jonathan Aitken; quite the reverse. But Roger Gale is a former producer of
Blue Peter rather than a lawyer, so I suppose he can be forgiven his ignorance.)
One Tory rebel, who was quite chatty at first, became distinctly frosty when I
asked if either he or his wife had been 'at fault' in their divorce. 'As a matter of
fact she was: she went off with a colleague. But you can't print that.' Toby
Jessel was slightly more cooperative. 'I believe in the ideal of happy marriage,'
he cooed. 'I've been very happily married since October 1980. I had an early
unhappy marriage which took place in 1967.' Was he humbled by the
experience? Apparently not. 'However much the experts may say there is
often if not always fault on both sides, people at large do believe "it was his
fault" or "it was her fault".' Maybe so; but how can 'people at large' ever

comprehend what goes on inside other people's marriages?

John Wilkinson, the twice-wed MP for Ruislip, supported the extension of the cooling-off period but missed the previous vote because he had to attend a constituency surgery. 'Abstention was probably the best thing for me,' he admitted, 'as I should be reluctant to cast the first stone.' Nevertheless, he would have voted against the principle of 'no fault' divorce. 'Fault does lie at the heart of divorce,' he told me, without revealing who had been the transgressor in his case. 'Having gone through this traumatic experience, one may be better qualified to deliberate on these matters. But that is not in any sense to adopt a high moral posture – that's the last thing one wants to do.'

Well, you could have fooled me. Perhaps Wilkinson should have a word with his preening, sanctimonious colleagues on the Tory benches, and with the nanny-state enthusiasts at the *Mail* – a paper whose proprietor, Lord Rothermere, is such a devoted 'family man' that for many years he commuted between a wife in London and a mistress in Paris. With such an exhausting domestic routine, I'm surprised he never felt the need for a 'cooling-off' period himself.

(*Guardian*, 1 May 1996)

Crash, bang, wallop

HOW DELICIOUS THAT the chairman of Westminster Council's licensing subcommittee, which has banned David Cronenberg's film *Crash* from all cinemas in the West End of London, should be called John Bull. 'My taste has always been right English,' Robert Southey confessed almost 200 years ago, 'and I grow more John Bullish every time I look into a newspaper.' Were Southey alive today, the newspaper in question would undoubtedly be the *Daily Mail*, which has been advising its readers on 'what YOU can do to keep this revolting film off our screens'. Refusing to watch *Crash* isn't enough. According to the *Mail*'s hysterical film critic, Christopher Tookey, we should 'hit them where it will hurt the most'. Since the movie's British distributor, Columbia TriStar, is a subsidiary of Sony, *Mail* readers are being urged to boycott all Sony electrical goods this Christmas.

It is gratifying to see that the *Daily Mail* has belatedly come round to the idea of sanctions and secondary picketing. But why should it advocate these methods of protest against something as piffling as a Cronenberg film, which was likely to be only a minority taste anyway? Allow Tookey to explain: 'Copycat crimes do happen. *Natural Born Killers* triggered a string of crimes, including a murder and near-fatal shooting.' Actually, it did nothing of the kind. Before deciding to grant a certificate to *Natural Born Killers*, the British Board of Film Classification investigated every single case of alleged 'copycat' crimes. 'We did a thorough search of media reports in America and also in France, where another rumour had started,' the BBFC revealed in its annual report for 1994, 'and we followed up every alleged link by telephoning the FBI or local police. In no instance were they prepared to attribute any of the killings to this film or any another film.' Blithely ignoring this awkward fact, in traditional *Mail* fashion, Tookey blunders on: 'So easily imitable were scenes in *The Good Son*, where two young boys caused a motorway pile-up, that the film has never received a general release.' Wrong again. *The Good Son*'s release was delayed because of certain alleged but unproven parallels with the Jamie Bulger case. By the time the BBFC was ready to pass it, the distributors had lost interest. It is now freely available on video.

'Ideally,' Tookey argues, 'film-makers and distributors would practise self-restraint. Director Stanley Kubrick banned his film *A Clockwork Orange* from being shown in Britain after some youths raped a young woman while performing "Singin' in the Rain", an act they had imitated from the movie.' Not so. As the film lecturer Julian Petley has pointed out in a letter to the Press Complaints Commission, objecting to Tookey's feverish fantasies, Kubrick suppressed the movie because he was sick of being blamed for copycat crimes by papers such as the *Mail*. Britain is the only country in which he withdrew *A Clockwork Orange*, since it is the only country in which the press campaigned against the film – just as it is now doing with *Crash*. The rape story is nothing more than a convenient myth.

Even if it were true, however, would this really justify blanket censorship? Mark Chapman, the man who shot John Lennon, was said to have been clutching a copy of *The Catcher in the Rye*. Should J. D. Salinger have pulped all his novels merely because of the effect they might have on one deranged reader? If we follow Tookey's logic, the answer must be yes. But he goes further, arguing that it isn't only lone nutters who are susceptible. 'Whether consciously or not, people do imitate what they see in the movies. When Joan Crawford wore a ruffled dress in the 1932 film *Letty Lynton*, the New York department store Macy's sold 50,000 exactly like it.' The implication is that if we are allowed to see *Crash*, thousands of us will immediately yearn to have sex in a multiple pile-up on the M25. If Tookey believes that, he'll believe anything.

What, then, will our moral guardians permit us to watch? After his private screening of *Crash* last week, John Bull of Westminster council complained that film-makers no longer produce wholesome fare 'like *The Wizard of Oz*'. Huh! When I first saw *The Wizard of Oz*, as a boy, I spent much of the performance hiding under my cinema seat howling in terror. In the very first scene, we learn that Dorothy's little dog, Toto, has been violently attacked by Miss Gulch. The ghastly Gulch is later transmogrified into the Wicked Witch of the West – a green-faced, long-nosed, sharp-chinned old monster with a demonic grin, who looks like a hideous hybrid of Edwina Currie and John Redwood. Worse is to come. When Dorothy and her chums are halfway down the yellow brick road, the Wicked Witch lures them into a vast field of poppies. 'What's happening?' Dorothy asks, becoming more spaced-out by the moment. 'I feel so sleepy.' Just as the intrepid travellers are sinking into a blissful, opium-induced trance, the Good Witch revives them by showering them with white powder – or 'snow', as she slangily terms it. In short, the film is a non-stop orgy of drugs and violence; and yet its video is still certified as 'U – Suitable For All'. Will no one – not even the *Daily Mail* – protect us from this filth?

(Guardian, 27 November 1996)

***

A NEW VOICE HAS entered the debate about *Crash*, David Cronenberg's film of auto-erotica. It belongs to Bel Mooney – novelist, broadcaster and sometime yurt-dweller. 'As a sixties person,' she announces, 'I confess I have always been proud to be called a liberal, a firm believer in tolerance and free speech.' Since her essay is published in the *Daily Mail*, you will already be anticipating the dread conjunction 'but'; and sure enough, here it comes. 'The artist may think it his/her duty to push against what seem to be limits, but the limits must be there for the creative push to take place.' Is she trying to do artists a favour – assisting their muse by giving them a few pricks to kick against? Er, not exactly. When they push against the limits, they should be banned. 'Over many a dinner table I have argued that unless people like myself take a stand against the seemingly endless downward spiral of sex and violence in books, films and on television, the world that I was born into will disappear for ever.' What world is this? She offers a few clues. 'Recently, I talked to a leading liberal-Left historian...' Well done, Bel! 'One of my friends is a distinguished liberal publisher.' Better still! But this listing of eminent acquaintances isn't done merely for boastful effect. Both the historian and the publisher, she reveals, are now having misgivings about freedom of expression. 'Are these good signs?' she wonders. 'Maybe at last the liberal establishment (of which I consider myself a part) will have the courage to change its mind and cry "Enough!"'

I have consulted the membership committee of the liberal establishment, but no one can recall inviting Bel to join. Nor is her name on the records of that even more exclusive club, the liberal intelligentsia – even though, elsewhere in her essay, she uses the phrase 'we in the liberal intelligentsia'. True, she has some of the requisite qualifications (sitting at 'many a dinner table', for instance), but a minimum condition of entry, to either the establishment or the intelligentsia, is that one must be a liberal. Anyone who earns a living by writing 2,000-word justifications for censorship in the pages of the *Daily Mail* is automatically ineligible.

It isn't even as if Mooney has the merit of novelty. The author Bryan Appleyard – another self-styled 'liberal' who is anything but – made much the same points in an article for the *Independent* on 1 December 1993. Here, for instance, is Bel Mooney on the history of censorship: 'In the fifties, the battle was to free the theatre from the sway of the Lord Chamberlain. The great and the good argued then and in the sixties that most forms of censorship should be overthrown in the name of...individual choice.' And here is Bryan Appleyard, three years earlier: 'Ever since the battle in the fifties to free the theatre from the grip of the Lord Chamberlain it has been assumed that we were moving steadily and healthily from oppression to liberalisation; that most forms of censorship should be overthrown in the name of...individual choice.' Back to Mooney: 'Once you accept the freedom of the artist/producer to shock...the noble concept of freedom of expression will find itself debased in every video shop in the land, through satellite and now the Internet.' Over to Appleyard: 'The freedom of the artist to shock is expressed...in every cinema, video shop and through every satellite receiver.' Appleyard's argument was that free speech may be harmless enough in 'the narrow world of high art', but it is quite unsuitable for 'the masses'. Mooney seems to agree: 'It is no longer good enough for the people I meet to sigh: "Of course we all hate the idea of censorship" – while out there in the darkness, where the privileged never poke their heads, people suffer and die in a savage chaos.'

Tantalizingly, she doesn't tell us where the 'darkness' is to be found. Still, we can all think of places where people have indeed suffered and died in savage chaos during the past few years – Bosnia, Rwanda, Algeria and so on. Was all this murderous mayhem really inspired by the films of David Cronenberg?

(Guardian, 3 December 1996)

Sodomy and the lash

THE END OF Tony Blair's honeymoon, so long predicted, can now be officially confirmed: his beloved mentor and dining companion Paul Johnson is threatening to file for divorce. 'In his faultless handling of events after Diana's death, Tony Blair seemed to be aligning himself with the decent majority,' he writes. 'But sometimes he is less clear about where he stands.' According to Johnson, who has long boasted of his friendship with the Prime Minister, we are witnessing a millennial struggle between two 'images of Britain'. One is the 'tender and beautiful' country which wept for Princess Diana. But there is also 'the nightmare Britain' of pop groups, Booker Prize authors and sensation-seeking artists – 'perverted, brutal, horribly modish and clever-cunning, degenerate, exhibitionist, high-voiced and limp-wristed...'

A suggestive selection of epithets, wouldn't you say? What he is trying to tell us, with untypical coyness, is that he can't stand poofters. Hence his rage at Blair's recent message of support for the Gay Pride march – 'an affront to ordinary Londoners'. Hence, too, his reminder of what happened to the artists and writers of the last *fin de siècle*: 'These precious creatures were riding high until, in 1885, the conviction and imprisonment of Oscar Wilde, the paedophile, brought the edifice of fashionable degeneracy down in shameful ruin.' Actually, Wilde was convicted in 1895; but this is the least important of Johnson's clod-hopping errors and idiocies. 'In Oscar Wilde's nineties,' he claims, 'the decadents had to operate with limited resources and spoke to a restricted audience. Wilde's West End plays were tailored to the moral tastes of the Victorian middle class – he kept his vices private until they were exposed by his own folly.' Today's degenerates, by contrast, receive 'huge publicity'. More publicity than Oscar Wilde? I think not. Gilbert and Sullivan wrote an entire opera satirising his flamboyant aestheticism. W. H. Smith refused to sell *The Picture of Dorian Gray* – described by Richard Ellmann as 'one of the first attempts to bring homosexuality into the English novel' – because it was deemed too 'filthy'. One might add that a man who wished to ingratiate himself with the Victorian bourgeoisie would not have written a book called *The Soul of Man Under Socialism*.

What of the plays? Wilde's first West End success, *Lady Windermere's Fan*, deliberately inverts middle-class morals by giving the devil all the best lines. 'As a wicked man I am a complete failure,' Lord Darlington comments. 'Why, there are lots of people who say I have never really done anything wrong in the whole course of my life. Of course they only say it behind my back.' A dunderheaded alderman who praised the playwright for 'lashing vice' was swiftly and publicly corrected. 'I can assure you that nothing was further from my intentions,' Wilde declared. 'Those who have seen *Lady Windermere's Fan* will see that if there is one particular doctrine contained in it, it is that of sheer individualism. It is not for anyone to censure what anyone else does, and everyone should go his own way, to whatever place he chooses, in exactly the way that he chooses.' At the first night, Wilde took his curtain-call wearing a green carnation and mauve gloves. His next play, *Salome*, was banned by the Lord Chamberlain. This scarcely suggests that he tried very hard to appease the Paul Johnsons of his day.

A century later, depravity stalks the land once more and our own Paul Johnson is in an apocalyptic frenzy. 'Will the Decadent Nineties end with an evil elite taking charge of our culture?' he wonders. 'The phenomenon I call the Diana Revolution – the birth of Diana Power this month – makes me suspect that the decadents are not going to have it all their own way. There is a stirring of decency at the grassroots.' By decency, of course, he means heterosexuality.

The idea that the Princess's admirers are all decent, wholesome queer-bashers is certainly original. It is also quite barmy. The most obvious manifestation of 'Diana Power' is the huge popularity of 'Candle in the Wind' – performed by one of the most famous homosexuals in the world. Though Johnson assures us that all but 'a few thousand' Britons share his foaming homophobia, he then explodes his own premise by grumbling that 'scarcely a day goes by without an MP or even a government minister "coming out" as a sodomite or a lesbian, introducing his or her partner to the world and receiving not public obloquy but approval and praise for his or her "courage" and "honesty".' Er, quite.

'It is,' Johnson concludes, 'high time for Tony Blair...to make up his mind where he stands.' Indeed it is. On the one hand there are the millions of people who have bought Elton John's record and are sublimely untroubled by Angela Eagle's lesbianism; on the other, alone and ridiculous, is Paul Johnson, gibbering like the ghost of the 9th Marquess of Queensberry. If forced to choose between his country and his friend, the PM may well decide – however reluctantly – that a certain red-haired, red-faced adviser has outlived his usefulness.

(Guardian, 24 September 1997)

***

WHO WAS THE ONLY woman ever to sit in Mrs Thatcher's Cabinet, apart from the PM herself? Baroness Young (for it was she) might have expected that this unique achievement would guarantee her lasting fame, but it didn't. Now she is making another bid for political immortality. In the House of Lords today she will invite the assembled backwoodsmen, bishops and bigots to throw out amendments to the Crime and Disorder Bill, passed by a huge majority in the Commons last month, which would lower the age of consent for homosexuals to sixteen. 'I think there will be a lot of support on the Conservative benches,' she says. Since most of the long-suffering benches in the Upper House are occupied by Tory bottoms, she may well succeed.

Baroness Young justifies her attempted sabotage by grumbling that 'there was no chance for a proper debate' when the amendments came before the Commons. On the contrary: there was a long debate on the evening of 22 June. Not a very good debate, I agree, but that's because politicians who oppose an equal age of consent are the same people who usually thunder against the 'nanny state' and insist on the sacred importance of 'equality before the law'. To get round this inconsistency, they were therefore obliged to talk in non sequiturs throughout. Nevertheless, the opinions of those who belong to the Baroness Young school of thought – more of a borstal, really – were thoroughly aired. Sir Patrick Cormack MP warned Honourable Members to remember 'the old description of the Navy, "rum, sodomy and the lash" '. To Sir Patrick's annoyance, this provoked sniggers. 'There is nothing funny about it,' he snapped. 'It is a perfectly reasonable point to make in support of my argument'. Another perfectly reasonable point came from Nicholas Winterton. 'Am I not correct,' he asked, 'in saying that a homosexual act is unnatural and if the Lord Almighty had meant men to commit sodomy with other men, their bodies would have been built differently?'

'I hope I shall be acquitted of the charge of being antagonistic to the homosexual community,' Sir Norman Fowler told the House. To prove his lack of antagonism, he then went on to confuse gays with paedophiles, citing 'the case of Roger Gleaves, the self-styled "Bishop of Medway"', as an argument against changing the law. Rather absent-mindedly, Fowler forgot to add that an age of consent set at twenty-one did nothing to stop Gleaves's sexual abuse of boys. Crispin Blunt MP was also worried about vulnerable teenagers, since much homosexuality 'depends for its gratification on the exploitation of youth'. Although girls need no legal protection from older men, 'the everyday experience of adolescents, combined with scientific observations, make it clear that boys of this age are self-evidently less mature, sexually and in judgment, than their female counterparts...My conclusion is that we have a duty to protect boys of sixteen and seventeen.' Girls of sixteen and seventeen, by contrast, would presumably still be free to go to bed with Bill Wyman or the Tory politician Piers Merchant.

I expect that today's discussion in the House of Lords will reach the same high standard of unprejudiced ratiocination. But there will be one element missing. The Commons debate included a deeply pious speech against the new age of consent by the Labour MP Stuart Bell, who pointed out that he was expressing both his own views and those of the Church of England, whose interests he represents in the House as a Second Church Estates Commissioner. It was not 'morally right or socially desirable' to give homosexuals the same rights as heterosexuals, he said. Instead, we need 'a broader agenda of moral vision'.

Bell set out his own sexual agenda some years ago when he wrote a novel called *Paris 69*. Though it is now sadly unavailable, here's a sample: 'And she keeps on sucking, sucking and nibbling and filling me with yearning, with desire to thrust her back on the bed now, strap her to it the way the schoolteacher had shown me...I wanted that she be tied to the bed and I dominate her, rape her, burst inside her and be cleansed.' The narrator, I need hardly add, is a man; there's nowt queer about our Stuart. Perhaps, during today's debate, someone from the Bench of Bishops will tell us whether the 'moral vision' of their parliamentary spokesman is also the Church of England's official policy.

(*Guardian*, 22 July 1998)

Reefer madness

T IS AN OLD and enjoyable summer ritual, as predictable as the invasion of Stonehenge on Midsummer's Eve or a defeat for the English
cricket team. A public figure suggests that cannabis ought to be decrimi-
nalized – or, at the very least, that a committee of eminent persons should be
allowed to brood and cogitate on the subject. Grateful for any distraction
during the silly season, MPs and tabloid editors work themselves up into a
state of foaming apoplexy. Then the whole thing is forgotten again for another
year.

So far as I can discover, the tradition began in July 1967, when such well-
known revolutionaries as Jonathan Aitken, David Dimbleby and Brian
Walden signed a full-page advert in *The Times* calling for a review of the law
on cannabis. The Home Office minister Alice Bacon duly professed herself
'horrified' by their irresponsibility – as did the president of Leeds University
Students' Union, one Jack Straw. 'I am opposed to the legalization of
cannabis,' he told the campus newspaper (which was edited, fittingly enough,
by the man who now edits the *Daily Mail*). 'It has not been conclusively
proved that the taking of cannabis is not harmful...It is also not enough to say
that drug-taking in general, and cannabis-taking in particular, is something
which must be left to the individual.' The same old pantomime has been acted
out at regular intervals ever since. In September 1994, for instance, Michael
Howard claimed that the Liberal Democrats were 'unfit for public office'
because their annual conference had proposed the establishment of a royal
commission on soft drugs. Even Charles Kennedy, the party's outgoing president – outgoing in every sense of the word – thought it necessary to chide
delegates for their 'frivolity'.

Five years on, Kennedy himself is in the line of fire for suggesting that, er, a
royal commission might be a good idea. 'Charles Kennedy clearly has yet
to learn how a responsible party leader should behave,' fumes Ann
Widdecombe, a latter-day Tory version of Alice Bacon. Not to be outdone, a

Downing Street spokesman informs us that 'Tony Blair is against decriminal-
ization of cannabis and sees no value in a royal commission.' In one respect,
Blair is right: why go to the trouble and expense of an official inquiry when the
job has already been done? All he needs to do is reprint the voluminous report
of the Indian Hemp Drugs Commission, set up in 1893 at the behest of the
British government to consider whether cannabis should be prohibited in
India. Although the descriptions of drug use in colonial Madras and Mysore
may be inapplicable to Britain at the end of the twentieth century, the general
conclusions are impressively timeless and universal.

The commission's seven members – four British officials and three 'Native
non-official gentlemen' – took their duties very seriously indeed, interviewing
1,193 witnesses from all over the country. Far from damaging one's health,
they found, 'it has been clearly established that the occasional use of hemp in
moderate doses may be beneficial' – a point confirmed by recent medical
research. (Ann Widdecombe would be shocked to learn that Queen Victoria
took cannabis to ease period pains.) They noted that hemp was used 'to give
staying-power under severe exertion' – particularly by wrestlers and musi-
cians, palki-bearers and porters, divers and postal runners, dhobis and night-
watchmen, mendicants and pilgrims.

Did the drug weaken one's character? 'The commission are of the opinion
that [its] moderate use produces no moral injury whatever.' Nor did it cause
insanity.

What of the alleged link between cannabis and crime, which so alarms
Messrs Straw and Blair? 'The general opinion is that hemp drugs have per se
no necessary connection with crime,' the commissioners reported. 'It is true
that some witnesses assert that habitual consumers sometimes spend more
than their poverty renders reasonably possible, and are then tempted to
commit petty thefts...The same is true, however, of any unwise expenditure
beyond what one can afford, and of any extravagance which intensifies
poverty.' Just so. In recent years there have been many cases of scratchcard
addicts who rob or embezzle to finance their habit, yet our government still
regards the National Lottery as a wholesome institution.

'When the basis of the opinions as to the alleged evil effects of the moderate use of the drugs is subjected to careful examination, the grounds on which
the allegations are founded prove to be in the highest degree defective,' the
commission concluded, after an exhaustive review of the evidence. 'Total prohibition of the hemp plant for narcotics, and of the manufacture, sale, or use
of the drugs derived from it, is neither necessary nor expedient.' This may
explain why Messrs Blair and Straw won't permit a similarly scrupulous

inquiry into their assertions that law reform will provoke an epidemic of crime, degeneracy and reefer madness. They are secretly afraid that, as in 1893, it would come up with the wrong answer.

(*Guardian*, 18 August 1999)

The people's wine is deepest red

'WHERE ARE THE *New Statesman*'s priorities?' demands an indignant letter in the magazine's current issue from a reader in Whitstable, Kent. It describes the *NS*'s excellent food and wine correspondents, Bee Wilson and Victoria Moore, as 'intelligent, elegant writers on worthless themes', whose 'trivial, indulgent musings have no place in a journal that is supposed to explore social justice'. The writer cannot understand how a left-wing journal allows space for articles on such 'selfish and silly concerns'.

The idea that socialists shouldn't enjoy the pleasures of the table is remarkably hard to dislodge. In the 1930s, Lord Beaverbrook wrote a sneering article for the London *Evening Standard* about 'Café Communists', whom he defined as 'the gentlemen, often middle-aged, who gather in fashionable restaurants, and, while they are eating the very fine food that is served in those restaurants and drinking the fine wines of France and Spain, are declaring themselves to be of Left Wing faith'. (One of the Café Communists named in the piece replied, with admirable presence of mind, that he didn't see why he should be 'a victim of the malnutrition which is an endemic disease of capitalism'.) When Aneurin Bevan was dining with him, Beaverbrook used to bawl at the butler: 'Bring the Bollinger Bolshevik a bottle of young, fizzy, cold champagne!'

As the letter in the *New Statesman* demonstrates, it isn't only rich right-wingers who believe that champagne socialism is an oxymoron. The left in this country has its own regiment of puritan zealots who regard any form of fun as a decadent distraction from more urgent tasks. The late Cyril Ray, a lifelong socialist who edited the *Compleat Imbiber* annuals, had a simple reply to these killjoys: 'There is no more virtue in not minding what you eat and drink than in not minding whom you go to bed with.' Though he refused on principle to allow the *Daily Telegraph* into his house, and once resigned from *The Sunday Times* because of an editorial supporting capital punishment, Ray saw no incongruity in his authorship of a book on Bollinger. As he pointed out: 'They don't say "How dare you call yourself a socialist and love good books, good painting and good music?" Socialism is about a fuller and richer life for everybody, and God knows there's plenty of good cheap wine about today.' His *Guardian* obituary – written by Christopher Driver, another radical foodie – was headed: 'The people's wine is deepest red.'

Raymond Postgate, founder of *The Good Food Guide*, was jailed as a conscientious objector in the First World War, took to the picket lines in the General Strike and received a fan-letter from Lenin for his book on *The International During the War*. None of this was enough to save him from being regularly attacked by pious fellow lefties for his gastronomic enthusiasms. 'Confounded nonsense,' he retorted. 'I should like to remind puritanical objectors that Major Cartwright, the first of the Reformers, was an expert on raisins and on gin; and that Marx himself on occasion even got drunk.' Just so; when Karl Marx had had a few he sometimes behaved in a manner more usually associated with Bertie Wooster on boat-race night. Engels, too, was a serious tippler who admitted that in 1848, the year of revolutions, he 'spent more time lying in the grass with the vintners and their girls, eating grapes, drinking wine, chatting and laughing, than marching'.

What Marx and Engels understood, even if some of their grim-faced followers didn't, was that there's nothing selfish and silly about shared pleasures, whether in the long grass or at the kitchen table. There are few things more conducive to comradeship than decent food and drink. It is, I think, no coincidence that the creator of the first top-class champagne was not some bloated plutocrat but Dom Perignon, a Benedictine monk of the seventeenth century who devoted his life to caring for the sick and needy. 'He loved the poor,' according to his epitaph, 'and he made excellent wine.' Note the conjunction: 'and', not 'but'. Those who yearn for a better future need all the sustenance they can get. Pessimism of the intellect, Antonio Gramsci advised, must be accompanied by optimism of the will; and how can one not feel optimistic at the sound of a popping cork, or the taste and texture of a perfect peach?

(*Guardian*, 20 April 2000)

THE PARANOIA PANTOMIME

Letters in green ink

S HOCKING NEWS FROM the United States: Daniel Patrick Moynihan, the veteran senator from New York, has proposed that the Central
Intelligence Agency should be closed down. Nor is his a lone voice: in
the *International Herald Tribune* the other day, the eminent columnist William
Pfaff argued that the CIA 'is at the end of its useful life'.

What damned impudence. If Messrs Moynihan and Pfaff were to study
The CIA Catalog of Clandestine Weapons, Tools and Gadgets, a copy of which I
obtained recently, they would see that there's still plenty of life in the Agency.
The forty-eight items described in the brochure include a miniature hacksaw
disguised as a belt buckle, a pistol that looks like a glasses case, a felt-tip pen
filled with mustard gas, and a 'suppository escape kit' containing a saw, a file,
a drill and knife blades ('a small container of surgical lubricating jelly is issued
along with the kit'). Oh, and a gold Rolex watch: although this has no hidden
compartments or concealed weapons, it 'could be used to finance escape and
assist an agent on the run'. As the preface points out, these devices 'are but a
small part of the CIA's global effort to be of service to those brave souls who
search and listen for "the truth that makes us free"'. Do Daniel Patrick Moynihan and William Pfaff really not appreciate the necessity of maintaining the
West's arsenal of lethal suppositories? Have they never heard of that wise old
motto, 'The price of liberty is eternal constipation'?

CIA agents awaiting their redundancy cheques must look with envy at
their counterparts in MI6, otherwise known as the Secret Intelligence Service.
Sir Michael Quinlan, the former permanent secretary at the Ministry of
Defence, was recently commissioned by the government to report on
whether SIS had been rendered obsolete by the end of the Cold War. He has
now delivered his verdict: MI6 is a national treasure that must be preserved at
all costs. These costs include an annual budget of £150 million, plus the
£230 million bill for building and equipping the Service's huge, Babylonian
new HQ on the south bank of the Thames at Vauxhall Cross, designed by

the post-modernist architect Terry Farrell. Unkind souls may point out that Farrell was also responsible for the eggcup-topped offices of TV-am, which came to a sticky end a couple of years ago; but there is no reason to suppose that history will repeat itself. MI6's licence to kill is an open-ended franchise.

Besides, the Service enjoys the public blessing of no less a figure than the head of state. As the Court Circular quietly revealed earlier this month: 'The Queen, accompanied by the Duke of Edinburgh, this morning opened the new headquarters of the Secret Intelligence Service at Vauxhall Cross, London, and was received by the Chief of the Service (Sir Colin McColl).' I trust that Sir Colin, who retires next month, reminded her of MI6's many achievements. There was Kim Philby, who for years ensured that all MI6's secrets were swiftly passed on to the KGB. There was Buster Crabb, the wheezy, ageing frogman who drowned while carrying out an underwater reconnaissance of a Russian ship, thereby provoking no end of diplomatic embarrassment for his employers in the Service. Then there was George Blake, one of the senior MI6 men in charge of Operation Gold, the secret tunnel under Berlin which enabled British intelligence to eavesdrop on Russian military communications in the mid-1950s: since he was in fact a Soviet agent, the Russians knew from the outset that they were being monitored, and all the thousands of hours of tape-recordings so painstakingly acquired by MI6 turned out to be worthless.

Perhaps Sir Colin confined himself to more recent triumphs, such as MI6's inability to anticipate the fall of the Shah of Iran, and its failure to persuade the British Government that Argentina might invade the Falklands – or, some years later, that Saddam Hussein was about to march into Kuwait. Bringing Her Majesty fully up to date, he may even have alluded to his colleagues' role in the arms-to-Iraq scandal. As a Foreign Office official has revealed in evidence to the Scott Inquiry, MI6 told ministers that machine tools supplied to Iraq by Matrix Churchill were unlikely to be used 'for direct manufacture of munitions'. And how did MI6 know this? Why, it had been given an assurance by one of Matrix Churchill's directors, Dr Safaa al-Habobi – who happened to be the head of Iraq's arms procurement operation, and was therefore assumed to be an honest and upright gent.

Do Sir Colin and his 2,000 staff ever get anything right? Of course not. Uselessness is one of the great traditions of the Service, like the green ink in which the MI6 director writes all his letters. When William Pfaff notes that the principal activity of Western intelligence during the Cold War 'was always the effort to penetrate Soviet intelligence, while Soviet intelligence was spending its time penetrating Western intelligence', he is quite right; but the conclusion he draws from this – that the enterprise was a waste of time and money – is mistaken. Intelligence work is a stately gavotte, or perhaps a *danse macabre*; it achieves nothing. So what? No one ever argues that *Come Dancing* should be abolished merely because it is 'unproductive'.

At a time when other public services are being privatized or subjected to competitive tendering, MI6 remains, thankfully, a protected species. The 'intelligence' it supplies could be procured, at a tiny fraction of the cost, from any averagely well-informed newspaper reader or from Reuter's news agency. But it provides a lot of harmless pleasure – and financial security – to hundreds of overgrown adolescents who enjoy donning false noses, writing in invisible ink and turning up the collars of their raincoats. One of the job-creation schemes suggested by John Maynard Keynes in his *General Theory* was for the Government to fill old bottles with banknotes, bury them in disused coalmines and then encourage workers to dig them up again. That, more or less, is what MI6 does. It may be pointless, but at least it gives sheltered employment to people who would otherwise be unemployable.

Which leaves only one question: how does one join this admirable organization? Following in Her Majesty's footsteps, last week I paid a visit to Vauxhall Cross. Ignoring the suspicious looks of several men who were emerging from the building (they could tell I wasn't a spook since I wasn't wearing the obligatory sunglasses), I strode through the front door and up to the front desk. 'Can I have a job please?' I asked. 'No, I'm sorry,' the rather startled man at reception told me. 'We're full up.' Yes, but there must be openings from time to time. Could I see the personnel officer? 'Er, no. There isn't one.' So how do they recruit new staff? He declined to explain. Still, he did agree to take my name and address, in case an unexpected vacancy should occur.

Beside the desk I noticed an internal memo. Sensing that it might be a classified document, I grabbed it and scarpered. Thus I became the proud owner of a sheet of paper advertising MI6's 'health and fitness club' – complete with a floor plan of the new HQ, which I shall probably sell to Russian intelligence for a small fee. 'Whether you need to "let off steam", improve your fitness, lose weight, train for a sport or rehabilitate after an injury,' the Club Manager boasts, 'our impressive array of facilities provides the ideal solution. Your social life may receive a boost as well!' Impressive is certainly the word. The new MI6 office has its own sports hall (suitable for basketball, mini-hockey, football, badminton and table tennis) as well as a gymnasium, an aerobics studio and a squash court.

Espionage has long been known as 'the great game'. The game in question, I now realize, is ping-pong.

(*Observer*, 31 July 1994)

Secrets and lies

Aᴅꜰᴛᴇʀ ᴀ Qᴜɪᴄᴋ ɢʟᴀɴᴄᴇ at the Scott Report, Stephen Glover of the *Daily Telegraph* concludes that 'we are dealing here with decent and moral men who behaved rather incompetently.' He continues: 'There is no evidence that their incompetence derived from any moral lapse.' He is struck, indeed, by 'how strong the moral impulse was in British foreign policy'. Reluctant though I am to argue about morality with Stephen Glover – who was described recently as the most formidable moralist in Britain – I think he may be pushing his luck. The index to Scott's magnum opus includes entries for machine tools, magnets, marine pyrotechnics, military trade fairs, mine clearance systems, missile launchers, mortars, munitions and mustard gas; but not a dickybird about morality.

Still, the dread word is not entirely neglected in the text itself. During the Iran-Iraq war, we learn, it cropped up in an internal memo written by Keith Haskell, the head of the Middle East department at the Foreign Office. 'The Americans (and the Arabs) may wish that we were tilting more to Iraq,' he noted. 'But we have consistently and publicly emphasized our even-handedness and impartiality in this conflict, and I think it would be inadvisable and morally wrong to be tempted down the primrose path of short-term expediency.' Morally wrong! Haskell had exceeded his brief, and was rightly rebuked by one of his Foreign Office bosses, Sir Stephen Egerton. While concurring with Haskell's general attitude, Egerton deplored the reference to morality. 'It is better to steer clear of this...concept now that we are so far into the arms supply game,' he wrote.

And that was that – until Sir Stephen was summoned to give oral evidence to the Scott Inquiry, whereupon he did a hasty volte-face, agreeing that 'morality had a part to play in decisions regarding the supply of weapons, particularly those of a chemical or nuclear type'. Jolly decent of him, I'm sure. But what 'part' was allotted to morality by the men at FO central casting: one of the romantic leads, or merely a cameo role? Anyone who has read the Scott Report will know the answer. Although most debate in Parliament and the press has concentrated on whether Waldegrave was a knave, and the Attorney-General a proven Lyell, the most fascinating sections of Scott's epic are those in which we see just how civil servants behave when they think no one is looking. Take the submission of 13 April 1984 prepared by the deeply moral Mr Haskell for his minister, Sir Richard Luce. It began promisingly enough: 'Our present policy is that we are neutral in the conflict between Iran and Iraq and do not sell lethal equipment to either side.' However, he added, 'we have so far refused to be drawn into detailed discussions of what constitutes "lethal" and "non-lethal", so as to retain some flexibility to adjust our supply of equipment and parts to the ebb and flow of the conflict.'

Yes, Mr Haskell, I think we see what you're getting at. Alan Collins, another official at the FO, developed this delightfully feline point in a memo of 29 October 1984, in which he brooded over 'the loss of future defence sales business' in Iran and Iraq as a consequence of Britain's surfeit of morality. 'To overcome these difficulties, which are at present uppermost in MoD and DTI eyes, we should need a measure of flexibility in interpreting our policy. We would have to avoid being forced into exact definitions of what we were prepared to supply to either side. The well-established principle of refusal to reveal the details of individual transactions would be helpful in this respect.' I bet it would.

Michael Petter of the DTI summed up his department's opinion thus: 'We accept that existing policy is difficult to present convincingly but it has enabled British firms to secure valuable defence orders and to continue to pursue profitable civil business in both markets. Its practical advantages, whatever its presentational shortcomings, are therefore not to be lightly discarded.' The echo of the Christian service of marriage ('not by any to be enterprised, nor taken in hand, unadvisedly, lightly, or wantonly, to satisfy men's carnal lusts and appetites, like brute beasts that have no understanding') is presumably deliberate. Nevertheless, there was no sign of the M-word in Petter's memo; merely a determination to satisfy the carnal lusts and appetites of British exporters without incurring 'presentational' difficulties.

No wonder the brute beasts were so alarmed when politicians started muttering about 'guidelines'. On 2 November 1984, the Foreign Office minister Sir Richard Luce proposed that Britain should 'permit no new supply commitments to either party which would appreciably increase its ability to prolong or to exacerbate the conflicts'. Christopher Sandars, a senior official at the

Ministry of Defence, swiftly suggested an amendment, which was accepted: that the words 'appreciably increase its ability' should be replaced by 'significantly enhance the capability'. It was an inspired semantic adjustment, almost invisible to the untrained eye. Any supplies whatsoever to either side might 'appreciably' increase its belligerent ability, for those who can appreciate such things; but who could say, in the context of such slaughter, whether our contribution was 'significant'?

There was one more task for the wordsmiths of Whitehall. Luce's original draft suggested that the government should scrutinize all applications for export licences with the utmost rigour, 'accepting that this may lead to the relinquishment of our role as a supplier even of non-lethal equipment to Iran and Iraq as long as the present conflict continues'. For a brief moment, morality reared its ugly head; but it was soon decapitated. By the time Luce's text had been turned into the famous 'Howe guidelines', the clause beginning with the words 'accepting that...' had been omitted altogether.

It is true that Whitehall's finest minds agonized long and hard over British policy towards Iran and Iraq. But, in spite of what Stephen Glover and some other commentators seem to think, these public servants were not fretting over the moral consequences of prolonging a ghastly war. Their writhings and squirmings had only one cause: they wanted to keep supplying equipment to the combatants without being found out. Or, as Bernard Shaw observed long ago, 'An Englishman thinks he is moral when he is only uncomfortable.'

(*Guardian*, 21 February 1996)

Significant skulduggery

IN HIS OFFICIAL BIOGRAPHY of Harold Wilson, published in 1993, Philip Ziegler dealt briskly and dismissively with Peter Wright's allegation that MI5 officers had plotted against the Prime Minister. 'The present head of MI5,' he wrote, 'after long experience in the service, is...convinced that the bureaucratic machinery of the department would have made it impossible for any significant skulduggery to have taken place, even at the lowest level.' Ziegler's source was identified in a small footnote at the back of the book: 'Interview with Mrs Stella Rimington.' Ziegler was so delighted by his little scoop – the first on-the-record interview given by a serving head of MI5 – that he didn't pause to consider how utterly worthless her testimony was. If her subordinates had engaged in 'significant skulduggery', would she know? And even if she did know, would she tell us?

The libel laws being what they are, one normally hesitates before accusing people of concealing the truth. But spies and spooks are a special case, since mendacity is one of their essential skills. As the former MI6 officer Anthony Cavendish has written: 'An SIS officer lies from his first day in the service. It is part of his cover.' Stella Rimington acknowledged the point when she emerged from the shadows to deliver her Dimbleby lecture in 1994. 'A cynic,' she said, 'may ask: "How can I know that what you're saying is true?" Well, it is difficult.' It certainly is. Rimington's lecture sought to dispel the 'fairly wide-spread misunderstanding' that 'the Service monitors high-profile people'. She also insisted, at great length, that MI5's targets are only those 'subversives' who would undermine democracy. 'It does not include political dissent...the allegation that the Service sought to investigate organizations which were not subversive is quite untrue.' Thanks to the MI5 whistleblower David Shayler, we now learn that these threats to democracy include Jack Straw, who was deemed a 'communist sympathizer' merely because he had been president of the National Union of Students. If the blithering idiots at the security service had any political nous whatever, they would know that young Straw was tediously well scrubbed and well behaved. It is a typical MI5 triumph to take almost the only student from the '68 generation who was not remotely radical and mark him down as a dangerous troublemaker.

This is the sort of frazzle-brained logic we have come to expect from the spooks. As one ex-MI5 officer of my acquaintance complained a few years ago, some of her colleagues 'thought people who wore jeans were potentially sub-versive'. Sir Edward Heath, that well-known revolutionary firebrand, has revealed that when he was Prime Minister, 'I met people in the security serv-ices who talked the most ridiculous nonsense and whose whole philosophy was a ridiculous nonsense. If some of them were on a Tube and saw someone reading the *Daily Mirror* they would say: "That is dangerous, get after him, find out where he bought it." ' MI5 apologists tell us that it is quite different now. They note that the monitoring of Straw and Mandelson predated the 'reform' of the Service in the late 1980s. The old guard has been cleared out since then, and the days when Peter Wright and his chums bugged and bur-gled their way across London are long gone.

I think not. According to Shayler, MI5 was tapping the telephone of my

Guardian colleague Victoria Brittain even as Rimington delivered her reassuring Dimbleby lecture in 1994. 'Then, in 1995, a decision was taken to try and plant a bug in her Islington home and search the premises,' he reports. 'A specialist MI5 "recce" team surveyed the house and brought in a team of lock-pickers to assess how easy it would be to break in. In the end we backed out because the break-in team feared the risk of being caught was too high.' Shayler estimates that this surveillance, which continued for several years, cost the taxpayer about £750,000.

Cloak-and-dagger work has always tended to attract paranoid fantasists who see even the mildest dissent as rank treachery, and it will take more than a powerless parliamentary committee or an ineffective ombudsman to alter MI5's habits. As long ago as 1711, Parliament tried to 'regularize' the behaviour of official mail-tamperers by insisting that no letter could be opened without a warrant from a Secretary of State; but the government snoops within the Post Office carried on regardless. Their antics were satirized by Jonathan Swift a few years later in *Gulliver's Travels*, in a passage that is eerily similar to Shayler's account of modern MI5 methods. While Lemuel Gulliver was visiting the Academy of Lagado, a professor showed him

> a large paper of instructions for discovering plots and conspiracies against the Government. He advised great statesmen to examine into the diet of all suspected persons; their times of eating; upon which side they lay in bed; with which hand they wiped their posteriors; to take a strict view of their excrements, and from the colour, the odour, the taste, the consistence, the crudeness or maturity of digestion, form a judgment of their thoughts and designs.

It seems no more ludicrous than preserving a set of John Lennon's handwritten lyrics for 'Working Class Hero', as MI5 apparently did.

Gulliver repaid the academy's hospitality by explaining how the security services operated in his own country. He told the professor:

> in the kingdom of Tribnia, by the natives called Langden, where I had long sojourned, the bulk of the people consisted wholly of discoverers, witnesses, informers, accusers, prosecutors, evidences, swearers. It is first agreed and settled among them what suspected persons shall be accused of a plot; then effectual care is taken to secure all their letters and other papers...These papers are delivered to a set of artists very dexterous in finding out the mysterious meanings of words, syllables, and letters. For instance, they can decipher a closestool to signify a Privy Council, a flock of geese a senate, a lame dog an invader...

I need hardly point out that Tribnia and Langden were anagrams of Britain and England. They still are.

(*Guardian*, 27 August 1997)

Spies, lies, old school ties

W HAT IS TO BE DONE with Richard Tomlinson, the renegade intelligence officer? 'My old employer, the KGB, would simply have kidnapped him, executed him, or locked him up for ever after his first offence or put him in a lunatic asylum,' Oleg Gordievsky commented last weekend. 'This must be one of those occasions when it is very frustrating for MI6 not to have the KGB's powers.' Most frustrating, I'm sure. But the Secret Intelligence Service has only itself to blame. If Tomlinson really is a loose cannon, as countless security experts now assure us, how did he ever get through the well-guarded portals of Vauxhall Cross?

The answer has been provided by the historian Andrew Roberts, who knew Tomlinson at Cambridge University and was himself nearly recruited by SIS. 'I sat a series of extremely testing exams,' Roberts reveals. 'Some were straightforward written questions: my spirits rose when I was asked to place, in order of precedence, Viscount, Duke, Marquess, Earl and Baron (this one in particular would have played on Richard's social chippiness).' It may also explain why the list of SIS officers published on the Internet last week includes one viscount plus umpteen chaps with names like Peregrine Plantagenet Wykehamist-Twytte.

Having sailed through these exacting tests, Roberts was summoned for an interview with SIS's doctor. ' "Homosexual, are you?" he inquired. When I said I wasn't he almost apologised for being so personal. "We have to ask. Silly, really, as of course no one says Yes. With Oxford it's drugs, with Cambridge it's boys." ' What it is with Lampeter or Bangor we shall never know and nor will the chieftains of SIS, since their procedures are carefully designed to exclude provincial oiks and encourage public-school fantasists. As Roberts confirms, the only serious qualifications for a job in British intelligence are an Oxbridge degree and boundless self-confidence, both of which Richard Tomlinson had.

Now that Tomlinson has turned against his former employers, it is no surprise that his cause should be taken up by Lyndon LaRouche, the veteran American conspiracy theorist, and our own dear Mohamed Al Fayed. A year ago, Fayed's sidekick Michael Cole advised TV producers who were investigating the death of the Princess of Wales that they should interview one Jeffrey Steinberg, a 'senior reporter' on the magazine *Executive Intelligence Review*. Steinberg duly appeared in several Diana-related television programmes, but viewers were not told that *Executive Intelligence Review* is in fact the weekly propaganda sheet for Lyndon LaRouche.

Like Fayed, LaRouche has some interesting theories about the British establishment. He believes that the Queen runs an international cocaine-smuggling cartel and that Lord Rees-Mogg was responsible for the Oklahoma massacre in 1995. 'The mouth of Lord William Rees-Mogg,' he wrote recently, 'has become the world's largest open sewer-pipe of demented ravings...the guiding hand behind the deployment of the new terrorist wave.' Fair enough – though I was slightly peeved when LaRouche wrote to me a few years ago alleging that Rees-Mogg was also the secret author of my own column. During the 1996 presidential campaign, *Executive Intelligence Review* carried the splendid headline: 'US Election is also a Referendum on Britain's Lord Rees-Mogg'.

But the villainous Rees-Mogg is no more than an accomplice to the real Napoleon of Crime, otherwise known as Prince Philip. According to LaRouche, the royal family wants to terrorize the United States into becoming a British colony again, thus giving the House of Windsor a monopoly in the American cocaine market. The only person powerful enough to foil this plot was the Princess of Wales, which is why she had to be eliminated. After the bombing of the US embassy in Nairobi last summer, LaRouche instantly detected the Duke of Edinburgh's fingerprints. 'If Satan considered his darling, Adolf Hitler, to be relatively a wimp, Satan must be gloating over his selection of Prince Philip as Hitler's successor. As I shall demonstrate, this view of Prince Philip as quite literally a satanic figure is no hyperbole...' LaRouche's latest pamphlet, *The Pure Evil of Al Gore*, adds that the American vice-president is a secret agent of the Windsors, committed to 'the British monarchy's longer-range strategic policy for the planet as a whole'.

This may seem barmy but is no barmier than many of the 'intelligence assessments' provided by MI6 over the years. Lyndon LaRouche thinks that the Italian banker Roberto Calvi was murdered by the Duke of Kent; those fine public servants at Vauxhall Cross are convinced that only someone who knows the difference between an earl and a marquess is fit to be initiated into the mysteries of trade-craft. Which is the more eccentric?

(*Guardian*, 19 May 1999)

Dr Strangelove, I presume

ALL POLITICIANS LIE from time to time. But in the long and lurid annals of parliamentary mendacity there have been few lies bigger than that uttered by Willie Whitelaw, Margaret Thatcher's Home Secretary, on 12 February 1980. 'Most houses offer reasonable protection against radioactive fallout from nuclear explosions,' genial Willie told the House of Commons. 'Protection can be quite substantially improved by a series of quite simple do-it-yourself measures.' He then published a pamphlet called *Protect and Survive*, which described some of these DIY defences. 'If you can reach home in a couple of minutes, try to do so,' it suggested. 'If you live in a caravan or other similar accommodation which provides very little protection against fallout, your local authority will be able to advise you on what to do.'

The manifest lunacy of *Protect and Survive* had a most salutary effect. By the end of the year, Labour had adopted a non-nuclear defence policy and the Campaign for Nuclear Disarmament had recruited thousands of new members. One was the young Tony Blair. 'We don't need dangerous and costly Trident and Cruise missiles, which just escalate the nuclear arms race,' he declared during the 1983 general election. Three years later he signed a CND advert supporting 'the removal of all nuclear weapons from British territory'. How long ago it all seems. The Cruise missiles have gone, and last Saturday the perimeter fence at Greenham Common was ceremonially dismantled. Later this month a card-carrying CND member, Peter Hain MP, will fly to New York to represent the British government at a 'review conference' on the Nuclear Non-Proliferation Treaty (NPT). To judge by the latest defence white paper, which scarcely mentions our nuclear arsenal, you might think that Blair had achieved his ambition of beating warheads into ploughshares.

Not so. 'The fact that I happen to be a passive CND member doesn't at all conflict wth my own strong commitment to the government's agenda,' Hain says. And this 'agenda', like that of previous Labour governments, is dictated by Washington. No sooner has the fence come down at Greenham than we learn that the Pentagon hopes to use the early-warning station at Fylingdales, Yorkshire, for its new National Missile Defence (NMD) programme. 'We have received no formal request from the US administration regarding Fyling-dales,' Geoff Hoon, the invisible Defence Secretary, announced in a written answer on 9 February, 'nor would we expect any until after a US decision on whether or not to proceed towards deployment of the NMD system.'

This was a classic bit of MoD obfuscation: why would Bill Clinton bother with 'formal requests' when he can have a private word with his friend Tony? Sure enough, by the end of last month, 'Cabinet sources' were informing lobby correspondents that Tony Blair 'has already spoken to President Bill Clinton about the missile system, dubbed "son of Star Wars", and given assur-ances of his support'. As one minister asked: 'How can we turn down a request from our closest ally?' Quite easily, I'd say. If Blair had an ounce of gumption, he could reply that the NMD system breaches the USA's obligations under the Anti-Ballistic Missile Treaty of 1972. He could also ask Clinton, and Al Gore, whether it is really worth spending $50 billion on a nuclear shield whose sole purpose is to repel an attack from North Korea. (Kim Jong-Il must be hugely flattered.) Finally, he could recall something he must have learned in his days as a CND supporter: that there is no fully effective protection against a nuclear strike, just as there is no sense in rushing down to the Citizens' Advice Bureau when the third world war starts. 'If you look at world history,' Presi-dent Chirac said last December, in a thoughtful interview with the *New York Times*, 'ever since men began waging war, you will see that there's a perma-nent race between the sword and the shield. The sword always wins.' The National Missile Defence system, he predicted, is 'just going to spur sword-makers to intensify their efforts'.

The only absolute defence against nuclear weapons is to do away with them. Some of the most senior brass-hats in the US military establishment admitted as much in Jonathan Schell's book *The Gift of Time*, published at the end of 1998. Robin Cook's old colleague Michael Foot made the same point a few months later in *Dr Strangelove, I Presume*, a passionate polemic against what Foot calls 'the bloody Bomb'. I am told that Peter Hain accepts the argu-ment. But will he dare say so when he goes to New York? At the last NPT review conference, five years ago, Britain was represented by its Foreign Secre-tary, Douglas Hurd, rather than a mere junior minister. This failed to mollify Robin Cook, who was then still an angry oppositionist. 'Douglas Hurd's claim to have made progress on disarmament is a travesty of the truth,' Cook wrote in the *Guardian* on 20 April 1995. 'The defence select committee has described Trident as a "significant enhancement of the UK's nuclear capacity". The non-nuclear states agree and are unimpressed by Hurd's claims to the contrary.'

Since then, the Labour government has commissioned a fourth Trident submarine. Each of its forty-eight warheads has a 'yield' of 100 kilotons, five times as powerful as the bomb that destroyed Nagasaki. After the Strategic Defence Review of 1998, which concluded that 'it would be premature to abandon a minimum [*sic*] capability to design and produce a successor to Trident', several staff from the atomic weapons establishment in Aldermaston were seconded to the American laboratory at Los Alamos to 'assist with the technical development of facilities of mutual interest', in MoD-speak. Last summer, the ministry revealed that it was investing £100 million in an 'enhancement programme' for Trident. Whatever happened to Robin Cook's outrage at governments that enhance the UK's nuclear capacity?

As Cook noted in his 1995 article, the non-proliferation treaty was essentially a bargain struck between countries without nuclear weapons, which gave up the option of acquiring them, and the five nuclear powers, which undertook in return to get rid of theirs through negotiation. 'The security assurances offered by Douglas Hurd to the non-nuclear states are inadequate,' he thundered. 'They will remain so until the nuclear powers give a commitment to no first use of nuclear weapons against any country. It would never be rational or legitimate to use nuclear weapons first, and we should not hesitate to announce formally such a basic principle as official policy.' No hesitation, eh? After nearly three years in office, Labour has yet to proclaim a 'no first use' policy. Quite the opposite: at last year's NATO summit, Tony Blair insisted that Britain and the US must retain the right to threaten a pre-emptive nuclear strike. Does Robin Cook still think that this isn't 'rational or legitimate'? Or has he, like Dr Strangelove, learned to stop worrying and love the Bomb?

(*Guardian*, 12 April 2000)

Buddy, can you spare a tank?

THE DROOLING ADMIRATION of British right-wingers for George Bush's missile defence system is matched by their sneering contempt for Vladimir Putin's suggestion that Russia and Europe should cooperate on an alternative scheme. 'The Russian plan is fantasy ballistics, having no existence in the real world,' a *Sunday Telegraph* editorial declares. 'And besides, does anyone want our defences against rogue states to be left in the hands of the people responsible for the sinking of the *Kursk*?' Perhaps not. But does anyone – other than the *Sunday Telegraph*, the Conservative Party and Tony Blair – have much faith in the technological and managerial efficiency of our own military-industrial complex?

Why, for instance, did British troops in Kosovo use insecure mobile phones to communicate? Answer: because their Clansman radios, in service since the 1970s, were so antiquated as to be useless. Why didn't they have new radios? Because the army was waiting for its modern battlefield communications system, Bowman, which had been ordered a mere twelve years earlier. Since then, Geoff Hoon has scrapped Bowman and invited new bids, effectively writing off the £330 million already invested. A report from the National Audit Office, with mandarinesque understatement, describes the whole chaotic saga as 'extremely disappointing'.

Not very surprising, however. Last April, more than fifty Lynx helicopters were withdrawn from service because of faulty rotorheads. In July, Britain pulled out of a European anti-tank missile project, which was ten years behind schedule and seemed likely to produce a weapon that would be out of date before it was delivered. (The MoD had already spent £100 million on it.) A month later, the RAF grounded eighty-four Tucano trainer aircraft after discovering 'fatigued parts' in the rudder assembly. In October, the Royal Navy's entire fleet of nuclear-powered submarines was taken out of service for 'urgent safety checks' following a leak in HMS *Tireless*'s propulsion system. On 1 November, several newspapers published photos of the only submarine on duty in British waters the previous day – a 32-year-old German U-boat, hired by the Royal Navy for £6,500 an hour. The *Sun*'s headline writer rose to the challenge: 'All Hans on Deck'.

Nor should we forget the army's SA80 assault rifle, which went back to the firing ranges for testing last month having undergone no fewer than eighty-two revamps since 1986. The MoD describes it as 'probably the most reliable rifle in the world' but I have yet to meet a soldier who agrees. Despite the vast sums spent on repairs and modifications, it still tends to seize up at awkward moments – as in Sierra Leone last year, when British paratroops who were fired at by the Revolutionary United Front found that their safety catches had jammed. (Another delightful feature of the SA80's design is that spent cartridges are ejected next to the soldier's head, which means that left-handed users have to fire it right-handed.) Then there's the aptly named Challenger, Britain's accident-prone battle tank, which is finally coming into use two years late and at £55 million more than its original estimated cost. And the Eurofighter, three years behind schedule and £1.5 billion over budget. And does anyone remember the Nimrod early-warning aircraft, which was aborted after consuming £1 billion of taxpayers' money?

Still, no need to worry: at least we can rely on our American allies. The National Missile Defence system (NMD) failed its last two tests. The Thaad missile, designed to intercept medium-range ballistic missiles, missed its target in six consecutive test shots. Lt Gen John Costello, commander of the US Army Space and Missile Defense Command, admitted that 'we can do better in reliability and quality control'. The same can be said, fortissimo, of the V-22 Osprey, a hugely expensive helicopter-aeroplane whose record over the past year was summarized by the *Washington Post* thus: 'Two crashes, twenty-three dead marines, numerous waivers of required tests, and allegations of lying by senior officers.' Although an official report found that the Osprey had 'dangerous aerodynamic defects' and was 'not operationally suitable', the Pentagon pressed ahead with production, preferring to jeopardize the lives of its marines rather than incur the wrath of the contractors and their friends in Congress. In the words of the *Post*'s headline: 'Great Idea! Buy First, Then Find Out if It Flies'.

I wouldn't want my defence to be in the hands of those responsible for the *Kursk*. Nor would I entrust it to the knaves and fools responsible for military procurement in Britain and America. The Cold War doctrine of mutual assured destruction is being succeeded by an equally grim balance of terror: Mutual Assured Incompetence.

(*Guardian*, 28 February 2001)

CRIMES, FOLLIES AND MISDEMEANOURS

Schooled for scandal

MANY YEARS AGO, shortly after making a hasty exit from secondary education, I sent my old housemaster a postcard explaining why I would not be returning. It consisted of a quote from one of Henry Fielding's novels: 'Public schools are the nurseries of all vice and immorality.' In a brief and bad-tempered reply, the housemaster pointed out that Fielding was describing conditions more than two centuries ago. 'It is quite different today,' he insisted, 'as you know perfectly well.'

Oh yeah? I wonder if he noticed a front-page news story last weekend, revealing that Scotland Yard detectives 'are investigating allegations of a paedophile network involving teachers from some of Britain's top public schools'. The network is said to include 'Charles Napier, a former treasurer of the Paedophile Information Exchange and a former staff member of the British Council in Cairo, who was jailed last year for sex assaults on youngsters in London'. Charles Napier was my gym-master at prep school – and a very good gym-master too, always willing to lend a hand (quite literally) as the boys practised their backflips and headstands. From time to time he would invite his favourites into a small workshop next to the gym, where he plied us with Senior Service untipped and bottles of Mackeson before plunging his busy fingers down our shorts. Although I rejected his advances, I continued to help myself to beer'n'cigs from his secret depot when he wasn't around.

It never occurred to me to report him to the authorities. Why? Because he was the authorities. Complaining about a teacher was as unthinkable as refusing to participate in cross-country runs. Anyway, no eleven-year-old boy wishes to parade his sexual innocence: Napier warned me – and many others – that by refusing to cooperate we were merely demonstrating our immaturity. 'X lets me do it, you know,' he said, naming a classmate of mine. For weeks afterwards, X sneered at me for my squeamishness.

I don't know where X is now (running a prep school of his own, probably), but I'm glad to learn that Napier has been taken out of circulation at last. As his half-brother told me a few years ago, 'Charles is such a trial to my mother. Every time he gets sacked, she asks him why he can't find some work which doesn't involve children. And then, after being on the dole for a while, he rings her up in great excitement and says, "Marvellous news, Mummy, I've got a new job – it's in a youth club..."' The half-brother, by contrast, has delighted his mother by staying on the straight and narrow. Very narrow indeed, actually: he is a Tory MP.

(*Guardian*, 28 August 1996)

The bottom line

'If parents are anxious to have their children well educated, they must not be afraid of a little castigation on the place which nature has ordained for the purpose.' – Editorial in the Family Herald, *January 1846*

'Referring to Gary Paul he said: "In my view I did my best to strike him on the buttocks where it would hurt but not cause any physical damage. I did not consider I gave him any excessive caning." Judge Bertrand Richards commented: "Buttocks were ordained by nature for the purpose."' – Court report in Daily Telegraph, *August 1975.*

T AKE A BABY INTO a trattoria in Florence or Rome, and you will be greeted by squeals of delight from the staff and customers. Repeat the experiment in a London restaurant – or, worse still, a pub – and the maître d' or landlord will fix you with a poisonous glare of disapproval. When Evelyn Waugh grumpily described children as 'defective adults', he was articulating a common national prejudice. We are a nation of child-haters; and, as the size of the prison population demonstrates, we are a nation of punishment freaks. Put the two together and you have a society where physical violence against tiny tots is not only acceptable but a bounden duty. Hence the undisguised glee of Tory backbenchers when Gillian Shephard indulged her flogging fantasies on the *Today* programme this week. 'I think there is so much value in proper corporal punishment,' Harry Greenway MP raved. 'I don't mean beating boys until they bleed...' Of course not; merely scarring and bruising will be quite adequate. It was entirely predictable that Britain should have been the last country in Europe to ban corporal punishment in state schools, in 1987 – and then only because the European Court of Human Rights gave us no choice. I don't doubt that we shall be the last country in Europe to outlaw the beating of children by parents, too.

No wonder spanking is known throughout the world as the English vice. Exactly a century ago, a book about virtue by the French author Josephin Aimé Peladan included a whole chapter on 'le vice anglais'. It concluded: 'The Anglo-Saxon will always represent human depravation – the race which stains pleasure with blood, which conceals an assassin's knife in the bed of love.' One hundred years on, we are still spanking away like billy-o – and still pretending that we do so in the name of love. 'You say "Don't do this", "You mustn't do that" and you gently slap them if they transgress,' the Archbishop of Canterbury advised his flock last weekend, 'and there is nothing wrong with that as long as it is done with love and firm discipline within the family set-up.' Many a stern Victorian paterfamilias must have thought that he too was exercising 'love and firm discipline within the family set-up' when he walloped his wife or housemaid. If he tried it today, however, he might well find himself up on a charge. It is bizarre but true that the only British citizens who have no legal redress against domestic violence are those who are most vulnerable.

As children grow up, according to Archbishop Carey, 'they learn and understand those rules and of course it has to be lived out. We older people must practise what we preach. So I don't think we pontificate from on high. We actually live the kind of discipline we are wanting a future generation of people to grow up with.' Oh really? I find it inconceivable that George Carey would take a swipe at an archdeacon who had been 'misbehaving'; the disciplinary code observed by grown-ups doesn't allow recourse to physical assault. Why, then, do we believe we are setting children an example, and preparing them for adult life, by whacking them every time they stray from the path of righteousness? The answer is depressingly simple: because we know we can get away with it. If George Carey saw a pet poodle piddling on his carpet at Lambeth Palace, perhaps he would administer one of his 'loving slaps'; if the miscreant mutt was a sabre-toothed rottweiler, he might think twice. It is nothing to do with 'discipline', and everything to do with the balance of power. As Penelope Leach comments in her recent book *Children First*, 'When a big child hits a small child in the playground, we call him a bully; five years later he punches a woman for her handbag and is called a mugger; later still, when he slugs a workmate who insults him, he is called a troublemaker; but when he becomes a father and hits his tiresome, disobedient or disrespectful child, we call him a disciplinarian. Why is this rung on a ladder of interpersonal violence regarded so differently from the rest?' I can already hear George Carey pointing out one difference: when he spanks, he does so for the child's own good. But good intentions are no justification, merely paving stones on the road to hell. Does a police officer's desire to convict criminals justify violence to an obviously guilty suspect? The other distinction, Carey may say, is that the smacking of children is administered in 'a private, loving family context'. Following that logic, we might as well legalize wife-beating and granny-bashing as well.

'If the whole concept of punishment is foreign to the self-discipline parents want children to acquire,' Penelope Leach concludes, 'then physical punishment cuts at its very foundations, highlighting people's reluctance to regard children as fully human – as people just like themselves except for youth and inexperience – and their ultimate readiness to abandon cooperation for the naked assertion of painful power.' Listening to the beguiling understatement of George Carey, Gillian Shephard and their supporters, who murmur about 'loving slaps' and 'gentle taps', one could easily forget that the point of smacking is to inflict pain. 'We are not talking about beating [children] up,' says David Clark, the shadow defence secretary, 'but a little slap doesn't do them any harm.' But it hurts them, doesn't it? His colleague David Blunkett, who was so scathing about the Education Secretary's yearning for the cane, has nevertheless endorsed the Archbishop's 'perfectly reasonable' remarks, adding that it is 'important to distinguish between smacking and physical violence'. Has this supposedly intelligent fellow never twigged that smacking, however mild, is indeed physical and violent? And where are all these calm, caring, cool-headed spankers anyway? Almost every time I visit the supermarket I witness some harassed and frustrated parent yelling at an errant child: 'You stop that right now or I'll belt you.' I have never heard a shopper say: 'Now look, darling, I think it's important to impress on you that you mustn't pull the bottles of Virgin Cola off the shelves, and so I intend to deliver a light slap – in a loving context, of course.' This isn't a wallop; it's codswallop.

The Tory MP Sir Ivan Lawrence, who applauds the Archbishop's 'common sense', has seen fit to inform us that 'I got a good hiding at home and at school if I was bad. It didn't do me any harm; in fact, I like to think it probably did me some good.' Students of Sir Ivan's parliamentary career may wonder how beneficial it really was; but at least he is honest enough not to take refuge in euphemisms. One other politician who has spoken bluntly on this subject, though he probably won't wish to be reminded of it, is Michael Meacher. I have a friend who was a pupil at Berkhamsted School when Meacher was a cane-wielding prefect. 'Now, boy,' the future Labour frontbencher warned, as he ordered my friend to bend over, 'you are going to understand the meaning of pain.' It may not have done Meacher any harm; but the recipient has never quite forgotten the ordeal.

There is one final point about corporal punishment, which is seldom mentioned in these discussions: spanking is sexy. Go into any telephone box in central London and you'll find dozens of calling cards from prostitutes advertising 'strict discipline' in one form or another. When George Ryley Scott wrote his pioneering *History of Corporal Punishment* in 1938, the publishers restricted its sale to 'members of the medical and legal professions, scientists, anthropologists, psychologists, sociologists, criminologists and social workers', precisely because they feared his treatise might otherwise be used as S&M pornography. 'It would have been easy to ignore the sexual side and all its implications,' he admitted in the preface. 'But this ostrich-like attitude would have been not only to evade one of the main issues, but to permit a distortion of the truth. One of the most pernicious features of corporal punishment lies in the possibility, on the one hand, of pandering to the sadistic element in mankind, and, on the other, of awakening or developing sexual libido.' Nothing has changed since then: how could it, human nature being what it is? On the paperback edition of Ian Gibson's *The English Vice*, the most exhaustive study of flagellomania ever written, there are admiring reviews from the *Times Educational Supplement*, *The Sunday Times*, the *Scotsman* – and *Janus*, the magazine for spanking fetishists, which notes that 'it should command the attention of every close student of corporal punishment'. Alas, there are few 'close students' whose interest isn't wholly lubricious. Perhaps it is too much to expect a busy Archbishop of Canterbury or Secretary of State to read Ian Gibson's book before sounding off about the harmlessness of slapping and slippering; but as educated people they must surely be aware of Jean-Jacques Rousseau's *Confessions*, published posthumously in 1782.

If not, let me enlighten them. Rousseau, whose mother died in childbirth, spent much of his boyhood being brought up by a Protestant priest, M. Lambercier, and his unmarried sister. 'Since Mlle Lambercier treated us with a mother's love, she had also a mother's authority,' he recalled, 'which she exercised by inflicting on us such childish chastisements as we had earned.' After his first beating, he was startled to find the experience 'less dreadful' than he had anticipated; in fact, he discovered in the shame and pain 'an admixture of sensuality' which left him eager for more.

Who could have supposed that this childish punishment, received at the age of eight at the hands of a woman of thirty, would determine my tastes and desires, my passions, my very self for the rest of my life, and that in a sense diametri- cally opposed to the one in which they should normally have developed? At the moment when my senses were aroused my desires took a false turn and, confin- ing themselves to this early experience, never set about seeking a different one...How differently people would treat children if only they saw the eventual results of the indiscriminate, and often culpable, methods of punishment they employ!

More than two centuries later, George 'Spanker' Carey and Gillian 'Thrasher' Shephard still can't see it. Perhaps someone should slap them about a bit, firmly but lovingly, until they come to their senses. After all, as they have so confidently reassured us, it can't do any harm.

(*Guardian*, 31 October 1996)

From Budleigh Salterton to Pyongyang

'YOU KNOW WHAT Scousers are like – always up to something,' Jack Straw quipped earlier this year. One might say the same of the Home Secretary himself. When not abolishing jury trials, he amuses himself by tormenting asylum seekers; when bored with trying to extradite David Shayler, he privatizes a few more prisons. And, when there's nothing else to occupy his time, he introduces yet another terrorism bill.

The only glimmer of humour in this sinister new legislation is the title of Schedule 8, Part II: 'Inchoate and Related Offences'. Perhaps the joke is unin- tentional, but I can't be the only reader of the bill to recall Sydney Smith's famous line: 'Many inchoate acts are innocent, the consummation of which is a capital offence.' Until now, British governments have regarded this as an important distinction. Nearly 150 years ago, for instance, the Austrian ambas- sador in London complained to Sir George Grey, the Home Secretary, that Karl Marx and other members of the Communist League were discussing 'the murder of princes'. By way of reply, Grey treated the ambassador to a rather lofty lecture on the nature of liberal democracy: 'Under our laws, mere discussion of regicide, so long as it does not concern the Queen of England and so long as there is no definite plan, does not constitute sufficient grounds for the arrest of the conspirators.'

It does now. Under Clause 57 of the bill, it will be a criminal offence to 'incite another person to commit an act of terrorism wholly or partly outside the United Kingdom...It is immaterial whether or not the person incited is in the United Kingdom at the time of the incitement.' And what precisely is an act of terrorism? Let me remind you of the bill's remarkable definition: 'In this act "terrorism" means the use or threat, for the purpose of advancing a political, religious or ideological cause, of action which involves serious violence against any person or property.' In other words, if someone in Budleigh Salterton 'incites' a friend in Baden Baden to issue a 'threat' to hurl paint over a statue of Kim Il Sung in Pyongyang, a crime will have been committed.

This country has a long record of offering shelter to displaced agitators: refugees as diverse as V. I. Lenin and General de Gaulle lived as exiles in London, scheming and dreaming, before returning in triumph to their native lands. It is a typical New Labour triumph to take the one British tradition of which we can feel unequivocally proud and turn it into a criminal offence. If the Straw law had been in force twenty or thirty years ago, every supporter of the African National Congress in Britain would have been liable to prosecution. Anyone who demanded the eviction of Indonesian troops from East Timor, or spoke in support of the Sri Lankan Tamils, could also have expected a visit from Sergeant Straw and his brigade of plods. And what of John Major – who, after the Gulf War, urged Iraqis to rise up and overthrow Saddam Hussein? A letter in the *Guardian* even asks if we could use the new law to indict Tony Blair, 'for plotting to use Trident'. Not so, alas. Straw has wisely added a line at the end of Clause 57 which effectively places himself – and Blair and Major – above the law of the land: 'Nothing in this section imposes criminal liability on any person acting on behalf of, or holding office under, the Crown.' So it's OK for British ministers to support counter-coups in Sierra Leone, but if the rest of us follow their example we shall be thrown in the slammer.

When Sir Keith Joseph was spreading the gospel of Thatcherism to hostile university audiences in the mid-1970s, he often used the story of Karl Marx to win round left-wing hecklers. 'I am proud that such a man found sanctuary in England,' he would shout over the hubbub. 'That's why I believe so passionately in Western democratic values: without them *Das Kapital* would never have been written.' Having already achieved the impressive feat of making Michael Howard look like a bleeding-heart liberal, Jack Straw is now determined to prove himself even more right-wing than the late Keith Joseph. What on earth will he do for an encore?

(Guardian, 8 December 1999)

A law unto himself

W HO ARE THESE woolly-minded lawyers and Hampstead liberals that oppose Jack Straw's splendid plan to save time and money by abolishing a defendant's right to jury trial on such piffling charges as theft and burglary? It's time to name and shame the guilty wimps.

Here's one. *The Times* of 7 July 1993 carried a feature by Gareth Williams QC, a former chairman of the bar, reviewing the report of the Royal Commission on Criminal Justice. 'The serious blemish in an otherwise admirable report,' he wrote, 'is the proposal that in those cases where the accused can now opt for trial by jury, this right should be removed...This would be madness. There are delays and inefficiencies at the moment, but the way to deal with them is to improve the mechanics, not to erode a fundamental liberty...I hope that Parliament will refuse to countenance legislation of this kind.' In an interview at the time, he added that there were 'no circumstances' under which he could agree to such a proposal. 'I am adamantly opposed.' Gareth Williams QC, otherwise known as Lord Williams of Mostyn, is now the government's Attorney-General, and adamantly in favour of what he once called 'madness'.

Williams was not the only lawyer to criticize the royal commission. The then shadow home secretary, a promising young barrister, said it was 'totally unsatisfactory' to prevent defendants from choosing trial by jury: 'Fundamental rights to justice cannot be driven by administrative convenience.' Tony Blair (for it was he) is now, I believe, some sort of minister, and apparently no longer cares two hoots about fundamental rights to justice.

But why go all the way back to 1993? Here's what another Labour lawyer told MPs as recently as 27 February 1997: 'Let me now refer to [Michael Howard's] proposal to end the right of many defendants to elect for trial by jury, even though they may face charges of dishonesty, and their reputation and their whole future may be at stake. Surely, cutting down the right to jury trial, making the system less fair, is not only wrong but short-sighted and likely to prove ineffective. Is it not the case that that is not only the view of the opposition and many practitioners and jurists but was the view of the Home Secretary, at least until today?' The speaker was, as you may have guessed, Jack Straw, who now sneers at 'practitioners and jurists' who still believe what he believed three years ago. But did he really believe it, even then? According to the old right-wing joke, a neo-conservative is a liberal who has been mugged. In Straw's case, however, there was no need for a mugging: he never had a liberal bone in his body.

Even as a student in the sixties he was a grim authoritarian, calling for crackdowns on cannabis users. When he became an Islington councillor in the early seventies, he had an ingenious idea for dealing with violence on local housing estates: set up impromptu 'tenants' courts' which could run trouble-some neighbours out of town. Even some of the most grizzled reactionaries in the Labour group were gobsmacked, and gently informed Straw – supposedly a qualified lawyer – that there might be a few legal problems with his lynch-mob scheme. 'I don't think he's moved on at all,' one old Islingtonian told me this week. 'Kangaroo courts are still all right by Jack.' There have been some pretty ghastly Home Secretaries in the past fifty years or so – David Maxwell Fyfe, Henry Brooke, David Waddington, Michael Howard – but none, I think, quite so proudly contemptuous of liberty. What makes Straw's behaviour all the more odd is that there's no need for it, since his reasons for curbing jury trial are manifestly bogus.

Even if Straw's justifications were true, they would be outweighed by the need to preserve the right to be tried by one's peers. He may think that charges of theft, burglary or handling stolen goods are trivial, but for those in the dock they can be career-shattering and life-wrecking. As he said in February 1997: 'If a police officer, an MP or even a Secretary of State were charged with an offence of dishonesty, would they not insist upon being tried by a jury? If that is the case, why should others be denied that right of election?'

But his justifications are not true, and he should certainly be hauled up on a charge of dishonesty if he persists with them. The claim that his 'reform' will save £100 million a year has been thoroughly exploded, not least in a *Guardian* article last November by Professor Lee Bridges of Warwick University. Straw's suggestion that more and more defendants are 'abusing the system' by insisting on their right to jury trial is equally false. As David Wolchover and Anthony Heaton-Armstrong have pointed out in the *New Law Journal*, the proportion of cases committed to crown courts because the

defendants elect for jury trial – rather than because magistrates decline jurisdiction – actually fell from 53 per cent to 28 per cent over the past decade. If
Straw wants to deal with 'inefficiencies' in the justice system he should turn
his attention to the real culprits. Only last month, the National Audit Office
revealed that delay and incompetence at magistrates' courts wasted more
than £40m a year, of which half 'resulted from failures within, or in liaison
between, the police, the Crown Prosecution Service and the courts or other
public bodies'.

Why, then, is Straw so determined to curtail trial by jury instead? Because
he can, I guess; and because he gets a kick out of annoying Hampstead liberals. When two journalists from the *Observer* interviewed the Home Secretary
last autumn, they pointed out that sacrificing liberty and justice in the name
of efficiency was the argument of the tyrant: Mussolini made the trains run on
time. Most Labour politicians would be deeply offended by the comparison
with a fascist dictator, but not our Jack. He merely smiled, apparently happy
to take it as a compliment. 'Well,' he said, 'I am trying to make the courts run
on time.'

Like Mussolini, Straw won't stop there. As he said last year: 'It must be
possible to change one's mind.' He has already abandoned his commitment to
a full-blooded Freedom of Information Bill, his opposition to 'three strikes
and you're out', his promise that asylum seekers would not have their benefits
withdrawn, his conviction that privatized prisons are 'morally repugnant', his
distaste for 'draconian' Prevention of Terrorism Acts – and, of course, his
belief that people 'whose whole future may be at stake' should be able to
choose trial by jury. Is anything sacred? I assume that he won't change his
mind on capital punishment. Looking at his record so far, however, I wouldn't
bet on it.

(*Guardian*, 12 January 2000)

Britain's executioners

A LTHOUGH IT'S OFTEN said that British politics is becoming
more American – two main parties which are almost indistinguish-
able on many issues, both financed by influence-buying tycoons and

pressure groups – there is still one great difference; and it's a matter of life and death. Every leading politician in the US, whether Republican or Democrat, supports capital punishment. In 1992, Bill Clinton broke off his primary campaign and hastened back to Arkansas to execute a brain-damaged black man, Rickey Ray Rector, solely to forestall any suspicion that he was 'soft'. This time round, the champion killer among the candidates is the Texas Governor, George W. Bush, who takes great pride in the fact that his state accounts for one third of all executions in the US. Last week he granted a temporary reprieve to a man awaiting lethal injection, Ricky McGinn: no big deal, given how many others he sends to their deaths, but extraordinary enough to earn long cover stories in both *Newsweek* and *The Economist*.

In Britain, by contrast, it is hard to find any politician who thinks we shall ever bring back hanging. Even William 'Battling Billy' Hague, who yearns for the return of the gallows, has admitted it's a lost cause. 'We have to be realistic,' he says. 'It is now highly unlikely that any Parliament would vote to bring back capital punishment.' And yet, though surprisingly few people seem to know it, British judges are still condemning people to death. At 7 Downing Street, almost within earshot of Leo Blair's nursery, the judicial committee of the privy council meets regularly to hear final appeals from prisoners on death row in Britain's old Caribbean colonies.

A glance at Amnesty International's annual report, published last week, shows the consequences of these deliberations. In Trinidad and Tobago, for instance, no fewer than nine men were hanged during one weekend in June last year. A tenth man was 'hanged in July in violation of an order of the Inter-American Court of Human Rights not to execute him until "such time as the court has considered the matter". There were approximately eighty people on death row at the end of 1999.' As the report's preface points out, Amnesty International campaigns vigorously for the abolition of the death penalty. 'Pending abolition,' it adds, 'AI calls on governments to commute death sentences, to introduce a moratorium on executions, to respect international standards restricting the scope of the death penalty and to ensure the most rigorous standards for fair trial in capital cases.'

This ought to make uncomfortable reading for Lord Hoffmann, a director of Amnesty International's fund-raising arm. You may remember Hoffmann: he is the Law Lord whose vote in favour of extraditing General Pinochet was later annulled by five other Law Lords because his Amnesty links 'were so strong that public confidence in the integrity of the administration of justice would be shaken'. But he is also one of the privy council's hanging judges, and in the last twenty months he has helped to send thirteen Caribbean prisoners to the gallows. One was Trevor Nathaniel Pennerman Fisher, a convicted murderer from the Bahamas who appealed to the privy council in October 1998, just one month before Hoffmann's ruling against Pinochet. Fisher's argument was simple: he should not be executed while a petition against his sentence was still being investigated by the Inter-American Commission on Human Rights (IACHR), to which the government of the Bahamas is a party. Two judges, Lord Slynn and Lord Hope, agreed with him, stating that 'it was hard to imagine a more obvious denial of human rights than to execute a man, after many months of waiting for the result, while his case was still under legitimate consideration by an international human rights body'. But they were outvoted by the three other judges – including milord Hoffmann of Amnesty International. Fisher was executed soon afterwards.

It seems incredible that someone can be deprived of his life on a three to two split decision; you might as well decide his fate on a penalty shoot-out. But such verdicts have become increasingly common. Last December, again by a three to two vote, Hoffmann and two colleagues dismissed another appeal from the Bahamas. John Junior Higgs and David Mitchell, convicted murderers, pointed out that each of them had a petition pending before the IACHR – though after the Fisher decision their lawyers must have guessed that this wouldn't impress Hoffmann and Co. But there was a second ground for appeal. Higgs and Mitchell said that their long confinement in one tiny, insanitary and unfurnished cell, from which they were let out for only twenty-five minutes' exercise four days a week, constituted 'cruel and unusual punishment', thus violating the principle that a man condemned to hang should not suffer further cruelties. (Higgs claimed that he had also been subjected to a 'mock execution' in 1997.) In the words of Lord Steyn, one of the dissenting judges: 'The conditions in which the appellants were held for the last three years were an affront to the most elementary standards of decency. The Bahamas had, over a long period, treated them as subhuman and had forfeited the right to carry out the death sentences.' Lord Cooke said that the men's treatment in jail was 'completely unacceptable in a civilized society'.

This is pretty strong language for senior judges to use. But Lord Hoffmann was unmoved by his colleagues' bleeding-heart whimperings, ruling that 'it would create uncertainty and be detrimental to the administration of justice in the Bahamas' if the privy council started bothering about whether local prison conditions were 'inhuman'. Perhaps he'd better skip the bit in Amnesty's latest report that details just how appalling they are.

David Mitchell was hanged three weeks later, on 6 January 2000. John

Junior Higgs cheated the gallows by committing suicide the previous day. He left a note thanking his warder for 'turning a blind eye' while he slashed his wrists.

(*Guardian*, 14 June 2000)

Doublethink for halfwits

I T I S S U N D A Y A F T E R N O O N . The wife is already asleep in the armchair, and the children have been sent out for a nice long walk. You put your feet up on the sofa, settle your spectacles on your nose, and open the *News of the World*...

Thus begins George Orwell's essay on the decline of the English murder. Were he writing today, the wife and children would be peering over dad's shoulder, hoping that the newspaper had identified a few more nonces. Later, having had their tea and fashioned a suitable placard (KILL ALL PERVS), the family would set out for a nice long riot – smashing windows, setting cars alight and screaming threats through the letter box of a tenant who has a vaguely similar name to someone once rumoured to be a child-molester.

Here's a passage from another famous essay by Orwell, explaining why no really strong fascist movement arose in Britain during the 1930s: 'Material conditions were not bad enough, and no leader who could be taken seriously was forthcoming.' Turn now to an article by Dr Theodore Dalrymple in the *Sunday Telegraph* last weekend: 'All it would require for authentic fascism to develop is a severe economic downturn and the rise of an evil demagogic genius. The *News of the World* has already given us an intimation of what can be done in that direction...' Fascism is a minority taste in this country. Nevertheless, our eruptions of mass hysteria, which seem to have become far more frequent and noisy since the death of Princess Diana, suggest an emotional volatility that is ripe for exploitation. Genuine fascists certainly understand this – not least the National Democrats, a far-right party, which until 1995 was better known as the National Front and is led by the former NF chairman and Holocaust-denier Ian Anderson.

In January 1998, Anderson accompanied members of the anti-paedophile campaign People Power when they delivered a letter to Downing Street demanding tougher action against child-abusers. Since then, the National Democrats have launched a 'Paedophile Watch' on the Internet. 'If you have any information regarding convicted paedophiles living in your area,' the website advises, 'please telephone...' Someone who rang the number last week was told that if he provided names and addresses, the party would distribute leaflets in their neighbourhood. It comes as no surprise to learn that reporters from the *News of the World* sought information from Ian Anderson for their 'name and shame' stunt.

It is only just over three weeks since the newspaper began its calamitous crusade. 'There are 110,000 proven paedophiles in the UK,' it declared. 'Today we start by identifying the first of these offenders but we make a pledge that we will not stop until all 110,000 are named and shamed. Week in, week out, we will add to our record...' The solemn pledge was broken within a fortnight, but its incendiary consequences cannot be halted so easily. As the Scottish journalist Charles Mackay remarked in his book *Extraordinary Popular Delusions and the Madness of Crowds*, published more than 150 years ago, 'Men, it has been well said, think in herds; it will be seen that they go mad in herds, while they only recover their senses slowly, and one by one.'

What does the *News of the World*'s editor, Rebekah Wade, think of her handiwork now? 'The decision to start the campaign by naming paedophiles living in the community was a considered one,' she wrote last Sunday, in a 'personal message' to readers. 'I was aware that it could prompt some passionate reaction, because we at the *News of the World* have always known how deeply people feel about the threat these sick individuals pose to children...Reaction against them, sometimes violent, has happened frequently in the past.' This may turn out to be a rather rash admission if Wade is prosecuted for inciting public disorder, or for conduct likely to cause a breach of the peace. Nor is it entirely cancelled out by her protestation that 'throughout the campaign we have counselled strongly against vigilante action'. True, in the first week of naming and shaming, her newspaper did warn that 'our campaign will be counter-productive if it provokes any display of animosity to those we name'. But the same editorial began with this ringing declaration: 'There must be no hiding place for the evil perverts who prey on our children... We are taking the first step to publish the names and addresses.' Did Wade honestly believe that she could print mugshots of these 'monsters' – ranging from a man who abducted and assaulted a five-year-old girl to a woman who was impregnated by a fourteen-year-old boy – without provoking displays of animosity? Didn't she realize that the likeliest effect of her reckless antics would be to drive known offenders underground and thus increase the likelihood of sexual assaults on youngsters? If so, she's a congenital halfwit.

She is also a coward. Throughout this episode Wade has refused all requests for interviews, subcontracting the task to hapless boxwallahs and understrappers from Wapping. But she is no more cowardly than government ministers, who are so terrified of offending the Murdoch press that not one has issued a forthright condemnation of Wade or her rag. The best Jack Straw could manage was a comment that 'in our judgment the press in these matters ought to act on the advice of the police'. Home Office minister Paul Boateng daringly opined that the *News of the World*'s behaviour was 'unhelpful' – but then praised the paper for making 'an important contribution to the debate'.

Finally, while naming and shaming, let us not forget William Hague – a man who can't see a bandwagon without leaping nimbly aboard, even after fourteen pints of bitter. 'TORY LEADER HAGUE BACKS OUR CAMPAIGN', the paper announced jubilantly last weekend. One of his proposals was that certain paedophiles should be 'subject to automatic life sentences'. Can this by any chance be the same William Hague who, in April this year, proposed abolishing automatic life sentences for murder?

(*Guardian*, 16 August 2000)

CORNERS OF A FOREIGN FIELD

Once more unto the beach

'IT IS AN AMUSING SIGHT, when staying at Dover, in the end of September, to watch the boats coming from Calais,' the Rev. E. J. Hardy wrote just over a century ago in his book *Manners Makyth Man*. 'What an army of tourists!...But did not all these tourists "go to the continent" for the sake of their health? And if so, why do they look so pale and worn? Why do they give one the impression that they are returning from war, rather than a pleasure trip?' Summer's lease hath all too short a date, and the modern descendants of Hardy's late-vacationing stragglers are now limping back from the continent in an equally battle-weary condition. In the offices of our great tabloid newspapers, the seasonal clichés are having one last outing before being put back into storage until next summer. 'Holiday Hell of Double-Booked Brits'. 'Couple Find "Holiday Hell" at Hotel'. 'Trapped in Costa Colditz'. 'Brits Win War of Sun Loungers'. 'Mayhem for Britons at Austrian Hotel'. 'Shocked British holidaymakers told last night of their nightmare...' 'Ring the *Daily Mirror* hotline to tell us about your holiday horror stories...' 'Have you been booked into a horror hotel? Been misled by tempting promises? We'd like to hear your holiday nightmares...'

Britons have always found Abroad a hellish place. 'The object of travelling,' William Hazlitt wrote, 'is to see and learn; but such is our impatience of ignorance, or the jealousy of our self-love, that we generally set up a certain preconception...and are surprised at and quarrel with all that does not conform with it.' Or, as Hugh and Pauline Massingham observed more than thirty years ago in their excellent book *The Englishman Abroad*: 'We admire what we recognise and guffaw like a donkey at anything that would not happen in the cosy, familiar whirl of Deal and Bournemouth and Blackpool. Because we drink beer, we mock the Frenchman for his addiction to wine. And because we like a cut off the roast and two veg, we despise an Italian's love for what we regard as contemptible pap.' But all that has changed, hasn't it? Cross-Channel ferries and Spanish beaches are now clogged with Britons. Even the most hardened xenophobes seem to accept that insularity is a lost cause: Margaret 'Batting for Britain' Thatcher was happy to put her signature to the Single European Act, and the *Sun* regales its readers with recipes for spaghetti carbonara and gazpacho.

Plus ça change, however, *plus c'est la même chose*. From the era of the Grand Tour to the age of the package charter flight, Britons have usually been disappointed – sometimes outraged – to discover that Abroad is not in every respect identical to Skegness. One of the 'holiday horrors' unearthed by the *Sun* this summer was a tale of British tourists in Spain who had been stricken with the runs and spent most of their time queueing for the loo. This old chestnut would have been familiar to any Victorian who had read Thomas King Chambers's *Manual of Diet in Health and Disease*, published in 1875: 'In almost all country places out of England it is impossible to avoid the greasy dishes which are apparently preferred by all except our own countrymen; and a frequent consequence is rancid indigestion, with a nauseous taste in the mouth, and flatulence or diarrhoea.'

Talking of flatulence, I wonder if editorial executives at the *Sun* ever dip into William Hazlitt? If so, they will know that one of their newspaper's regular charges against the 'Frogs' – that they have foully unhygienic habits ('ZEE FRENCH ARE FEELTHY – OFFICIAL') – was anticipated in Hazlitt's *Notes of a Journey Through France and Italy*. 'If the French have lost the sense of smell,' he protested, in a passage of which any tabloid leader-writer would be proud, 'they should reflect (as they are a reflecting people) that others have not. Really, I do not see how they have a right in a public vehicle to assault one in this way by proxy...One does not expect from the most refined and polished people in Europe grossness that an Esquimaux Indian would have too much sense and modesty to be guilty of.'

Not only are foreigners smelly and rude, they are also unwilling to provide us with the comforts we demand. In May this year the *Daily Mirror* ran a two-page 'News Special' in which British tourists in Majorca grumbled about the quality of their hotel rooms. 'You can't tell if it's night or day as there are no windows,' one said. 'All the carpets are sticky and stained. It's diabolical.' Three months later, the papers were full of the story of Martin Mears, whose holiday hotel room in the Canaries had been 'full of cockroaches...it was sheer hell.' He added: 'Our bed had a two-inch thick foam mattress so we didn't sleep.' Now where have we heard that before? Turning to Robert Southey's *Letters Written During a Journey in Spain*, I find the following eerily familiar whinge: 'Jacob's pillow of stone was a down cushion, compared to that which bruised my head last night; and my bed had all possible varieties of hill and vale, in whose recesses the fleas lay safe; for otherwise it was so hard that I should inevitably have broken their bones by rolling over them. Our apartment is indeed furnished with windows; and he who takes the trouble to examine may convince himself that they have once been glazed.'

What is so pernicious about all these travellers' moans is that they seem to be having some effect. In a hilltop taverna on the Greek island of Lemnos last week, I asked a waitress what was for dinner. 'We have schnitzel,' she replied, 'and pizza, and hamburgers, and spaghetti Bolognese.' When I explained that I wanted something Greek – tzatziki and spanakopita, perhaps, followed by grilled fish with garlicky skordalia, rounded off with a slice of honey-soaked baklava, all washed down with plenty of chilled retsina – she looked amazed. 'Oh no, we don't do Greek food,' she told me with lofty distaste. And who can blame her? In the *AA Guide to Greek Islands*, written by the venerable Arthur Eperon, the section on restaurants announces bluntly that 'no one goes to Greece for the food or wines'. When even the doyen of British travel writers tells them that their culture is worthless, is it any wonder if the natives eventually abandon the unequal struggle and reconstruct Abroad in the cosy, familiar style of Bournemouth and Blackpool?

(*Observer*, 11 April 1994)

Verily, she spake unto them

'God separated Britain from mainland Europe, and it was for a purpose.' – *Margaret Thatcher, speaking at the Centre for Policy Studies last week*

IN THE BEGINNING God created the heaven and the Earth. And God said, Let there be light: and there was light. And God called the light Britain, and the darkness he called Abroad. And God said let there be a firmament in the midst of the waters that shall divide the children of Albion from those that dwell in the darkness; and he created Dogger, Fisher and German Bight; yea, and also Channel Light Vessel Automatic. And God saw that it was good, especially when read by Charlotte Green.

And God said, Let us make a man in our own image, after our likeness; but then he changed his mind and created William Hague. And the Lord God commanded the man, saying, of the tree of knowledge thou shalt not eat, for thou art a blithering idiot; upon thy belly shalt thou go, and dust shalt thou eat all the days of thy life. But I shall give unto thee Margaret, who shall be thine helpmeet. And Margaret and William were both naked and were not ashamed, since they were utterly shameless.

And the woman did tempt the man, and therefore the Lord sent them forth into the wilderness, where he visited them with many torments and plagues, not least Jeffrey Archer and Michael Ashcroft. But Margaret comprehended it not; for she had long since lost the plot. And upon her forehead was a name written, MYSTERY, BABYLON THE GREAT, THE MOTHER OF ABOMINATIONS, and she was drunken with the blood of the martyred Senator Pinochet. But still William failed to notice that the old girl was off her rocker.

And it came to pass in those days that a decree went out that all the Eurobond dealers should be taxed, and there was great lamentation in the land. The hand of the Lord was also upon the cattle which is in the field, and there was a grievous murrain and pestilence upon them. And the French said that British beef would be no more welcome to them than hath been the plague of frogs that the Lord visited upon the Pharaoh of Egypt. And so the scribes and pharisees of the *Sun* and *Daily Mail* said, Hop Off You Frogs.

And Margaret warned the children of Albion, saying, The fish in thy sea shall die, as it is written in the common fisheries policy; and thou shalt be forced to yield thy power of veto, as the Hagarites yielded to the sons of Reuben and the tribe of Manasseh; and thy budget rebate shall be cut, even as Zipporah hath cut off the foreskin of her son and cast it at his feet. And she said, Verily, it is all the fault of Johnny Foreigner, who is envious of this other Eden, this demi-paradise, this precious stone set in a silver sea. Let us make of Albion a refuge and a fortress for our people. For is it not written in the scriptures that Britain arose from out the azure main at heaven's command? And someone said, No, I think that was James Thomson in 'Rule Britannia'.

But Margaret heeded not, saying, It is the Lord's will that we should leave Europe, for He hath separated us from the mainland for a purpose. And a still small voice pointed out that, by this logic, she should also support independence for the Isle of Wight; yea, and even the Isle of Thanet, where Billericay Dickie hath had his rendezvous with Janet.

And another voice asked, Was it not the Blessed Margaret who agreed to the Single European Act and hath given the go-ahead to the Channel tunnel which linked this sceptr'd isle to the rest of the continent? And the people rose up and said to her, Thou hypocrite, first cast out the beam from thine own eye.

But Margaret heeded them not, as per usual.

(Guardian, 22 December 1999)

Wakening the spirit of Bankside

T ODAY, ON HIS EIGHTY-THIRD BIRTHDAY, General Pinochet will learn whether the House of Lords has confirmed his immunity from prosecution. Even if he does have to face extradition proceedings he can be assured of a most comfortable custody: his 'London friends' are clubbing together to rent a rural retreat for their favourite torturer. These friends include Robin Birley, the sandwich tycoon and sometime Referendum Party candidate; Taki Theodoracopulos, the Greek comedian; and Paul Johnson, the septuagenarian naughty boy. Nor should we forget Pinochet's professional PR man, Patrick Robertson, who previously applied his image-enhancement skills to Jonathan Aitken and Sir James Goldsmith with such conspicuous success. The House of Lords may decide that Pinochet has suffered enough, bearing in mind that he has already taken tea with Margaret Thatcher and visited Madame Tussaud's. Forcing an old man to endure the company of Taki and Paul Johnson through the long winter nights would almost certainly constitute cruel and unusual punishment.

If he is allowed to go home, human rights campaigners will grumble that nothing can be done about murderous dictators who come to England for their holidays. Not so – as one of Pinochet's spiritual forebears, Field-Marshal Baron von Haynau, learned to his cost nearly 150 years ago. Haynau was a brutal Austrian commander known as 'the Hyena' who had fully earned the nickname by torturing prisoners and flogging women while suppressing revolts in Italy and Hungary. In August 1850, as a respite from these exhausting duties, he took a short vacation in London, where his sightseeing itinerary included a tour of Barclay and Perkins's Brewery on the south bank of the river. As soon as the Baron entered the brewery, draymen chucked horse-manure and hay-bales at him. He fled into the street, where lightermen and coal-heavers then joined the chase – ripping his clothes, yanking out tufts of his bushy moustache and shouting 'Down with the Austrian butcher!' Haynau tried to hide in a dustbin at the George Inn on Bankside, but was soon routed out and pelted with more dung.

By the time the police reached the pub, rowing him across the Thames to safety, the bedraggled and humiliated butcher was in no fit state to continue his holiday. Within hours, a new song could be heard in the streets of Southwark:

> Turn him out, turn him out, from our side of the Thames,
> Let him go to great Tories and high-titled dames.
> He may walk the West End and parade in his pride,
> But he'll not come back again near the 'George' in Bankside.

Messages of congratulation arrived from workers' associations as far afield as Paris and New York. Even Lord Palmerston was secretly amused, reckoning that the Field-Marshal could only be improved by a sip of his own medicine.

The spirit of Bankside has been dormant ever since. But perhaps it should be remembered the next time a wandering despot turns up at Madame Tussaud's.

(*Guardian*, 25 November 1998)

Lamont's animal magic

L ORD LAMONT, the man who almost bankrupted us all on Black Wednesday, has several unusual talents. He is a surprisingly fleet-footed dancer, and his imitation of the call of a scops owl is one of the ornithological marvels of the age. Since the arrest of General Pinochet he has revealed another side to his remarkable character: Norman Lamont, South American magical realist.

The first outing of this implausible figure came on *Newsnight* immediately after the Law Lords delivered their verdict on Pinochet, when Norman tried to outflank the playwright Harold Pinter by claiming that he knew all about Chile because he had been in Argentina more than a quarter of a century ago. Now he has given us a few more details, in an article for *The Times*. 'I visited

South America several times in the early 1970s,' he recalls, 'and was in Buenos
Aires when Allende formed his government. I saw the refugees fleeing from
terror who were arriving there. I remember a little old lady in brown tweeds
with her furniture piled on the back of a donkey who asked me, a complete
stranger, if I could help her reach Europe.' Even allowing for Norman's magical realist skills, I think we should assume that it was the lady and not her
donkey who asked the young Lamont for directions to Europe. We can also
deduce that the encounter took place in the street, since she would have been
unable to take her donkey to a social event. (Most people in Buenos Aires live
in high-rise apartment buildings with lifts, and invitations to Argentine cocktail parties seldom say 'bring bottle and burro'.) So how did she get there? The
border between Argentina and Chile runs along the highest peaks of the
Andes, one of the toughest mountain ranges in the world. Even in summer,
night temperatures are sub-zero, and it takes days for experienced walkers to
make the crossing. Those brown tweeds were formidable indeed.

After entering Argentina, the old lady must have trekked more than a
thousand miles across the Pampa to reach the capital – where she would have
discovered that Buenos Aires is a busy metropolis in which you simply can't
lead a donkey down the streets. The traffic will kill you, and a municipal regu-
lation even older than Norman Lamont forbids it. How much furniture can
you load on a donkey anyway? There were Chileans arriving in Buenos Aires
in 1970, but they came by plane. Their furniture (usually genuine Louis XV or
Chippendale pieces) followed by van or in a container. Nor were they 'fleeing
from terror': they left because they expected Chile to go the way of Cuba and
become a communist state. The major newspaper proprietors in Buenos
Aires, all anti-Allende, would certainly have printed tales of horror and atroc-
ity if there were any to be had; but there weren't.

Talking of Cuba, Lamont informs us that there were '17,000 Cubans' in
Chile at the time of Pinochet's coup. What, I wonder, became of them? Did
they go to Santiago airport, in spite of the roadblocks, and fly back to
Havana? It would have taken sixty 747s to spirit them back to the Caribbean.
Did they fall into Pinochet's hands? If so, he has killed 20,000 people, not
3,000. Or did he send them all to jail to learn carpentry along with the error of
their ways? Are they still there? The Anglo-Argentine writer William Gill, who
was living in Buenos Aires at the time, tells me that an architect friend of his
was put in touch with one of the victims of Allende's 'terror' – a Chilean who
had bought the most expensive apartment in the city, a duplex of 12,000
square feet. As they stood in the monumental emptiness of the drawing room,
and the client explained where he wanted to place sculptures or pictures that

required special lighting, his face clouded over with sadness. 'I've told my children that these are hard times, and things are very different,' he said. 'Every now and then, they must be prepared to take the bus.'

William Gill was not an Allende sympathizer. Nevertheless, he is outraged by Lamont's fantastical blatherings. 'Norman Lamont is entitled to defend any fascist he admires,' he wrote to *The Times* last week. 'What he can't do is misrepresent the facts of history that led to the death of thousands in appalling circumstances. A few of the thousands of people killed by neo-Nazi generals in Argentina (who were as monstrous as Pinochet and his cronies) had been friends of mine at school or university. I owe it to them to put the record straight.' *The Times* refused to let him do so, but I am happy to oblige. Not that anything is likely to make Lamont see sense. 'One of the criteria on which the Home Secretary will base his decision,' he claims, 'is whether the alleged offences are political. That is why the French government refused to extradite David Shayler.' It seems astonishing that milord Lamont of Lerwick can't tell the difference between a whistleblower exposing illegal actions by his employers and an omnipotent dictator who tortured and murdered his own citizens. But what can you expect from a tubby former Chancellor who thinks that he's a scops owl?

(Guardian, 9 December 1998)

Sweet talk at the White House

ACCORDING TO WILLIAM BLAKE, 'He who would do good to another must do it in Minute Particulars.' Thanks to the Starr Report we can now see just how much good Bill Clinton did to Monica Lewinsky – and she to him. He sent her Walt Whitman's *Leaves of Grass*; she reciprocated with *Vox*, Nicholson Baker's novel about telephone sex.

'Many of the thirty or so gifts that she gave the President,' Kenneth Starr reveals, 'reflected his interest in history, antiques, cigars and frogs.' Frogs? This was a new one on me and I half suspected a misprint: 'frigs' would certainly make more sense. But no; the present list includes 'a frog figurine' and 'a letter opener depicting a frog'. From some distant recess of memory I recall a speech by George Bush in Oshkosh, shortly before polling day in 1992, in which he said that 'being attacked on character by Governor Clinton is like being called ugly by a frog'. Did Bush know about Clinton's fellow feeling for slippery, croak-voiced amphibians? Whereas Hannah Arendt saw in Adolf Eichmann 'the banality of evil', Starr wants to persuade us that Clinton represents the evil of banality. But this lets the old brute off far too lightly. The interminable catalogue of minute particulars – the frogs, the thongs, the cigar, the blue dress – seems entirely incongruous with a charge of 'high crimes and misdemeanours'. Without any added context, the President stands condemned as a petty liar rather than what he is – a whited sepulchre of hypocrisy and corruption.

Clinton, lest we forget, has long tried to impose a stern code of private morality on others. He sacked his first Surgeon-General, Jocelyn Elders, because she had the temerity to inform the nation's teenagers that masturbation wouldn't make them go blind. 'We can't renew our country unless more of us, I mean all of us, are willing to join churches,' he told a joint session of Congress in 1994, during a puritanical homily about family values and sexual responsibility. In his State of the Union address of January 1996 – a month when he had two 'sexual encounters' with Lewinsky – he called for a national crusade against promiscuous youngsters and unmarried mothers.

No doubt Starr would say that such matters are beyond his remit. But since he has somehow managed to extend that remit from a property-deal in Arkansas to a blow-job in the White House, I feel sure that his dextrous legal mind could have found a way round the problem. As it is, the report is one long coitus interruptus: just as something interesting is about to happen, Starr suddenly remembers a pressing engagement elsewhere. Lewinsky claims, for instance, that while she was in the Oval Office between noon and 2 p.m. on 19 February 1996 the President took a phone call from a sugar-grower in Florida whose name was 'something like Fanuli'. Starr notes that this is corroborated by the official log: 'The President talked with Alfonso Fanjul of Palm Beach, Florida, from 12.42 to 1.04 p.m. Mr Fanjul had telephoned a few minutes earlier, at 12.24 p.m. The Fanjuls are prominent sugar-growers in Florida.' And, er, that's it; without further ado Starr scampers off in search of more titillation.

Alfonso and his brother Jose 'Pepe' Fanjul are probably the richest sugar-barons in the United States, and at least $65 million of their annual income comes from a government restriction on imports, which gives the Fanjuls a captive market and obliges American shoppers to pay twice as much for sugar as anyone else in the world. Now and again, some malcontent wonders why these squillionaires should enjoy such a lavish subsidy at the expense of the consumer, but since most members of the House and Senate agriculture committees have received generous donations from the Fanjuls, the boondoggle continues. In February 1996, however, when Clinton took that phone call, the Fanjuls were worried men. Senator Richard Lugar – one of the few politicians not in their pay – had proposed a $100 million levy on the Florida sugar-kings to help clean up the Everglades, whose ecosystem has been all but ruined by the fertilizer-rich run-offs from their fields. More alarmingly still, Clinton supported the scheme.

What sweet nothings did Alfonso whisper to his chum in the Oval Office during that twenty-two-minute conversation? Did he point out that he had been co-chairman of Clinton's Florida campaign in 1992 and a big-time donor ever since? Did he mention that, only a few months earlier, he had attended one of Clinton's influence-peddling 'coffee mornings' in the White House, at which about $27 million was raised for the Democratic National Committee? Nobody knows. What I do know is that the sugar-levy was quickly dropped, and the bill for cleaning up the Fanjuls' mess had to be met by the long-suffering American taxpayer instead.

To me, at least, Clinton's insatiable lust for tycoons and their chequebooks is far more interesting than his desire for frog figurines and fellatio. Starr's justification for pursuing the Lewinsky story is that it establishes a 'pattern of behaviour'. In his blinkered prurience he fails to notice that the dalliance with Alfonso Fanjul suggests a pattern of behaviour far more incriminating than a weakness for young women in thongs.

(Guardian, 16 September 1998)

Dumbo v. Pinocchio

D URING THE AMERICAN election campaign of 1992, President Bush delivered a scathing verdict on Messrs Clinton and Gore: 'My dog Millie knows more about foreign affairs than these two bozos.' Now the United States may be about to elect an even bigger bozo – George W. Bush.

'Dubya' could certainly use some expert advice from Millie. Last November, a TV interviewer asked him to name the leaders of a few countries that were in the news. 'The new Pakistani general,' Bush replied, having already failed with India and Chechnya, 'he's just been elected – not elected, this guy took over...' 'And can you name him?' 'General, I can name the general.' 'And it's...?' 'General.' Liberal Washingtonian sophisticates were vastly amused. The online magazine *Slate* began compiling an archive of Bushisms ('updated daily'), which now runs to eleven long pages. Some of these are essentially malapropisms – 'hostile' for 'hostage', 'anecdote' for 'antidote', 'cufflink' for 'handcuff', 'preservation' for 'perseverance', or (my favourite) 'terrier' for 'tariff barrier'. Others are expressions of plain ignorance, such as his admission that he thought Slovakia was the same place as Slovenia.

A few, rather like Dan Quayle's best lines, have their own surreal splendour: 'I know the human being and the fish can coexist peacefully'; 'Families is where wings take dream'; 'I am a person who recognizes the fallacy of humans'; 'It is clear our nation is reliant upon big foreign oil: more and more of our imports come from overseas'; 'You can't take the high horse and then claim the low road'; 'Will the highways on the Internet become more few?'

At the start of this year, the American punditocracy seemed to assume that Bush's dunderheadedness would guarantee his eventual defeat. Yet he has now overtaken the studiously cerebral Al Gore, the self-proclaimed creator of the Internet, who can probably identify the capital of Slovenia or the President of Pakistan in his sleep. Why? One reason is that many voters apparently don't want a president who makes them feel stupid. Bush himself is clearly aware of this, and now cracks self-mocking jokes about his linguistic incompetence at every opportunity. He was also quick to deny a suggestion in this month's *Vanity Fair* magazine that he has severe dyslexia, even though it might have won him some sympathy and disarmed his tormentors. (Mustn't mock the afflicted, must we?) The implication of his rebuttal seemed to be: I ain't ill or disabled, I'm just a good old American dimwit – an amiable chump, a genial goof, a second Ronnie Reagan.

But there is another message, albeit largely subliminal (or 'subliminable', as Bush would say): You can trust me, 'cos I'm not smart enough to be devious and dishonest. Even when he is caught telling a whopper – as in last week's presidential debate, when he boasted of pushing through a patients' bill of rights which he had in fact vetoed – people seem willing to blame it on his feeble, faulty memory rather than wilful deceit. Al Gore, by contrast, is not only a smart alec whose head bulges with hard-disk capacity but also a liar. Last month he told the Teamsters union that when he was a baby his mum lulled him to sleep by singing 'Look for the Union Label' – a song which was written when Gore was twenty-seven years old and had presumably outgrown his cradle. The story is about as plausible as Tony Blair's recollection of watching Jackie Milburn play football for Newcastle.

As with Blair, however, Gore's inventiveness isn't limited to harmless and endearing childhood anecdotes. Blair has repeatedly claimed, falsely, that he voted for Mike Foster's Anti-Hunting Bill; Gore says that he was 'the author' of the earned income tax credit, even though it was passed by Congress in 1975, two years before he entered the house. According to Andrew Rawnsley's book, Tony Blair lied about Bernie Ecclestone's £1 million gift to the Labour Party; Al Gore's mendacity about his own fund-raising activities is eerily similar. Three years ago, he flatly denied that he had ever attended meetings at the White House to discuss illegal 'hard-money' donations. When documents later surfaced showing that the vice-president had indeed been present, he told the FBI that he 'drank a lot of iced tea during meetings, which could have necessitated a rest-room break'. (This ingenious alibi was promptly exploded by Harold Ickes, the former deputy chief of staff, who testified that he had always stopped the meetings when the vice-president left the room.) Under interrogation by the justice department in April this year, Gore was asked about more than thirty fund-raising 'coffee mornings' which he had hosted at the White House before the last presidential campaign. He said he had 'no concrete recollection' of any such events. Perhaps all those cups of coffee had kept him almost permanently in the lavatory.

Since the fall of the Berlin Wall, various wiseacres have asserted that we are now at the End of History: that American-style democracy is the unimprovable culmination of human achievement, a universal model, which all countries will henceforth copy. A glance at this year's contest between Dumbo and Pinocchio might make even Francis Fukuyama wonder if he spoke too soon. The one serious and substantial candidate, Ralph Nader, has been excluded from the televised debates and largely ignored by the mainstream media, perhaps for fear that he'll show up his rivals as a couple of bozos. Potential Nader supporters are being warned by liberal Democrats that unless they vote for Gore as 'the lesser of two evils' they will be responsible for letting Bush into the Oval Office. This is a counsel of despair and desperation – 'like a man on a raft facing the decision of whether to drink seawater or his own urine', in the words of Alexander Cockburn.

Yet the American media is still gamely and patriotically pretending that the election confirms the sublime superiority of their version of democracy, and that the electorate should thank Gore and Bush for forcing it to decide between piss and the deep blue sea. A *Washington Post* editorial this week argued that although many aspects of the campaign were 'squalid' and 'corrupt', and although neither candidate had any obvious principles or 'inner conviction', nevertheless both Gore and Bush were decent, admirable fellows: 'The nation this year is fortunate in its choice.' The latest issue of *Time* magazine piles on the flattery: 'The Lover vs The Fighter...With just two weeks to go, the campaigns have made the choice clear: Do you want Bush's pledges of civility or Gore's crusading punch?'

The lover versus the fighter! Oh brave new world, that has such titans in it. The real 'choice', alas, is rather less alluring: the flubber versus the fibber.

(*Guardian*, 25 October 2000)

Unfinished business in the Balkans

TELEVISION SELDOM PAYS much attention to the wider world, so I was pleasantly surprised to find a ninety-minute discussion about Kosovo on Channel 4 last week – even if the programme, Jon Snow's *Weekly Planet*, did go out at an hour when only drunks or insomniacs were watching. Surprise turned to astonishment, however, when I saw the two experts lined up to explain British policy in the Balkans. They were General Sir Michael Rose and Dame Pauline Neville-Jones, billed respectively as 'head of UN operations in Bosnia, 1994–5' and 'political director of the Foreign Office, 1994–6'.

The descriptions scarcely do justice to the careers of this gruesome twosome. Though the programme never examined their credentials, someone should – if only because those who forget the past are condemned to repeat it. As Neville-Jones said of Kosovo in last week's TV programme, 'I have that terrible sinking feeling of watching something happen again...' General Rose presented himself as a humble soldier at the mercy of politicians. 'In Bosnia I was working for the United Nations, and I was constrained by UN Security Council resolutions,' he said. His tasks had been to alleviate suffering, stop the war spreading and create the conditions for peace. 'I did not have any other agenda while I was there.'

Too modest, my dear fellow. Under Security Council Resolution 836, for instance, Rose had a mandate to 'deter attacks against the safe areas'. But when the Serb artillery launched a fierce bombardment against the safe area of Gorazde, in April 1994, he seemed remarkably unconcerned. It was, he insisted, no more than a 'minor' and 'tactical' operation by the Bosnian Serbs, who had 'no serious intention' – even though his HQ in Sarajevo received daily reports from UN military colleagues in Gorazde warning that the death toll was rising fast. 'If this is "not serious", I hope I don't see a serious situation develop,' one UN monitor complained to Rose. 'Saying it is a minor attack into a limited area is a bad assessment, incorrect and shows absolutely no understanding of what is going on here.'

While Rose twiddled his thumbs, scores of people were killed and hundreds wounded. He then suggested that the Bosnian troops defending Gorazde hadn't fought hard enough – 'a strange comment,' as the historian Noel Malcolm has pointed out, 'from someone who both supported and enforced an arms embargo against the Bosnian army, the ultimate aim of which was to prevent them from fighting at all.' More insultingly still, a few months later he claimed that most of the damage to buildings in Gorazde had been caused by the Bosnian forces themselves, whom he accused of driving 12,500 Serbs out of the city and destroying their houses. To quote Noel Malcolm again, 'Since the entire administrative district of Gorazde, an area covering 383 square kilometres, had contained only 9,844 Serbs, and since half of these had lived in villages outside the city itself, it seemed reasonable to conclude that General Rose was acting here, however unwittingly, as little more than a conduit for Serb propaganda.'

Pauline Neville-Jones's performance last week was even more shameless and disingenuous. Why, Snow wondered, had Britain done nothing sooner about Kosovo? 'I don't hold responsibility for that,' she said, apparently forgetting her earlier admission that the Foreign Office had been well aware of the looming conflict throughout her term as political director. When Snow asked if the Foreign Office was now worried that the fighting in Kosovo would spread to Macedonia and elsewhere, she reminded him that she had retired from Whitehall some time ago: 'I don't honestly know precisely what they think today...' Yet I have it on excellent authority that Dame Pauline was given a thorough briefing by the FO only hours before the broadcast.

Still, let's give her credit for something: Dame Pauline has noticed, at long last, that President Milosevic is a menace. 'Primarily I have to say I blame the authorities in Belgrade,' she admitted. Why then, Snow inquired, do we want Milosevic to remain in power? 'I've never actually put that proposition down on the table.' Actually, that is just what she has been doing for years. Throughout the war in Bosnia, she and her colleague Douglas Hurd treated Milosevic as a moderate and necessary middleman, refusing to accept that he was in fact the genocidal thug who had instigated the violence. At the Dayton peace talks, where Neville-Jones was the chief British representative, she argued energetically – and successfully – for an end to sanctions against Serbia. What no one at Dayton knew, but Hurd has since confirmed, is that at the same time she was in touch with NatWest Markets about the possibility of a job in the private sector. Hurd himself had become deputy chairman of the bank shortly after resigning as Foreign Secretary, and Neville-Jones joined him as managing director in July 1996 – whereupon they jetted off to Serbia to cash in on the abolition of sanctions. At a 'working breakfast' in Belgrade, Milosevic signed a lucrative deal whereby NatWest Markets would privatize Serbia's post and telephone system for a fee of about $10 million. For a further large fee, they agreed to manage the Serbian national debt.

Hurd and Neville-Jones claimed that this hideous partnership with the Butcher of Belgrade was 'in the interests of the West', since it committed Milosevic to a process of 'liberalization'. Two years on, he is now so liberal that he uses tanks and heavy artillery against his own citizens. When Snow asked if Britain should take some of the blame for encouraging Milosevic, Dame Pauline sounded suddenly nervous: 'No, well, look, er, er, well, you can always beat your own breast, but...' But indeed. Pauline Neville-Jones and General Sir Michael Rose have never beaten their own breasts, nor even rapped themselves lightly over the knuckles. Instead, Rose has just collected a hefty advance for his self-congratulatory memoirs, while Neville-Jones is fêted and honoured by a grateful establishment. Only a few months ago she was appointed a governor of the BBC, 'with special responsibility for the BBC World Service'. If these are the rewards of failure, who needs success?

(*Guardian*, 24 June 1998)

***

IS THERE A single *Guardian* reader who supports NATO's action against the genocidal Serbian war machine? Apparently not, to judge by the letters to the editor published during the last week. Some of these are from genuine pacifists, tender-hearted souls to whom the swatting of a wasp and the bombing of a munitions dump are equally obscene. Fair enough. Other opponents of the war take the Alan Clark line of self-interested isolationism, arguing that the Balkans are not worth the bones of a Pomeranian grenadier, let alone the life of an RAF pilot. Fair enough again, if that is really what they believe. But most other critics, particularly on the Left, deserve no such indulgence.

Last week's parliamentary debate on Kosovo has been widely praised, not least by those who participated in it. 'Sombre, serious, passionate and crossing party lines, it has done a lot of credit to the House of Commons,' according to the Defence Secretary. In fact it was a rancid stew of insincerity, ignorance and plain codswallop. 'There is great opposition to the war,' Tony Benn boasted. 'Henry Kissinger is against the war.' Well, of course he is: massmurdering war criminals have a tendency to stick together. Benn also complained that 'the House suffers from its lack of knowledge of history', and then proved the point by declaring that 'Kosovo has been in Yugoslavia for centuries' – no mean feat, given that the state of Yugoslavia didn't exist until the twentieth century.

If historical amnesia now afflicts even old-timers such as Benn himself, not to mention Denis Healey, what hope is there for the next generation? The Labour MP Harry Barnes and the Tory Bowen Wells both claimed that the conflict in Yugoslavia 'began' with the German-inspired recognition of Slovenia and Croatia. 'That is what started it,' Wells added. 'At that point the Serbs, or all those who wanted to keep Yugoslavia together, were perfectly justified in taking up arms...' Not one Honourable Member pointed out that the true sequence of events was the other way round: by the time the EEC agreed to recognize Croatia, in December 1991, Milosevic's forces had already been bombarding Dubrovnik for three months, and the town of Vukovar had long since been reduced to rubble.

Benn and his chums on the Labour Left are outraged that Britain or anyone else should 'act as the policeman of the world'. Yet these same voices have for many months been pleading with the Law Lords and Jack Straw to act as the world's policeman in the case of General Pinochet, rightly rejecting the argument that Pinochet's crimes are none of our business and should be dealt with by the Chileans themselves. Again and again in last week's debate, MPs maintained that it was always wrong to 'intervene' in the internal affairs of a sovereign state, even if that state is massacring its own people. Did Tony Benn protest at the overthrow of the murderous Idi Amin in 1979? This was undoubtedly an infringement of Uganda's territorial integrity, since Amin was toppled only because Tanzanian forces came in on the side of Ugandan rebels; nevertheless, most of us thought that the breach of sovereignty was outweighed by the urgency and rightness of the cause. The same could be said of the Vietnamese invasion that put an end to Pol Pot's genocide. If Benn saw a woman being raped by a group of thugs, he would (one hopes) rush to her aid. As Ken Livingstone asked last week: 'Why should we as a nation stand back when the same thing has been happening on our doorstep for the best part of a decade? My socialism and driving moral force are not defined by lines drawn on a map, certainly not when they were drawn by imperial powers at Versailles in 1919.'

It is reassuring to know that the spirit of internationalism is not entirely dead on the British Left. Many other Labour MPs – and *Guardian* letter-writers – seem to think that anything happening beyond the cliffs of Dover is *ultra vires*. We have no right, they claim, to involve ourselves in other people's civil wars. Very well then: can we now expect them to condemn those British socialists who enlisted to fight in the Spanish Civil War sixty years ago?

(*Guardian*, 31 March 1999)

***

'HAVE YOU BEEN got at by MI6?' a reader asks, horrified by my comments on Yugoslavia. 'Right here, right now, in my city, on the streets of Glasgow, the Labour-controlled council is threatening to sack librarians. Meanwhile, George Robertson is stroking the fuselage of a fighter plane in Italy. Ray Bradbury could not make this up. George Orwell would be stuck for words.' Oddly enough, shortly before this letter arrived I too had been wondering what George Orwell would make of the present imbroglio. 'Yugoslav politics are very complicated and I make no pretence of being an expert on them,' he admitted in *Tribune* on 12 January 1945. Nevertheless, I think he might have had some useful observations to offer.

First, let's take the argument, often heard in the last fortnight, that NATO's onslaught has united even the Serbian opposition behind Milosevic, thus scuppering any chance of a more humane and liberal regime ever emerging in Belgrade. As Orwell pointed out in 1940, dictators have often enhanced their power by imposing intolerable burdens on their citizens. 'Whereas socialism, and even capitalism in a more grudging way, have said to people "I offer you a good time", Hitler has said to them "I offer you struggle, danger and death", and as a result a whole nation flings itself at his feet. Perhaps later on they will get sick of it and change their minds, as at the end of the last war.' And so they did. Though Hitler's hegemony over his people seemed unchallengeable at the time, as soon as he and his gang were defeated the Germans transformed their nation into a model social democracy with remarkably little grief. Is it vain to hope that history might repeat itself once Belgrade's own little Hitler has gone?

Orwell would, I'd guess, be contemptuous of those who blame NATO for the horrific exodus from Kosovo. It has long been clear that Milosevic's intention is to make the area uninhabitable for Muslims (or, indeed, Roman Catholics); what is happening now is merely a speeded-up version of what would have happened anyway. If the mass expulsions were the fault of Messrs Blair and Clinton, one would expect the refugees to feel very bitter towards their self-styled saviours. But they don't. During the past week many hundreds of weary, weeping fugitives have been interviewed as they cross the borders into Macedonia, Montenegro and Albania; none has called for NATO to withdraw. In fact, they have unanimously supported the military action against Belgrade, however awful the immediate consequences for themselves. Opponents of the war who claim to have the best interests of the Kosovars at heart should shut up for a minute or two and listen to what these people are actually saying.

Besides, what is the alternative? Summon yet another conference at a French château, plead the pacifists; send in yet more jet-setting mediators, monitors and special envoys. This is, of course, precisely the policy that the international community has followed for the best part of a decade, and what do we have to show for it? Hundreds of broken ceasefires and promises, and thousands of corpses in Srebrenica, murdered under the very noses of blue-helmeted UN soldiers. ('Despotic governments can stand "moral force" till the cows come home,' Orwell noted in September 1942. 'What they fear is physical force.') Throughout all the 'ethnic-cleansing' atrocities committed by Serbian troops and paramilitaries, from Vukovar in 1991 to Racak in 1999, Western politicians continued to insist that Milosevic was a man they could do business with. The essential thing, as both the Conservatives and the Socialist Workers' Party agreed, was 'not to take sides'.

Orwell would certainly not have fallen for the nonsense that one should remain impartial between the oppressor and the victim. 'There is no such thing as neutrality in this war,' he wrote in 1941, arguing that 'if you don't resist the Nazis you are helping them'. The same can be said of the modern National Socialists in Yugoslavia. When Tony Benn and Diane Abbott set up the apparently neutral Committee for Peace in the Balkans four years ago, they claimed that their only purpose was to oppose external involvement in Bosnia and to lobby for a continuation of the arms embargo. But the logic of this position was that Bosnia should become part of Milosevic's Greater Serbia. It was therefore no surprise to learn that the founding supporters of the committee included not only Benn and Abbott but also Sir Alfred Sherman, who had spent the previous couple of years advising Radovan Karadzic and Ratko Mladic, the well-known war criminals and ethnic-cleansing experts.

Again and again in the last decade, those grandees who proclaimed their even-handedness – Douglas Hurd, Malcolm Rifkind, David Owen, Sir Michael Rose – proved in effect to be accomplices of Serb aggression by treating the Butcher of the Balkans as a reasonable statesman who should be indulged and flattered at every turn. Most have had the good sense to keep quiet since the bombing began – the notable exception being General Rose, who has used his *Sunday Times* column to contrast NATO's ineffectiveness with his own triumphant record as head of the UN protection force in Bosnia, where he 'succeeded in vastly reducing the level of slaughter and ethnic cleansing'. Oh yeah? Like so many people who ostentatiously declined to take sides, Rose failed to realize that the only beneficiaries of his inaction and spurious neutrality were Slobodan Milosevic's goon-squads.

Douglas Hurd accidentally gave the game away in April 1993, when explaining why the arms embargo against Bosnia shouldn't be lifted. Although 'at first sight it seems an act of justice', he said, in practice it would merely create a 'level killing field'. The only possible inference to be drawn was that he preferred an uneven killing field, on which Milosevic provided the Bosnian Serbs with troops and weapons while the Bosnian government had to make do with whatever equipment it could buy on the black market or grab from captured enemy soldiers. Confirming this interpretation, Hurd said that allowing the Bosnians to defend themselves would 'only prolong the fighting'. Hurd's successor, Malcolm Rifkind, maintained this tradition of appeasement-by-default. And as recently as January this year, Robin Cook told the House of Commons that although the massacre of Kosovar civilians in Racak was 'a war crime', the blame 'lies with both sides' – thus earning himself a rare tribute from Tony Benn, who praised the Foreign Secretary for 'the balanced way in which he presented the background'.

The ghastly pictures from the Kosovo border are evidence not of military failure but of political failure. The culprits are those shoulder-shrugging fatalists who have forced us to spend ten long years striking a 'balance' between murderer and murderee – and who continue to excuse or ignore Milosevic's wickedness. I know what George Orwell would have thought of them. 'The choice before human beings is not, as a rule, between good and evil but between two evils,' he wrote in October 1941. 'You can let the Nazis rule the world; that is evil; or you can overthrow them by war, which is also evil. There is no other choice before you, and whichever you choose you will not come out with clean hands.' Perhaps some people genuinely believe that genocide is a lesser evil than bombing military installations. But, as Orwell concluded, the choice has to be made: 'We do not have the chance, in a time like this, to say "Tomorrow we can all start being good". That is moonshine. We only have the chance of choosing the lesser evil and of working for the establishment of a new kind of society in which common decency will again be possible.'

(*Guardian*, 7 April 1999)

***

AT A RATHER right-wing lunch last Friday, I expressed my pleasure at the popular uprising in Serbia which had toppled Slobodan Milosevic. 'Popular?' a Tory gent harrumphed, in the way that only old Tory gents can. 'I think there's something deeply suspicious about it. Look at those cars and buses driving into Belgrade, led by a bulldozer to deal with police roadblocks. It wouldn't surprise me in the least to learn that the drivers had all been paid by the CIA.'

Those who uphold the existing order can never accept that ordinary citizens might be able or willing to challenge it, and so any manifestation of 'people power' is always followed by a search for the hidden hand that has been pulling the strings. I was, therefore, unsurprised by my lunch companion's conspiracy theory; what surprises me is that it isn't more widely believed. How can there be genuine rejoicing in the streets of Belgrade? Haven't countless British politicians and pundits, from both Left and Right, assured us that President Milosevic enjoys near-universal support in his own country?

In May last year, only a few days before the Serb withdrawal from Kosovo, Martin Bell MP told the House of Commons why the NATO intervention had nevertheless failed: 'My feeling is that, as far as his domestic political situation is concerned, Milosevic has been strengthened.' In the House of Lords, former defence minister Lord Blaker warned that 'the determination of the Serb people to support Mr Milosevic would be increased'. The political journalist Paul Routledge wrote in the *Mirror* that 'the tyrant Milosevic is still in power, and more popular with his people than ever', while *Times* readers learned from Simon Jenkins that 'Mr Milosevic may be "degraded" but he is politically impregnable'. The *Daily Mail* agreed: 'There is no doubt the country is now united behind Milosevic.' A *Panorama* programme on 'The Mind of Milosevic' interviewed Dr Jerrold Post, who was director of the CIA's political psychology centre from 1989 to 1998. 'I believe,' he intoned gravely, 'that the NATO strike designed to weaken him will strengthen him and will very much add not only to his support but to his mystique.' Tony Benn, Henry Kissinger and a large battalion of historians and retired ambassadors claimed that NATO's onslaught had scuppered any chance of a more democratic regime emerging in Belgrade for many years to come. In the words of Denis Healey, 'All observers agree that the bombing has strengthened Milosevic's political position in Yugoslavia.'

Not all observers, actually. Even during the NATO campaign, Milosevic was never as 'politically impregnable' as the pundits claimed. At the end of April 1999, Deputy Prime Minister Vuk Draskovic appeared on state television to denounce the President for dragging the nation into a war it couldn't win. Other opposition leaders started demanding Milosevic's resignation, and by early May there was evidence of widespread public discontent: the journalist Maggie O'Kane reported on it at length, which may be why she was promptly expelled from Belgrade.

After the ceasefire of June 1999, it became clearer still that the population which had supposedly flung itself at Milosevic's feet was sick of him. More than 10,000 Serbs took to the streets of Cacak on 29 June to demand the immediate resignation of the dictator. In the southern city of Prokuplje, which had hitherto been regarded as a Milosevic stronghold, only five people turned up on 8 July for the first pro-government demonstration since the end of the Kosovo War – while 4,000 staged a rival rally in the main square, chanting 'Slobo like Saddam' and 'Slobo out'. A month later, 150,000 anti-Milosevic protesters marched through the centre of Belgrade. The president's downfall had become a question of when, not if.

Why, then, did so many allegedly perceptive experts maintain that he was invincibly popular? The answer, I'd guess, is that they took Milosevic at his own estimation. It's an all too common error: throughout the 1990s, he convinced foreign politicians and diplomats that he was the bringer of peace in the Balkans, rather than the father of strife. Hence the willingness of successive British Foreign Secretaries to peddle the fiction that the Bosnian conflict was a 'civil war', even though they knew perfectly well that it had been instigated and directed from Belgrade. Despite all the atrocities committed by Serb troops and paramilitaries, from Vukovar in 1991 via Srebrenica in 1995 right up to Racak in 1999, international negotiators insisted that Milosevic was 'a man we can do business with', in the words of the US envoy Richard Holbrooke. (Did Holbrooke know that Neville Chamberlain had used the same phrase after his first meeting with Adolf Hitler?) Although his promises were continually shown to be as flimsy and worthless as a devalued dinar, still the old mantra was recited: Slobo's the chap with whom we can make deals – literally so, in the case of Douglas Hurd and Dame Pauline Neville-Jones.

Where are they now, all these eminent and culpable oafs who so consistently misjudged Milosevic? Shut away in their kitchens, gorging on humble pie? Of course not: this is a breed that knows no shame. Lord Owen could be heard on the World Service last Thursday night, pontificating grandly about the future of Yugoslavia while modestly omitting to mention his own inglorious role in its past. The following morning, Neville-Jones gave Radio 4's *Today* programme the benefit of her own expertise. Since she is a governor of the BBC, it was probably wise of the interviewer not to ask the obvious question: how dare these ministers and mandarins, who helped Milosevic to stay in power for so long and to wreak such ghastly havoc, now presume to lecture us on the inevitability of his demise?

(*Guardian*, 11 October 2000)

SNAKE-OIL SALESMEN AND
MUMBO-JUMBO MERCHANTS

2K: The number of the beast

S UMMER FELL ON a Friday this year. Friday 24 June, to be precise. At Wimbledon, where the temperature topped 100 degrees, spectators were collapsing from dehydration. 'HOTTEST DAY – AND IT'S HERE TO STAY', the evening paper's front-page headline announced. Aboard a train to East Anglia, my fellow passengers gasped and sweated as they discussed their weekend barbecue plans. The first flash of lightning came about two hours later. 'Don't worry,' I reassured a nervous young member of our household. 'It's only a little storm. It's not the end of the world.' At which moment the heavens blazed and thundered, and all the lights went out.

Oddly enough, that very morning I had received a letter from Father Neil Horan, a Roman Catholic priest in south London, warning me that Armageddon was imminent. 'There were many mistakes made in the past, in trying to predict the end of time,' he wrote. 'The evidence suggests that this time, people who are predicting the end are on sure ground. The long-awaited arrival of Jesus cannot, surely, be now too far off.' He drew my attention to Chapter 16 of the Book of Revelation: 'And there were voices, and thunders, and lightnings...And there fell upon men a great hail out of heaven.' Father Horan certainly seems to have predicted the spectacular eruption that Friday rather more accurately than the Meteorological Office. Lighting a candle, I took myself off to bed and settled down to read the documents that came with his letter. They included a message of support from Lady Thatcher, praising 'your sterling and imaginative efforts in the cause of promoting world peace'.

Imaginative they certainly are. The Queen, for instance, may be surprised to learn that the Second Coming depends on her not abdicating before the end of the millennium. 'Your Majesty,' Father Horan informs her, 'you have the great honour and distinction of being foretold by the Divine Writer who wrote Psalm 45, more than 2,500 years ago. May God bless you as you take your crown to the Holy City, to present to his Divine Majesty, Jesus Christ, who will then be king of kings. Do not even think of giving up the throne to

Prince Charles, or any member of your family.' What Psalm 45 actually says is that 'the daughter of Tyre shall be there with a gift'. No mention of the daughter of Elizabeth the Queen Mother, nor yet of the mother-in-law of Fergie and Di. But Father Horan has it all worked out. 'Tyre was the chief city of the ancient Phoenicians...They were leading seafarers and traders. The Phoenicians have died out as a people and as a seafaring power. The Psalm demands that Tyre exists at the end of days, but present-day Lebanon simply does not fit the prophecy, in any way. Britain seems to come closest to fitting it. Up to the early twentieth century, Britain was both a greater trading nation, and a seafaring one.' Ergo, Tyre is in fact Buckingham Palace. It seems that prophecies, whether in the Old Testament or the *Daily Mirror*'s horoscope column, are much the same as policy statements from the Liberal Democrats – capable of sustaining any interpretation that the credulous wish to place upon them.

It would be easy to dismiss Father Horan's message as the babblings of a lone eccentric. Easy, but wrong: for the ranks of the credulous are alarmingly large. An opinion poll in 1984 revealed that 39 per cent of Americans believe there will soon be a nuclear battle between Christ and the Antichrist at Armageddon, followed by a new age of 'Rapture'. More disturbingly still, the 39 per cent included the man who was head of state at the time. 'We may be the generation that sees Armageddon,' Ronald Reagan informed the TV evangelist Jim Bakker during his 1980 presidential campaign. Talking to a California state senator a few years earlier, Reagan had confided: 'For the first time ever, everything is in place for the battle of Armageddon and the Second Coming of Christ.' Several of the President's senior colleagues were similarly afflicted. James Watt, his secretary of the interior, told Congress in 1981: 'I do not know how many future generations we can count on before the Lord returns.'

How different, you may say, from our own dear government. I wouldn't be so sure. John Major doesn't issue apocalyptic statements about the 'end-time', but there are signs that he, too, suffers from a chiliastic obsession. One could point to his choice of the year 2000 as the deadline for creating a 'classless society'. More striking, I think, is his creation of a 'Millennium Fund', which, with a budget of over £250 million a year, will be the twenty-second-biggest quango in Britain. Major recently appointed seven 'millennium commissioners' to help Michael Heseltine and Peter Brooke distribute this loot over the next seven years. They include the *Times* columnist Simon Jenkins, the astronomer Heather Couper and the chairman of Newcastle United FC, Sir John Hall. The only reaction to his announcement was a rather sniffy editorial in the *Financial Times*, complaining that the decision on how to spend the millennial billions 'should not be made by such a narrow group of individuals'.

Ah, but it should – if, as I suspect, the Prime Minister is taking his cue from his namesake, St John the Divine. Reading the Book of Revelation by candle-light during the thunderstorm, I saw immediately why Major wished to hire seven lay commissioners to work for seven years.

> John to the seven churches which are in Asia; Grace be unto you, and peace, from him which is, and which was, and which is to come; and from the seven Spirits which are before his throne...And I saw the seven angels which stood before God; and to them were given seven trumpets...And the seven angels which had the seven trumpets prepared themselves to sound...And I heard a great voice out of the temple saying to the seven angels, Go your ways, and pour out the vials of the wrath of God upon the earth.

The more one studies St John's predictions, the louder the contemporary resonance becomes. Look at Chapter 10, in which an angel appears carrying some sort of pamphlet: 'And I took the little book out of the angel's hand, and ate it up; and it was in my mouth sweet as honey: and as soon as I had eaten it, my belly was bitter.' Can there be any doubt that this 'little book' is the Citizen's Charter? Now move on to Chapter 12. 'And there was war in heaven: Michael and his angels fought against the dragon; and the dragon fought and his angels, and prevailed not...And the great dragon was cast out.' Until now, scriptural scholars have assumed that Michael the dragon-destroyer probably refers to the president of the Board of Trade, Michael 'Tarzan' Heseltine. My own theory is that the Chief Secretary to the Treasury, Michael Portillo, is a likelier candidate. In his tirade on behalf of the 'silent majority' two months ago, Portillo said that we now lived 'in a world turned upside down'. No report of the speech pointed out the significance of these words: they first appeared in the Acts of the Apostles ('Those that have turned the world upside down are come hither also') and were later popularized by the Ranters and other millennial sects in seventeenth-century England, who were convinced that the Second Coming was just around the corner.

In several interviews during the past year, the Prime Minister has said that he will 'go when people least expect it', thus echoing Chapter 3 of Revelation: 'I will come on thee as a thief, and thou shalt not know what hour I will come upon thee.' But the decision may not be his to take. If last month's European elections are any guide, the British electors have already decided that his time is up. Their verdict on Major is perfectly summarized elsewhere in Chapter 3: 'I know thy works, that thou art neither cold nor hot; I would thou wert cold or hot. So then because thou art lukewarm, and neither cold nor hot, I will spue thee out of my mouth.' This is the way the world ends: not with a bang, but with a technicolour yawn.

(*Observer*, 3 July 1994)

Thanks a lot

M ARXISM IS DEAD. It has been disproved, debunked, exploded; it has rung down the curtain and gone to join the choir invisible; it is an ex-parrot. Or so we are told. But every time I see an Innovations mail-order catalogue – and it's hard to avoid them at this time of year, as they fall out of magazines like so many autumn leaves – I realize that Karl Marx was largely right. Capitalism, he pointed out, depends for its survival on constantly extending people's needs. To quote from Ernest Mandel's excellent summary, *The Marxist Theory of Alienation*: 'The system must provoke continual artificial dissatisfaction in human beings because without that dissatisfaction the sales of new gadgets which are more and more divorced from genuine human needs cannot be increased.'

Marx's only mistake was to assume that consumers would eventually become so alienated by this process that they would rebel against it. Instead, they have embraced it as an invaluable source of Christmas gifts, jamming the credit-card hotline with their orders for revolving shoe-racks, pyjamas that glow in the dark, a see-through alarm clock ('highly original'), a clock with no face or hands, an hourglass with 'digital sand' ('uses two button-cell batteries') and a 'gleaming FM/AM/LW radio' that not only looks like a motorbike but also emits 'the emotive throb' of a Harley-Davidson when switched on. (Quite why anyone would want the background noise of a revving engine while listening to *The Archers* or *This Week's Composer* is not explained, though I can see that it might come in useful for drowning out the pious flannel of *Thought for the Day*.)

Even Marx might have raised a bushy eyebrow at the ingenuity with which capitalism continues to create 'needs' that don't exist. Look at the treats on offer from Innovations this autumn: 'The world's first microchip-controlled home Drinkscentre' dispenses gin and tonic 'at the touch of a button' and costs £149.99. Thanks a lot. For a fraction of that price, one could buy a bottle of Gordon's and several litres of Schweppes, unscrew the tops, tip them into a glass and get stuck in. Or how about the Micromix? 'This beautifully simple British invention automatically stirs food while it cooks in the microwave. Perfect for dishes like scrambled eggs.' There is, of course, an even more beautifully simple way of making scrambled eggs: put egg mixture in saucepan, heat, stir with spoon – and eat.

'Accurate to within one second in a million years!! Jungham's remarkable clocks are the most accurate timepieces in the world. The mantel clock has an internal antenna that picks up a radio signal from a transmitter in Rugby controlled by the National Physical Laboratory, guaranteeing absolute precision…The digital alarm clock is controlled by a radio signal generated by the German atomic caesium clock in Frankfurt and works within a radius of 900 miles.' Who wants to be accurate to one second within a million years? How do we know that the National Physical Laboratory in Rugby will still exist in a million years' time? What happens if you take the clocks on holiday to America? Answer comes there none.

'Take the fun out of Scrabble with the CZ704 Scrabble Computer! This astonishing new electronic miracle from Taiwan brings an end to hours of Scrabble enjoyment. Simply tap in your seven letters and within seconds the 40-megabyte RAM chip will give you on-screen access to all possible combinations to achieve maximum score value. Reduces playing time of game to ten minutes.' Actually, that last item comes from Gnome's Xmas Mail Mart, a satirical feature that appears in *Private Eye* every Christmas. But satire, as so often, is matched stride for stride by reality. Here's a genuine entry in the Innovations catalogue: 'The ultimate aid for crossword puzzlers. Franklin's new pocket computer is an essential for all crossword addicts. When stuck for an answer, enter the letters you know and "?" for those you don't. In seconds, Crossword Solver fills in the blanks. £49.99.' Great – except that the whole point of doing crosswords is to work out the answers for oneself. By eliminating this satisfaction, Franklin (whoever she or he may be) has come up with something as alluringly 'essential' as alcohol-free lager, or pleasure-free sex.

The Patent Office informs me that it receives 27,000 applications for patents every year. Which ones are born to blush unseen, and which will earn a fortune? The answer is that it's a lottery: for every successful good idea, such as Catseyes in the middle of roads, there is an equally successful clunker, such as hot-air hand dryers (instructions for use: hold hands under air stream for a minute, give up in despair and dry hands on back of trousers instead) or

Tetrapak milk cartons (instructions for use: try to pull cardboard wings apart; fail; pull harder; watch with bemusement as cardboard rips and milk spills over kitchen table). The creators of Tetrapak, Gad and Hans Rausing, are now worth £5.2 billion – which makes them the richest people in Britain, well ahead of the Queen, the Sainsbury family and John Paul Getty II. And all because they devised a milk carton that I can't use.

'Inventions that are not made, like babies that are not born, are rarely missed,' J. K. Galbraith wrote in *The Affluent Society*. He has a point. Before Innovations started filling our houses with expensive but worthless clutter, did people say, 'Oh, how I wish we had an electronic crossword-solver and a digital hourglass'? I think not. However, there are a few necessary inventions that have not been made yet, for which I am waiting with some impatience: a device to stop me dozing off in the bath and dropping my book in the water; a way of getting my hair cut without being asked whether I've been on holiday; a digital display on my radio which reveals, when I turn on halfway through *Desert Island Discs*, who the castaway is; a homing device which locates missing cats; coffee that tastes as good as it smells; an umbrella whose spokes won't break at the first gust of wind; a television with a built-in lie detector, which flashes every time a politician tells a fib on *Newsnight* or *Question Time*; a washing machine that doesn't swallow socks. If the boffins at Innovations will forswear their pointless gadgets and satisfy these basic human requirements, I shall eat my words (after stirring them with a Micromix first, of course). Meanwhile, if you're looking for a truly original Christmas present, buy a paperback copy of Karl Marx's *Grundrisse*. It's cheap, it's useful – and it doesn't need batteries.

(*Observer*, 25 September 1994)

A theory to end all theories

W HO KILLED PRESIDENT KENNEDY? After at least a hundred books on the subject, we are still waiting for a conclusive answer. Two weeks ago, however, a young arts impresario named Giri Tharmananthar told me that he had cracked the case. In a converted warehouse near King's Cross station in north London, he was presenting 'the first ever public showing in the UK of leaked video footage of the Kennedy assassination'. The video, he boasted, 'reveals without doubt that the driver of Kennedy's car turns and shoots the fatal blow, explaining why Mrs Kennedy launched herself out of the rear of the car...' Alas, the revelations and explanations did not quite live up to their billing. The 'leaked video footage', which turned out to be an image from the famous Zapruder film, was so blurred that one could scarcely see the driver, let alone witness him swivelling in his seat to take a pot-shot at the President. Still, Tharmananthar's cunning stunt achieved its main purpose, by luring customers in to see a play that he was promoting in the same warehouse.

More than thirty years after the event, the shooting of President Kennedy still 'has legs', as they say in Hollywood. Look at the cover headline on the December issue of *Vanity Fair*: 'JFK: CASE REOPENED. New evidence on the death of a President'. Oddly enough, the driver of the presidential car doesn't earn a mention in the magazine's twenty-one-page article, but plenty of other suspects are rounded up – the Mafia, the KGB, the CIA, the FBI and, for good measure, Fidel Castro. Trying to follow the logic of this investigation is like playing an exhaustive and exhausting game of consequences. The mother of Lee Harvey Oswald, for instance, used to know a corrupt lawyer who was 'linked to' a crime operation run by the New Orleans mobster Carlos Marcello. One of Marcello's oldest friends was Nofio Pecora, who, three weeks before the assassination, was telephoned by Jack Ruby – the same Jack Ruby who later shot Oswald dead in the Dallas police headquarters. What does it all add up to? Search me. But *Vanity Fair* feels sure that it must mean something.

'Only connect' is the conspiracy theorists' guiding principle. Back in the 1960s, some of them even found a sinister synchronicity between JFK's death and the assassination of President Lincoln a hundred years earlier: both men were shot in the head, on a Friday, in the presence of their wives; their alleged murderers were both killed before coming to trial; both Lincoln and Kennedy were succeeded by Southern Democrats called Johnson. Like Casaubon in *Middlemarch*, who thought that a lifetime of research would eventually yield up the key to all mythologies, assassination buffs are convinced that by doggedly collating every scrap of fact or speculation they will one day solve the mystery of who did what in Dallas on 22 November 1963.

'When you have eliminated the impossible,' Sherlock Holmes used to remind Dr Watson, 'whatever remains, however improbable, must be the truth.' But the whole point of conspiracy theory is that nothing is impossible. What remains is everything, and so everything must be true: Shakespeare's plays were written by Francis Bacon, aided by four monkeys with typewriters; John Major is really an alien invader from the planet Vulcan. Like most journalists, I am often contacted by people who assure me that they are being persecuted by a cabal led by the Lord Chancellor, the Archbishop of Canterbury, the Special Branch and the Princess of Wales; many of them also believe that MI5 has planted tiny transmitters inside their skulls. 'I'm not paranoid, you know,' they say – and their menacing manner makes it clear that disagreement would be inadvisable.

In his excellent study, *The Paranoid Style In American Politics*, Professor Richard Hofstadter suggested that the paranoia of the conspiracy theorist isn't necessarily a psychological abnormality. 'I am not speaking in a clinical sense, but borrowing a clinical term for other purposes,' he explained. 'I use the term much as a historian of art might speak of the baroque or the mannerist style. It is, above all, a way of seeing the world and of expressing oneself.' Just so. The amateur detectives and freelance obsessives who devote their lives to the JFK saga are not fruitcakes – well, not all of them. They are artists, and the canvas they have painted is as vast and teeming as a crowd scene from *Where's Wally?*

Consider the following facts. One of President Kennedy's lovers, Mariella Novotny, was a protégée of Stephen Ward, the man who introduced John Profumo to Christine Keeler. Profumo was a minister in the government of Harold Macmillan. Macmillan's wife, Dorothy, was the lover of Lord Boothby, who was an associate of the Kray twins. Another chum of the Krays was the Labour MP Tom Driberg, who wrote an authorized biography of the KGB agent Guy Burgess. Eugene Ivanov, the Soviet diplomat who had an affair with Christine Keeler, was also a KGB man. Between 1959 and 1962 Lee Harvey Oswald lived in Moscow, where, it has been reported, he was recruited by the KGB.

Only connect? We've hardly started. Another of Kennedy's alleged mistresses, the actress Suzy Chang, was a friend of Lord Snowdon – who in turn was an old friend of Jeremy Thorpe. The scandal which forced Thorpe to resign as leader of the Liberal Party was, according to Harold Wilson, orchestrated by the South African intelligence service BOSS. Wilson also believed that he himself was the victim of a plot by both BOSS and MI5 to smear him as a KGB agent. And he may have been right: in September 1963 the Soviet defector Anatoly Golitsyn told John McCone, the director of the CIA, that Wilson was working for the Russians. McCone owed his job at the CIA to...John F. Kennedy.

Sooner or later, if the conspiracy artists stick to their task, the picture will include almost every crime or scandal of the twentieth century. You want to prove a 'connection' between the Kennedy assassination and the Nazis? No problem. One of the earliest revisionist studies of JFK's murder, Mark Lane's *Rush to Judgment*, had a preface written by the historian Hugh Trevor-Roper. This is the same Trevor-Roper who, some years later, verified the bogus Hitler diaries on behalf of Times Newspapers. Before the Second World War, *The Times* was an advocate of appeasement. So was the American ambassador in London – a certain Joseph Kennedy, father of you-know-who...

Yes, yes, you will say, but where's Wally? Where's the smoking gun? Nobody has yet spotted it; and nobody ever will.

(*Observer*, 4 December 1994)

Who would have thought it?

I T I S A L I T T L E - K N O W N fact that, when not writing these articles, I attend to my duties as chairman of a large multinational conglomerate. Statements of the Obvious plc – also known by the acronym 'SO?', since that is what cynics usually say when they see our products – was set up a few years ago to meet the ever-growing demand by many consumers to be told what they already knew.

You have probably seen the work of SO? without realizing it. One of our most profitable subsidiaries produces all those market research 'surveys' which are such a boon to news editors with space to fill. 'Unemployment is damaging families...according to a survey published yesterday' (*Guardian*, 13 April 1994). That was one of ours. Then there was the research we conducted for the Women's Royal Voluntary Service a couple of weeks ago, which found that many old people 'said that there had been opportunities they wish they could have taken'. Yet another of our recent triumphs was the disclosure that many children are 'more familiar with computer game heroes Sonic the Hedgehog and Super Mario than with childhood literature characters such as Alice in Wonderland and Little Red Riding Hood'. In February, great public-ity was given to our startling discovery that many undergraduates find it diffi-cult to live on their student grants. A couple of months earlier, after interviewing 1,500 people, we revealed that few men share household chores equally with their female partners.

But we don't spend all our time brandishing clipboards on windswept street corners, asking passers-by if they would agree that rich people tend to have more money than poor people, or that nice things are better than nasty things. We are just as likely to be found in the oak-panelled lairs of senior politicians, providing them with ringing phrases for their manifestos ('We must face the challenge of the future' – that always seems to go down well) or tweaking up their rhetorical flourishes. Perhaps you recall John Smith's speech to the Labour Party local government conference last year? Promising 'a new political approach for a new political era...a new politics that puts people first, that rejects dogma and embraces practical commonsense solutions', he argued that Labour should 'embody the hopes and aspirations of the ordinary people of this country for a better life for themselves and their families. When you get right down to it, that is what they want from politics.' This bold oration was hailed by the press as 'radical' and 'astonishing'; the trade union leader John Edmonds praised it as 'a new vision' which 'burst through some of the tired historical dogma of the Labour Party'. We were happy to let Smith take the credit; but we got the fee.

Our vast database of sonorous but uncontroversial phrases is suitable for use by all political parties on every conceivable occasion. 'We must build, but build surely...We must grasp the opportunities...Let us go forward together.' I shouldn't be telling you this, but many of these are pinched from an old Peter Sellers sketch parodying the vacuousness of political rhetoric. Another of our secret sources is Sellers' character Chauncey Gardener, whose simple maxims so impressed the Washington political elite in the film *Being There*. When Bill Clinton was writing his inauguration speech last year, he asked us if we could lend a hand. In a spirit of slight mischief, we dug out one of Chauncey Gardener's best lines: 'After the winter comes the spring.' Imagine our delight when Clinton put the words straight into his address...and nobody sniggered.

Why should they? The market for platitudes is the one sector of the American economy which has continued to thrive throughout the recession. Look at those 'how to be a millionaire' manuals which are such a perennial feature of the *New York Times* best-seller list – *The Seven Habits of Highly Effective People*, *The Art of the Deal, Things They Don't Teach You at Harvard Business School*, and so forth. Almost all of them are assembled by keen young trainees at our American head office and then sold on to the 'author'. Our biggest success so far is *The Leadership Secrets of Attila the Hun*, which is to be found on the bookshelves of every middle-manager in the United States, and has been described as a 'fantastic' guide, which 'will help you make the most of your leadership potential'. It includes some of our most thought-provoking suggestions: 'You must have resilience to overcome personal misfortunes, discouragement, rejection and disappointment'; 'When the consequences of your actions are too grim to bear, look for another option'. Who could disagree?

Like any world-beating corporation, we are sometimes the victims of industrial espionage. I was irritated recently to read *Keep Going for It*, in which Victor Kiam – he who liked Remington's razors so much that he bought the company – passed on the ideas which had propelled him to success. 'Turn those negatives into positives!' 'A little bit of courtesy and caring. It goes such a long way.' 'Business is a game. Play it to win.' 'When you're an entrepreneur, you don't look a gift horse in the mouth.' 'When opportunity knocks, the entrepreneur is always home.' 'Any job worth doing is worth doing well.' All these *aperçus* were stolen from us. Still, as the senior vice-president of our cliché department often observes, imitation is the sincerest form of flattery.

Besides, we remain ahead of the game. Recognizing that not everyone wants to be Victor Kiam or Donald Trump, we have lately diversified into the even more lucrative market for New Age books about 'self-help' and 'personal growth'. Our top title at the moment is Jonathan Lazear's *Meditations for Men Who Do Too Much*, aimed at workaholics who have burned themselves out by reading *Keep Going for It* and *The Leadership Secrets of Attila the Hun*. Here are some of Lazear's wise words, which he bought off-the-peg from Statements of the Obvious. 'Our families, our partners, our extended families, our children will always be there for us if we can make the decision to be there for them.' 'We need to learn to pace ourselves.' 'Wealth doesn't really translate to happiness.' 'Trusting no one can be as dangerous as trusting everyone.' 'We can learn from our failures.' 'No one is happy all of the time.'

Finally, a word about ethics. Some consumer groups have suggested that it is 'immoral' for our company to make a fortune by selling truisms which had hitherto been treated as common property, like the air we breathe. What nonsense. More than 200 years ago, the authors of the American Declaration of Independence prefaced their statement of human rights by announcing, 'We hold these truths to be self-evident.' If Thomas Jefferson and his colleagues didn't flinch from stating the obvious, why should we?

(*Observer*, 1 May 1994)

Dancing elephants and boiled frogs

E VER SINCE BILL CLINTON was elected to the presidency, the great debate has raged: is he as stupid as he looks? The answer, we now learn, is yes. Any lingering doubts were quelled once and for all earlier this month by the revelation that the President had spent a whole day at Camp David listening to the advice of Stephen Covey and Anthony Robbins, 'two of the nation's leading motivational and personal development gurus', both of whom make their living by peddling banal truisms to ambitious but doomed middle-managers who dream of becoming chief executives. Bill Clinton, of course, is a chief executive already. But his invitation to Covey and Robbins proves that he is, at heart, another dim-witted no-hoper in an ill-fitting suit who is going nowhere.

Messrs Covey and Robbins, by contrast, are chortling and whooping all the way to the bank. Covey earned $70 million last year from his book *The Seven Habits of Highly Effective People* (5 million copies sold so far) and his lectures on 'Principle-Centred Leadership', for which he is paid £250,000 a time. Robbins, a 34-year-old Californian who once worked as a school janitor, charges a mere £100,000 a day for his services. His best-selling books include *Awaken the Giant Within* and *Unlimited Power*. He is now worth about $80 million.

So what are the seven habits of highly effective people? How do we awaken the giant within? In short, where can I get some of this loot? The answer is obvious: write a self-help manual for simpletons. Covey used to be a Mormon missionary; now, to judge by *Seven Habits*, he is a missionary for morons. 'Did you ever consider,' he writes, 'how ridiculous it would be to try to cram on a farm – to forget to plant in the spring, play all summer and then cram in the fall to bring in the harvest? The farm is a natural system. The price must be paid and the process followed. You always reap what you sow.' The echo of Chauncey Gardener, the idiot savant who dispensed horticultural wisdom in Jerzy Kosinski's satire *Being There*, is presumably unintentional.

Robbins prefers to take his metaphors from the kitchen rather than the farmyard. 'If someone makes the greatest chocolate cake in the world, can you produce the same quality results?' he asks. 'Of course you can, if you have that person's recipe...if you follow the recipe to the letter, you will produce the same results, even though you may never have baked such a cake before in your life.' Easy, isn't it?

The man ultimately responsible for all this lucrative twaddle is Dale Carnegie, who published *How to Win Friends and Influence People* almost sixty years ago. Countless best-sellers in the same vein have been produced since then – *The One-Minute Manager, The Leadership Secrets of Attila the Hun* and so on – but most of them stick pretty closely to the formula (oh, all right, recipe) invented by the guv'nor. It was certainly Carnegie who cottoned on to the selling power of animal analogies, peppering his prose with such undeniable aphorisms as 'No one ever kicks a dead dog' and 'If you want to gather honey, don't kick over the beehive'. Studying the titles on display in the management section of Waterstone's nowadays, you might think you'd stumbled into the natural history department by mistake. There's Debra Benton's *Lions Don't Need to Roar: Stand Out, Fit In and Move Ahead in Business,* Harvey Mackay's *Swim with the Sharks without Being Eaten Alive* and James A. Belasco's *Teaching the Elephants to Dance: Empowering Change in Your Organization.* Charles Handy's *The Age of Unreason* has a picture of a leaping frog on its front cover. Why? 'If you put a frog in water and slowly heat it, the frog will eventually let itself be boiled to death,' he explains. 'We, too, will not survive if we don't respond to the radical way in which the world is changing.' Not to be outdone, Stephen Covey has included a section on fish in his latest book, *Principle-Centred Leadership.* 'I've long been impressed,' he reveals, 'with the many parallels between fishing and managing. In reality, senior-level executives are really fishing the stream. That is, they're looking at the business in the context of the total environment and devising ways to "reel in" desired results...' Yes, yes, I think we get the picture.

Apart from dancing elephants and boiling frogs, the other essential ingredient of these books is lists. Following the distinguished example of God, who condensed the laws of righteousness into ten easy-to-understand commandments, the authors of business manuals seek to persuade their readers that the secrets of success are finite and can be briefly enumerated. Again Carnegie was the pioneer, offering 'seven ways to peace and happiness' and 'four good working habits that will help prevent fatigue and worry'. Having hit the jackpot with *The Seven Habits of Highly Effective People,* Covey went even further in his sequel, whose chapter headings include 'Three Resolutions', 'Six Days of

Creation', 'Six Conditions of Empowerment', 'Seven Deadly Sins' (didn't someone else think of that first?), 'Seven Chronic Problems', 'Eight Ways to Enrich Marriage and Family Relationships' and, generously enough, 'Thirty Methods of Influence'. Meanwhile, Anthony Robbins has come up with 'Five Keys to Wealth and Happiness' and 'Seven Lies of Success'. More ambitiously still, his book *Giant Steps* provides no fewer than '365 lessons in self-mastery' – though some of them are pretty skimpy. Here is Lesson 364, in its entirety: 'Remember to expect miracles...because you are one.' Gee, thanks, Tony. I bet President Clinton appreciated that.

Why is the leader of the most powerful nation on earth susceptible to the platitudinous bromides dished out by these latter-day quack-doctors? Does he really suppose that he can now swim with the sharks and roar with the lions? Apparently so. Apart from proving that Clinton is an incorrigible berk, it also goes to show that (as Messrs Covey and Robbins would put it) there are two rules for making a fortune in America: never look a gift horse in the mouth – and don't kill the goose that lays the golden eggs.

(*Observer*, 22 January 1995)

The stars are out

S EE IF YOU CAN guess the source of the following: 'According to the mystic meteorological mirror, Peter Pans born under the sign of Virgo possess the secret of eternal youth...Librans are cocksure creatures. They know what they want and they usually get it...With Mars as its ruling planet, Aries is naturally the sign of soldiers and sportsmen – men and women of action and dynamic resolve. Their element is Fire. They tend to live in the here and now...' Mystic Meg's New Year message? No: these are extracts from leading articles in *The Times* during the past week. 'Over our next twelve issues,' the paper announced in a Boxing Day editorial, 'we shall consider what the next year holds in store for famous and less famous people born under each of the zodiac's signs.' It has been as good as its word. And the menace is spreading: two other 'serious' broadsheets, the *Sunday Telegraph* and *Sunday Times*, now give houseroom to horoscope pedlars.

Why are so many otherwise intelligent editors and readers in thrall to this drivel? A common explanation links it to the decline in religious faith, and suggests that once people cease to believe in God, they do not believe in nothing: they believe in anything, including gibberish about the Age of Aquarius. But a likelier reason is the imminence of the year 2000, which is causing a worldwide outbreak of pre-millennial tension among those of a superstitious turn of mind. In a respectable London bookshop last week, I was astonished to find an entire section given over to works by or about Nostradamus, the sixteenth-century mumbo-jumbo merchant. One paperback, *The Prophecies of Nostradamus* ('edited and interpreted by Erika Cheetham'), has been reprinted twenty-three times since its first publication in 1973, from which one must deduce that an alarming number of Britons take his babblings seriously.

Even if judged on their own terms, Nostradamus's interpreters seem to have only the haziest idea of what they are talking about. 'When Saturn and Aquarius are in conjunction with Sagittarius in the ascendant, towards the end of the century,' Cheetham writes, 'we should expect a great war.' But since Saturn is a planet and Aquarius a sign of the zodiac, such a conjunction is astronomically impossible – a category mistake, as philosophers would call it.

Nostradamus himself had little faith in the competence of most stargazers. 'Let the profane and ignorant herd keep away,' he warned in one of his verses. 'Let all astrologers, idiots and barbarians stay far off.' Erika Cheetham is puzzled and rather hurt by this incantation. 'Why,' she wonders, 'does Nostradamus include astrologers among the people he damns? Is this yet another example of his trying to bluff the authorities?' Or, as I prefer, is it a sly admission that he knew his celestial prophecies were all hooey?

In *Nostradamus: The Final Reckoning*, Peter Lemesurier broods on another of the old boy's forecasts: 'Once he for seventeen years has held the see, They'll change the papal term to five years' time.' If Nostradamus is right, he argues, 'then we are faced with the distinct possibility that on 16 October 1995 (or possibly 22 October) Pope John Paul II will be asked to stay on for another five years.' A moment's thought will show that this 'distinct possibility' is quite absurd, since popes – unlike British prime ministers or American presidents – are elected for life. But anyway, as Aneurin Bevan used to say, why look in the crystal ball when you can read the book? October 1995 has been and gone, and no announcement has come from the Vatican.

Horoscopes are often said to be 'harmless fun', but I can't see anything either funny or harmless in a lucrative con-trick which preys on people's ignorance and fear. As the great Professor Richard Dawkins pointed out last weekend, a pharmaceuticals manufacturer who marketed a birth-control pill that had not the slightest demonstrable effect on fertility would be prosecuted under the Trades Descriptions Act, and sued by trusting customers who found themselves pregnant. 'If astrologers cannot be sued by individuals mis-advised, say, into taking disastrous business decisions, why at least are they not prosecuted for false representations under the Trades Descriptions Act and driven out of business? Why, actually, are professional astrologers not jailed for fraud?' Quite so. But why stop at professional astrologers? Those who aid and abet them are equally guilty. Fond though I am of Peter Stothard, editor of *The Times*, I think six months in Wormwood Scrubs might be just what is needed to bring him to his senses.

(*Guardian*, 3 January 1996)

Mystic Mogg

A FTER FRIDAY'S PLUNGE on Wall Street, share-dealers had an uncomfortable weekend wondering if meltdown had begun or if this was merely a 'correction'. They would not know until Monday morning, when the world's greatest market guru was due to pronounce. William Rees-Mogg (for it was he) duly obliged. 'Last week's falls on Wall Street are likely to be followed by further falls in New York,' the Somerset sage announced in *The Times*. 'This is...the end of the bull market of the 1990s.' Frabjous day, calloo callay! The Dow-Jones and the Nasdaq bounced back immediately. For, thanks to his prognosticatory skill, Mogg has become something of a legend on Wall Street. Nine years ago he published a book called *The Great Reckoning: How the World Will Change in the Depression of the 1990s*. As he noted recently, few heeded his warning: 'Indeed, people got rich during the boom by rejecting it.'

An infallibly fallible tipster is just as useful as one who always picks the winner. 'Although Mrs Thatcher's majority was not quite large enough to avoid a second ballot, the victory was clearly a decisive one,' Mogg wrote after the first Tory leadership election in 1990. 'Of course many people will doubt that she really has won...I take the contrary view that a mandate is a mandate

and that she will derive real strength from having overcome so tough a challenge.' I quickly placed a large bet that Thatcher would resign at once, and so
she did. In May 1993 he tried again: 'It is now as probable that Mr Major will
have to go as it was nine months ago that Mr Lamont would have to.' This
time I bet my entire life savings that Major would lead the Tories into the next
election; once again, thanks to Mystic Mogg, I cleaned up.

In his latest oracular bulletin, Mogg admits that 'many of us have been
wrong in the past decade about the durability of unsustainable growth in the
Western stock markets'. Too modest, my dear chap: you have been wrong
about absolutely everything – which is why we punters love you so.

(*Guardian*, 19 April 2000)

A spot of lateral sinking

I F OUR BELOVED GOVERNMENT has a fault – something which
many people are apparently reluctant to believe – it is a tendency to leap
aboard bandwagons whose wheels have fallen off. Blair invited Noel Gal-
lagher to Number 10 soon after the release of *Be Here Now* had exposed Oasis
as derivative duds; he discovered the joys of capitalism at the very moment
the system began devouring itself. Now, following his demand for more creativity in Whitehall, the Department of Education has called in Dr Edward de
Bono 'to develop bright ideas on schools and jobs'.

More than 200 officials from the department recently attended a lecture in
which de Bono described his 'Six Thinking Hats system' of decision-making.
The idea is that civil servants should put on a red hat when they want to talk
about hunches and instincts, a yellow hat if they are listing the advantages of a
project, a black hat while playing devil's advocate, and so on. 'Without wishing to boast,' he says, 'this is the first new way of thinking to be developed for
2,400 years since the days of Plato, Socrates and Aristotle.' Without wishing
to boast, de Bono claims also to have invented 'lateral thinking' and 'water
logic'. Here's an example of how they work, from his suggestively titled book
I Am Right, You Are Wrong: 'How often does someone who is using a traditional wet razor stop to consider whether instead of moving the razor it might

be easier to keep the razor still and to move the head instead? In fact it is rather better. But no one does try it because there is "no problem to fix".' Men at the Department of Education who attempt this shaving technique will soon discover why it hasn't caught on: the result looks like an out-take from *The Texas Chainsaw Massacre*. What other useful tips can they expect? 'You can't dig a hole in a different place by digging the same hole deeper.' 'With a problem, you look for a solution.' 'A bird is different from an aeroplane, although both fly through the air.' 'Gloves make a poor Christmas present for a man with no hands.' I made that last one up, but its water logic is undeniable.

In another manual, *Tactics: The Art and Science of Success*, de Bono offered the lessons that might be learned from a number of people who 'would generally be regarded as "successful" '. The millionaires he invited us to emulate included US hotelier Harry Helmsley (later convicted of massive tax evasion) and Robert Maxwell. 'At the end of the book,' de Bono advised, 'the reader should say, "Why not me?" ' If millions go missing from the Department of Education's pension fund, we shall know Whitehall has risen to the challenge.

(Guardian, 2 December 1998)

Chumps talking to chimps

F REPORTS FROM Georgia State University are to be believed, a simian equivalent of Desmond Morris may shortly be writing a book called *The Hairy Human*. The likeliest candidate is Kanzi, a pygmy chimpanzee who has learned to tap out messages in symbol-language on a computer keyboard. 'Kanzi is perfectly capable of talking about what he wants to happen tomorrow,' says his teacher, Professor Sue Savage-Rumbaugh. 'He is capable of answering questions about what happened yesterday.' However, Kanzi may be beaten to it by Chantek the orang-utan, who 'already has a 2,000-word vocabulary in sign language' and is now learning to use a voice synthesizer.

But should we believe it? About twenty years ago a chimp called Washoe was said to have acquired a vocabulary of 'hundreds of words' in American Sign Language (ASL), which she could use to create meaningful and original sentences. As Steven Pinker notes in his book *The Language Instinct*, this pre-posterous claim was based on the myth that ASL is a crude system of pan-tomime gestures rather than a full language with complex syntax. Pinker quotes the candid admission from the one deaf member of the Washoe team: 'The hearing people were logging every movement the chimp made as a sign. Every time the chimp put his finger in his mouth, they'd say "Oh, he's making the sign for drink" and they'd give him some milk...When the chimp scratched himself, they'd record it as the sign for scratch...' When Jane Goodall visited the project, she pointed out that all these so-called signs were used by chimps in the wild.

I presume that science correspondents have studied the inglorious history of previous experiments in this field, and may even have read Noam Chomsky on Universal Grammar. Why, then, does Professor Savage-Rumbaugh merit such such lavish and uncritical coverage, long before any of her claims have been properly tested? No doubt the advent of the Silly Season has something to do with it. But the story would probably be irresistible at any time of year, since the talking ape is one of our most enduring and appealing myths.

In Angela Carter's novel *Nights at the Circus* (1984) we are introduced to Lamarck's Educated Apes, a troupe of performing chimps who can write mes-sages on blackboards and negotiate their own pay rises. In John Collier's comic masterpiece *His Monkey Wife* (1930) an African ape called Emily falls in love with an English schoolmaster, Alfred Fatigay, follows him back to London and educates herself in the British Museum Reading Room. Though Alfred already has a fiancée, Emily's decency and devotion win through in the end: 'Into the depths of those all-dark lustrous eyes, his spirit slid with no sound of a splash. She uttered a few low words, rapidly, in her native tongue. The candle, guttering beside the bed, was strangled in the grip of a prehensile foot, and darkness received, like a ripple in velvet, the final happy sigh.'

For every tale in which apes represent humanity's most bestial and atavis-tic urges, from *Gulliver's Travels* to Aldous Huxley's *Ape and Essence*, there are just as many in which their good manners and sensibility are contrasted with the brutishness of our own 'civilization'. (Even King Kong, lest we forget, was more victim than villain.) This version of the fable was already well estab-lished by the time Darwin revealed our common ancestry – most amusingly in Thomas Love Peacock's novel *Melincourt* (1817), where an orang-utan arrives here from Angola and is soon transformed into Sir Oran Haut-Ton, baronet and Member of Parliament. Though Sir Oran never acquires the power of speech, his 'grave and dignified silence' is taken as proof of great wisdom. Sir

Oran is 'a specimen of the natural and original man – a genuine facsimile of the philosophical Adam'.

This idea of the Noble Savage – popularized by Rousseau and, in Britain, by the eccentric Lord Monboddo – has now been taken up and embellished by environmentalists. Professor Peter Singer, the guru of the animal liberation movement, argues that the ability of great apes to reason and communicate entitles them to the same rights as humans. In New Zealand, several MPs have proposed that we should accept chimpanzees, gorillas and orang-utans as fellow members of a 'community of equals'. I expect that Professor Savage-Rumbaugh's alleged breakthrough will hasten the formation of a Votes for Apes campaign.

However well intentioned, this is a dangerous anthropomorphic fallacy. 'What an irony it is,' Steven Pinker comments in *The Language Instinct*, 'that the supposed attempt to bring *Homo sapiens* down a few notches in the natural order has taken the form of us humans hectoring another species into emulating our instinctive form of communication, or some artificial form we have invented, as if that were the measure of biological worth.' As I have occasionally pointed out, few defenders of the cute and cuddly fox extend the same passionate sympathy to the cold, scaly carp. If legal rights are to be granted only to those creatures that can mimic us or win our affection, what hope is there for the poor old scorpion and jellyfish?

(*Guardian*, 28 July 1999)

Black men can't jump

IS JACK STRAW UNDEREMPLOYED? It seems unlikely: persecuting asylum seekers, curtailing trial by jury and drooling over MI5 ought to be a full-time job. And yet he somehow found the time yesterday to share a platform at Church House in London with the American author Charles Murray, at a debate sponsored by *The Sunday Times* on 'The Growing Threat of the Underclass'. Straw is unapologetic. 'I deplore many of the views Mr Murray has espoused,' he told anti-racists who had asked him not to attend, 'but I also believe in argument.'

Murray's best-known book, *The Bell Curve* (1994), runs to more than 800 pages but can be summarized in a few sentences. Black people are more stupid than white people: always have been, always will be. This is why they have less economic and social success. Since the fault lies in their genes, they are doomed to be at the bottom of the heap now and for ever.

If Jack Straw were invited to discuss the innate intellectual inferiority of black people with, say, a member of the Ku Klux Klan or the British National Party, would he wish to dignify the event with his presence? What sort of 'debate' can one have about such manifest and malign claptrap? The appearance of a senior minister from the British government at yesterday's colloquy pays Murray a wholly undeserved compliment. One might say the same about *The Sunday Times*' involvement – except that this is what we have come to expect of that absurd and half-witted newspaper, which has for some years been promoting Murray as the most brilliant soothsayer of our time.

Murray does not belong to the Klan or the BNP, of course, though both organizations have derived much comfort and pleasure from his work. His insidious achievement has been to make racism respectable by dressing it up in the alluring garb of science and dispassionate scholarship. More than 400,000 Americans bought *The Bell Curve*, delighted to find their prejudices confirmed by apparently irrefutable statistical research. Very few of them, I guess, subsequently read the obscure academic journals in which Murray's methodology was systematically discredited. To the American public – as well as *The Sunday Times* and Jack Straw – he remains a figure to be reckoned with.

Murray's work depends on crude definitions of two indefinable concepts, intelligence and race. He thinks that our place in the social pecking order depends on our IQ, which is genetically and racially predetermined and cannot be much affected by schooling, environment or class. (We must assume, therefore, that Prince Andrew and Prince Edward have very high IQs indeed.) The measure of intelligence used in *The Bell Curve* is the Armed Forces Qualifying Test; and, if you accept his premise that IQ is 'innate', then the figures do indeed seem to show that black people are fated to be less intelligent. If, however, you take the trouble to seek out the test paper, you will find sample questions such as this: 'Solitary most nearly means a) sunny; b) being alone; c) playing games; d) soulful.' Or this: 'If a cubic foot of water weighs 55lb, how much weight will a 75½ cubic-foot tank trailer be carrying when fully loaded with water?' If young African-Americans find it hard to answer these questions, might this have something to do with the quality of their education? Not according to Murray, who attributes it entirely to the curse of their ancient and immutable genetic inheritance.

As for race, his belief that 'Africans' are genetically homogeneous is even more ludicrous – the exact opposite of the truth, in fact. After exhaustive study of DNA samples, Professor Kenneth Kidd of Yale University has discovered that 'in almost any single African population – a tribe or whatever you want to call it – there is more genetic variation than in all the rest of the world put together.' The explanation is simple: Africa is where early humans evolved, and where they stayed for the first 100,000 years of their history – time enough for wide genetic variations to develop.

Though often described as a social scientist, Murray took his Ph.D. in politics. Behind the scientific camouflage he is essentially a right-wing polemicist peddling a familiar myth: that nothing can or should be done to ameliorate racial and economic inequality. He gave the game away three years ago in a brief personal manifesto, *What it Means to Be a Libertarian*, which proposed the abolition of all social security and welfare and the repeal of all legislation protecting civil rights or outlawing racial discrimination. 'In a free society, freedom of association cannot be abridged,' he argued. 'Implicit in this freedom is also the freedom not to associate. Individuals and private groups may accept, reject, embrace, ignore, hire for, fire from, lease to, evict from, anyone for any reason. In other words, free people must be free to make judgments about their fellows and to act upon them.' Which is merely a rather cumbersome and highfalutin way of saying that banks, restaurants, doctors and bus companies should be free to stick up their old Jim Crow signs, announcing: 'No blacks will be served.'

It's hard to believe that this is a man whose views are taken seriously by many American politicians and our own *Sunday Times*. To disprove Murray's theories about the superior intelligence of white people, one need look no further than his own lamentably inadequate brain. As George Orwell wrote, 'There are certain things one has to be an intellectual to believe, since no ordinary man could be so stupid.'

Alas, Murray's success in dictating the terms of debate has emboldened other polemicists to launch their own racial theories under a guise of pseudo-scholarship. A new book by the American writer Jon Entine, *Taboo: Why Black Athletes Dominate Sports and Why We're Afraid to Talk About It*, claims that the preponderance of black boxers and basketball players in the United States must be all down to DNA – and nothing to do with the fact that professional sport is one of the few available routes out of poverty for some African-Americans. Although Entine may appear to be praising black people rather than denigrating them, his assumptions are no less racist (in the strict sense of the word) than those of *The Bell Curve*. Reviewing the book in the *New York Times*, the biological anthropologist Jonathan Marks asked: 'How can we accept a genetic basis for athletic ability and reject it for intelligence? The answer: we can't. Both conclusions are based on the same standard of evidence. If we accept that blacks are genetically endowed jumpers because "they" jump so well, we are obliged to accept that they are genetically unendowed at school-work because "they" do so poorly.' Marks added that if professional excellence or over-representation were to be regarded as evidence for genetic superiority, 'there would be strong implications for Jewish comedy genes and Irish policeman genes'.

A gentler but no less damning critique appears in the latest *Scientific American*, which points out that Entine's pretence at 'scientific method' is disingenuous, since his book 'does not even attempt to evaluate a robust data set' but uses a few individual cases – Mike Tyson, Michael Jordan – as justification for extravagant racial generalizations. The journal's same issue carries a most salutary piece about the dangers of half-baked extrapolation from dodgy data. It examines the overcrowding-causes-crime scare, which has been fanned for many years by conservative underclass-pundits who maintain that 'behavioural deviancy' in inner cities is the fault of feckless parents producing too many children. The theory, based on experiments with rats in a confined space, turns out to be wholly unsupported by statistical evidence when applied to humans. What actually causes crime and social disorder, the authors find, is not population density but 'scarcity of resources' – or, if you prefer, gross inequalities in the distribution of wealth.

For obvious reasons, such a conclusion is unpalatable to right-wing doom-mongers. So they blame the victims instead. And who better to blame than...well, we all know who lives in those overcrowded inner-city ghettoes, don't we?

(*Guardian*, 10 May 2000)

PLAY POWER

Nevermind

A COUPLE OF MILLENNIA AGO, the Greek writer Menander argued that anyone whom the gods love dies young. The gods in question must, I suspect, work in the publishing industry. 'WHY KURT COBAIN HAD TO DIE,' yells a front-page headline on the June issue of *Q*. The cover of *Vox* promises, 'COBAIN: In Bloom, In Utero, In Memoriam.' Or you may prefer *Select*: '"I hate myself and I want to die" – THE LAST DAYS OF KURT COBAIN'. *The Face*, in a rather more modest type size, has 'Kurt Cobain remembered'. Meanwhile, less than two months after the event, the first full-length book about Cobain's suicide is already in the shops.

Much the same thing happened with the deaths of Elvis Presley and John Lennon. But their passing was also marked by tributes from heads of state and eminent professors; even the squarest old fuddy-duddy could probably have hummed at least a couple of their songs. The mourning for Kurt Cobain, though no less intense, is far narrower. If President Clinton paid his respects, I missed them. (Perhaps he was too busy composing his 'eulogy' to Richard Nixon.) While millions of teenagers and twentysomethings are distraught with grief, almost nobody else can understand what all the fuss is about.

Or so I thought, until I read an article the other day by Bernard Levin, who was apparently so moved by Cobain's death that he hastened to Tower Records and bought Nirvana's best-known albums, *Nevermind* and *In Utero*. Having listened to them all the way through, he 'realized that this stuff is not just shouting, and is even up to making a musical point'. Indeed, Levin seems to have experienced some sort of spiritual awakening while sitting through such ditties as 'Rape Me' and 'Territorial Pissings'. Grunge music, he concluded, was a necessary purgative for the anger and violence of its youthful devotees – 'a kind of solace amid the carnage' of the modern world. 'Shall the young lead us back to sanity via the howling and screaming of pop singers?' Levin wondered. 'Shall Kurt Cobain be remembered not for the terrible blackness that drove him to his death but for the realization that he had another, and much more important, task to do on this earth?'

What surprised me about Bernard Levin's article was not its semi-mystical optimism – this is, after all, the same Levin who once thought that the Bhagwan Shree Rajneesh might save the world – but the fact that he was aware of Nirvana's existence at all. I began to wonder if there were other undiscovered Cobain-worshippers among the great and the good.

'It's a rock group, is it?' Dame Barbara Cartland replied when I sought her views. 'We don't know anybody who likes rock music. No, wait – what about Katie Boyle? She moves with so many different people. She might know...Unless you ask that man – what's he called? Buddy Greco, that's it. Do you think he'd know? He's a funny little man...'

Twenty-five years ago, the suicide of a teen icon would probably have elicited an earnest, anguished sermon from the Archbishop of Canterbury. So I rang Lambeth Palace to ask whether Dr Carey felt there were lessons to be learned from Kurt Cobain. 'I honestly couldn't tell you,' a woman in his office replied. 'Let me see if anyone here knows.' A minute later, she returned. 'I've just had a word with the Archbishop's press secretary and she says she's never heard him mention Nirvana at all.'

Undaunted, I then tried the uncrowned queen of Britain's liberal intelligentsia, Baroness Warnock. She told me that she had been 'amazed by Bernard Levin's piece'; beyond that, however, she had little to offer. 'As far as I'm concerned I knew this person [Cobain] existed, but that was about all.'

Next stop was Terry Eagleton, the incurably modish media don who is now Warton Professor of English at Oxford. 'I'm afraid you've drawn a blank here,' he said, with perhaps a tinge of regret. Nirvana 'never meant anything very much to me. Not my kind of thing, I'm afraid, Oh dear no. I don't actually work in popular culture.'

I decided to skip a generation and speak to some of the baby-boomers who grew up on rock music and rebellion. Derek Hatton was, in his time, a hero of sorts to disaffected young people – though his clothes were rather snazzier than those of the irredeemably scruffy Cobain. What, I asked, was his favourite Nirvana song? He paused for about half a minute. 'Have I got a favourite? No, I haven't really. It's one of those things, if it's on I'll listen to it and say that's nice, but...just a minute.' There was another long pause. He sighed heavily several times. The thought occurred to me that he probably hadn't heard any of Nirvana's records but was unwilling to confess as much. 'Um, no.' (Another loud sigh.) 'I can't think...It's something I've never grabbed hold of, you know what I mean? I still like a lot of sixties stuff...And I like U2, Status Quo...' But not grunge, perhaps? 'No,' he finally conceded, 'not so much grunge.'

In desperation, I turned to a bona fide rock writer – Dave Hill, the biographer of Prince. He, at least would have something to say about poor old Kurt, wouldn't he? Apparently not. 'I'm a 36-year-old former rock critic and I couldn't name you a single song by Nirvana,' he told me. 'I listen to my old Al Green records and occasionally get the Clash out. The Nirvana thing just passed me by.' In mitigation, he pointed out that 'the audience for popular music is so diffuse now'.

It certainly is. Thirty years ago, when there were just three radio stations and two television channels, we all suckled at the same cultural teat. 'Come mothers and fathers throughout the land/And don't criticize what you can't understand,' Bob Dylan used to sing, but in fact many of the pop groups of the time appealed equally to mums and teenagers. Look at the list of performers who appeared in the Beatles' Christmas shows in 1964 and 1965: the inane Freddy and the Dreamers, the ultra-hip Yardbirds – and Rolf Harris, who was basking in the success of his song 'Tie Me Kangaroo Down, Sport'. One need only try to imagine an equivalent line-up today – Pearl Jam sharing the bill with Kylie Minogue, perhaps, or Barry Manilow gigging with Snoop Doggy Dogg – to realize just how fragmented pop culture has become.

During the 1960s, the Beatles were praised by Harold Macmillan as 'our best export'. Harold Wilson, not to be outdone, awarded them MBEs. The Master of Brasenose College, Oxford, invited them to dine at high table; the music critic of *The Times*, William Mann, went into raptures over their 'pandiatonic clusters' and 'flat sub-mediant key switches'. Even the noisier and naughtier Rolling Stones were granted a certain respect by the establishment: in August 1967, immediately after appearing in court on drugs charges, Mick Jagger attended a 'secret rendezvous' (later broadcast on peak-time television) with the Bishop of Woolwich, the editor of *The Times* and Malcolm Muggeridge.

The parents of the 1990s seem to have no such curiosity about their children's heroes. After dozens of phone calls, I have still not found anyone over the age of thirty-five – apart from Bernard Levin and myself – who knows what Kurt Cobain sounded like. Recalling that John Major has teenage offspring, I even put the question to 10 Downing Street. 'Has he ever listened to Nirvana?' a spokesman repeated incredulously. 'I'll try to find out.' Given how reluctant the PM usually is to commit himself to anything, I am not expecting an early answer.

(Observer, 29 May 1994)

The Macaulay Culkin effect

ALTHOUGH DAVID LODGE'S television adaptation of *Martin Chuzzlewit* has another five weeks to run, we already know how the story ends. Lodge wanted to round the film off with a triple marriage ceremony but was overruled by his director, Pedr James, who preferred a Forrest Gump-ish soliloquy from Tom Pinch. On one point, however, the two men were in full agreement: that Charles Dickens' own closing scene, in which the inappropriately named Charity Pecksniff was jilted on her wedding day, would be unacceptable to a prime-time audience. As a result, the BBC now stands accused by some critics of being 'willing to sacrifice the integrity of literary works to boost ratings'.

The irony would not have been lost on Dickens. For it was largely 'to boost ratings' that he sent young Martin Chuzzlewit to the United States, after learning that the novel's early chapters – published in serial form – had been selling poorly. An interlude of knockabout comedy at the expense of the Americans would, he reasoned, be popular with his British readers. More ironically still, these episodes have been dropped from the television adaptation, lest they harm the BBC's chances of selling the series in America. Professor John Carey has described this omission as 'astounding', but it is nothing of the sort. It is what happens whenever film producers buy the rights to a novel: in return for a large cheque, the author is expected to sit and watch as his or her beloved work is torn to shreds, hurled into a salad bowl and smothered with Thousand Island dressing. As my friend Ian McEwan has said of his experiences in Hollywood: 'It's an opportunity to fly first-class, be treated like a celebrity, sit around the pool and be betrayed.'

He should know. Eight years ago, under commission from Twentieth Century Fox, McEwan wrote *The Good Son*, a story about a twelve-year-old orphan who has a psychotic cousin. The studio bosses sat on the script for ages, fearful that neither children nor psychotics were crowd-pullers. After the success of *Home Alone* and *The Silence of the Lambs*, they changed their minds and put

McEwan's film into production. All was going swimmingly until Kit Culkin, whose gruesome son Macaulay had recently been signed up by Fox, suddenly insisted that his boy be given the lead part. For good measure Kit Culkin also brought in a different director – who, without bothering to tell McEwan, hired a new scriptwriter to ladle on the Thousand Island dressing. 'I found myself basically sacked from my own script,' Ian recalled. 'By any standard of behaviour – even Hollywood standards – that's pretty poor.'

I should have thought it was par for the course. A crime writer of my acquaintance was surprised a few years ago to hear that an American film company wanted to use one of her books as a 'vehicle' for Sigourney Weaver. When the author pointed out that her heroine was English, the film moguls replied: 'Yeah, well, of course we'll have to make a few changes...' My friend turned down the proffered fistful of dollars.

More often, however, the lure of the loot proves irresistible. The British writer Pat Barker also expected 'a few changes' when Hollywood bought the rights to her book *Union Street* – and boy did she get them. Iris King, the main character in the novel, is an eighteen-stone widow in her mid-fifties who lives in a squalid council house in Middlesbrough; when she discovers that her daughter is pregnant, she is so horrified that she supervises a back-street abortion. Barker first suspected something was amiss when the film company told her that Barbra Streisand and Mary Tyler Moore were being considered for the part. She told the producer that she thought both women were grotesquely unsuitable, and they were duly dropped – to be replaced by Jane Fonda. Barker was gobsmacked: 'A woman who has had her breasts augmented and a couple of ribs extracted wasn't exactly my idea of perfect casting for Iris.' An even bigger surprise was in store, when her agent gave her the glad tidings that Robert de Niro was going to play Stanley, Iris's lover. The agent was slightly puzzled, since she didn't remember a character called Stanley in the book. Barker explained that this was because there wasn't a character called Stanley.

From then on, the 'few changes' came thick and fast. Iris's hovel in the North of England was transformed into a smart house with a garden in New England. The climactic scene of the novel – the daughter's abortion – vanished without a trace. Instead, Iris and Stanley rode off happily into the sunset, with Fonda sitting on the bars of de Niro's bicycle – no mean feat for a woman who should have been eighteen stone. Before Charles Dickens starts turning in his grave at the liberties taken with *Martin Chuzzlewit*, he should bear in mind that at least the BBC didn't cast Madonna as Mrs Gamp.

Why do film people mess about so recklessly with the stories which they

have acquired at such expense? The usual explanation is that they are insensitive philistines who can't appreciate the writer's art. But I wonder if they
aren't playing a far more intellectual game. Modern literary theory is a hotbed
of arguments about the 'death of the author', the 'privileging of the text' and
the need to resist 'closure'. Could it be that Hollywood, in its mischievous
way, is trying to put the theory into practice? The circumstantial evidence is
strong. Bertolt Brecht, for instance, used to complain that traditional bourgeois drama is presented as a complete, unalterable 'art-object', thereby pre-
venting its audience from 'reflecting critically' on the 'mode of
representation'. To quote Professor Terry Eagleton's summary: 'The play does
not stimulate them to think constructively of how it is presenting its characters and events, or how they might have been different.' This is certainly not a
charge that anyone could level at *Stanley and Iris* – or the BBC's multiple-
choice endings for *Martin Chuzzlewit*.

I can't prove that the director of *Stanley and Iris* is a student of Brecht's
'alienation effect', or Walter Benjamin's essays on 'The Author as Producer'
and 'The Work of Art in the Age of Mechanical Reproduction', or Roland
Barthes's 'Introduction to the Structural Analysis of Narrative', or Pierre
Macherey's 'Theory of Literary Production'. But I know of at least one person
in the film industry who certainly is. In between adapting classic novels for
television, this man has produced a string of books with such titles as *The
Modes of Modern Writing, The Novelist at the Crossroads* and *Working with Struc-
turalism*. His name? David Lodge.

I rest my case.

(*Observer*, 13 November 1994)

Shove ha'penny, live from Wembley

TONY BLAIR MAY not have won many friends by tinkering with
Clause Four and dabbling in devolution, but with his crusade to save
the soul of British sport he seems to have stumbled upon a genuinely
popular cause. Even the *Daily Telegraph* concedes that 'when it comes to football, Mr Blair has found a winner'. Cheered on from the touchline by his new

fans in the Tory press, Blair argues that the £7 million transfer of Andy Cole to Manchester United is an unacceptable manifestation of 'sport's growing obsession with money-making' – an obsession that has also given us pyjama cricket, sponsors' slogans on shirts, corporate hospitality boxes and other delights. He is, of course, quite right. Where he goes badly wrong is in assuming that the trend can be reversed – that, if only we elect a Labour government, we shall return to those happy, foggy days when you could buy a bag of chips, a pint of milk stout and a match-winning centre forward and still have change from half a crown.

Once a sport has nibbled at the fruit of the tree of knowledge, it can never again return to Eden. Footballers are no more likely to forgo their six-figure salaries than is Cedric Brown of British Gas. If it is true, as Tony Blair says, that 'the values that make soccer the people's game are being eroded', then the people will have to find a new game. It's a job for which we are well qualified. Although modern Britain has little to boast about in most departments, we can still take pride in having invented – or reinvented – more sports than any other nation on earth: squash, snooker, football, rugby, lawn tennis, table tennis, badminton, cricket, golf, racquets and even water polo.

But do we take pride in it? Not often. On a holiday in Switzerland last month, I mentioned to my companions that skiing was introduced to the country by Sir Arthur Conan Doyle. They refused to believe me, suspecting that this was some sort of hallucination brought on by a surfeit of *glühwein*. Faced with universal incredulity, I even began to doubt the story myself. Having checked with Sir Arthur's memoirs, however, I find that it's true: staying in Davos in the winter of 1894–5, Doyle asked a local shopkeeper to make him a pair of wooden skis – on which, to the great amusement of the natives, he then hurtled downhill through the snow. As one of Doyle's biographers later observed, he thus devised 'a form of sport which in after years became the chief pastime of Switzerland, though there is no evidence that the people who made fortunes out of it acknowledged his pioneer work with cash, or even thanks'.

His lack of reward was, to use a cliché from another of our sporting exports, par for the course. American baseball players have been on strike for the past season in protest at the inadequacy of their seven-figure salaries; but has anyone spared a thought for the poor British, who have never received a penny – still less a million dollars – in royalty payments from the game we created? Instead of acknowledging our copyright, the Americans have simply stolen it by rewriting history. In the early years of the twentieth century, an American tycoon set up a seven-man commission of inquiry (including two senators) to 'learn the real facts concerning the origin and development of the game'. The commission's report, published in 1907, insisted that baseball was a pure-bred American idea, which owed nothing to 'foreign' influences such as the English game of rounders. This has been the received wisdom ever since – in spite of the fact that the first published rules of baseball, which appeared in Robin Carver's *Book of Sports* in 1834, were copied out verbatim from the chapter on rounders in *The Boys' Own Book*, printed in London five years earlier.

So it goes: sporting pioneers cannot expect gratitude. True, there is now a marble plaque at Rugby School commemorating 'the exploit of William Webb Ellis who with a fine disregard for the rules of football, as played in his time, first took the ball in his arms and ran with it, thus originating the distinctive feature of the rugby game, AD 1823' – but when he actually committed his historic foul the reaction was far less complimentary. His captain gave Ellis a severe dressing-down, and apologized to the other team for the boy's shamefully unsportsmanlike behaviour.

In Rugby Union, at least, we can still hold our own against international opposition – which is more than can be said of our footballers, cricketers or tennis players. I suspect this may well be because Rugby Union remains a quasi-amateur game, and amateurishness is one quality which this country has always had in abundance. Once professionalism creeps in, however, we're doomed. A century ago, when transfer fees were illegal, England was the pre-eminent footballing nation; now, for all the millions of pounds invested in the game, we can't even qualify for the World Cup. Instead of grumbling about the unfairness of it all, Tony Blair should come up with an alternative; as he is so fond of pointing out, we live in a changing world and must adapt accordingly. Since Labour has used this argument to justify ditching most of its commitments – on Europe, nuclear weapons, trade unions – it can surely be persuaded to shed its sentimental attachment to soccer as well. There is no shortage of ancient British pastimes that could, with a bit of encouragement from the People's Party, be established as the new People's Game – caber-tossing, egg-rolling, up-helly-aa, Long Alley bowls, conkers, marbles, shove ha'penny.

In due course one of them might become as big a crowd-puller as football – whereupon competitors could demand huge salaries, politicians would bemoan the corruption of a noble game and sports editors would demand the sacking of the English team manager after our humiliating defeat by Albania. No matter: we have an inexhaustible supply of replacements. Anyone for pancake-racing?

(Observer, 29 January 1995)

Men about the house
behaving badly

'LIKE MOST PEOPLE,' the television scriptwriter Andrew Davies told an interviewer last month, 'I've always dreamed of writing a sitcom.' How very true. Virginia Bottomley dreams of little else; so, I suspect, does Sir Isaiah Berlin. If Shakespeare were alive today, he'd undoutedly be writing sitcoms. 'A new double-whammy of comedy on BBC1 from the master of mirth!' the *Radio Times* would announce. 'In *Love's Labour's Lost*, four men vow to have nothing to do with women; but then a bevy of beautiful ladies arrives – with hilarious consequences! The fun-feast continues with *A Midsummer Night's Dream*: lovely Hermia is told by her father to marry Demetrius, but she really loves Lysander; so the sweethearts elope to the woods where they meet a host of zany characters – including a "rude mechanical" called...Bottom!'

Since Shakespeare is not alive today, we shall have to make do with Andrew Davies, who brought us *Middlemarch* and *House of Cards*, and whose commitment to 'excellence' and 'quality' is second to none. 'Drama is all about making masterpieces,' Davies said in his recent Huw Wheldon Memorial Lecture, 'not chasing tired old shows downmarket after ratings.' Now that he has turned his hand to sitcom, however, he seems to have come badly unstuck. The unanimous critical opinion is that Davies's new series, *Game On!*, is not a masterpiece at all; it is, rather, an attempt to chase a very tired old format indeed.

The 'situation' of his comedy is that two sexually frustrated young men are sharing a flat with a gorgeous woman. This should not be confused with *Men Behaving Badly*, in which a gorgeous woman lived in a flat immediately above the one occupied by two sexually frustrated young men. Nor is there any resemblance to *Man About the House*, where the flatmates were two gorgeous women and one sexually frustrated young man. After an exhaustive search in the invaluable *Guinness Book of Sitcoms*, I am pleased to report that Andrew Davies has indeed come up with something original.

Not very original, I agree; but it's no easy task to find an entirely new angle for a flat-sharing farce. Put four young men in the flat, and some smart alec will point out that *The Young Ones* beat you to it. Three young women? Been there, done that: it was called *Take Three Girls*. Two young women? *The Liver Birds*. So you try something really wacky: four elderly women living together. And then, too late, you remember *The Golden Girls* – not to mention the disastrous *Brighton Belles*.

Authors are often advised to 'write about what you know'. But what do the creators of sitcoms know? Most of them are middle-aged, middle-class white men who worry about their mortgages, mow the lawn at weekends and occasionally help out at the Residents' Association barbecue. Every morning they get up, engage in jokey banter with the wife and children over breakfast and then retire to the study to seek inspiration. Inevitably, the first image that comes into their head is a suburban house with a surburban family. Some writers go no further: witness *2Point4 Children* and *Ever Decreasing Circles*.

But the true pro will want a gimmick or an inversion which can provide the necessary comic tension. Glance at the titles of a few sitcoms and you'll see how the trick is worked: *And Mother Makes Three* (young widow bringing up children), *Father, Dear Father* (divorced dad bringing up precocious daughters, sharing house with his eccentric mother), *Bachelor Father* (single man bringing up foster-children), *My Son Reuben* (possessive Jewish mother forever worrying about her ageing bachelor son), *My Old Man* (grumpy old chap living with his daughter and son-in-law), *My Wife's Sister* (widow living with sister and grumpy brother-in-law), *Two Plus Two* (couple moving into new house only to find another couple living in the front bedroom), *My Wife Next Door* (separated couple accidentally moving into neighbouring cottages). Any fool can play the game, and many fools do. No wonder the poor viewers are in a permanent state of déjà vu.

It is often argued these days that pop music has reached the end of its natural life, since the three-chord song has a finite number of permutations. The same could be said of sitcoms – except that, because they predate rock'n'roll, they reached saturation point rather earlier. Look at *The Upper Hand*, ITV's prime-time entertainment for Friday nights: the woman of the house is a power-suited executive; her lover is a house-husband; and, to increase the chuckle quotient, the woman's mum lives with the couple. The 'humour' here depends on two assumptions: that the notion of a female breadwinner is self-evidently absurd, and that mother-in-law gags are still funny. If you didn't know that *The Upper Hand* was written and recorded in the 1990s, you'd assume it had been conceived sometime between the Suez crisis and the Beatles' first LP.

In his famous book *Le Rire*, published almost a hundred years ago, the French philosopher Henri Bergson defined comedy as 'any arrangement of acts and events...which gives us, in a single combination, the illusion of life and the distinct impression of a mechanical arrangement'. But sitcom writers have long since abandoned the struggle to create an illusion of life, thereby leaving their mechanical arrangements as glaringly obvious as the pipework outside the Beaubourg building. When even an author as talented as Andrew Davies has to resort to minor variations on the old flat-sharing formula, the genre must be doomed.

Well, almost. There is, surprisingly, still one plotline that has never been used. In a chapter on 'The Comic in Situations', Bergson proposed the following scenario: a henpecked husband escapes by divorce from the clutches of his wife and mother-in-law; the wife then marries a man with a grown-up daughter – who in turn weds the henpecked husband. 'Lo and behold,' Bergson concluded, 'the double combination of marriage and divorce brings back to him his former wife in the aggravated form of a second mother-in-law!' You can almost hear the studio audience's hysterical guffaws.

Poor old Bergson. His treatises on consciousness, vitalism and other important philosophical concepts may have been highly influential – but what he really wanted, like Andrew Davies and the rest of us, was to write a sitcom. Perhaps some television company will belatedly take up his rib-tickling idea.

(*Observer*, 19 March 1995)

Pay up! Pay up! And play the game!

A FTER ENGLAND'S MEDIOCRE performance in the Second Test against New Zealand in 1994, Mike Atherton issued a characteristically gloomy verdict: 'We were substandard in all departments.' Unduly modest, I'd say. Although many of England's bowlers are trundling dullards, and our batsmen often turn out to be accident-prone prodders, we are still the undisputed world champions in one department – our ability to come up with excuses for failure.

Sometimes these excuses are merely farcical, as when the *Cricketer* magazine complained in 1992 that Pakistani players had been swigging orange squash from bottles placed just beyond the boundary during their Test victories over England. 'Allowing bowlers to swig away at the edge of the field cannot be conducive to the public good,' it thundered. After a disastrous tour of India the following winter, the chairman of selectors, Ted Dexter, announced that his men weren't shaving often enough: 'We have to look at the whole matter of facial hair.' By the summer of 1993, when England lost the Ashes series, Dexter had decided that supernatural forces must be at work. 'We may be in the wrong sign or something,' he said after Australia's victory in the Lord's Test. 'Venus may be in the wrong juxtaposition to somewhere else.' The preposterous Dexter – the embodiment of the old cricketing 'gentleman'– gave way soon afterwards to the gritty Yorkshireman Ray Illingworth, an archetypal professional. But some things didn't change. Although England managed to win the first of the 1994 Tests against New Zealand, it took rather longer than Illingworth would have wished. His reaction? He fired the English team's chaplain, the Reverend Andrew Wingfield-Digby, and banned the use of mobile telephones in the dressing room.

Harmless idiocy, perhaps. But the subtext to these absurd whinges is rather less amusing. 'Questions have been asked at Lord's these last few days to which it is hard to find reassuring answers,' John Woodcock, the reactionary doyen of cricket writers, announced in *The Times* after England's dismal performance against the South Africans two years ago. After rounding up the usual scapegoats ('Why do England wear their beach clothes on the balcony? Why don't England captains shave in the morning?'), he reached his main point: 'Why is the advice of a great patriot and bowler like Alec Bedser never sought?'

This is the same 'patriotic' Bedser who chaired the meeting of the English Test selectors in 1968 which chose to omit Basil D'Oliveira from the English squad to tour South Africa. President Vorster's government had made it clear for months that it would cancel the tour rather than play against a team that included a 'coloured' man, and the decision by Bedser and his colleagues was greeted with jubilation by South African racists: the minister of the interior said that it was a great day for apartheid. In the 1970s, Bedser was a founder member of the National Association for Freedom, an extremely right-wing outfit that was rather keen on South Africa. Perhaps because its acronym was too embarrassingly apposite, NAFF later changed its name to the

Freedom Association, but its politics remained the same.

The administrative elite of the MCC and TCCB has long been stuffed with men such as Alec Bedser, who could never see the point of boycotting apartheid and who now speak of having 'resumed' our contests with South Africa, as if the past quarter of a century had been nothing more than a tiresome and unnecessary interruption. English cricket is, God knows, in a sorry state, but the last thing it needs is advice from flannelled fools of his kidney. Alas, that is just what it gets, and the fools in question are as likely to be found in the Cabinet room as in the committee-members' boxes at Lord's. It is no coincidence that Alec Bedser's greatest admirer – often seen sharing a joke with him at the Oval – is the Rt Hon. John Major, PC, MP. Just as the game's administrators have long treated cricket as an extension of their own brand of politics, so our political leaders like to imagine that government is merely sport by other means.

John Ruskin coined the phrase 'pathetic fallacy' to describe the Romantic poets' habit of attributing emotions to inanimate nature – happy flowers, mournful skies and so on. A related syndrome, which one might call the athletic fallacy, is the tendency to see English sporting performances as somehow symptomatic of the nation's health. In 1993, after the English football team had suffered the ultimate humiliation of being beaten by the US, the *Independent* juxtaposed photographs of John Major and the then England coach Graham Taylor at the top of its front page. 'Two leaders faced their critics yesterday, determined to carry on come what may,' a headline announced. An editorial in the same day's *Sun* made the connection even more explicitly. 'Did you wake up this morning with pride in your heart?' it asked. 'You probably didn't...Whether it is football, cricket or politics, we seem to be on a losing run...Why is Britain playing below form, why are our heads down? Because we are not being led. The British people are a great crew. What we need now is a great skipper.'

The earnest belief in sporting triumph as an essential precondition for political recovery is an ancient and enduring one. As Orwell commented, if it's true that the battle of Waterloo was won on the playing fields of Eton, it's equally true that every subsequent battle has been lost there. And no game lends itself more easily to analogy and metaphor than cricket, with its exotic lexicon of googlies and long-hops, no-balls and sticky wickets. In nineteenth-century England, the future of the empire was often thought to depend on whether one could keep a straight bat, and the phrase 'it's not cricket' entered the language as a lofty put-down of those lesser breeds who refused to accept the Lex Britannica as holy writ. Many people over a certain age can probably still recite Sir Henry Newbolt's 'Vitaï Lampada', which proceeds from a school cricket pitch ('Ten to make and the match to win') to a bloodstained battle-field where a young officer rallies the ranks by crying: 'Play up! Play up! and play the game!'

To give him his due, Newbolt was not quite as frivolous or foolish as he may sound to modern ears. What he was trying to suggest, perhaps rather clumsily, was that war should be conducted according to proper rules – a rea-sonably humane point of view with which no supporter of the Geneva Con-vention could disagree. 'War, like life itself, is a game or else a brutality worse than bestial,' he explained. 'To win a game makes the pulses leap, but not to massacre – that only chokes and disgusts.' No such excuses can be offered for most of his contemporaries. Although 'Vitaï Lampada' is the best-known manifestation of the athletic fallacy from Victorian and Edwardian England, it was merely part of a vast literature on the subject. In 1859, a correspondent in *The Times* blamed the British army's poor performance in the Crimea on defi-ciencies in the cricket system at Eton. On the outbreak of the Boer War, the *Lorettonian*, a public-school magazine, printed a poem called 'To Loretto from Her Volunteers', which promised:

> For the bowling we are ready
> And will keep the right foot steady
> And try to not flinch as they hum past our head.

The supposed correlation between skill at games and martial prowess was still thriving at the time of the First World War, when Old Stonyhurstians in Kitchener's army were told by their school mag that 'the name of English sportsmen lies at stake'. E. W. Hornung, the creator of Raffles, extended the conceit yet further in his poem 'Lord's Leave, 1915':

> No Lord's this year: no silken lawn on which
> A dignified and dainty throng meanders.
> The schools take guard upon a fiercer pitch
> Somewhere in Flanders.
> Bigger the cricket here: yet some who tried
> In vain to earn a colour while at Eton
> Have found a place upon an England side
> That can't be beaten.

It reads like parody, but Hornung's intentions were wholly sincere. In later verses, the Germans are presented as demon bowlers firing their Krupp shells from 'a concrete grandstand far beyond the boundary'. Although the conditions are dreadful – 'no screen and too much mud for cricket lovers' – this is one match in which appeals against the light are not permitted.

Now that few Britons go to war, political success is measured not in military victories but in the opinion polls; and the sporting analogy has been adjusted accordingly. In 1994, a leader in *The Times* argued that the English cricketers who capitulated to the West Indies in Port of Spain had taken their cue from 'the John Major Ramblers' at Westminster. 'As Tory MPs leave for their Easter break,' the *Daily Express* editorialized, 'it is not events at Westminster they should have uppermost in their minds but those in the West Indies, where the England cricketers have just lost the Test series.' With both Mike Atherton and John Major, the paper explained, it had been assumed that a change of leader would be enough to end Britain's losing streak. 'Alas, Test cricket is not like that. And nor is politics.'

In a variation on the pathetic fallacy, the philosopher Gilbert Ryle invented the term 'category mistake' for the yoking together of two incompatible concepts – 'love is a rectangle', say, or 'Thursdays are crimson'. The juxtaposition of the English cricket eleven with Her Majesty's government is undoubtedly a category mistake but, under the captaincy of the sports-mad John Major, it has become hard to avoid. One could even argue, only slightly fancifully, that he was propelled into Downing Street by a cricket metaphor. In the autumn of 1990, Margaret Thatcher announced at a dinner in the City of London that she expected some fast bowling from her critics but would hit it to the boundary. Her Deputy Prime Minister, Sir Geoffrey Howe, resigned in a huff shortly afterwards, explaining to the House of Commons that he had gone to the European wicket only to find that Mrs Thatcher had broken his bat. Howe's speech precipitated the downfall of Mrs T and the elevation of John Major, a man who in 1956 had been named as the London *Evening Standard*'s 'cricketer of the month' after taking seven wickets for Rutlish Grammar School.

And so the metaphor became flesh. In the summer of 1995, while preparing to announce his challenge for the Tory leadership, John Redwood took himself off to Lord's to watch the West Indian batsmen in action. The following day, not to be outdone, John Major emerged from Conservative Central Office brandishing a cricket bat. He was then whisked away to Lord's. How could Redwood top that? Easy: he had himself photographed in cricket whites (which always make a man look better anyway), and let it be known that he had just returned from playing in a real game – something Major hadn't managed for several years, unless you count his brief innings in a charity match in Zimbabwe and a few balls delivered in South Africa for the benefit of the cameras. Both candidates were so keen to boast of their cricketing enthusiasm that I half expected them to dispense with the election and settle their differences in a single-wicket contest at Lord's instead.

Major's belief in the magical potency of cricket goes way beyond the metaphorical. Inspired by his twin dreams of a classless society and a revival of competitive games in schools, the Headmasters' Conference proposed last year that the government should fund private education for working-class children who are good at sport, as public schools can 'foster the spirit of fair play and sportsmanship exemplified by models such as C. B. Fry, who played football and cricket for England after leaving Repton'. The public-school heads could hardly have chosen a more convincing refutation of their theory that healthy bodies make for healthy minds. Brilliant athlete though he was, Fry was also a nincompoop. In his autobiography, he paid fond tribute to the 'innate dignity' of Adolf Hitler, whom he described as a 'great man'. The Führer had many attributes, but a spirit of fair play was not one of them.

Nevertheless, Major and his colleagues were clearly attracted by the idea of reviving the Corinthian spirit. The sports minister Iain Sproat, who edits *The Cricketers' Who's Who*, has claimed that if we had more organized sport in schools 'we'd have fewer little thugs like those who murdered James Bulger' – thus echoing the conclusion of the Royal Commission on Public Schools, as long ago as 1864, that 'the cricket and football fields are not merely places of exercise and amusement; they help to form some of the most valuable social qualities and manly virtues'.

This view of the game as a force for moral hegemony – devised by the upper classes of Victorian England, now perpetuated by the 'classless' John Major – is astonishingly tenacious. C. L. R. James, who as a Trinidadian Marxist might have been expected to take a radically different perspective, was utterly seduced by it: the heroes of his seminal work *Beyond a Boundary* were Thomas Arnold, the nineteenth-century headmaster of Rugby, Thomas Hughes, the author of *Tom Brown's Schooldays*, and W. G. Grace. James was dazzled by the 'grandeur' and 'moral elevation' of Arnold's ideas, apparently happy to overlook the fact that these ideas included a contempt for the working class and a terror of universal suffrage. What mattered, in C. L. R.'s view, was that Arnold introduced compulsory games for his pupils, 'the only contribution of the English educational system of the nineteenth century to the general educational ideas of Western civilization'. One can almost hear Major applauding.

Even Mike Marqusee, another expatriate Marxist, gave his book *Anyone But England* the ominous subtitle *Cricket and the National Malaise*. Thankfully, unlike James, Marqusee is not in thrall to the Victorian public-school ideology. He is scathing about the quasi-feudal system that governed cricket until well into this century, with its distinction between gentlemen and players, and its determination to perpetuate 'the myth of an enduring and natural social hierarchy'. The game's aristocratic administrators, who pretended to be guided by a sense of 'fair play', were in fact anything but fair to the working-class players whose talents they exploited. 'Pray God no professional may ever captain England,' said Lord Hawke, Yorkshire CCC's president, as recently as 1924.

All most deplorable. Does Mike Marqusee rejoice, then, that patrician amateurs such as Hawke – who kept vulgar commerce out of cricket, or at least at a safe distance from it – have been replaced by hard-headed professionals? Like many cricket-loving socialists, he is in something of a quandary. 'To the war between modernizers and traditionalists, there is no end,' he writes. 'But a socialist would be foolish to take sides in it.' This is for fear that his love of leg-spin bowling and uncovered wickets might place him on the same side of the barricades as 'the crusty old traditionalists'. Too timid, my dear fellow. Some things are true even though the *Daily Telegraph* says they are true; similarly, one should allow that some things in this country are worth conserving, even though crusty old traditionalists happen to think so too.

The trouble with the potentates of the MCC is that, in certain important respects, they are not nearly reactionary enough. Given their hostility to almost everybody outside their own magic circle – black people, women, undeferential foreigners – one would expect them also to shun the barbarian hordes of PR consultants, marketing whizz-kids and corporate-hospitality merchants. Go to any county ground and you will see that this is not the case. While devoting its energies to keeping women out of the Long Room at Lord's, and banishing free spirits such as David Gower from the Test side, the MCC has done nothing to prevent rich corporations from disfiguring the Arcadian scene – the boundaries, the players' shirts, the very pitches themselves – with logos and huckstering slogans. Even the umpires now wear the colours of a privatized electricity company. 'There is no doubt,' the promotions manager of the Test and County Cricket Board said recently, 'that it is primarily the image of the game and its track record of successful association with the business world which continue to attract corporate advertisers.' Silly me. I thought the attractions of the game were its guile and grace, and those other qualities sketched so evocatively by Mike Marqusee: 'the arc of a straight six, the crisp, dismissive sound of a square cut, the sudden savagery of a stump uprooted by pace...the solace of an empty county ground on a bright weekday morning...the sublime waste of an entire day on something with no redeeming purpose whatsoever'.

But perhaps I'm being unfair. In their willingness to let the money-changers into the temple, the blazered buffoons at Lord's may have unwittingly proved themselves to be true traditionalists after all. Although it is tempting to see the history of English cricket as a transition from feudalism to capitalism via imperialism – without any intervening period of civilization – the story is slightly more complicated than that. Look at this cutting from the *St James's Chronicle* of 26 July 1796: 'Yesterday a cricket match was played on Hounslow Heath between the Westminster Scholars and those of Eton for 100 guineas a side, which was won by the Westminster Scholars.' So much for the equation of amateurism with the public-school spirit. A month later, the astounding sum of 1,000 guineas was put up as prize-money for a game between eleven one-legged pensioners and eleven one-armed pensioners – a stunt that even Rupert Murdoch's Sky TV might hesitate to repeat.

The lure of lucre spread far beyond these freak-shows. In 1815, the following advertisement appeared in the *Morning Herald*: 'A grand match will be played in Lord's New Cricket Ground, St John's Wood, Marylebone, on Wednesday July 12th, and the following days, between the county of Surrey against All England, for 1,000 guineas a side.' It was only at the start of the Victorian age that this rampant commercialism – which included bets for huge stakes and plenty of skulduggery and nobbling – was extinguished. In his book *The Cricket Field*, published in 1851, the Reverend James Pycroft referred to that now-forgotten era as 'a dark chapter in the history of cricket'. Eric Parker's *History of Cricket*, written a hundred years later, also described money as the 'curse' that 'blackened the game' in the early nineteenth century. But,' he concluded cheerfully, 'the game was greater than the curse...Cricket was nobler than some of its players, and the straightness of it, in the balls bowled and in the bats that hit them, won in the end.'

Parker's belief that cricket's evolution ended sometime in the mid-nineteenth century, having reached an unimprovable state of perfection, is almost touching in its imbecilic innocence. It reminds me of the final chapter of *1066 and All That*, in which 'America was thus clearly top nation and history came to a .' Nevertheless, he is half right. Cricket may be a relic of a pre-industrial age, a version of pastoral, a colonial legacy, a continuation of the class war by other means, a gimmick for vote-hungry politicians and an alluring investment opportunity. But the game is greater than the curse, whether that curse be the oligarchs of the MCC or the predatory magnates of satellite television. George Orwell's description of England as 'a family with the wrong members in control' applies equally well to cricket: those of us who play or spectate will always find a way of preserving its subtle delights from the irresponsible uncles and bedridden aunts who seek to thwart us. On visits to India and Sri Lanka I have often watched children hurling themselves into the game with joyous abandon, equipped with little more than a set of makeshift stumps and a dust-track wicket. These youngsters have probably never heard of Lord Hawke, or Kerry Packer. What they do know is the thrill of a well-struck drive, a perfectly pitched yorker, a soaring catch. With such pleasures still available, even to the poorest citizen, who needs metaphors?

(*New Statesman*, 31 May 1996)

THE MEDIUM IS THE MESS

The debaucher

WHEN HE WAS A SCHOOLBOY, Rupert Murdoch supplemented his pocket money by catching water-rats and selling their skins at sixpence a time. His other wheeze was to collect horse manure from the Murdoch family's paddocks, put it in bags and sell it to neighbours for their gardens.

William Shawcross, Murdoch's biographer, cites these enterprises as proof of the lad's 'business flair', without noticing quite how appropriate they are for a man who went on to found an empire built on rats and filth. Today, the Dirty Digger earns his millions from, *inter alia*, the following: Fox TV, an unspeakably vulgar American television network whose most popular programme is *Studs*, a 'game show' in which young people leer at one another and brag about their sex lives; the *Sun*, which not so long ago filled its front page with a snatched photograph of Lord Gowrie entering a massage parlour; the *News of the World*, which performed the same service for Major Ronald Ferguson; and the *Sunday Times*, which published the Hitler diaries without bothering to establish their authenticity.

Rupert Murdoch has made a fortune from selling excrement and, in the process, has debauched our culture and corrupted our youth, producing a generation of lager louts, sex maniacs and morons – or 'New Britons', as their proud godfather, Andrew Neil, prefers to call them. When Murdoch dies, I trust he will be buried in a graffiti-spattered riot-zone in Newcastle or Rochdale, preferably in an area where every house is defaced by a Sky satellite dish; his headstone can then carry the simple message *Si Monumentum Requiris, Circumspice*. More than 2 million houses have Sky dishes already, and it is predicted that by 1997 the figure will be 12 million. William Shawcross evidently thinks that this is good news. Indeed, Shawcross seems to admire almost everything about his subject. Much criticism of Murdoch, he tells us, 'has been repetitive, and uninteresting – or made by political opponents'. He quotes, with an entirely straight face, Anna Murdoch's claim that her husband 'is a very good and moral human being'.

This may come as a surprise to those who remember the Willie Shawcross of the 1970s, the passionate young radical who was forever denouncing Henry Kissinger for warmongering in Cambodia. But like his father, a politician who lurched from Left to Right and earned himself the nickname of 'Sir Shortly Floorcross', young Willie has now moved on. He quotes approvingly the crappy old cliché, which holds that anyone who isn't a socialist at twenty lacks a heart, but anyone who is still a socialist at forty lacks a head. One can see why he wishes to believe it. In his twenties, Shawcross was married to the socialist feminist Marina Warner, and his journalism was a sustained attack on the rich and powerful. Now, minus heart but plus head, he is to be seen around town with the Hon. Mrs Olga Polizzi, a Conservative member of Westminster City Council who is one of Lady Thatcher's best friends, and he earns his living by eulogizing a multimillionaire press baron and pornographer.

But there is more to it than mere floor-crossing. When Shawcross began work on this book [*Rupert Murdoch: Ringmaster of the Information Circus*], Murdoch refused to cooperate in any way, preferring to save his best stories for his own memoirs, for which he had been paid an advance of $1 million by the American publisher Random House. Towards the end of 1990, however, Random House appointed as its president Harold Evans, the man whom Murdoch had sacked as editor of *The Times* almost ten years earlier. 'The wheel of fortune makes me your publisher as you used to be mine,' Evans wrote to Murdoch. 'I think it will be a happier experience for you than it was for me. But please don't pull any punches.' Murdoch, understandably miffed at being delivered into the hands of his enemy, went off the whole idea of writing an autobiography. Instead he repaid his advance and got on the blower to Shawcross, offering him every assistance. What happened next is, unwittingly, rather well described in Shawcross's account of Harry Evans's first encounter with Murdoch:

> Harry Evans had fallen in love...There was nothing unusual about that. Murdoch would become immensely, sometimes disproportionately, enthusiastic for a new recruit or adviser. For them his attention could be overwhelming. His charm was so intense and yet so unaffected, so natural and yet so strong, that few people came away from their early meetings with him other than mesmerised. Harry Evans was susceptible.

And so, to judge by his book, was Willie Shawcross. Having fallen in love with Murdoch, whom he describes as a 'genius', Shawcross has produced a long, tedious chronicle of the Dirty Digger's business triumphs, written in a species of American thrillerese which is as euphonious as a pneumatic drill. Here is his account of the great financial crisis of 1990, when Murdoch nearly drowned in debt but was saved by an American banker, Ann Lane:

> News Corp was a company that had never known serious financial covenants. The whole company's ethos was to wing it. Ann Lane wanted to put a stake through the company's heart...Lane was playing hardball...Murdoch told her, 'I think it's over. I don't think I'm going to get there with this bank. I'm coming over. I can't deal with it on the phone.' Lane knew how he felt. This roll on 7 December was for a total of A$1 billion. But Pittsburgh could turn the roll into a dive. She felt as if they were falling over a cliff in slow motion...In any restructuring there are always creditors who do not want to help. Often they have good reason to get out. Sometimes they are just playing chicken...Any federal regulator could 'launch'. If a huge warhead were needed, the chairman of the Federal Reserve could do it, and indeed Murdoch tried to reach him on that day...

Every so often, when not blithering about chickens who dive over cliffs while playing hardball with huge warheads which have a stake through their heart, the author recalls his subtitle and treats us to a page or two about the 'Information Circus' of which, so he says, Rupert is the ringmaster. 'The Information Age offers fabulous opportunities, but there is no guarantee that they will be seized,' Shawcross gibbers excitedly. 'What matters are the choices of those barons who control the fantastic new holdings in the global village. Companies like [Murdoch's] News, Sony, Bertelsmann, Time-Warner, are now in a position to set the agenda for the millennium.' I expect their ethos will be to wing it.

Notwithstanding its oppressive length, this book is an extended feature article rather than a biography. There is no attempt to fathom Murdoch's character or discern patterns of behaviour – and I can see why. For Murdoch's most consistent characteristic is that he is a liar and a hypocrite, a man who cannot be relied upon to keep his word. Shawcross cannot bring himself to believe such a thing of his new sweetheart, and so episodes which would reveal Murdoch's dishonesty are skipped lightly over, ignored altogether or – most alarmingly – rearranged to suit the author's prejudice in favour of the Dirty Digger.

Let me give an example. In December 1990, Channel 4 broadcast a documentary which alleged that Murdoch's empire had been 'kept alive by questionable accounting policies and tax dodging on a world scale' and that 'Murdoch personally has been involved in suspect share dealings'. It was a brilliant and damning exposé. Shawcross, however, pretends it was a fuss about nothing. 'It insinuated that he [Murdoch] had dealt in the company's shares at a time when he had possessed "price-sensitive information",' he writes. 'But these transactions were already matters of public record and in Australia, unlike in Britain, there was no ban on directors dealing in options in their own company.' I wonder who gave Shawcross that idea. In fact, Section 128 of the Australian Securities Code specifically prohibits share-trading by any company director (or employee) who has 'price-sensitive information' about the company – which Murdoch undoubtedly had at the time of the dubious deals.

I suspect that the person who misinformed Shawcross about insider dealing was probably the same rat-and-manure merchant who fed him another lie, namely that the circulation of *The Times* did not rise during Harry Evans's editorship. Shawcross accepted this 'fact' without checking. In the original manuscript of his book, which was circulated to various interested parties earlier this year, he wrote: 'Furthermore, as the months went by, Evans's changes [at *The Times*] did not produce any significant rise in circulation.' In fact, to quote from the 1981 annual report of News Corporation, signed by Murdoch himself, 'With no promotion, circulation [of *The Times*] has begun to move upward from 276,000 to more than 300,000 today.' When this was pointed out to Shawcross (by Evans himself, I believe), the manuscript was hastily amended. A piffling matter, perhaps, but it suggests an alarming willingness on Shawcross's part to believe whatever the Digger tells him. Which, in turn, suggests that Shawcross has not understood Murdoch at all.

The book is so disfigured by inaccuracies – sins of omission as well as commission – that it would take me all year to list every one of them. But perhaps one more example will suffice to show both Murdoch's unreliability and Shawcross's myopic focus. It concerns Messrs William Collins, the publishers. In 1981, having tried unsuccessfully to take over Collins, Murdoch was left owning 41.7 per cent of the company's voting stock. Ian Chapman, the chairman and chief executive, asked him to promise that he wouldn't launch another unwelcome takeover bid. At a meeting in the London flat of his solicitor, the blessed Lord Goodman, Murdoch duly gave an 'unequivocal undertaking' to Ian Chapman and Sir Charles Troughton, the deputy chairman of Collins. And, surprise, surprise, Murdoch then betrayed them, making a hostile bid for Collins.

You would not learn much of this from Shawcross's book. There is no mention of the meeting in Goodman's flat, and only a passing reference to the undertaking – 'Chapman said Murdoch assured him he would not make a hostile bid for the company' – which implies that this is an unsubstantiated claim by Ian Chapman, rather than undisputed fact. During the same period, Murdoch made other 'unequivocal' promises to the Australian Broadcasting Tribunal (when buying a television station in Sydney) and to the British government (when buying Times Newspapers); in both cases, his word turned out to be written in wind and water. Doesn't this begin to look like a habit, one that a biographer might profitably discuss? Not to Shawcross.

Which is a pity, for Murdoch is an interesting figure – or would be, in the hands of a more perceptive biographer. A penny-pinching spendthrift, an anti-establishment power-groupie, a licentious prude: the man throbs with contradictions. There was a glorious moment in June this year when the head of Fox TV was summarily fired by Murdoch for bringing a male stripper on to the podium at a News Corp seminar in Aspen, Colorado. 'One thing this company has to stand for,' the owner of the *Sun* and the *News of the Screws* said gravely, explaining the severity of the punishment, 'is that there are limits.' Amazingly, nobody sniggered,

(Review of *Rupert Murdoch: Ringmaster of the Information Circus*,
by William Shawcross. *Literary Review*, September 1992)

Rupert's cultural revolution

R UPERT MURDOCH'S LOVE AFFAIR with China operates on the good old-fashioned principle of give and take. Rupert took BBC World Service TV off his Star network; the Chinese government gave him permission to start a cable TV station in Guangdong. Rupert ditched Chris Patten's book *East and West*; President Jiang Zemin returned the favour by allowing the film *Titanic* into Chinese cinemas, to the delight of Twentieth Century Fox (prop. R. Murdoch). Rupert celebrated the fiftieth anniversary of the Universal Declaration on Human Rights last December by visiting Beijing and expressing his 'admiration for China's tremendous achievements in every respect over the past two decades'; President Jiang has now repaid this compliment by granting an exclusive interview to *The Times* on the eve of his state visit to London.

For such an important assignment the newspaper naturally sent its best reporter, Lord Rees-Mogg. This could have been a serious diplomatic faux pas. Five years ago, the Chinese ambassador to London wrote to *The Times* protesting at Rees-Mogg's 'gross misjudgments', and as recently as April 1996 Moggie was still attacking China's 'insensitive and repressive' regime. Luckily, however, he is now fully on-message. During their meeting in the Great Hall of the People last week, the Sage of Somerset and the Butcher of Beijing were soon giggling like a couple of schoolboys. 'We are almost at the same age, but I'm two years older than you,' President Jiang chuckled. 'I was told you are a Lord. What's the difference between a Lord and a Sir?' They went on to chat about their families. 'He obviously has a very warm affection for his grand-children,' Mogg wrote. 'Overall I found the President very relaxed, very friendly, very intelligent, a man at ease with himself...Among world statesmen he reminds me most of President Eisenhower, a natural conciliator.'

Eventually the banter had to stop. Mogg knew there was a question he must ask, but wasn't sure how to put it without causing offence. He phrased it thus: 'With globalism, the whole world is involved with issues of nationality and ethnic tension. In Britain we have our own controversies with our national relationship with Europe. You have the problem of the minorities. I have met the Dalai Lama on a number of occasions and regard him as a distin-guished religious leader. Is there any prospect of reconciliation?' There was a moment's tense silence. Had Mogg been too fearless, too hard-hitting? 'I was not expecting to be asked that question,' Jiang replied at last, 'but you have asked it in a very friendly way, so I will answer it.' The President then revealed that his country's influence on Tibet had been entirely benign. Mogg was deeply impressed by this evidence of 'humanity' and 'respect for religious beliefs'.

Perhaps Rees-Mogg hasn't read a 1,000-page report published by the US state department last month, which highlighted the 'particularly severe' viola-tions of religious freedom in China and six other countries. Or perhaps he agrees with President Jiang's spokesman, who issued this enigmatic statement through the Xinhua news agency on 14 October: 'The problem of "religious persecution" does not exist in China...Faced with the sound conditions of reli-gion in China, they [the American government] throw stones at China like a blind man feeling a giant elephant.'

Very well. If the blind elephant-groper is a tainted source, what do Rees-Mogg and Murdoch think of Amnesty International, which has produced copious evidence of Jiang's 'respect for religious beliefs' – the torture of Bud-dhist monks and nuns, the rounding up of prominent Muslims, the detention of Christians? The only religious groups tolerated in China are those which register with the government and submit themselves to the authority of the official religious affairs bureau. Worshippers who refuse to obey these conditions are sent off to do forced labour in 'thought reform' camps until they renounce their faith. As a devout Roman Catholic, Rees-Mogg must surely know about Father Yan Weiping, a priest in Beijing, who was arrested in May while celebrating Mass. Later that night he was found dead in the street, having apparently been thrown from a fifth-floor window by his interrogators.

Even worshippers who do sign up with a registered group aren't immune. Early this summer, in the northern capital of Xian, the government ordered the state-run Christian organization to demolish the city's biggest and oldest church, because 'the growing congregation posed a threat to stability'. When about fifty parishioners occupied the building to protect it from being razed, a huge goon-squad of police stormed in and arrested them. Political dissidents could also tell Lord Rees-Mogg a thing or two about their President's 'humanity'. As Amnesty points out, hundreds of people are still in jail for their part in the pro-democracy protests that were crushed in Tiananmen Square ten years ago. Liu Xin was just fifteen years old when he was arrested in June 1989; by the time he is let out, in June 2004, he will have spent half his life behind bars. Liu Baiqiang, thirty-one, who was already serving a ten-year jail sentence in June 1989, allegedly wrote 'Long Live Freedom' on tiny scraps of paper in his cell; according to the official indictment, he then 'attached these to the legs of locusts and released the insects into the air'. He was given a further eight years for 'counter-revolutionary incitement and propaganda', and is not due for release until December 2003.

All this is ignored by milord Rees-Mogg and *The Times*, which instead fills a whole page with sycophantic drivel about Jiang Zemin's 'peace and goodwill' towards his people. 'Confucius made it the first of his five universal rules that "justice ought to be practised between an emperor and his subjects",' Mogg drools. 'This idea of a direct contract between ruler and people – one interpreted in a very different way from modern Western understanding – still stands at the heart of Chinese government.'

A rather different picture of this Confucian justice can be found in Isabel Hilton's brilliant new book, *The Search for the Panchen Lama* – which, in the words of one reviewer, 'illustrates with stark clarity the true intentions of the Chinese government with regard to their unfortunate Tibetan neighbours'. The book has had glowing notices: 'excellent' (*Observer*), 'compelling' (*Daily Mail*), 'fascinating' (*Independent*), 'deeply felt and carefully researched... damning' (*Sunday Telegraph*). Oddly enough, however, no review of *The Search*

for the Panchen Lama has yet appeared in any newspaper owned by Rupert
Murdoch. I do hope that President Jiang finds some way of expressing his
gratitude.

(*Guardian*, 20 October 1999)

Black power

'THE NEWSPAPER INDUSTRY in London has long attracted proprietors of immense ego,' Conrad Black once observed, reviewing a
biography of Lord Beaverbrook. He should know. Although the proprietor of the *Telegraph* has not yet been admitted to the circle of hell reserved
for great Fleet Street megalomaniacs – the first Lords Northcliffe and Rothermere, Robert Maxwell, Beaverbrook himself – he is on the waiting list. At a
time when many media moguls (Rupert Murdoch, for one) seem curiously dry
and desiccated, Black is a tycoon of the most old-fashioned kind – noisy, iras-
cible, flamboyant, pugnacious and hugely opinionated. While his rivals accel-
erate down the infobahn, he restricts his business to the printed word. In the
age of the soundbite, he continues to deliver his own views in lengthy, thun-
derous philippics. He has been well described by one critic as 'a man who
rejoices in the intellectual and financial status of not giving a damn, of living
in a kind of Basil Fawlty wet dream in which Basil has not only won the football pools but has also swallowed a thesaurus and somehow acquired another
fifty points of IQ'. While still in his forties he wrote a 522-page autobiography;
a mere two years later, he is the subject of a 468-page study – unauthorized,
but sympathetic – by the financial journalist Richard Siklos. Not bad going for
a man who, until a decade ago, had scarcely been heard of outside his native
Canada.

True, he doesn't yet have a peerage, but according to Siklos he has drawn
up a short list of titles he might adopt. He would be in the House of Lords
already if Margaret Thatcher were still PM; alas, she was driven from office
too soon to reward him for his devotion. 'John Major, I don't call upon him in
the same way,' he informs Siklos. 'While our relations are perfectly cordial
there's not the same or even slightly comparable rapport that there was with

her. I had considerable admiration for her and she knew that. And she was much more comfortable with people in my – if I may put it this way – socioeconomic echelon...' I take this to mean that Major is less overawed by excessive wealth than his predecessor was. If true, it is rather to his credit.

Nevertheless, I can see why Black would regard it as a defect, since he himself is one of the most slavering power-groupies of modern times. To get a picture of his 'echelon', one need look no further than the Hammer-horror cast he has assembled for the international advisory board of his holding company, Hollinger – Lord Hanson, Sir James Goldsmith, Lord Rothschild, Lord Carrington, Henry Kissinger, Zbigniew Brzezinski, Richard Perle, Paul Volcker, Giovanni Agnelli, Chaim Herzog and, of course, Baroness Thatcher. In 1992 he acquired a new wife to match his new status, in the mini-skirted form of Barbara Amiel, a reactionary glamour-puss who confesses that she finds powerful men 'sexy'. She too is now a director of Hollinger, and has lately been hired to write a weekly column for one of her husband's newspapers, the *Daily Telegraph*. 'Barbara Amiel will speak her brilliant mind,' the paper boasted; no doubt flunkeys of the Emperor Caligula said something similar when he appointed his horse to a consulship.

The Canadian squillionaires who preceded Black in Fleet Street, milords Thomson and Beaverbrook, offer two distinct models of newspaper ownership. Thomson was a benign conservative who never interfered with his editors; according to rumour, the only section of the paper he read with close attention was the classified advertising. Asked why he kept buying newspapers, he replied: 'To make more money.' When the same question was put to Beaverbrook, by the Royal Commission on the Press, he explained: 'I ran the paper purely for propaganda, and with no other purpose.' A tease, perhaps, but also the truth. Like so many press barons, Beaverbrook was a man of passionate but loopy convictions which would have been unlikely to find their way into print had he not happened to own the printing works. As Hugh Cudlipp has commented, of Beaverbrook's campaign for Empire Free Trade, 'he merited no more attention than a bearded nut in Trafalgar Square carrying a placard proclaiming that "Judgment is Nigh"; but he owned newspapers.'

If Black's admirers are to be believed, he is Thomson and Beaverbrook rolled into one – a brilliant businessman and a serious student of politics and history, who can pursue both propaganda and profits with equal panache. But I have my doubts. Although his purchase of the *Telegraph* at a bargain price was an undeniable coup, Siklos's book confirms that this owed more to luck than judgment. Certainly there has been little evidence of his management

genius in the past year or two. Having announced that he would not rise to
Rupert Murdoch's challenge by cutting the cover price of the *Daily Telegraph*,
he then did just that, infuriating his City backers. Last autumn, quite unneces-
sarily, he precipitated the resignation of the *Telegraph*'s editor. Since then, he
has been obliged to issue a public warning that his company's profits are
plummeting.

What of his political nous? As one might expect of someone whose men-
tors are Henry Kissinger and Margaret Thatcher, he sees only the world as it is
reflected in the polished mahogany of boardroom tables. In October 1991,
shortly after buying the *Spectator*, he fired off an angry letter protesting at the
magazine's 'unbalanced' coverage of George Bush. 'In recent years,' he added,
'the *Spectator* has published an error-riddled cover piece on the Reichmanns
and Canary Wharf and a gratuitous sketch of Lord Carrington. Lord Carrington and Paul Reichmann would have the right to expect to be treated fairly by
the *Spectator* even if they were not directors of the companies that ultimately
owned it and friends of its proprietor.' A year later, after Bush had lost to Bill
Clinton and Canary Wharf's troubles had forced the Reichmanns' main company into bankruptcy, Black took up his pen once more. 'Subsequent events
demonstrate that Stephen Robinson was not mistaken in taking the Democratic quest for presidency seriously and Edward Whitley, the author of the
Canary Wharf piece, was essentially correct...I would like to retract those
aspects of my letter.' This is pretty rich coming from a newspaper proprietor
who is forever berating reporters for their slipshod methods. ('My experience
with journalists,' he testified to a Canadian Senate Committee, 'authorizes me
to record that a very large number of them are ignorant, lazy, opinionated,
intellectually dishonest and inadequately supervised.') As the episode shows,
his own sense of reality is no more reliable than that of the drunkest hack in
the gutters of Fleet Street – or, for that matter, of a bearded nut in Trafalgar
Square.

But he owns newspapers.

(Review of *Shades of Black: Conrad Black and the World's Fastest-Growing Empire*,
by Richard Siklos. *Observer*, 28 January 1996)

Megaboob man

I NCREDULITY AND OUTRAGE were the main reactions to the deal between Express Newspapers and a multimillionaire pornographer. Journalists resigned in protest, questions were asked in the House; thousands of readers cancelled their orders; and several large supermarket chains withdrew their advertising.

That was in 1987, when the owner of the *Sunday Sport*, David Sullivan, was invited by Lord Stevens of Ludgate to revamp the *Daily Star*. Within two months the partnership was cancelled. Thirteen years on, milord Stevens' successor – sensitive, Labour-supporting Lord Hollick – has handed over the entire Express Group to Richard Desmond, the publisher of *Asian Babes* and *Horny Housewives* as well as *OK!* magazine. If there was any incredulity or outrage (except from jilted bidders such as the *Daily Mail*), I missed it. Not a murmur from the House of Commons or Downing Street; merely one or two brief, regretful editorials suggesting that Lord Beaverbrook might be turning in his grave.

One must be careful to avoid false nostalgia here. Beaverbrook told the Royal Commission on the Press that he ran his newspapers for the sole purpose of making propaganda. He also had a list of people he disliked, including Lord Mountbatten and Noël Coward, whose names were never to be mentioned in the *Daily Express* or the London *Evening Standard*. Nevertheless, Beaverbrook had certain redeeming qualities as a newspaper owner: he liked journalists and editors; he was beholden to no one; and, in practice, he preferred mischief to propaganda. (Hence his recruitment of trouble-making mavericks such as Michael Foot, Tom Driberg, A. J. P. Taylor, James Cameron, and Vicky and David Low.) True, Beaverbrook assured *Express* readers in the late thirties that 'Britain will not be involved in a European war' and ordered the *Evening Standard*'s editor, Frank Owen, to stop being beastly to the Nazis. But Owen ignored the instruction; and with two other Beaverbrook favourites (Michael Foot and Peter Howard) he then wrote *Guilty Men*, a ferocious pamphleteering attack on appeasers.

I cannot see Desmond tolerating such independence or insubordination. On the day after he bought the *Daily Express*, his chief boxwallah Paul Ashford added a large panel plugging *OK!* magazine to the top of the front page without bothering to tell the editor. 'The *Express* will probably expand most quickly if it is a well-liked newspaper, and people do not like newspapers that pick fights,' Ashford told the *Sunday Telegraph* last weekend. 'People will do business with the *Express* because we give them the best deal, we will be nice to you and look on it as a long-term relationship.' In other words, celebrities who have done deals with *OK!* – Posh and Becks, Catherine Zeta Jones and Michael Douglas – can expect full immunity from any criticism in the *Express* newspapers. Harmless enough, perhaps, but once the principle has been established it can be extended. Not so long ago, Desmond invited William and Ffion Hague to pose for *OK!* magazine. The Hagues did not reply, much to Desmond's annoyance. Suppose they had agreed to his request, however. Would the Tory leader also have a guarantee that the *Express* 'will be nice to you and look on it as long-term relationship'?

It was the Empire Free Trade campaign run by Lords Beaverbrook and Rothermere which provoked one of the strongest attacks ever made on British press barons. 'What the proprietorship of these papers is aiming at,' Stanley Baldwin told an election meeting in 1931, 'is power, and power without responsibility – the prerogative of the harlot throughout the ages.' He was wrong, of course: power without responsibility is the prerogative of the customer. The harlots are the public figures who sell themselves to these rich and grubby men. One such is Tony Blair, who has been shamelessly prostituting himself to the right-wing tabloids ever since he became leader of the Labour Party. He flew all the way to Australia to speak at Rupert Murdoch's annual corporate shindig; he paid extravagant homage to Sir David English of the *Daily Mail*, a newspaper which has never faltered in its determination to destroy the Labour Party by fair means or foul.

Now, all of a sudden, he complains that 'the anti-European press' is 'fundamentally dishonest'. But a prostitute who has continually encouraged a favoured punter to keep returning for more can't turn round after a few years and denounce him for cheating on his wife. Blair surely hasn't forgotten one of the services he performed to satisfy the *Sun* during the 1997 election campaign: an 'exclusive' interview, published two weeks before polling day, in which he tickled all the paper's erogenous zones.

'I know exactly what the British people feel when they see the Queen's head on a £10 note,' he murmured seductively. 'I feel it too. There's a very strong emotional tie to the pound which I fully understand. Of course there are emotional issues involved in the single currency. It's not just a question of economics. It's about the sovereignty of Britain and constitutional issues too. I do understand how passionate people are about the pound.' Understandably enough, the *Sun* was thrilled by these fond endearments. 'His remarks were aimed at boosting his image as Blair the patriot,' it reported. 'Mr Blair accepted that millions of voters are opposed to ditching one of the nation's most historic symbols.' Like a Soho punter in the throes of ecstasy, the newspaper persuaded itself that this was True Love rather than a financial transaction.

Many prostitutes have testified that it is depressingly easy to go on the game – and horribly difficult to escape from it thereafter. As the publisher of top-shelf magazines such as *Megaboobs* and *Nude Readers' Wives*, Desmond ought to understand the nexus of sex and commerce better than most. When he proposes that Tony and Cherie invite *OK!* magazine into their delightful home in return for 'a long-term relationship' with the *Express* and the *Daily Star*, will Blair have the strength to say no?

(*Guardian*, 29 November 2000)

***

RICHARD DESMOND, the porn baron who now owns the *Daily* and *Sunday Express*, gave £5,000 to the Conservatives in 1997. Shocking, eh? The *Independent on Sunday* seems to think so, describing its revelation as 'a further blow to the Tory leader William Hague'. Never again, it suggests, can Hague claim the 'moral high ground'. But a small donation four years ago is pretty negligible when compared with the shameless wooing of Dirty Desmond by our clean-living, church-going Prime Minister. Shortly before Christmas, the *Express* owner was invited to Number 10, where Tony Blair and Alastair Campbell plied him with cups of tea and flattery galore, and assured him that they were looking forward to a beautiful new friendship.

Is there any tycoon, however disgusting, before whom Blair won't genuflect? Apparently not. But let's try to give him the benefit of the doubt: if the PM studied the porn website fantasy121.com, which is owned by Richard Desmond, he might have truly believed that the *Express* boss was indeed a New Labour kinda guy.

Desmond is, for instance, determined to end the misery of social exclusion. Hence the appearance on his website of nude photos of Grace, a 79-year-old woman who would like to meet men under the age of twenty for sex. She doesn't want our pity, just the opportunity for fair trade ('Would you like a pair of my wet panties?'), and finishes with this touching appeal: 'If you are planning a sex party, don't forget to invite me.'

The *Express*'s proprietor is also disturbed by the pressure on women to conform to male ideas of female perfection. Women such as Karen of Croydon, who admits, 'I have always been fat and a little shy. I always thought that men would not find me attractive. I am poor too. I live in a horrid little room and I don't work because I can't find a job. It's pretty miserable really...Until a week ago I was still a virgin.' Then Desmond's tireless social workers came to the rescue. 'When the time came for the photographer to fuck me I was so wet he didn't need to bother with foreplay.'

It isn't only in the UK that Desmond performs his little deeds of kindness. He has an ethical foreign policy too. As a blurb on the website notes, 'It's hard to believe that we found Shaheeda in the slums of Bombay in India. She was begging in the streets so we offered her $100 to strip for us.' Now hear her reaction as Desmond's special envoys distribute much-needed clothing: 'Oh, these clothes are so soft. These panties feel so good and I find myself becoming sexually aroused. I have never done this before.' Unlike some aid workers, the chaps from fantasy121.com don't believe in quick fixes. Proper advice is needed so that she can stand on her own two feet – preferably with legs akimbo. 'As a beggar, men never ask you for sex,' she says. 'If I could earn money having sex, I would. It is not easy to appear sexy when you are dressed in rags and cannot wash. I don't know how to thank you for this day.' Moved by her gratitude, Desmond's men reach for their wallets again. 'We gave Shaheeda an extra $100,' they reveal, 'because she let all of us fuck her. We are trying to arrange for her to go to America and become a major porno movie star. Watch this space.'

I hope that Blair and Campbell will do so. While exploring the site, they'll find further evidence of how effective the private sector can be in tackling third world debt: 'We found Maria on the beach at Rio de Janeiro. We offered her $5 and she agreed to come back to our hotel and to pose for these pictures.' While she disrobes, Maria looks rather puzzled – as well she might. 'I am just a poor peasant. I live by collecting rubbish. Why do you want to see my pants? OK, I will take my pants off, for $5 I will do anything. It is much money. Do you all want to fuck me? OK, but I want five more US dollars, OK? How many of you will fuck me? Twelve of you? Holy Mother of God! OK, let's get started then.'

This is the charitable side of Desmond, which he is too modest to talk about. Five years ago his magazine *New Talent* even ran a competition called

'Win a Shag', in which the prize was a night in a London hotel with a buxom 'model' called Carol. Another of *New Talent*'s wheezes was to offer its readers conducted tours of the office. A former employee of Desmond's porn mags tells me that 'you could always tell which days they were because all the female staff would be out of the office, hiding in toilets or smoking outside. I once saw a series of photos of these days which culminated in readers eating sugar cubes out of models' vaginas – right on Desmond's £80,000 boardroom table!'

Who knows? If Desmond's *Express* titles back New Labour in the next general election, perhaps Blair will repay the debt by offering their readers the chance to try something similar in the Cabinet room.

(*Guardian*, 17 January 2001)

Don't mention it

I N AN EDITORIAL MARKING the fiftieth anniversary of VE Day, the *Daily Mail* advised that 'the colours in which this pageant is painted should be strong. It is a wonderful chance for indifferently taught children to learn what their grandsires did in the war and why.' One year on, the paper has belatedly decided to reveal what the grandsire of its proprietor, Viscount Rothermere, got up to during the crucial years before the war. All last week the *Mail* was serializing an authorized biography of the first Lord Rothermere and his barmy brother Lord Northcliffe – 'The Men who Made the *Mail*'. Old man Rothermere, we learned, was 'under no illusion as to the nature of the Nazi Party': it was led by ruthless expansionists who would 'stop at nothing'. By 1935, he was in a state of near-despair 'because of Britain's steadfast refusal to rearm even in the face of conclusive evidence that the Nazis were dangerous men bent on war'.

Anyone reading this would have assumed that Rothermere and his newspaper spent the 1930s alerting the nation to the Nazi threat – which isn't quite the case. He was certainly in favour of rearmament; but, with the crackpot logic for which the *Daily Mail* has long been famous, he was also a raving anti-Semite under whose guidance the *Mail* became the only paper in Fleet Street to offer Hitler its enthusiastic support. As early as September 1930, Rother-mere wrote a long article praising 'the services that the National Socialist Party has rendered to Western Europe'. Three years later, he reassured his readers that so-called 'Nazi atrocities' were nothing more than 'a few isolated acts of violence such as are inevitable among a nation half as big again as ours'. The persecution of the Jews was a wise precaution: 'In the last days of the pre-Hitler regime there were twenty times as many Jewish government officials in Germany as had existed before the war. Israelites of international attachments were insinuating themselves into key positions in the German administrative machine...It is from such abuses that Hitler has freed Germany.'

What of Hitler's territorial ambitions? 'We cannot expect a nation of "he-men" like the Germans to sit for ever with folded arms,' Rothermere argued in 1934, 'under the provocations and stupidity of the Treaty of Versailles.' In January 1936, he greeted the third anniversary of Hitler's accession as 'a memorable date in the history of Europe'; the Führer's 'magnetic influence' had placed Germany 'in the forefront of nations'. As late as March 1938, the Anschluss was hailed as proof of the 'speed and effectiveness' of Nazi power. 'Today the resolve of the British people will have nothing to do with the situation in Central Europe. Not one British soldier, not one penny of British money, must be involved in this quarrel which is no concern of ours.'

How does the *Daily Mail* square all this with its insistence that the first Lord Rothermere was an unwavering anti-Nazi? It doesn't; in all the thousands of words it carried about him last week, the *Mail* never once found the space to mention these embarrassing panegyrics – presumably on the old principle that you shouldn't let the facts stand in the way of a good story.

(*Guardian*, 24 April 1996)

His nibs of the fibs

TONY BLAIR'S EXTRAVAGANT tribute to Frank Sinatra may have raised a few eyebrows, but his comments on Sir David English, the former editor of the *Daily Mail*, scaled new heights of hyperbole. 'I counted David English as a friend. He was a truly outstanding journalist. He never lost his love and enthusiasm for his chosen profession and never lost his eye for a good story.' I don't doubt that Sir David English was devoted to his wife and children, nor that he was an expert dancer who once won a gold medal for Latin American Samba at the old Bournemouth Palais. I fully accept that he made pots of money for both himself and his employer, Lord Rothermere. But there must be some limit to the rule about *de mortuis nil nisi bunkum*.

'He was so good at the job,' Roy Greenslade wrote in the *Guardian* last week, 'that it was possible for many to say, as I did, that they disliked his politics, and therefore often loathed his paper, but they had nothing but deep admiration for the man. Why? Because he was the finest practitioner of modern journalism.' Some may say that exaggerated praise is both natural and pardonable in valedictions. But the eulogizing of this 'supreme professional' is an insult to anyone who believes that journalism ought to have some slight connection with telling the truth.

Fittingly enough, even his obituaries were spiced up with falsehoods. They claimed, for instance, that as a foreign correspondent for the *Daily Express* 'he was there when President Kennedy was assassinated in 1963, turning in brilliant copy'. The source for this is an article written by English himself, twenty-five years later, about the indelible impressions left on those people who were 'in Dallas, Texas, with the President. I was one of them.' He had watched the final motorcade and 'witnessed the whole unbelievable scenario spiralling out of control in a frenzy of hysterical violence'. In fact, English was not 'in Dallas, Texas, with the President'; he was more than a thousand miles away, in the *Daily Express*'s New York office. By the time our hero arrived in Dallas, early editions of the *Express* were already cascading from the presses in London with a report filed from Washington by his colleague Robin Stafford. All English did was to find a telephone at the airport, ring his office and shout 'I'm here!' There was no time for him to make any inquiries, let alone send an updated dispatch. The front page of the final edition was unchanged – except for the byline. 'From Robin Stafford, Washington' had become 'From David English, Dallas, Friday'.

The point, however, is not that David English deliberately embellished or falsified his part in the drama. When I exposed his memory lapse in 1988, he was genuinely nonplussed. He really thought he had been in Dallas with JFK, he told a friend, but now he realized that he was wrong. 'There is this peculiar mind which sees things differently,' the friend explained to me at the time. 'When people say the *Daily Mail* is a Tory propaganda sheet, for instance, he just can't see it.' Thus in 1977 he tried to smear the Labour government by publishing a letter that suggested that the National Enterprise Board had approved a 'British Leyland slush fund'. Although elementary checking would have shown him that the letter was a fake, the finest practitioner of modern journalism went ahead anyway. The paper had to pay £100,000 in damages, but even in his front-page apology English couldn't resist introducing yet another lie. 'There is genuine and deserved criticism and anger,' he wrote. 'But on top of that there is the ugly bully-boy campaign of intimidation and fear...We can take the first. The second is an orchestrated campaign to silence us.' In fact, the only bullying and intimidation was being conducted by his own newspaper.

In that same apology, English angrily denied that he had been led astray by political spite. 'Does anyone believe that if we had had a Tory government for the past three years, the paper would have been a sycophantic lapdog silently adoring our rulers with moist and worshipping eyes?' Er, yes. One of his front pages during the 1979 general election was headlined: 'LABOUR'S DIRTY DOZEN: Twelve Lies They Hope Will Save Them'. These lies – such as Labour's allegation that the Tories would increase VAT and prescription charges – were entirely true. So where did the bogus 'story' come from? It had been copied out, almost verbatim, from a press release issued by Conservative Central Office.

Mrs Thatcher gave him a knighthood three years later, and he repaid the favour in the 1983 election campaign with another helpful scoop. 'The Japanese car giant Nissan is to scrap plans for a £500 million British plant if Labour wins the election,' the *Mail* reported. 'Up to 35,000 new jobs are at stake in areas of high unemployment which are Labour strongholds.' This wild fabrication was memorably satirized in a *Private Eye* spoof: 'AIDS THREAT TO LABOUR VOTERS'. Even after his beloved Thatcher was toppled, Sir David was still willing to put the fiction-factory on overtime when duty called. In the 1992 campaign a desperate John Major rang English to plead for more support and the *Mail* obliged with a torrent of mendacity – 'Labour Votes to Tax Poor', 'Labour Leader Defends Extremist Policies' and so on. In the early hours of 10 April, after writing the headline for his final election-night edition ('NICE GUYS DO FINISH FIRST'), he set off for Conservative Central Office to receive the nice guy's gratitude. 'Thank you very much,' John Major said. 'You won the election.' When Neil Kinnock made the same point in his bitter resignation speech a couple of days later, Sir David was loftily dismissive. 'To suggest, as Mr Kinnock has done, that the *Daily Mail* single-handedly won the election for the Conservatives and brought about a Labour defeat is very flattering,' he sneered. 'It ascribes far more influence to us than we would give to ourselves.' Yet he seemed happy enough to accept the compliment on election night when it came from John Major.

Now, only a few years later, a Labour Prime Minister tells us that Sir David English was a dear friend and an outstanding journalist. This, as Winston Churchill nearly said, is the sort of English up with which we should not put.

(*Guardian*, 17 June 1998)

VANITIES OF PUBLISHING

Curling up with a Trollope

ORGET THE LOCAL ELECTIONS: the most important political battleground of the moment is the Trollope Society, whose annual dinner was held last month in the Great Hall at Lincoln's Inn. Just as diplomacy is (according to Zhou Enlai) the continuation of war by other means, so the current vogue for Anthony Trollope is a continuation of politics by other means. Sitting at one end of the top table, resplendent in their dinner jackets, were Robin Cook MP and the Labour-supporting thriller writer Ken Follett, who cheerfully described himself to me as 'a hedonist socialist'; a few places further down I spotted Lord Young of Graffham, one of the more gruesome relics of the Thatcher years. P. D. James, stalwart Tory, and Ruth Rendell, socialist feminist, were both there, engaged in a vigorous struggle for the soul of the bearded Victorian gent who is now more fashionable than Vivienne Westwood or Snoop Doggy Dogg.

If the Left-liberal intelligentsia is at last attempting to reclaim Anthony Trollope from the embrace of Conservatives, it is not a moment too soon. He was in fact a Liberal, who once stood for Parliament on a robustly anti-Tory platform; but since the great revival began, with the formation of the Trollope Society in 1987, the Right has been allowed to claim him by default. Lord Rees-Mogg led the successful campaign for a Trollope monument in Poets' Corner; John Major chose *The Small House at Allington* as his castaway's book when he appeared on *Desert Island Discs*. The Labour Party, as so often these days, has failed to offer any persuasive opposition. In a BBC *Bookmark* programme last October, Roy Hattersley dismissed Trollope as 'an author who is attractive to people who don't really like books and don't really like literature'.

Hattersley is not entirely wrong, of course. There is certainly something fishy about John Major's sudden emergence as a devoted Trollopian; the only other authors he has publicly praised are Robert Goddard (a writer of mediocre adventure yarns) and Jeffrey Archer – whose *As the Crow Flies* Major enjoyed so much that he read it twice. All the more reason, however, to challenge the Prime Minister head-on, rather than merely withdraw from the fray with a sulky shrug as Hattersley has done. The joy of Trollope is that he wrote so much, and about so many subjects, that his works include plenty of ammunition for use against the Majors and Rees-Moggs. Like Shakespeare's plays or the Bible, he provides evidence to support any case one wishes to argue.

It would, for instance, be easy to demonstrate that last month's dinner would have met with Trollope's disapproval. Grace was said before the meal, although he was known to dislike the practice. There were speeches afterwards; yet in *Barchester Towers* Trollope proposed that 'speech-making on festive occasions [should] be utterly tabooed and made as it were impossible'. Diners were served individually by waitresses; Trollope detested this system (known as '*à la Russe*' in his day), preferring to have dishes put in the middle of the table so people could help themselves. He insisted that dinner should always begin with soup; we kicked off with 'Scallops Silverbridge'. Even the venue was suspect: in his short story 'The Spotted Dog', the narrator wanders through Lincoln's Inn – 'than which,' Trollope observes, 'we know of no place in London more conducive to suicide'.

A similar feeling gripped me when I arrived at Lincoln's Inn for the Trollope Society bunfight and caught sight of my fellow guests, many of whom were thin-lipped men with grey hair and spectacles. 'They all look like judges,' my companion murmured – and it turned out that they were. (One judge, who sits on the East Anglian circuit, roamed the hall after dinner cadging cigarettes from strangers. So much for the dignity of the law.) My spirits sank further when I discovered that my seat at table put me opposite a panelled wall on which hung a group portrait of Margaret Thatcher, Lord Hailsham and Lord Widgery – a triple whammy of modern monsters. Gazing around, I wondered how many Trollope-loving legal grandees have ever read, say, *Orley Farm*, in which lawyers are depicted as rogues and the criminal justice system is shown to be a conspiracy to suppress the truth. Precious few, I'd guess. As Roy Hattersley said in that *Bookmark* programme, 'You can talk about Trollope without ever having read him.'

Which brings us back to John Major, who assures us that he has digested 'a large number of his books...well over half of them'. (No mean feat, given Trollope's prolificacy.) Major missed this year's dinner – a pity, as I had hoped to confront him with a few choice morsels from *The Small House at Allington*, his desert-island book. Such as this: 'It is very hard, that necessity of listening to a man who says nothing.' Or this: 'A self-imposed trouble will not allow itself to be banished' – a neat summary of the PM's idiotic antics over qualified majority voting. I had also hoped to cross-examine Major about his even more puzzling fondness for another Trollope novel. 'I'm delighted,' he said recently, 'that *The Way We Live Now* is now a text in school examinations. I think there's a great deal in Trollope that would be ideal for people to study.' Yes indeed. *The Way We Live Now* is a scathing satire on deceit and corruption in public life. As Trollope explained in his autobiography, 'a certain class of dishonesty, dishonesty magnificent in its proportions, and climbing into high places, has become at the same time so rampant and so splendid that there seems to be reason for fearing that men and women will be taught to feel that dishonesty, if it can become splendid, will cease to be abominable.' Isn't this the very dishonesty exemplified by William Waldegrave, whose smirking justification for ministerial mendacity was endorsed by the Prime Minister not so long ago?

And what of the novel's memorable villain, the financier Augustus Melmotte? Those schoolchildren who, with John Major's blessing, are studying *The Way We Live Now* may be interested to learn about the real-life inspiration for Melmotte and his crimes. As John Sutherland writes in his introduction to the Penguin edition: 'About the period 1869–73 British authorities had become seriously alarmed about abuses of international financing operations which, if not actually criminal, made nonsense of traditional business ethics. A select committee of the House of Commons was set up, and was investigating loans with foreign states as Trollope wrote.' Today, a select committee is once again investigating unethical foreign loans, particularly that for the Pergau dam project in Malaysia. Does this ripe historical irony ever trouble John Major when, after a hard day of defending the Pergau deal, he curls up in bed with a good Trollope?

Probably not. For, to quote Major's favourite novelist, nothing 'stinks so foully in the nostrils of an English Tory politician as to be absolutely irreconcilable to him. When taken in the refreshing waters of office any such pill can be swallowed.' When the report of the Scott Inquiry is published, those words would make a splendidly appropriate epigraph.

(*Observer*, 17 April 1994)

Memoirs are made of this

———————————

Y OU HAVE PROBABLY SEEN the advertisement: a photo of a wild-
eyed femme fatale, under the menacing slogan, 'She's back...' It looks
like a teaser for a new horror movie ('Just when you thought it was safe
to go back in the water...she's back'; or 'She's back...and this time it's personal'). In fact, it is promoting a shocking true-crime story – the paperback
edition of Margaret Thatcher's memoirs, *The Downing Street Years*.

There is worse to come. Thatcher is publishing a second volume this
autumn, dealing with her childhood (*Nightmare on Downing Street: The
Prequel*); by the time we have recovered from that, the Tories may well have
lost a general election – whereupon we can expect a full-scale bombardment
of memoirs from embittered ex-members of the Major government. If you
don't believe me, look at the number of ministers from the Thatcher era who
have gone into print – Norman Tebbit, Cecil Parkinson, Nigel Lawson, Geoffrey Howe, Willie Whitelaw, Norman Fowler, Edwina Currie, Lord Carrington, Jim Prior, even Francis Pym for heaven's sake. Chancellors do it;
ministers of state at the Department of Transport do it; educated fleas do it. It
therefore seems reasonable to assume that, in due course, John Selwyn
Gummer and Virginia Bottomley will do it too.

If you are a politician who is past the sell-by date, there are several good
reasons for penning an *apologia pro vita sua*. It provides a 'contemporary
source' for political scientists, thus ensuring that historians yet unborn will
allow you at least a passing mention in their chronicles of *fin-de-siècle* Britain.
It gives you another burst of publicity – chat shows, literary lunches, signing
sessions – at a time when you might otherwise have been sliding out of public
consciousness into the black hole inhabited by James Chuter Ede and Ray
Gunter. And then there's the dosh: Nigel Lawson was paid a six-figure
advance for the *The View from No. 11*, and even a ferrety little nonentity
like Norman Fowler managed to wangle about £40,000 for his riveting
autobiography, *Ministers Decide*.

What advice can we offer to Gummer and Bottomley – apart from begging them to desist? First, get the title right. Flippancy must be avoided, as you will learn by studying the masters of the genre: Lord Hailsham (*The Door Wherein I Went*), Jim Callaghan (*Time and Chance*), Douglas Jay (*Change and Fortune*), Oswald Mosley (*My Life*), Leo Amery (*My Political Life*) and, most admirable of all, Anthony Eden (*Memoirs of the Rt Hon. Sir Anthony Eden KG, PC, MP*).

And so to the text. The opening words are all-important, since they have to grab the attention. Page one of *Against Goliath: David Steel's Story* shows how it should be done: 'David Steel was shot dead outside his house in front of his wife and child. The date was 20 December, 1686. Doubtless there have been times when some wished that his descendant might suffer the same fate.' The first chapter of Denis Healey's *The Time of My Life* is another good model: 'No comet blazed when I was born. But there was a storm all over England.' Do not follow the example of Sir Geoffrey Howe, whose *Conflict of Loyalty* begins with the deeply unexciting news that 'Aberavon was until 1921 the name of the Welsh borough of Port Talbot, where I was born'.

How you fill the rest of the book is up to you, but some conventions ought to be observed. It is bad form to criticize MPs from other parties; by praising them instead, you prove your statesmanlike magnanimity. 'Michael Foot is a highly principled and cultivated man, invariably courteous in our dealings,' Thatcher writes in *The Downing Street Years*. 'If I did not think it would offend him, I would say he was a gentleman.' She vetoed a Tory election poster which carried a 'particularly unflattering' picture of Foot – because 'I do not like personal attacks'.

With MPs on your own benches, however, you can be as rude as you like. 'Nigel had pursued a personal economic policy without reference to the rest of the government. How could I possibly trust him again?' (Thatcher on Lawson). 'Margaret behaved little better to her colleagues after the July 1989 reshuffle than she had before' (Lawson on Thatcher). 'Nobody could complain that I was not giving strong support to the Prime Minister...That certainly did nothing to diminish the signals emanating from Number 10 that could be seen as attempts to downgrade my role' (Howe on Thatcher). 'Geoffrey Howe was now also making mischief...I was not best pleased' (Thatcher on Howe).

Lest readers suspect that you're a narrow-minded thug who is interested only in settling old scores, you must emphasize that you also have what Denis Healey calls a 'hinterland'. Perhaps you once went to an opera; if so, be sure to mention it. And if you have ever met any distinguished figures from the arts world, tell us about them. In *Conflict of Loyalty*, Geoffrey Howe records with pride that he was at Cambridge with Julian Slade, author of the musical *Salad Days*. Not to be outdone, Nigel Lawson once attended a dinner-dance with 'our good friends Adam Faith and his wife Jackie...the film actress Joan Collins was also at our table'. Norman Tebbit trumps them all by revealing that his first girlfriend was Wendy Craig, later the star of such imperishable master-pieces as *Butterflies* and *Nanny*.

Finally, what about your love life? Casting an envious glance at Alan Clark's royalty statements, you may think that bedroom romps are essential. But Clark is an exception to the rule. The two raciest memoirs by politicians in the past thirty years – Woodrow Wyatt's *Confessions of an Optimist* (plenty of womanizing) and Tom Driberg's *Ruling Passions* (even more of the other thing) – were not best-sellers, whereas Willie Whitelaw's indescribably tedious *The Whitelaw Memoirs* sold by the megaton. Sex should be confined to the chapter about your 'difficult' adolescent years, where you can describe how you were seduced by a prefect on the art-room sofa at school. Assuming you were, that is. You may also reminisce about your 'hard drinking and wild parties', as Norman Tebbit did in *Upwardly Mobile*. It was all a long time ago, you explain, and you have grown out of that sort of thing.

Assuming you have, that is.

(Observer, 26 March 1995)

Unteddybearable

TWO POSTS BECAME vacant when Sir John Betjeman died. The Poet Laureateship (salary: £100 and a butt of sack) went to Ted Hughes, who in due course proved himself a worthy heir to Alfred Austin with a toe-curling poem in honour of the Queen Mum's ninetieth birthday. But the more important office – that of National Teddy Bear – was filled by Alan Bennett.

The only other candidate, Philip Larkin, was far too mordant. The National Teddy Bear is allowed (expected, in fact) to be gloomy, but his grumbles must be instantly defused by a wry smile and a self-deprecating shrug. 'I'm not happy,' says a character in Bennett's play *The Old Country*, 'but not unhappy about it.' It might be the author himself speaking. In 1988 he was asked to deliver a lecture on 'Happiness' at Birmingham University. 'I said to them, it wouldn't matter if it was all about unhappiness, would it?' In the event he used the occasion to propound his theory that 'the only time you're really happy is when you're looking back'.

With his nostalgic bathos, his ear for the absurdities of everyday chit-chat, his enjoyment of the petty paraphernalia of class distinctions and his fascination with humdrum suburban lives, he was a natural successor to Betjeman. True, his native Yorkshire was far from Metroland – but vulgarity and snobbery aren't so very different, North or South. (Betjeman, like Bennett, was an addict of *Coronation Street*; both carried a torch for Hilda Ogden.) Anyway, surprisingly few of Bennett's works are Yorkshire-based: *Forty Years On* takes place in a public school on the South Downs, and *Habeas Corpus* is set in 'Brighton's plush, silk-stockinged district of Hove'. Like Betjeman, Bennett had no apparent enemies. 'It's terribly difficult talking about Alan without reeling off a litany of virtues,' Richard Eyre said. 'He's a really lovely man.' He was so cuddly that not even *Private Eye* had ever attacked him.

As in life, so in plays: the mockery was always fond, and the satire celebrated what it seemed to be guying. One of the sketches that made his name in *Beyond the Fringe* was a sermon on the theme 'My brother Esau is an hairy man', which was thought by some in the God-brigade to be offensive until Bennett assured them that it was 'done out of affection'. Thirty years later, when he introduced the Queen as a character in *Single Spies*, he forestalled any protests from royalists by again announcing that 'it's done out of affection'. And, he added tellingly, 'If it isn't, it doesn't work.'

He receives this affection back in abundance. Everybody adored his *Wind in the Willows* at the National Theatre, so much so that it has become an annual Christmas institution. His book of essays and occasional jottings, *Writing Home*, has sold an amazing 200,000 copies in hardback since its publication six months ago. *The Madness of King George*, a film based on his play, won rave reviews and an Oscar nomination. At a time when most other British institutions are sliding into terminal disrepute, the National Teddy Bear is still cherished and respected.

Or is he? Although the critics drooled over *The Madness of King George*, I have yet to meet a cinema-goer who agrees with their verdict. A prominent Thatcherite complained to me recently that the film was 'thoroughly republican, of course'; a couple of days later, a well-known left-wing writer told me it was 'disgraceful royalist tosh'; meanwhile, from the political middle ground, Gerald Kaufman MP has denounced Bennett's screenplay as 'schoolboy scatology' and 'smug pseudo-history'. This is deeply shocking: Alan Bennett is supposed to be above criticism. It's as if someone had mugged the Queen Mum. How could it have happened? And why? The answer was unwittingly provided by another playwright, David Hare, when he argued earlier this month that the source of Tony Blair's popularity – his ingratiating charm, his 'unwillingness to make enemies' – would ultimately prove his undoing. According to Hare, the Labour leader is hobbled by an 'immature desire to be all things to all men', thereby raising expectations which cannot be satisfied.

The same appears to be true of Alan Bennett. Like the Prince of Wales, the National Teddy Bear can bemoan modern architecture or sigh despairingly at the spread of hypermarkets and theme-parks, but he must remain above angry controversy. (As a character in *The Madness of King George* observes, being the heir to the throne 'is not a position, it is a predicament'.) Bennett was, fittingly, a founder-member of the SDP, the 'nice people's party'; but he dropped out as soon as the leaders started squabbling. During the miners' strike of the mid-1980s, he was predictably uncomfortable. 'In those villages where most of the miners were on strike, my sympathies would have been with those who were working,' he explained, 'and in villages where most of the miners were working, with those who were not.' Clear? When *The Madness of King George* was released, Bennett shyly admitted in the *London Review of Books* that he is indeed a supporter of the monarchy. 'Given my royalist inclinations,' he added, 'I haven't followed the goings-on over the break-up of the marriage of the Prince and Princess of Wales...like everything to do with the monarch, I'd just like to be able to take it for granted as one used to do.' But, of course, it can't be taken for granted. Now that a serious debate has begun about the future of our regal figureheads and the nature of our unwritten constitution, the limitations of the Bennett method have been fatally exposed: by striving to be all things to all people, he may end up being nothing to anybody. If he had written a screenplay which put the royalist case with passion and vigour, even republicans might have applauded, since at least it would have given them something to engage with and argue about. Instead, he continues to take refuge in Prufrockian pusillanimity and melancholy drolleries.

There is only one way out: he should resign from his unpaid public office. Teddy bears are all very well, but they have neither claws nor teeth. And, however much we love them, most of us eventually prefer to cuddle up with a real, breathing human being.

(*Observer*, 23 April 1995)

Tits and bums

JOHN LE CARRÉ'S NEW, cut-price novel, *Our Game*, is said by the *Guardian* to have had 'unusually bad reviews'. Really? The *Financial Times* called it 'a wonderful book', one of 'the best novels of our age'. The *Observer* was enraptured by its subtlety, 'the prose equivalent of shifting key changes and soft dissonant chords...an extraordinary novel'. The *Daily Telegraph* described le Carré as 'the essential voice of our time'. If those are bad reviews, most authors would think, give me excess of them. What is most 'unusual' about le Carré's recent novels is how overpraised they are. His last offering, *The Night Manager*, was crude, dull and implausible – but how the critics raved! 'Marvellous...sheer inspired prose-writing...lyrical...a never-ending delight...wonderful stuff, subtle, exciting'.

It is no coincidence, I suspect, that le Carré's adoring reviewers are all men: his male characters tend to be weary, morally ambivalent old coves who philosophize about decline and dishonour, death and despair – just the sort of thing ageing literary gents like to chew on. But what about the women? In *The Night Manager*, the female dramatis personae are differentiated entirely by their chest measurements. When the hero, Jonathan Pine, has his first encounter with Jeds, the mistress of a villainous arms dealer, his eye is immediately caught by 'her unsupported breasts inside the expensive shirt...Jonathan had a disgraceful urge to scoop one out.' Soon afterwards, he glimpses through the sleeve of her bathrobe 'a view of one perfect breast, its slightly erect nipple lifted to him by the action of her arms, the upper half golden-lit by the reading lamp above her'. A few pages later, a couple of 'nymphet nieces in trembling smocks' come 'bouncing up to him', one of them 'lifting her breasts in saucy indignation' as she addresses him. Later still, we meet the 'finely moulded' Marilyn Trethewey, who has 'strong high breasts, for she could not have been a day more than twenty'. Then there is Yvonne Latulipe: 'She was wearing her key chain like a necklace and as she straightened herself the keys settled with a clink between her breasts.'

His new book seems, at first, to be business as usual. Here is the 'beautiful young mistress' of retired secret agent Tim Cranmer: 'Emma is wearing the Watteau look that I encourage in her: wide hat, long skirt, her blouse unbuttoned to the sun...' But we soon discover that le Carré's focus has shifted downwards since the Russ Meyer-style orgy of bosom-ogling in *The Night Manager*: he has become a hip-and-thigh man. 'She had a young figure and a very English carriage. Bending from the hip...' 'She was seated at the Bechstein...with that strict posture she has that nips the waist and spreads the hips.' 'He had entered the territory he loved best. "Figure to kill for. Lovely little bottom. Legs all the way up. Sat there right in front of me, swingin' 'em at me."' 'Emma. Who are you being or seeming – with your hair up, swinging your legs at Jamie Pringle?' 'Not swinging her legs at me, though I do recognize that, even hunched in pain, she is a tall girl, and a very pretty one, and that her legs are remarkably good.' *Our Game*, which is being sold in supermarkets at half the cover-price, is not merely inexpensive: it's cheap.

John le Carré once told an interviewer that his novels are influenced by the German romantic movement, 'so I don't really expect, on an intellectual level, to be understood here anyway'. Is it too much to hope that he will try, one day, to understand women on an 'intellectual level' slightly higher than that of a Page Three caption-writer?

(*Guardian*, 3 May 1995)

Pooter, the party pooper

ALTHOUGH TORIES OFTEN accuse socialists of practising the politics of envy, they are pretty envious themselves – especially of the Left's cultural icons. And who can blame them? While progressive causes enjoy the support of Oscar-winning actresses and Booker-winning novelists, the Conservatives have to make do with Lynsey de Paul and Jimmy Tarbuck.

No wonder the poor dears keep trying to pinch other people's artistic property. Ever since the publication of *Animal Farm*, they have been claiming

George Orwell as one of their own; more recently, they sought to persuade us that the Ealing comedies were essentially Thatcherite in spirit; last year, we had the absurd spectacle of John Redwood taking the credit for Britpop. Now, in a robust editorial, the *Daily Telegraph* has appointed itself sole custodian of George and Weedon Grossmith's masterpiece, *The Diary of a Nobody*. 'Where,' it asks, 'does Mr Pooter choose to send one of his carefully composed letters of complaint, after suffering abuse from a cab driver? To the *Daily Telegraph*. This newspaper has always been honoured to be associated with such a decent fellow as Pooter. His values are timeless: he is thrifty, loyal, hard-working and distrustful of those on the make.'

He is also petty, snobbish and a crashing bore. Although I cannot prove that the Grossmiths intended the book as Marxist agitprop, their picture of suburban small-mindedness is strikingly similar to another great work of Victorian social observation, *The Condition of the Working-Class in England* – written by their near-contemporary, Fred Engels. In a chapter on 'The Attitude of the Bourgeoisie Towards the Proletariat', Engels paid a *Telegraph*-style tribute to Charles Pooter and his kind: 'These English bourgeois are good husbands and family men, and have all sorts of other private virtues and appear, in ordinary intercourse, as decent and respectable as all other bourgeois.' Nevertheless, he added, they are 'incurably debased' by self-interest: 'It is utterly indifferent to the English bourgeois whether his working-men starve or not, if only he makes money.'

This is certainly true of Pooter, who treated his maidservant abominably and was forever whingeing about the ghastliness of 'tradesmen'. Borset, the butterman, became so weary of the old fusspot that 'he said he would be hanged if he would ever serve City clerks any more – the game wasn't worth the candle'. Containing his rage, Pooter 'quietly remarked that I thought it was possible for a City clerk to be a gentleman. He replied he was very glad to hear it, and wanted to know whether I had ever come across one, for he hadn't.' Thanks to his pathetic pretensions, Pooter is despised by almost everyone.

The *Telegraph* ignores all these inconvenient facts, preferring to bask in the glory of having once received a letter from its hero. But even that story hardly justifies its adulation of this 'decent fellow'. What happened was that Pooter, after a long journey home from the East Acton Volunteer Ball, told the cabbie that he had forgotten to bring any money and therefore couldn't pay the fare. Understandably enough, the driver 'called me every name he could lay his tongue to'. The shameless Pooter then decided to write to the *Telegraph* demanding stricter government supervision of the cab-trade, 'to prevent civilians being subjected to the disgraceful insult and outrage that I had had to endure'.

It should be obvious to anyone but a halfwit that this episode is satirizing the spurious indignation of those prim, middle-class moaners who inhabit the *Daily Telegraph*'s correspondence page – the Herbert Gussetts, the Edna Welthorpes, the Disgusteds of Tunbridge Wells. And yet the *Telegraph* takes it as a huge compliment. 'Pooter is not only a comic archetype, but also a moral one,' it raves, praising him as one of the 'worthy and unglamorous figures' on whom this country's prosperity was founded. 'As Carrie Pooter says to her husband: "You are not handsome, but you are good, which is far more noble." Absolutely. More Pooters, please.'

I'd say we have quite enough Pooters already. For six years we have been governed by one, reincarnated in the equally gormless and risible form of John Major. How many more does the *Telegraph* want?

(*Guardian*, 28 August 1996)

The biggest snob in England

JAMES LEES-MILNE, the elderly aesthete, has published yet another volume of his diaries – and, as usual, the critics are ecstatic. 'What pleasure he has given,' sighs the royal biographer Kenneth Rose. From the New Labour camp, John Mortimer commends the 'courage' and 'elegance' of Lees-Milne's insights, adding that 'you can't help liking the sexagenarian diarist'. Val Hennessy finds the book 'an absolute delight'. Anne Chisholm praises him as 'an astute and informal chronicler of the human and social comedy of his life and times', with a 'keen appreciation of the beauties of the natural and the artistic world'. Why does Lees-Milne enjoy such unanimous acclaim? I suspect that he benefits from the toff-worship which afflicts so many literary types, even among the liberal intelligentsia. Brought up on Evelyn Waugh and Nancy Mitford, and parlour games about U and Non-U, they have an insatiable appetite for morsels of country-house gossip and snooty prejudice. (Captain Mark Phillips, on his marriage to Princess Anne, is dismissed by Lees-Milne as 'barely a gentleman'.)

Some toff-literature is indeed worth reading. But the justifiable praise for Alan Clark's diaries – and even the journals of Anthony Powell, with their enjoyably Pooterish record of every meal consumed, and their exhaustive genealogies of each passing acquaintance – becomes somewhat tarnished when the same superlatives are bestowed upon a witless second-rater such as Lees-Milne. Here, chosen at random, is a conversation with Lord Kinross: 'We watched the Trooping of the Colour on our colour television set, and were agreed that it was the most splendid spectacle, which no other country could stage with the same dignity and pageantry as ours.' Astute, eh? His more general observations are equally piffling. 'Why are feet cold immediately on getting into bed?' he wonders, without noticing that the date of the diary entry – 6 January – might supply a clue. The next day he has another brilliant *aperçu*: 'How is it that when one has collywobbles and longs to relieve oneself, one can usually hold out, sometimes five minutes, until one reaches a lavatory?' Bladder control, you old fool.

'Without doubt,' one critic declared last weekend, 'he is the greatest diary-writer of our age.' This seems to be the received wisdom: searching through the reviews of his earlier diaries, I cannot find a single dissenting voice. There is another point on which the drooling reviewers agree. 'The Politically Correct lobby should avoid this book,' Val Hennessy warns gleefully. 'You must look elsewhere for political correctness than in these diaries,' echoes Kenneth Rose. John Mortimer says Lees-Milne is 'fearlessly politically incorrect'. Anne Chisholm, absent-mindedly forgetting to mention PC, contents herself with noting that 'small snobberies and weaknesses are not excised'.

Small snobberies! Lees-Milne is the biggest snob in England – and a particularly vicious one. 'The Filipina forgets things one has told her five minutes before. And is unreliable,' he writes of a new housemaid. 'I suppose all coloured people are like this. They have to be watched over.' On servants in general, he writes: 'I loathe and detest them. All they want is less work and more money. They have no decent feelings, no regard for truth. They are spoilt and rotten. I hope unemployment leaps to astronomical proportions and that they are humiliated and come begging cap in hand for work.' These violent outbursts are not momentary aberrations. In his last book of diaries, published three years ago, Lees-Milne lashed out at Scotsmen ('savages') and socialists ('I have no sympathy for them at all. Let them burn'). A *Panorama* film about Bangladeshis convinced him that 'such people ought not to exist...These ghastly people are a sort of standing, or seething, pollution of the Western world's perimeter, of the civilisation that we have known.' And so on. Predictably enough, the book was lauded for its 'feline observation', 'unquenchable curiosity' and 'deeply felt appreciation of the beautiful and the lasting'.

I have sometimes argued that the much-mocked euphemisms of political correctness ('physically challenged', 'persons of colour') represent an attempt, however clumsy, to observe certain courtesies. It may be PC to refrain from abusing yids and nig-nogs and poofters; it is also simple good manners. Lees-Milne's admirers should be able to grasp this point, since he is – or affects to be – a stickler for etiquette and correct form. Paradoxically, those pundits who fulminate about the menace of political correctness are themselves its luckiest beneficiaries. Instead of being obliged to confess that Lees-Milne is a demented racist and bigot, his fans can now describe their hero as 'fearlessly politically incorrect' – a euphemism far more weaselly than any perpetrated by PC zealots. The next time you hear someone say, 'I have an unquenchable curiosity, I'm afraid, and am rather feline in my astute and informal observations on the human and social comedy of my life and times', you'll know exactly what to expect: a nasty, small-minded, misanthropic bore.

(*Guardian*, 9 July 1997)

Bad eggs and old beans

T HE NOVELS OF P. G. WODEHOUSE, which were banned in the Soviet Union seventy-five years ago, are now 'required reading' for Russia's right-wing intelligentsia, according to the *Sunday Telegraph*. If so, this suggests that the right-wing intelligentsia have missed the point as surely as Lenin did when he added Wodehouse to the proscribed list in 1922 after taking offence at 'The Clicking of Cuthbert', a short story about a Russian novelist called Vladimir Brusiloff. True, in the early pages of the tale Brusiloff seems to be a grim and gloomy cove, and since he is a friend of both Lenin and Trotsky it might appear that Wodehouse is mocking the dourness of Soviet communism. By the end, however, he is revealed to be an immensely jolly golfing fanatic – and therefore, in Wodehouse's view, a good egg. Far from mocking the Soviet Union, the story is a satire on Western misconceptions.

Although Wodehouse is usually treated as a reactionary simpleton, his politics were rather more sophisticated than that. When Bertie Wooster's friend 'Sippy' Sipperley was arrested for nicking a policeman's helmet on Boat Race night, he had the presence of mind to identify himself as Leon Trotsky – 'which,' the magistrate commented when sentencing Sippy to thirty days without the option, 'I am strongly inclined to think an assumed and fictitious name'. This was a double joke, of course, since Leon Trotsky was indeed an assumed name – even for Trotsky himself, who stole the moniker from one of his old jailers while escaping from Siberia with a false passport in 1902.

I can't prove that Wodehouse was a keen student of Marxist history, but there is plenty of circumstantial evidence. The message of his 1910 novel, *Psmith in the City*, has been neatly summarized by the Wodehousean scholar Benny Green as an 'irrefutable argument that most work is a distasteful necessity which nobody in his right mind would ever dream of performing unless he needed the money desperately'. This elementary fact of life – which has long been beyond the comprehension of economists, tycoons, headmasters, bishops and New Labour ministers – can also be found, almost verbatim, in Karl Marx's Paris manuscripts of 1844.

Psmith himself was converted to Marxism while still a boy, when he was removed from Eton and thus deprived of the honour of playing cricket against Harrow at Lord's; thereafter he addressed everyone as 'Comrade'. As Benny Green has pointed out, this was clearly a joke at the expense of H. M. Hyndman, the nineteenth-century English Marxist and sometime batsman for Sussex, who (in Barbara Tuchman's words) 'adopted Socialism out of spite against the world because he was not included in the Cambridge eleven'. But the real joke was on the Tories – as represented by Bickersdyke, a former red-hot radical who has become a repulsive and opportunistic Conservative candidate by the time of *Psmith in the City*. Psmith exposes Bickersdyke's humbug by digging out the minutes of a seditious speech he made to the Tulse Hill Parliament many years earlier.

> Psmith looked across at him with a bright smile. 'They report you verbatim,' he said. 'And rightly. A more able speech I have seldom read. I like the bit where you call the Royal Family bloodsuckers…Your political views have changed a great deal since those days, have they not? It is extremely interesting. A most fascinating study for political students.'

Indeed it is. Oddly enough, Tony Blair revealed a few years ago that Wodehouse was his favourite author – which leads one to wonder if Bickersdyke's betrayal inspired the entire New Labour project.

Certainly Wodehouse would have been shocked by Blair's eagerness to please the bullying Little Englanders of the *Sun* newspaper. His long-forgotten novel *The Swoop*, published in 1909, was a devastating satire on the 'German invasion' scare-stories put about by the Europhobic demagogues and leader-writers of the day. ('The troops of Prince Otto had done grievous damage. Cricket pitches had been trampled down, and in many cases even golf-greens dented by the iron heel of the invader, who rarely, if ever, replaced the divot.') In the 1930s, when appeasement was official policy and the *Daily Mail* was chanting 'Hurrah for the Blackshirts!', he sabotaged the pretensions of Oswald Mosley equally effectively by turning him into Roderick Spode, leader of the Blackshorts.

But then Wodehouse was an instinctive anti-authoritarian who always sided with the underdog against self-important bossyboots such as Roderick Spode, Roderick Glossop, Aunt Agatha and the Efficient Baxter. His most eloquent political treatise, in my view, is the short story 'The Aunt and the Sluggard', in which Bertie is forced to fend for himself in a hotel without Jeeves's assistance. As the young master stands in his lonely bedroom, trying to tie his white tie himself, it strikes him for the first time that

> there must be whole squads of chappies in the world who had to get along without a man to look after them. I'd always thought of Jeeves as a kind of natural phenomenon; but, by Jove! of course, when you come to think of it, there must be quite a lot of fellows who have to press their own clothes themselves, and haven't got anybody to bring them tea in the morning, and so on. It was rather a solemn thought, don't you know. I mean to say, ever since then I've been able to appreciate the frightful privations the poor have to stick.

This is, I need hardly add, a perfect précis of *The Communist Manifesto*.

(*Guardian*, 18 March 1998)

From a cool sequester'd vale

WHILE AGONY AUNTS dissect Margaret Cook's motives and political pundits debate whether she will harm the career of her former husband, Robin Cook, no literary critic has yet commented on the most remarkable feature of her book – its extravagantly antique prose. 'Those most ardently piling contumely on my head,' she wrote in the *Sunday Times* last weekend, 'are the same who came to me last year with honeyed words and flattering phrases.' Forsooth! Has anyone other than a lawyer used the word 'contumely' since the days of Mr Bonar Law? In the first instalment of her memoirs we learned that Robin Cook liked to read Browning. One guesses that his ex-wife's taste in poetry is even less modern. The passage above has a distinct echo of Sir Thomas Wyatt's most famous verse ('They flee from me that sometime did me seek') and more than a hint of the opening scene from Shakespeare's *Henry V*: 'the mute wonder lurketh in men's ears/To steal his sweet and honey'd sentences...'

Instead of condemning her for dishing the dirt, we are invited by Margaret Cook to 'consider what extraordinary forces would propel me so far out of the usual private tenor of my ways'. Sounds familiar? Turn to Gray's 'Elegy in a Country Churchyard': 'Along the cool sequester'd vale of life/They kept the noiseless tenor of their way.' When it comes to sex – as it so often does with the Foreign Secretary – Margaret's book is as coy as a Regency Romance. She tells us of Robin's 'problem', which made him 'less active in marital relations with me'. Searching for the cause of the trouble, she 'questioned him about a certain lady...He was fonder of her than he perhaps should be.' A year or two later, he confesses that he is having it off with his secretary, Gaynor Regan. Or, as Margaret prefers to put it: 'Sunday, 4 August, 1996 was the day on which the fates decreed that my life should begin to come apart.' Those fates, eh? Forever issuing decrees without allowing a proper debate, rather like our own dear government.

Robin promised to end the affair, and Margaret agreed to stay with him.

But 'on one thing I did not waver. I would never be a wife to him again in the physical sense.' Robin replied that he had 'no intention of going through life as a celibate and that our mutual recuperation would depend on a full married life'. What did Margaret say to that? 'I kept my counsel on this issue.' Privately, however, she accepted that it might be necessary to turn a blind eye 'when he found release with other women...If he was not having marital relations, either with me or his mistress, he could be in serious difficulties and might act foolishly in a state of deprivation.' The penultimate scene in this ghastly morality play occurs just after the general election, when the Cooks find themselves – almost accidentally – in a passionate clinch. 'Without another word, we went upstairs,' she reports. 'His delight in our rehabilitation was considerable and unfeigned.'

Unfeigned rehabilitation...full married life...marital relations...finding release...being a wife in the physical sense. Has Margaret Cook never heard of a three-letter word beginning with S and ending in X? Until now I had thought that Radclyffe Hall held the all-comers' record for the most excruciating sexual euphemism in English literature ('And that night they were not divided'), but at least Hall had the excuse that she was writing in 1920 and dealing with the taboo subject of lesbianism. I can only assume that Margaret Cook's computer is an early victim of the Y2K bug and has transported her back to the year 1900.

(*Guardian*, 21 January 1999)

The name's Lecter, Hannibal Lecter

THERE WAS ONCE an Oxford don who would read no modern authors except Iris Murdoch and Anthony Burgess. His life changed when he tried a crime novel and experienced an epiphany like that of Keats on first looking into Chapman's Homer. 'P. D. James is the greatest novelist of the age,' he told me, gibbering with excitement. 'She's like Iris Murdoch but with plots!' I was reminded of this when studying the hyperbolic reviews of Thomas Harris's *Hannibal*. Literary editors, most of whom seldom read thrillers, are so astounded by its page-turning qualities that they promptly hail it as great literature. Erica Wagner of *The Times* praises Harris for asking profound questions about 'the dark that inhabits all of us to a greater or lesser degree'. Her opposite number at the London *Evening Standard*, David Sexton, describes the book as 'a momentous achievement...a modern inferno, full of references both to the Bible and to Dante'.

Though no one has mentioned it, the more obvious influence is surely the early James Bond films. Dr Lecter, supposedly the baddie, is 007 to the life. Bond has his Aston Martin DB5, his dry martinis and his Walther PPK; Lecter has his supercharged black Jaguar Mark II, his Château Pétrus and his state-of-the-art kitchen knives. Just as Bond flaunts his effortless expertise in almost any subject M cares to mention, so Lecter has a professorial knowledge of art, music, mathematics, psychology, astrophysics, haute cuisine, anthropology and linguistics.

The man pitted against Lecter is the hideously disfigured Mason Verger, his only surviving victim, a man with no nose, no lips, no soft tissue on his face and only a single, lidless eye. He takes out his frustrations by tormenting orphans until they cry, using their collected tears to dilute his martini. He is, in short, a composite of Dr No, Ernst Stavro Blofeld and Goldfinger. Where Bond villains usually have a tank of piranhas, Verger keeps a huge and hungry eel. 'There's an even bigger one in captivity in Tokyo,' he tells Clarice Starling. 'This one is second biggest. Its common name is the Brutal Moray. Would you like to see why?' In the absence of Rosa Klebb he relies on his sister Margot, a fearsome bodybuilder who crushes walnuts with her bare hands.

Like any Spectre supremo, Verger has a taste for absurdly theatrical and fallible methods of execution. Instead of simply hiring a hitman to rub out his enemy, he spends seven years breeding a herd of killer pigs in Sardinia, which are then airfreighted over to the States to eat Dr Lecter from the feet upwards. (Echoes here of Hilaire Belloc's unlucky Jim:

> Now just imagine how it feels
> When first your toes and then your heels
> And then, by gradual degrees,
> Your shins and ankles, calves and knees
> Are slowly eaten, bit by bit.
> No wonder Jim detested it.)

According to Robert McCrum of the *Observer*, 'Lecter's embodiment of evil is truly awesome.' Actually, it becomes ever more ridiculous and risible: by the closing chapters Lecter is not so much James Bond as Austin Powers. But Thomas Harris does indeed seem to think that he is grappling seriously with the Big Issues of wickedness and redemption, which is why his novel – unlike, say, *From Russia with Love* – doesn't even qualify as enjoyable tosh.

McCrum salutes Lecter as 'a villain for our times: softly spoken, anonymous...his eyes are maroon; his tongue is red and pointed; there are six fingers on his right hand.' Anonymous, eh? I'd guess that even the Met could make an arrest with that many eccentricities to work on.

(*Guardian*, 23 June 1999)

THE GREAT AND NOT-SO-GOOD

Who's kidding whom?

I T WAS A SIMPLE ASSIGNMENT: go and interview the editor of *Who's Who*. I duly bunged in a request to Messrs A & C Black, the publishers. 'I'm afraid not,' the firm's spokeswoman, Charlotte Burrows, informed me sternly. 'All the editors have to remain anonymous, to protect them.' Protect them from what? 'From people wanting to be in *Who's Who*.'

Could she mean me? Having been listed in Debrett's *People of Today*, a rival reference work, for five years or so, I have occasionally wondered when *Who's Who* will catch up; but it has never occurred to me to wheedle or bludgeon my way into those dense, double-columned pages. As a warning in each edition points out, 'an invitation to appear in *Who's Who* has, on occasion, been thought of as conferring distinction; that is the last thing it can do. It recognises distinction and influence.' Quite so; and people of distinction and influence do not resort to such undignified methods as lobbying.

I promised Ms Burrows that I would be on my best behaviour: no attempted bribes, no concealed weapons. After some friendly haggling, she offered a compromise. 'I shall give you a telephone number. You can ring it and speak to someone. But you won't know their name.' This person would be an editor – perhaps even the editor – of *Who's Who*. In an age when Stella Rimington, the head of MI5, appears in *Hello!* magazine, it is odd that a company whose job is to disseminate information should be so fanatically secretive. *People of Today*, which has been competing quite successfully with *Who's Who* since its creation eight years ago, sees no need for security precautions: the editor, Jonathan Parker, is named on the title page, along with his senior editor and co-editors. Yet Parker is, if anything, at greater risk than his shadowy counterpart at A & C Black. Once you gain admittance to *Who's Who*, you are there for life: even Lord Lucan still has an entry, although it omits his current address and does not register any achievements since 1974. At *People of Today*, by contrast, you are only as good as your last performance. If Mr Parker and his colleagues decide that your eminence is waning, they throw you overboard. 'We have the members of Take That in, for example,' he says. 'But now that they've disbanded we wouldn't guarantee they'll be in next year.' Mr Parker must therefore cope with the indignation of the has-beens as well as the supplications of the wannabes. Does he vary his route home every evening, for fear of being waylaid by outcasts? 'People have suggested that we might like to review their case and put them back in,' he admits. 'But nobody's ever threatened us with physical violence.' I had assumed that he, at least, would know the identity of his opposite number at *Who's Who*, but no. 'I think it's a woman,' he ventured. 'We've read various descriptions of her, but we're not sure who she is.'

It was time to put a voice, if not a face, to this publicity-shy panjandrum. I rang the secret phone number. It was answered by a woman who sounded alarmingly like M, the spy chief played by Dame Judi Dench in the latest James Bond film, and who had obviously learned her trade-craft at the same school. Are you, I enquired, the editor of *Who's Who*? 'In a sense we don't have an editor, haven't had since 1900.' But you are in charge? 'Yes.' Any hopes that she might break down under interrogation were quickly dashed. How many staff do you employ? 'It's not something that we would normally say.' How many copies do you sell? 'We don't divulge that.' When were you appointed? Silence. Eventually, however, a few facts emerged. She joined *Who's Who* straight from college, has been there for 'decades' and intends to stay until retirement. What is the appeal of the job? 'No one's ever asked me that. Er, let me think. What appeals to me is...it's very orderly, it's tidy, things are in alphabetical order.'

Ah yes; so they are. When A & C Black bought the rights to *Who's Who* a century ago, the British empire was at its zenith and the solidity of our institutions seemed unshakeable. Now that the monarchy is crumbling, the Church of England suffers from rising damp, and Parliament is infested with death-watch beetle, the tidy-minded editor and her colleagues are struggling gamely to preserve the façade of an orderly nation. The very first edition of the book, published by Baily Brothers in 1849, had no biographies at all, but merely a list of names – the senior and collateral branches of the royal family, the Houses of Lords and Commons ('showing the Political Bias of each Member'), the judges, the directors of the Bank of England, and so on.

This conception of the establishment has changed little since. Although *Who's Who* issues an annual press release drawing attention to the celebrities who have been given houseroom for the first time – the class of '96 includes Lenny Henry, Sally Gunnell, Robbie Coltrane, Gary Lineker and Tom Jones – most new entries are ex officio: MPs, civil servants above a certain rank, senior partners of blue-chip legal firms. 'We're always surprised at how much publicity *Who's Who* gets for putting in people like Frank Bruno,' Jonathan Parker says. 'The expression "been there, done that" comes to mind: Frank Bruno's been in *People of Today* for years. It seems funny for someone from Debrett's Peerage to say, but we're less snobbish.' *People of Today* is certainly more hospitable to what Parker calls 'the younger professions', such as advertising, marketing, PR and showbiz. The editor of *Who's Who* is untroubled by the criticism. 'Because they take people out, they can put in more people who haven't yet reached the stage where we consider it appropriate to include them,' she told me. 'We are more cautious, preferring to wait until they have established themselves.' Paul McCartney and Elton John have crept in, but old stagers such as Mick Jagger and Eric Clapton, still waiting forlornly for the summons, may wonder what more they have to do to prove that they have 'established themselves'.

For all the differences, *Who's Who* and *People of Today* agree on one editorial principle: that the subjects should be allowed to write their own CVs. Looking at Lord Archer's entry, you would take him to be a man who had enjoyed a hiccup-free ascent to wealth and title: there is no mention of the financial disaster that precipitated his departure from the House of Commons in 1973, nor of the generosity to a prostitute which ended his brief period as deputy chairman of the Conservative Party, nor of his curious involvement with Anglia TV share deals. As a source of information, these reference books are often inadequate or downright misleading. How old, for instance, is Lord King of Wartnaby, the president of British Airways? In the 1975 and 1976 editions of *Who's Who*, he gave his date of birth as 'August 1917'. For the next three years it was 'August 1918'. Since then he has declined to give a date at all. In both *Who's Who* and *People of Today*, the actress Nanette Newman insists that she was born on 29 May 1939; a search at St Catherine's House discloses that her actual date of birth was a full five years earlier.

Precisely because they are self-serving, however, the entries are sometimes more revealing than they seem. In his biography of Margaret Thatcher ('d. of late Alfred Roberts, Grantham, Lincs'), Hugo Young observed that Beatrice Roberts 'played remarkably little part in the development of her younger daughter: a fact made manifest by her exclusion from Margaret's biographical entry in *Who's Who*'. When an interviewer for the *Radio Times* asked about the omission, in October 1993, Lady Thatcher became quite flustered: 'What do you mean? How could I not? She was my mother. Oh dear, didn't I? Well, I must correct that.' In the latest edition, poor Beatrice is still missing.

The history of Tony Benn's attitude to *Who's Who* is even more suggestive.

Until the early 1970s, he was conventional enough: 'BENN, Rt Hon. Anthony (Neil) Wedgwood PC 1964; MP (Lab)...' The first sign of a mid-life rethink appeared in 1973, when 'Educ: MA Oxford' was amended to 'Educ: since leaving university'. By 1976, the editors realized they had a problem. His entry, which the previous year had run to more than three inches, was suddenly pruned to little more than two lines. But he was still not satisfied. As the editor recalls: 'It got to the stage where all he wanted was "Benn, Tony, MP". We rather felt that wasn't awfully helpful to people using the book.' For the next six years, uniquely for such a senior politician, he was allowed to absent himself from *Who's Who* altogether. 'Then,' according to the editor, 'we noticed that he seemed quite happy to be in every other reference book that lists MPs.' After some cajoling, he agreed to return in 1983 – but on his own terms. Where once he had made only a passing reference to his inheritance of a viscountcy ('title disclaimed and never used'), there was a long and heroic account of his part in the class war: 'Having unsucessfully attempted to renounce his right of succession, 1955 and 1960, won a by-election in May 1961 only to be prevented from taking seat; instigated Act to make disclaimer possible, and disclaimed title for life, 1963.' Under the heading of education, Benn now has nothing at all, although there are plenty of examples he could usefully follow, such as the late Osbert Sitwell ('Educ: during the holidays from Eton'), Michael Holroyd ('Educ: Eton Coll; Maidenhead Public Library'), or even Lord Archer ('Educ: by my wife since leaving Wellington Sch., Somerset'). One example nobody should follow is that of the Tory MP Graham Riddick, who claims to have been educated at Warwick University. Perhaps he was, but he never took a degree there: having failed his first-year exams twice, he was asked to leave.

The joy of a publication such as *Who's Who* is that, by appealing to human vanity, it encourages the participants to condemn themselves out of their own mouths. In his memoirs, the literary agent Giles Gordon noted proudly that his *Who's Who* entry was 'exactly the same length as my male organ, which I've just measured for confirmation'. (Two and a half inches, in case you were wondering.) Length may not be everything, but it has its own fascination: while Ronald Reagan makes do with fourteen lines, Dame Barbara Cartland spreads herself over more than a page – as did her old friend Lord Mountbatten, whose list of 'clubs' alone occupied ten lines. For overweening conceit, it is hard to beat the late Tory MP Sir Nicholas Fairbairn, who gave his professions as 'author, farmer, painter, poet, TV and radio broadcaster, journalist, dress designer, landscape gardener, bon viveur and wit'. He compounded the offence by dreaming up new recreations every year. These included 'being blunt and sharp at the same time', 'snookering the reds and other proctalgias', 'draining brains and scanning bodies' and, most elaborately, 'serving queens, restoring castles, debunking bishops, entertaining knights, befriending pawns'. He could have achieved the same effect by simply wearing a badge, announcing, 'I'm insufferable; give me a wide berth.'

A note at the front of Who's Who boasts that the recreations 'have become a distinctive feature of the book'. True, a few of them arouse one's curiosity (General Colin Powell: 'restoring old Volvos'); but archness is the more usual style. Studying the entries for authors such as Emma Tennant ('walking around'), Deborah Moggach ('walking around London looking into people's windows'), Christopher Hope ('getting lost') and Jilly Cooper ('merry-making, wild flowers, music, mongrels'), one begins to wonder how any of them ever found a publisher. And whatever possessed David Wilkinson, a professor of psychiatry at Liverpool University, to list his recreations as 'family, rural pursuits, being a pimp of discourse'?

This counter-productive flashiness is as old as Who's Who itself. Leafing through the 1900 edition at random, I came upon an entry for the Hon. Stuart Erskine who 'is an author, and contributes pretty frequently to various periodicals; was principal proprietor and editor of the Whirlwind, and, in conjunction with Mr L. Cranmer-Byng, started the Senate magazine; is one of the Celtic so-called "school" of writers; is no party man but a staunch Jacobite and occasional follower of Lord Rosebery; has no recreations, but seeks diversion in wild and solitary places.' Bully for him. Elsewhere in the 1900 edition, we find 'Grace, William Gilbert, surgeon'; only after listing all his medical qualifications does he think to add that he played cricket for England. A few pages further back is 'Fry, Charles Burgess, BA, late Assistant Master Charterhouse', who gives his recreations as 'cricket, Rugby and Association football, running, etc'. You would hardly guess from this that he was probably the most outstanding all-round athlete Britain has ever produced. More recently, Sir Alf Ramsey used to record that he had played at right-back for Tottenham Hotspur and had managed Ipswich Town FC, but modestly forbore to mention his role in England's World Cup victory.

Of the two reference books, People of Today is probably the more useful. It has 34,000 entries (as against 30,000 in Who's Who) and, from this year, is also available as a CD-Rom disk; if you want to know how many Tory MPs went to Eton, a few keystrokes will supply the answer. The policy of ditching people who no longer count for anything – which could be a nuisance for those of us who like to keep track of forgotten grandees – does not seem to be applied too harshly. Take That fans may be comforted to learn that Robbie

Williams ('Recreations: rollerblading, Port Vale FC') has survived in the 1996 edition, although he left the group last year.

One thing *People of Today* cannot hope to match, at least for another century or so, is the longevity of the senior volume. See how quickly you can guess the subject of this entry from the 1945 *Who's Who*: 'b. Braunau on the Inn, Upper Danube, 20 Apr 1889, of an old Austrian peasant and artisan family; religion, Catholic. Educ: secondary schools in Linz and Graz; studied painting and architecture in Vienna; settled at Munich in 1912 to study painting, supporting himself as artisan in building trade...Publications: *Mein Kampf*.' Rather surprisingly, the Führer's details were updated punctiliously throughout the war: 'Personal commander of the Army since 1941; Supreme War Lord; Supreme Law Lord, since 1942.' No recreations, alas; but his chum Benito Mussolini had more than enough for two – 'violino, equitazione, scherma, automobilismo, aviazione'. What a pity he never met Sir Nicholas Fairbairn.

(*Sunday Telegraph*, 17 March 1996)

Memoirs of a fox-hunting man

I T WAS THE POLITICAL WEDDING of the season. In August 1957, a rising young barrister with parliamentary ambitions, John Ryman, wed Shirley Summerskill, daughter of the Labour MP Edith Summerskill, in the crypt chapel at the House of Commons. At the reception, held in the garden of the Summerskills' family house in Highgate, Clem Attlee toasted the couple and gave a little speech about how the young people of today differed from those in his day. 'The sun shone throughout,' Edith Summerskill recalled in her memoirs.

Both her daughter and her new son-in-law were graduates from Oxford, where they had met in the University Labour Club. Shirley had been a medical student; John had read Law. He had also proposed, unsuccessfully, the admission of women to the Oxford Union. He was the quintessential young Oxbridge politico, armed with a curling lip, a pair of know-it-all spectacles and a quite impregnable self-confidence. Imagine the late Dick Crossman,

Lord Rees-Mogg and Sir Robin Day all blended into one 26-year-old creature and you have John Ryman on his sunblest wedding day.

He dressed and spoke like a Tory. His favourite recreation was fox-hunting. And yet he was a socialist – or, what is not necessarily the same thing, he wanted to be a Labour MP. His bride beat him to it, becoming the Member for Halifax in 1964. At that election Ryman was unsurprisingly defeated in the safe Tory seat of Gillingham, where he had won the nomination by the simple ruse of promising to pay the salary of a full-time Labour agent should he be selected. At the election of June 1970 he fought Derbyshire South-East, and lost again. In the same year, he was divorced by Shirley Summerskill for adultery with an unnamed woman.

His career at the Bar was rather more successful. From 1970 to 1974 he was chief prosecuting counsel for the Inland Revenue at the Old Bailey, and in years to come newspapers would sometimes call him 'John Ryman QC', though he never in fact took silk. It was an understandable error: his courtroom manner certainly had nothing of the junior counsel about it. One beak before whom he appeared found him 'pontifical, self-opinionated and offensive'.

This was the style Ryman brought to Westminster when he was at last elected to the House of Commons, in October 1974. During the next thirteen years, as the Labour MP for Blyth in Northumberland, he railed against a large cast of villains, many of them on his own side: Harold Wilson was 'blinkered by apathy and bridled by indifference'; his ministers were 'pampered and overpaid'; Anthony Crosland was 'insane' and 'revolting'; Chancellor Helmut Schmidt was 'a patronizing Hun'; Margaret Thatcher was 'the high priestess of Tory original sin'; the deputy chairman of the Coal Board was 'a pinstriped twit'; the chairman of the Post Office was 'a man of proven incompetence'; the Foreign Office was 'a permanent upper-class cocktail party'; the EEC was 'an unmitigated disaster'; the Callaghan government was 'wet and feeble'; Labour peers were 'mediocre hacks and nonentities'. He backed Tony Benn for the party's deputy leadership in 1981, yet he campaigned for the police and Customs officers to be given stronger powers. He claimed to be 'very left-wing', yet he spent much of the early 1980s inveighing against 'left-wing infiltration' of the Labour Party. In 1979 he proposed the restoration of capital punishment; four years later he voted against it. He condemned the 'rich, idle females of Belgravia', who were 'the most promiscuous section of the community', yet he rode to hounds with such females twice a week.

Ryman continued his legal work – not least on his own behalf. In his first election campaign at Blyth, he had continually libelled the former Labour MP for the seat, Eddie Milne, a brave and decent man who had been deselected for daring to expose the Poulson-financed corruption of the Labour Party in north-east England. Milne sued, and Ryman had to stump up £6,250 in damages. In 1975 Ryman and his agent, Peter Mortakis, were in the dock at Newcastle Crown Court, charged with falsifying their election expenses; Ryman was acquitted, but Mortakis was fined £400 and banned from holding public office. Ten years later, Ryman was thrown out of the chambers in which he was the senior barrister, after colleagues accused him of managing their expenses improperly; the Director of Public Prosecutions asked Scotland Yard to investigate, but no charges were brought. In 1987, just after he had resigned from the Labour Party and stood down as an MP in protest at the Militant Tendency, Ryman issued a writ against his lover for the previous two years, Susan Snashall, demanding that she reimburse him for a holiday they had spent together in the South of France.

Last month, at Bristol Crown Court, John Ryman made what may have been his last appearance as an advocate. He was defending himself against charges of stealing £130,000 from two women whom he had seduced. The old rhetorical swagger had gone: this was a new Ryman, meek, monosyllabic and contrite. He admitted the offences and apologized for them, pleading in mitigation that he was now ill and destitute. Judge Rupert Bursell sentenced him to two and a half years in jail.

Few of John Ryman's former friends – or victims – seem willing to discuss his rise and fall. 'I'm afraid I have no interest in answering any questions about John Ryman,' says William Hebditch, a Somerset fruit farmer whose late mother was relieved of £14,000 by Ryman while having an affair with him in the late 1980s. 'I don't think I can say anything useful about him,' says Ryman's Oxford contemporary and former brother-in-law Michael Summerskill. 'We don't want to help you,' I was told by a relation of Ryman's fourth wife, Margaret Camsell, whom he married in 1981. Susan Snashall will admit only that she wasn't surprised by Ryman's crimes: 'I think it's in character, but I don't particularly want to get involved...I don't particularly want to go over that ground.' A few years ago, when Ryman was suing her, Snashall was more forthcoming. 'Despite his philanderings,' she told the *Mail on Sunday*, 'he is a really lonely man.' He once told a secretary that the only woman he had ever truly loved was his nanny. 'It's doubtful,' Jim Collyer, a former chairman of Blyth Labour Party, said last week, 'if he had any friends.'

Well, perhaps one: Peter Mortakis, the agent who was convicted for fiddling Ryman's election expenses, says he would be happy to offer the former MP bed and board when he comes out of jail. 'I'm desperately sorry for him, really. You can't condone what he's done to those women, but you can try to understand it.'

What's to understand? Ryman was a conman and a chancer. He preyed on lonely women, usually widows or divorcees, who were flattered by his attentions. Pauline Chalker, aged sixty-eight, met him on a train from London to Bristol in January 1988 and was immediately attracted by his 'enormous knowledge', his 'abundance of wit and charm', his 'impeccably dressed' appearance. An intensive two-month campaign of wining and dining tightened his grip. Ryman, who had professed to be an investment adviser to a Swiss bank, persuaded her to entrust him with her savings of £50,000, plus another £50,000 that she raised by remortgaging her house in Bath. Then he scarpered.

A 54-year-old music teacher who lived a few miles outside Bath, Nicola Eeles, was being wooed by Ryman in much the same fashion at the same time, and soon consented to become wife number five. Their honeymoon, in August 1988, was paid for with a cheque he had extracted from the unsuspecting Pauline Chalker the previous week. Like Chalker, Eeles had been widowed recently; she, too, lent him thousands of pounds for investment in 'high-yield Swiss bank accounts'. By the beginning of 1989, Ryman had gone – as had £11,500 from her bank account. Later that year he had a fling with Gladys Reynolds, a fifty-year-old divorcee whom he met in a Wiltshire hotel. Introducing himself as Philip Spencer, he told her his infallible story of Swiss banks and high-yield accounts. This time he pocketed £20,000.

Where did all the loot go? Bristol Crown Court heard last month that Ryman spent much of it on horses, clothes, a Jaguar XJS, a £400-a-week flat in Chelsea, trips on the Orient Express and parties at the Savoy Hotel. He also used some for maintenance payments to his first wife, Shirley Summerskill, who of course had no idea that the cash was ill-gotten.

Anyone who had observed Ryman's career more closely might have had suspicions, however, since he had been known to readers of *Private Eye* for many years as 'Rotter Ryman'. During the late 1970s the former chief prosecutor of income-tax defaulters was himself harried by the Inland Revenue for unpaid PAYE on the salary of his Commons secretary – or, rather, secretaries, since they seldom stayed for more than a few months. An employment agency, Central Appointments, had to threaten Ryman with bankruptcy proceedings in 1978 before he would pay the £400 fee the company was owed for having found a secretary who was prepared to work for him. Ryman would often go AWOL for weeks on end – in 1976 the Labour chief whip went on the radio and broadcast an appeal for the errant Member to attend a crucial vote – and his secretaries became adept at fending off irate creditors and constituents during his absences. By the time he retired from the Commons in 1987 he was being pursued by a firm of chartered surveyors (owed £500), Fortnum & Mason (£700-worth of food bought on account and never paid for) and a posse of court bailiffs and solicitors. During the hearing of one debt-enforcing case in the mid-1980s, he told Westminster County Court that he earned £620 a month as a barrister but had monthly living expenses of more than twice that amount.

He was the architect of his misfortune, and now he must inhabit it alone. No politician can be found who will admit to having liked the man. His wives and lovers are either silent or scathing. ('I'm glad he's behind bars,' says his fifth wife, Nicola Eeles. 'He's a danger to women.') Former comrades in Blyth say they hardly knew him.

Except, that is, for his old agent Peter Mortakis, who believes that Ryman was a victim of sinister, powerful forces – in a word, MI5. 'They've tried hard enough to put him into this situation,' he says darkly. 'Scotland Yard investigated his law practice. And there was the case of the election expenses – that was a set-up too of course. I don't believe my trial was without the influence of those people. It caused me to reflect on the powers and influences involved...When John Ryman resigned because of the Militants, a lot of people felt he should have stood and fought. But who do you think was financing and organizing the Militant people? I can tell you this now: we couldn't fight MI5 as well.' So it was just like Alan Bleasdale's *GBH*? 'Exactly.' But even the security service can't force a man to go round conning widows out of their life savings, surely? Mortakis concedes that Ryman did this unaided. 'But MI5 created the situation in which he found himself without any money. If you take away a man's crutch, he'll fall on his face.'

Pauline Chalker, having lost her home and her life savings, offers a more plausible explanation, which owes nothing to either conspiracy theory or psychoanalysis. 'Ryman,' she says simply, 'is a complete and utter shit.'

(*Independent Magazine*, May 1992)

Calling a Spode a Spode

S AY WHAT YOU LIKE about Sir James Goldsmith, he certainly knows how to throw a good party. Most of us haven't been invited to his £20 million blow-out known as the Referendum Party; Sir Jimmy has wisely hired a security firm, whose directors include Cecil Parkinson, to keep out weirdos and gatecrashers. Nevertheless, we can still press our noses against the pane and enjoy the antics of the braying revellers inside.

One such is the right-wing historian Andrew Roberts, a fully paid-up member of the Chelsea Conservative Association. 'If the local Tory candidate is inferior to the Referendum one in certain constituencies, true Tories can vote for the better man with clear consciences,' he declared in the *Sunday Times* last weekend. 'In my constituency of Kensington and Chelsea, the choice is fortunately abundantly clear. We have Sir Nicholas Scott, the corporatist, interventionist, pro-Maastricht Tory wet sitting member, being challenged by Robin Birley, the traditionalist, high Tory, anti-Maastricht usher at my wedding.' Birley's qualifications are indeed 'abundantly clear': not only is he a wedding usher of rare skill and dedication, but he also happens to be the stepson of Sir James Goldsmith.

In the early days of the Referendum Party, some observers predicted that its supporters would all be half-witted Old Etonians with double-barrelled names. As we can now see, this was most unfair. Many of them are half-witted Old Etonians with single-barrelled names; others, such as the Italian-born Lady Powell, are not Old Etonians at all. (The last time I saw Carla Powell, incidentally, she was still dithering over which constituency to honour with her presence. In a spirit of mischief, I suggested Hartlepool. 'Oh no, I couldn't do that,' she replied. 'I lurve Peter Mandelson – 'e is one of my oldest friends.' Strange but true.) In the annals of aristocratic political folly, there's been nothing like it since the brief career of Roderick Spode, another self-styled Man of Destiny. 'Watch out for Spode,' Bertie Wooster warns Emerald Stoker in *Stiff Upper Lip, Jeeves*. 'He's about eight feet high and has the sort of eye that can open an oyster at sixty paces.' Jimmy Goldsmith to the life, I'd say. Else-where in the Wodehouse canon, Spode is described thus: 'It was as if Nature had intended to make a gorilla, but had changed its mind at the last moment.' The simian Goldsmith has gone one better by choosing a candidate who thinks he is a gorilla – John Aspinall, the eccentric zookeeper who will contest Michael Howard's seat in Folkestone on behalf of the Referendum Party.

Like his friend Jimmy, Aspinall has strong Spodean qualities, managing to be both extremely sinister and utterly ludicrous at the same time. He is best known for his unswerving conviction that tigers, big apes and bull elephants are essentially pussy cats at heart – a belief that has cost several of his zookeeping staff their lives, and has left his fellow Referendum enthusiast Robin Birley permanently disfigured. (In 1970, when Birley was a small boy, he had part of his face bitten off by one of Aspinall's tigers.) The Aspinall elec-tion address should be a most interesting document. He regards human beings as 'vermin', and has long argued that the population of Britain should be reduced from 58 million to 18 million by a policy of 'beneficial genocide'. If Goldsmith and his cronies do come to power, a mass-extermination along these lines would undoubtedly simplify the administrative arrangements for their referendum. Aspers also advocates 'a right-wing counter-revolution, Franco-esque in spirit and determination'.

The voters of Folkestone are clearly a rum bunch – they have, after all, been returning Michael Howard to Parliament for the past thirteen years – but I'm not sure if even they are quite ready for out-and-out fascism. Still, it is an excellent Goldsmithian joke to select Aspinall as a standard-bearer of 'democratic values'. By doing so, Sir James has achieved what was hitherto thought impossible: he has made the Home Secretary look like a moderate.

(Guardian, 18 September 1996)

A whiff of grapeshot

<hr/>

E VEN PAUL JOHNSON'S ENEMIES – and he has a few – cannot deny that he is the most prolific and versatile writer of his generation. He would probably be nicknamed 'Magic' Johnson, had the title not already been bagged by an American sportsman. Almost every day, he entertains his readers with a lengthy essay on anything from why gay men fancy John Major to the joys of the English climate. While producing this torrent of newspaper articles, he has also found the time to produce about thirty 'serious' books, including a history of the modern world which was admired by such eminent scholars as Ronald Reagan and Colonel Oliver North, and a study of left-wing intellectuals, which proved that they were all sex-crazed lunatics.

Oddly enough, he used to be something of a left-wing intellectual himself: in his younger days, he even wrote a novel called *Left of Centre*. The hero, Henry Arnold, is a young English journalist working for a magazine in Paris – as Johnson was at the time he wrote the book. Finding himself alone in a flat with a sleeping woman, he tiptoes into her bedroom: 'She was stark naked, and Henry found his gaze straying to her round and rosy bottom, which rose and fell gently to the rhythm of her breathing...Dora's bottom invited him. Here was his chance, at one blow, to reassume his masculine, paramount role in their relationship.' Convinced that the way to a woman's heart is through her rump, he delivers a well-aimed smack. Alas! Instead of swooning in ecstasy, Dora leaps up and orders him out of the flat.

But it would be wrong to deduce that Johnson is – or was – a mere bottom-fancier. No, he liked bosoms as well: 'Her breasts pushed out fiercely from beneath her white silk shirt...culminating in hard, menacing points, like the tips of Howitzers poking out of pillboxes.' The theme was pursued further in his next novel, *Merrie England* (1964), which is set in a high-class brothel and is liberally seasoned with passages such as this: 'Felix Appleby, dressed for the office, sat on the edge of Lady Titty Ross's rumpled four-poster bed, his eyes anchored firmly on the ample cleavage displayed by her *négligée*...' And this: 'Penny opened her dressing-gown. "There, you don't see a pair like that every day, do you, darling? I can see your eyes are popping out of your head, but they're real, all right. Want to touch to make sure?" ' If he had persevered, he could well have become the next Jilly Cooper. But Paul Johnson decided to devote his life to exposing political hypocrisy instead, a task for which he was ideally qualified. He has supported Harold Wilson; he has supported Margaret Thatcher. He has supported Tony Benn; he has supported Tony Blair. 'What I cannot bear,' he revealed a couple of years ago, 'is humbug.'

Quite so. Here is Johnson in the *Spectator*, an anti-Major magazine, on 2 October 1993: 'A prime minister needs authority and Major has none...The Tories must put him out of his misery.' A month later in the *Daily Mail*, which at the time was supporting the Prime Minister, he seemed to be having second thoughts: 'His cry of "back to basics" suggests his heart and his head are in the right places...It indicates that he may still prove himself a worthy leader.' No humbug there, of course: he'd simply changed his mind, an exercise he performs with healthy regularity. By January 1994, he'd turned against the Prime Minister once again, announcing that 'the coming year will witness the end, I predict and hope, of the Major government, the most disreputable of my lifetime.'

Well, we all make mistakes, don't we? But Paul Johnson deals with the big issues – and so he makes big mistakes. A month after Robert Maxwell's death in 1991, he wrote a furious article for the *Daily Mail*: 'Since Maxwell had been judged unfit to run a public company as long ago as 1971, what were the various regulators doing while he built up his crazy pyramid of debt? How did a man like Maxwell, who had This Man Is Dangerous written all over him in letters two feet high, manage to persuade senior bank executives to hand over to him hundreds of millions of their depositors' money? Who exactly were these generous, gullible fellows? What is their explanation?' One explanation might be that they had taken the advice of Paul Johnson. This is what he said in July 1984, shortly after Robert Maxwell took over the Mirror Group: 'Maxwell is a hard man with a sharp nose for extravagance, waste and freeloading of any kind...I don't care a damn about his early business record or what the Board of Trade said about him umpteen years ago. That is all ancient history.'

Ancient history, as he should know better than most, has a habit of coming back to haunt us. Following the death of Lord Home, for instance, Johnson lamented the fact that there were no more 'gentlemen' and 'grandees' in the Conservative Party. 'That is why Conservatism is in danger of becoming the party of suburbia and sleaze.' Fair enough – except that in his book *The Offshore Islanders*, published in 1972, he had attacked the 'pernicious nonsense' and 'raging middle-class snobbery' that had created 'the grotesque cult of the "gentleman", assiduously propagated by renegade-progressives...' Similarly, whenever Johnson rails against the inaccuracy of gossip columnists – as he does, frequently – some of us recall what he wrote about gossip in the introduction to his *Oxford Book of Political Anecdotes*: 'Anecdotes are a valuable source of historical truth. Inaccurate in detail they may be, but more often than not they convey an essential fact about a great personage which more formal records ignore...I am always inclined to give an anecdote the benefit of the doubt: true (at least in spirit) until proved false.'

Digging deeper into ancient history, younger readers may be surprised to learn that he was a fervent admirer of the Paris student uprising in May 1968. 'The methods of the idealist intellectuals must be *la democratie de la rue*,' he declared in the *New Statesman*. 'The power of the bourgeois-communist or bourgeois-capitalist state will not surrender unless directly challenged. A wild theory? Yes: but it works!' The French, he concluded, 'have given birth to a new revolutionary spirit, which will ultimately enrich the lives of all of us'.

In spite of his ideological somersaults and backflips, however, there are some recurring characteristics. Although it is unimaginable that he would now applaud long-haired lefties who throw cobblestones at the police, he sometimes hints that he is still a street-fighter at heart. In his polemical book *Wake Up Britain!*, published as recently as 1994, he announced that the rulers of this country are weak cowards who can and should be overthrown. 'Cold steel, hot blood, a whiff of grapeshot, the roar of the mob – it is amazing how many things will scare them. It will not take much – or many – to get them on the run.'

Whether you agree with him or not – and few people can have followed his long career without parting company with him at some point – it's hard to resist his glorious and passionate inconsistency. If variety is the spice of life, Paul Johnson is our very own National Vindaloo.

(Unpublished article written for the London *Evening Standard*, 24 January 1996)

Better dead than Ted

WITHIN A COUPLE OF MONTHS, the electors of Bexley will be asked to return the octogenarian Sir Edward Heath to Parliament for yet another term. I hope that many of them were watching *Newsnight* last week when the old brute paid tribute to his dear friend Deng Xiaoping, the man who used tanks and machine-guns against thousands of peaceful protesters in Beijing eight years ago. 'There was a crisis in Tiananmen Square,' Heath recalled, 'after a month in which the civil authorities had defied and they took action about it very well.'

Old men forget, and Sir Edward has clearly forgotten what he told the House of Commons on 13 July 1989: 'How could those in authority have allowed the massacre to happen, or indeed authorized it?...I could not condone for one moment the massacre in Peking and the executions and shooting in the other cities that followed.' The amnesia set in soon afterwards. As early as October 1990, he was rebuking the great Professor Norman Stone for having the temerity to mention the massacre. 'There is,' Ted grumbled, 'nothing to be gained from constantly dwelling on the tragedy of Tiananmen Square.'

There is, however, plenty to be gained from sucking up to Chinese dictators. On his first visit to the country, in May 1974, Heath was met at the airport by 2,000 schoolgirls waving Union Jacks. He then enjoyed three days of friendly talks with Mao Zedong, Deng Xiaoping and Zhou Enlai, before departing with a pair of eighteenth-century vases and two giant pandas. As Heath's biographer, John Campbell, records: 'His unconcealed delight in his reception drew some cynicism: "Mao was the first person he had seen in months who was actually pleased to see him," a friend was said to have remarked unkindly.' After returning to the backbenches, he was hired as a consultant by the China Ocean Shipping Company, the China Investment and Development Fund and Kleinwort Benson China Management. He also joined the 'public review board' of Arthur Andersen, the accountancy firm, in which capacity he often visited the Chinese capital. 'My job,' he once explained, referring to his Beijing jaunts on behalf of Arthur Andersen, 'is to ensure that they maintain a high standard of ethics, integrity and performance.' No irony was intended.

Some people may suspect that Heath's business interests influenced his sycophantic attitude to Deng Xiaoping. This would be appallingly defamatory. Knowing his record, I am sure he would have been happy to defend the Butcher of Beijing even if he had had no financial incentive whatsoever.

(*Guardian*, 26 February 1997)

***

IF MARGARET THATCHER was the Iron Lady of British politics, Ted Heath is and always will be the Brass Neck. Having made a disgusting spectacle of himself on *Newsnight* after Deng Xiaoping's death, he now has the infernal cheek to rebuke those of us who accused him of sycophancy towards the Butcher of Beijing.

Last week I quoted Heath thus: 'There was a crisis in Tiananmen Square after a month in which the civil authorities had been defied and they took action about it very well.' This transcription, he now tells us, 'is absolutely wrong, as anyone who watched the interview would know'. The sentence actually ended after the words 'they took action about it'. His next sentence began: 'Very well, we can criticize it...' I have watched the interview half a dozen times, and I remain unconvinced. Here, without any punctuation at all, is what he said: 'There was a crisis in Tiananmen Square after a month in which the civil authorities had been defied and they took action about it very well (pause) we can criticize it...' In spoken English, a longish pause usually indicates the end of a sentence, or at least a semi-colon. If Sir Edward doesn't wish to be misunderstood, he really ought to take a few elocution lessons.

'This is not a pedantic point – it is a fundamental difference between truth and lies,' Heath complains. 'At the time of Tiananmen Square I made a speech in the House of Commons expressing my horror at the use of troops, which caused so many deaths – and I have been consistent in this view.' How often has he expressed this consistently held view? On *Newsnight* he was given plenty of opportunities to acknowledge the ghastliness of the massacre, but he refused to do so. Instead, he berated the brave and dignified pro-democracy campaigner Martin Lee for daring to mention China's disregard for human rights. 'The Asiatic countries have an entirely different view of political democracy from what we have in the West,' Heath announced grandly. 'What they are working on is not one man one vote as we have it but a system of consultation and argument and settlement and so on.' When Lee pointed out that some of the biggest Asian countries, including India and Japan, do in fact allow their citizens to vote, Heath accused him of being 'corrupt' and 'hypocritical'. 'The plain fact,' he added, 'is that the Chinese have different religious beliefs than what we have in the West' – as if this somehow proved that they were unfit for democracy.

After listening to Sir Edward gushing on about how much he liked and admired Deng Xiaoping, Jeremy Paxman gave him one more chance to condemn the events of June 1989: 'He killed rather a lot of people in Tiananmen Square, didn't he?' Did the former Prime Minister speak of his 'horror' at the deaths? Far from it. 'Well, of course this is just like the British,' he spluttered angrily. 'It's the only thing you can bring up and we're the only country that does still bring it up.' Not true, as he well knows: in Hong Kong there has been a ceremony of remembrance every year since 1989. But let Sir Edward continue, using his revised punctuation: 'There was a crisis in Tiananmen Square after a month in which the civil authorities had been defied and they took action about it. Very well, we can criticize it in exactly the same way as people criticize Bloody Sunday in Northern Ireland.' We now know that Heath does indeed criticize the 'action' in Tiananmen Square – which, of course, took place on the direct orders of Deng Xiaoping. So if we are to criticize Bloody

Sunday in 'exactly the same way', we must condemn the head of government who presided over it.

The date of Bloody Sunday was 30 January 1972. The Prime Minister at the time was Edward Heath. Happy now, Ted?

(Guardian, 5 March 1997)

The best of British

'MY REFUSAL TO fudge won me few friends,' Norman Tebbit boasted in his autobiography, *Upwardly Mobile*. It is how he would like us to see him – the lonely hero *contra mundum*, cussed and uncompromising. But it is only half true. Far from being unswayed by the roars of the groundlings, he has always been a shameless populist who plays to saloon-bar opinion – or, as he prefers to call it, 'the feelings of the average man and his family'. And, throughout a long political career, he has remained utterly certain that the average man and his family are thoroughgoing racists.

In 1969, while trying to persuade the Tories of Epping to adopt him as their parliamentary candidate, Tebbit told the selection committee that Commonwealth citizens were 'aliens without the right to come here except by invitation'. As a 'small, densely populated island with a closely integrated population living cheek by jowl sharing common ethics, ambitions and standards – and prejudices, too', Britain could not afford to 'import large numbers of immigrants' and 'allow them to set up foreign enclaves'.

He has been repeating this theme, with many ugly variations and embellishments, ever since. 'Would it upset you if I came to live next door to you?' the black television journalist Trevor Phillips asked him a few years ago. 'Why should it?' Tebbit answered, with that familiar sneer flickering on his lips. 'I am one of the very few English people that lives in my street in London.' It seemed unlikely that so few of his neighbours were born in Britain or had a British passport. But to Tebbit, apparently, there is no such creature as a black Briton. Last Sunday, talking to the indisputably white David Frost, Tebbit was rather more explicit. 'If you get different societies mixed up and living close, cheek by jowl, you will splinter our society,' he declared.

Full marks for consistency, at least. When the Emperor Claudius invaded Britain in AD 43, no doubt one of Tebbit's ancestors was warning that these Eyeties would outlaw the wearing of woad and smuggle Catullus's pornographic poetry into the national curriculum. When William the Conqueror was biffing his way through Sussex in 1066, a lone but prescient voice from Essex foretold that we would soon be chewing garlic and using bidets. Why, the filthy Frogs might even force us to call our children Norman...

Lord Tebbit's solution to the 'problem' of multiculturalism is not repatriation. 'No, not at all, the very reverse,' he told Frost. 'What we have to do with some of our more recent arrivals is imbue in them a sense that the Battle of Britain is part of their history and that we share that, otherwise we are not going to have a single society...You cannot have a whole load of different cultures in one society. You have one culture for one society.' During the 1980s Tebbit was the patron saint of both yuppies and lager louts, but I'm sure he wouldn't wish us to think that those youngsters represented his monocultural ideal. What, then, is this white British culture to which all must subscribe? Noticing that it encompasses Irvine Welsh and Andrew Lloyd Webber, Barbara Cartland and the Manic Street Preachers, newcomers may be understandably puzzled. Fortunately, help is at hand. Tebbit's autobiography is a most useful guidebook to those standards and values which he expects everyone to share.

'We enjoyed ourselves,' he writes of his days as an office-boy at the *Financial Times*. 'We were noisy and enthusiastic, particularly after lunchtime visits to city pubs.' Lesson One for the novice: drink a lot at lunchtime.

Tebbit did his national service in the RAF. 'Life in the mess was convivial,' he recalls. 'The tying together of the diners' shoelaces on opposite sides of the long trestle tables always led to chaos as officers leapt to their feet to drink the loyal toast – though the risk of being caught crawling under the table to perform the deed and being thoroughly kicked was pretty high. Mess games, always including such favourites as High Cockalorum, mess rugby and "around the room without touching the floor", normally followed dinner, becoming progressively wilder, usually until the mess secretary or the president closed the bar.' Lesson Two: if invited to dinner by an Englishman be sure to get drunk and tie his shoelaces together, to show how well you are assimilating yourself.

Though he was 'far more fond of the company of other males than girls', young Tebbit did have a few dates with a girl called Wendy Craig. 'For the last thirty-five or forty years I have seen her only through the TV screen, though with great admiration.' Lesson Three: study some of the uproarious sitcoms in which Wendy Craig has starred – *Butterflies, Nanny, Mother Makes Three* – and you too will learn to admire the famous British sense of humour.

After being demobbed from the air force, Tebbit joined the Herts and Essex Flying Club. A fellow member's Jaguar 'was the first car in which I exceeded 100mph on the road, following a dispute over his claim to "change down at ninety"...We acknowledged that alcohol and aeroplanes were a lethal combination but like most people at that time had a relaxed attitude to drinking and driving...Driving accidents and car write-offs were almost a part of the life!' Lesson Four: always have a few pints before driving a car. Police officers will respect this patriotic gesture.

'Another craze was indoor motor-cycling,' Tebbit continues. While he was riding his BSA Bantam up a flight of stairs, his friends loosened the carpet-clips and pulled the rug from under him, causing a spectacular crash. 'Remarkably, injuries in such escapades were few and little damage was caused. The injuries received scant sympathy, and the damage had to be paid for – a code of ethics well understood and decently honoured.' Lesson Five: remember the British sense of fair play, and don't blub or whine when you are crushed by a maniac on a motorbike.

Easy, isn't it? If you follow these simple rules, you too can be as brutish and mean-spirited – and quintessentially British – as Baron Tebbit of Chingford.

(*Guardian*, 8 October 1997)

A very minor Major

IAN MACLEOD'S FIRST LAW of politics was that all MPs are either bishops or bookies. It works, up to a point: Tony Blair is undoubtedly on the episcopal side, while John Prescott and Robin Cook could both have enjoyed prosperous careers as tick-tack men at Brighton racecourse. But only up to a point. Where, for instance, do we place John Major? When he is shouting the odds from his ludicrous soapbox, one naturally categorizes him as a bookie. But then he spoils it by coming over all pious. To deal with this problem, I have devised Wheen's first law of politics: the virtues pleaded in mitigation for Conservative leaders always turn out to be their worst vices. It may not be as neat as Macleod's formulation, but it does have the advantage of being true.

Let's try it on Margaret Thatcher. In her heyday, even her foes on the Left used to praise her consistency. 'Whatever you think of the old girl,' they would concede, 'at least she has the courage of her convictions.' If only. The European integration against which she now rants from her elder stateswoman's perch in the House of Lords is part of the process she herself set in train by signing the Single European Act. In spite of her noisy disapproval of the 'nanny state', it was she who forced us to wear safety belts in cars. For all her fine words about the beauty of competition, she bequeathed us all those ugly near-monopolies such as British Gas and the privatized water companies. She hated quangos, but created hundreds of new ones. In short, far from being a 'conviction politician', she was an opportunistic hypocrite.

Now let us apply Wheen's law to John Major. His clod-hopping gormlessness and dunderheaded dithering were apparent from the start, but even some Labour voters were prepared to allow him a few redeeming features. All of these have now been exploded:

'Say what you like about John Major, at least he's straight and honest – a palpably decent chap.' If the opinion polls are correct, there are still many people who cling to this belief. In fact, as my old sparring partner Paul Johnson has rightly pointed out, Major's government is the most corrupt administration of modern times. He has certainly set an all-comers' record for the number of ministers obliged to resign for one sleazy reason or another – and for the amount of money raised from dodgy millionaires. Major was quick to deny the allegation in Lord McAlpine's new book that he engineered a £500,000 donation from the unlovely Greek tycoon John Latsis; but I notice he hasn't issued a libel writ. Why not?

'Say what you like about John Major, at least he is loyal to his friends and colleagues.' Try telling that to the members of his own Cabinet who were denounced as 'bastards' – or to Tim Yeo, another of his many ministerial casualties. When Major heard that Yeo was giving an interview to the Mail on Sunday, he rang a senior executive at Associated Newspapers and urged him not to print the story. 'You shouldn't listen to Yeo,' the Prime Minister warned. 'He's a cunt.'

'Say what you like about Major, at least he's a nice man.' This seemed to be confirmed by his valedictory 'Goodnight – and God bless' at the end of that first Prime Ministerial broadcast during the Gulf War. Hence, I suppose, the frisson of excitement provoked by 'Bastardgate' (as it was immediately and inevitably called). The revelation that Major slagged off his comrades when he thought we weren't listening was as shocking as if Mother Teresa had been caught singing 'The Good Ship Venus' at a hen-night. Hence, too, the more recent sensation when he denounced our European partners as 'a bunch of shits'. For those who knew him, however, this evidence of touchiness and ill-temper came as no surprise. My own view of our supposedly sweet-natured PM was formed when a Tory veteran told me of an encounter with him at a City boardroom lunch in the 1970s, shortly after Major had been selected as the Tory candidate for Huntingdon. The host, a leading merchant banker, jocularly congratulated young John on his good fortune in landing the fourth-safest seat in Britain. 'Good luck?' Major shouted angrily, rising from his seat and banging his fist on the table. 'It wasn't luck. It was bloody hard work!' Whereupon he stormed out. 'Don't worry about it,' the host reassured his embarrassed guests. 'He's always doing that.' To judge by his petulant outburst after last week's disclosures in this newspaper, he still is.

'Say what you like about Major, he's still a Brixton boy at heart – an ordinary bloke who wears woolly jumpers when off-duty.' When I was six years old, I dreamed of becoming Prime Minister – or, better still, king – for all sorts of childish reasons: so that I could take revenge on the girl who used to pull my hair at infants' school; so that I could always get a seat at the Lord's Test match; so that I could use the apparatus of the state to track down my lost sweetheart, whose family had moved to another part of the country; so that I could ban junket from school menus. (What happened to junket, incidentally? It seems to have disappeared without my dictatorial assistance.) Unlike the rest of us, John Major has never quite shed these juvenile ambitions. I cannot remember a Prime Minister who took such obvious, greedy pleasure in the trappings and perks of office: installing himself in VIP seats at the Oval and Stamford Bridge; cherishing his party invitations from Andrew Lloyd Webber and Jeffrey Archer; dishing out CBEs and knighthoods to his childhood heroes; wallowing in the plush comforts of chauffeur-driven travel and weekends at Chequers.

And who can blame him? Lest we forget, this is a man who was turned down for a job as a London bus-conductor. If he weren't Prime Minister, no one would give him the time of day.

(*Guardian*, 26 March 1997)

***

JOHN MAJOR'S memoirs contain one genuine surprise – a photo captioned 'Supper with the Rolling Stones before their concert in Charlotte, North Carolina, October 1997'. The picture shows our ex-PM, in his smart blue blazer with brass buttons, sharing a joke with Keith Richards, who has one hand grasping a huge glass of bourbon and the other wrapped round Norma Major's shoulder.

Maddeningly, the book tells us nothing more about this unlikely friendship between the Humiliated Tory and the Human Laboratory. But one can't help brooding on the caprices of fate. Both Keef and John were born in 1943 and spent their formative years in the south London suburbs; had things turned out differently, Johnny Major and the Mugwumps might now be issuing a greatest hits CD while Lord Richards of Sidcup would be remembered as Britain's most unflappable Prime Minister.

He certainly couldn't have made a worse hash of the job than Major. Which would you prefer – the man who presided over Black Wednesday, or the man who gave us Ruby Tuesday?

(*Guardian*, 20 October 1999)

Bob-bob-bobbing along

TODOR ZHIVKOV, the Stalinist who ruled Bulgaria for thirty-five years and who is probably best known for his expertise in poisoned-umbrella technology, will go on trial in Sofia tomorrow. He is charged with 'grave malfeasance'. Since he was toppled in 1989, no one has had a good word to say for the old brute. As he complained last year, 'Zhivkov is to be blamed for everything.' (Like Arthur Scargill and Oliver North, Zhivkov often refers to himself in the third person.) Last week, in the first interview broadcast since his fall, he told Bulgarian television that 'the Todor Zhivkov case is a vandal act of certain political forces and figures...So far I have not laid the blame on anybody, but if I have a chance to speak at this engineered trial, I will speak, and I will speak my mind.'

I wonder whether he will mention the name of Robert Maxwell during the proceedings. For although Maxwell now likes to present himself as the friend of freedom in Eastern Europe, not so long ago he was an enthusiastic admirer and business partner of comrade Zhivkov and his government. In March 1985 the *Daily Mirror* revealed that Maxwell 'had just struck a huge deal with the Bulgarian government' to modernize the country's printing and packaging industries. (Strangely, in an interview with the *Independent on Sunday* last year, Maxwell said that he had not done any business in Eastern Europe until after the fall of the Berlin Wall. Perhaps he doesn't read his own newspaper.) To celebrate the occasion, a whole page of the *Mirror* was filled with an adulatory profile of Zhivkov – 'a tidy, impressive man...jokey style...wears his age so lightly...'

In the same year, Robert Maxwell's Pergamon Press published a 'second revised edition' of its 500-page hagiography *Todor Zhivkov: Statesman and Builder of New Bulgaria*. As Maxwell had explained in his foreword to the first edition, the book was intended 'to give the English-speaking reader the opportunity to learn of the heroic struggle of the Bulgarian people to free themselves from German occupation and to build a prosperous and happy nation under the leadership of the Bulgarian Communist Party and its General Secretary Todor Zhivkov'. It also included the transcript of a long interview by Maxwell with Zhivkov, the tone of which can be gauged from the first question: 'Dear Mr President, how do you explain the fact that you have been holding the highest political and state post in your country for such a long time?' Maxwell went on to praise Zhivkov's late daughter Lyudmila Zhivkova, a former Politburo member, for realizing 'the vital necessity to live according to the supreme laws of truth and beauty'. So enraptured was Maxwell by her work that on his return to England he created the Lyudmila Zhivkova Foundation – though no one from Maxwell's office has been able to explain to me precisely what this does.

Presumably Captain Robert Maxwell MC isn't a man who'd abandon his friends in their hour of need. So can we take it that he will appear at next week's trial as a character witness for dear Mr ex-President? His spokesman, Bob Cole, pondered this question for some hours before returning with a brief official statement: 'Robert Maxwell is in the United States.' That was all he would say on the subject.

Cole did reveal, however, that the Lyudmila Zhivkova Foundation is no more: Maxwell has renamed it 'The International Foundation St Cyril and St Methodius'. Whatever happened to the supreme laws of truth and beauty?

(*Independent on Sunday*, 24 February 1991)

***

ALL THE WORLD'S a stage; but few of us can hope to play quite so many parts as Lord Donoughue of Ashton – lecturer at the LSE, senior adviser to both Harold Wilson and Jim Callaghan, assistant editor of *The Times*, biographer of Herbert Morrison, life peer, head of research and investment policy at the bankers Grieveson Grant, and now a minister of agriculture in the Labour government.

There is one small embarrassment in this dazzling CV, an interlude when he sought the bubble reputation even in the cannon's mouth: 'Exec. Vice-Chm., London & Bishopsgate Internat. Investment Holdings, 1988–91.' The chairman of LBI at that time, one Robert Maxwell, used the company as a staging post for shares belonging to his employees' pension funds, which he then transferred to his other businesses. Now that Maxwell's auditors have been fined £3.5 million for failing to notice the old fraudster's legerdemain, Donoughue has some explaining to do. In an interview with *The Times* last Saturday, he said that he 'was duped, along with everyone else'. True, he did 'raise concerns' with Kevin Maxwell in April 1990. But this was merely 'a routine thing'. He resigned in April 1991, seven months before the plundering of the pension funds was publicly exposed. There was no cause for him to 'blow the whistle', since he was 'unaware of any wrongdoing'. Good old Donoughue: so trusting, so unsuspecting, so generous with the benefit of the doubt. And Maxwell was most generous in return. He paid the LBI vice-chairman a salary of £180,000, an annual contribution of £36,000 towards his pension, plus a £200,000 Christmas bonus.

What were those 'concerns' in 1990? For further details we turn to Maxwell's great biographer Tom Bower, who reveals that Donoughue was prompted by a colleague to write to Kevin Maxwell on 5 April, demanding that 'improprieties' must stop. 'I will not stay with an operation conducted in such a way.' (This is what he now calls 'a routine thing'.) The improprieties continued, of course. But Donoughue knew nothing about them until April 1991, when he sent a memo to Robert Maxwell about the stock-lending, warning that there was 'a reasonable prosecution case against LBI'. He handed in his notice the same month – though in fact he stayed on until the summer, negotiating a £280,000 pay-off. Maxwell drowned on 5 November and soon afterwards the truth about his crimes was revealed.

No thanks to Donoughue, however, who had remained silent throughout. Using a favourite New Labour phrase, he informs *The Times* that he is 'totally relaxed' about his record at LBI. I fear that he is telling the truth. 'No shame, no blame' is the motto of Maxwell's former associates, and it seems to work: almost all of them have survived, indeed flourished, without a blemish on their characters.

Take Helen Liddell MP, who claimed in 1994, 'I never worked for Robert Maxwell. It is a smear to suggest I was ever employed by him.' More recently, in an interview with the *Sunday Telegraph*, she said that although she was Maxwell's director of corporate affairs in Scotland from 1988 until 1991 she scarcely ever saw the man, because 'I was 450 miles away'. She added that it had come as a complete surprise when Maxwell rang to offer her a job.

The truth is slightly different. On 26 October 1987 Liddell sent a letter to Maxwell asking if he had any vacancies ('I hope you do not find this approach impertinent'), and after joining the board of his Scottish companies she became slavishly devoted to her benefactor. During the 1988 Commonwealth Games in Edinburgh she clung to him so closely that at one point she even followed him into the gents' lavatory – a scene that was recorded for posterity by a BBC TV documentary crew. In the next two years she often accompanied Maxwell on trips abroad and in 1991 was involved in the Mirror Group flotation, which is the subject of a DTI inquiry.

None of this has done her any harm. She is now a minister, often described as one of Tony Blair's 'high flyers'. How could she have guessed that Maxwell was a criminal, merely because he had the word 'crook' tattooed on his forehead? Like Lord Donoughue she was no more than a well-rewarded dupe – defined in the *OED* as 'a person who allows himself to be deceived or deluded'.

But at least one person had no such delusions, since he received advance warning of the crime. Vanni Treves, senior partner of the City lawyers McFarlanes, was consulted on 6 August 1991 by Peter Laister, a director of Maxwell Communications Corporation, who had become increasingly alarmed by the boss's habit of using the company as a private piggy bank. Treves's advice is recorded in Tom Bower's book: 'Don't make any statement.' Laister, who assumed that it was his duty as a director to expose Maxwell's looting, was puzzled. 'Who can we tell?' he asked. 'Nobody,' Treves replied. 'You must exercise absolute caution.' Laister returned to the lawyer's office two days later, accompanied by three other directors who were worried by Cap'n Bob's grand larceny. Once again Treves told them to keep quiet. 'You're in a dangerous position. You could be held liable for breaches of the Companies' Acts, which require you to protect the shareholders' interests. You must urgently get all the facts, but don't talk to anyone, including the auditors. Talking to others could mean leaks...' If Treves had advised them to go public, Maxwell might have been stopped in his tracks. Instead, the Cap'n was allowed to carry on stealing for another three months – until he fell off his yacht and the MCC enterprise sank with him.

There were, however, many survivors. Helen Liddell and Lord Donoughue are ministers of the Crown. Alastair Campbell, who defended Maxwell so forcefully after his death, is the chief gatekeeper at 10 Downing Street. Peter Jay, who as Maxwell's 'chief of staff' strove to prevent journalists from publishing the truth and hired private detectives to spy on Tom Bower, is himself now a senior journalist with the BBC. Oh, and last year the government appointed Vanni Treves – who cheerfully confessed to having 'little familiarity with the media world' – as the new chairman of Channel 4.

(*Guardian*, 10 February 1999)

The world's his playground

H AVE YOU SEEN the new television commercial for *The Economist* magazine? In case you missed it, the storyline goes like this. An airline passenger, Mr Burnside, finds himself sitting next to a familiar figure. 'Hey!' a voice-over chirrups. 'It's Henry Kissinger! Ready for a good chat?' Burnside shrinks back aghast – from which we are meant to infer that he hasn't read *The Economist* and is therefore out of his conversational depth. A likelier explanation, however, is that he doesn't wish to be trapped on a plane with a liar and mass-murderer.

It seems odd to choose President Nixon's old Secretary of State to front an expensive sales campaign. Can we now expect to see Saddam Hussein advertising dogfood, or General Ratko Mladic explaining the advantages of double-glazing? What makes it all the odder is that younger viewers probably have no idea who Henry Kissinger is, while the rest of us remember him only too well as a man who brought death and destruction to any country unfortunate enough to incur his attentions: Cambodia, Cyprus, Bangladesh, East Timor, Angola, Chile – the full list would take up most of this page.

But then *The Economist* has always been a strange institution. A few newspapers, in their more vainglorious moments, might like to think that they run the country; *The Economist* knows it does. From their tower block in St James's, the staff look down on Whitehall both literally and metaphorically. Many of them go on to senior posts in government or industry – Sarah Hogg to Downing Street, Rupert Pennant-Rea to the Bank of England, Andrew Knight to News International. It is this certainty of its own importance that has taken the mag's circulation from just over 100,000 in the 1970s to more than half a million today. In the words of a previous advertising campaign: 'I never read *The Economist*. Management trainee. Aged forty-two.' Insecure, ambitious middle-managers hastily invest in a subscription, convinced that it will transform them into cigar-chomping captains of industry.

Or even, perhaps, into world leaders such as Henry Kissinger. One advert from the early 1990s reprinted a photograph of George Bush rushing for his helicopter, clutching a copy of *The Economist*. The paper's executives were immensely pleased at this confirmation of its status. Had they paused for thought, they might have twigged that a disastrous American administration is not something for which most self-respecting journalists would take the credit. But writers on *The Economist* aren't journalists in the normal sense of the word. What it claims to offer is not news but 'intelligence'; not so much a magazine, more one's very own think-tank. When it was founded, in 1843, the paper promised to enter 'a severe contest between intelligence, which presses forward, and an unworthy timid ignorance, obstructing our progress'. Since then the manifesto has become even more glib, following the edict of Geoffrey Crowther, editor between 1938 and 1956: 'Simplify, then exaggerate.'

In the flip, narrow mind of *The Economist*, deregulation is the cure for everything and free-market solutions are always best. If its editorials often read like essays by a particularly bumptious Oxford undergraduate, this is because they are, more or less; many staff join straight from the varsity, untainted by exposure to life outside seminar rooms before they start laying down the law to Mozambique or the Baltic Republics. Until recently the main recruiting agent was R. W. Johnson, a don at Magdalen – which may explain why four of the nine short-listed candidates for the editorship in 1993 were Magdalen alumni.

Though not an Oxford man himself, Kissinger used to be a professor at Harvard, which is the next best thing. Like *The Economist*, he is an inveterate power-groupie who treats the world as an adventure playground for ethics-free games of realpolitik. Since retiring from office, he has earned a small fortune as a pundit for American newspapers and television – and a far larger fortune as a 'consultant' to large corporations for whom the bottom dollar is indeed the bottom dollar. After the Tiananmen Square massacre of 1989, for instance, he wrote a syndicated column attacking Congress for imposing sanctions on China 'in reaction to events entirely within its own domestic jurisdiction'. For good measure, he added that 'no government in the world would have tolerated having the main square of its capital occupied for eight weeks by tens of thousands of demonstrators.' What he forgot to tell his readers – but the *Wall Street Journal* revealed shortly afterwards – was that he had a powerful financial incentive, since he had been negotiating with the Chinese government on behalf of H. J. Heinz, Atlantic Richfield, ITT and several other American corporations.

By starring in this week's commercial, Kissinger is repaying an old favour. Seventeen years ago, he claimed in *The Economist* that the right-wing coup against Prince Sihanouk's Cambodian government in 1970 'took us completely by surprise' – the 'us' in question being himself, Richard Nixon and the American government. This provoked a letter to the magazine from Samuel Thornton, who had worked for American naval intelligence in Saigon and distinctly remembered planning Sihanouk's overthrow with the approval of 'the highest level of government' in Washington. *Economist* readers were not given the opportunity to study Thornton's interesting account: the then editor, Kissinger's chum Andrew Knight, refused to print the letter, explaining to Thornton that he had personally checked the allegations and found them to be untrue.

Knight's investigation consisted largely of conversations with two senior figures. One was Richard Helms – who as director of the CIA at the time of the coup was bound to deny the story. The other was Kissinger. As the American reporter Seymour Hersh has commented, 'If all journalists used Knight's method of asking those at the very top about their possible misdeeds, none of the major investigative stories of the past two decades would have become public.' *The Economist* knows no other method. It is accustomed to dealing only with 'those at the very top' – as is Kissinger. No wonder they love each other so dearly; and no wonder Kissinger's fellow passenger in the TV commercial looks so terrified. If Mr Burnside were a small and defenceless country, Kissinger would probably have invaded him by now.

(*Guardian*, 2 October 1996)

***

READING THE LIST of guests and homage-payers – Henry Kissinger, Margaret Thatcher, Taki, Paul Johnson, Rupert Murdoch, John Aspinall, Jonathan Aitken, Pat Buchanan, Chief Buthelezi – at Sir Jimmy Goldsmith's memorial service recently, I wondered when such a ripe collection of rogues and brutes had last gathered under the same roof. Then it occurred to me: many of these characters, and some even ghastlier ones, have also been under the roof of 10 Downing Street since Tony Blair moved in.

Margaret Thatcher came to call shortly after the general election, dispensing her expert advice on European policy. Paul Johnson has been a regular visitor, as has Rupert Murdoch – who took the precaution of arriving at the back entrance for his last tête-à-tête a few weeks ago, safe from the prying lenses of the gutter press. Then there was Blair's notorious invitation to Bernie Ecclestone and the malodorous Max Mosley. 'Who next?' you may ask. 'Henry Kissinger? Saddam Hussein? Jeffrey Archer?' Right first time. Last month, almost unnoticed, Dr Kissinger popped in to Number 10 for a chat with the Prime Minister. The only mention of this historic encounter came in a brief item from the Press Association, which noted that 'he and Tony Blair are friends'. According to a Downing Street spokesman, the two men spent half an hour 'looking across the spectrum of international relations'.

It's quite a spectrum. Let us recall the fine words of this year's Labour manifesto: 'Labour wants Britain to be respected in the world for the integrity with which it conducts its foreign relations. We will make the protection of human rights a central part of our foreign policy.' Perhaps Blair and Kissinger discussed violations of human rights in East Timor, which has been occupied illegally by Indonesian troops since 1975. The invasion took place just one day after Kissinger and President Gerald Ford visited Indonesia – and, as his biographer Walter Isaacson has revealed, Kissinger 'knew from US intelligence of Indonesia's planned action, which violated the laws governing its purchases of American arms, but...was quietly content to permit the Timor rebellion to be suppressed, so the administration did nothing to stop the invasion'. More than 100,000 residents of East Timor (almost a seventh of the population) were killed. After returning to Washington, the Secretary of State 'raised a little bit of hell with his staff' – not because of the deaths, by which he appeared unmoved, but because the state department had sent him a memo pointing out that Indonesia's use of American weapons was an outrage which would require an embargo against Jakarta. 'That will leak in three months,' Dr K raged, 'and it will come out that Kissinger overruled his pristine bureaucrats and violated the law...'

Since Tony Blair is a polite host, no doubt he avoided embarrassment by steering the conversation away from those areas where his guest had disgraced himself. But, rather like Basil Fawlty trying not to mention the war, he must have found it hard to think of anything else to talk about. Cambodia? A definite no-no, since Kissinger bombed its citizens to smithereens without troubling to inform the American Congress. Cyprus? Another taboo subject: as Christopher Hitchens proves conclusively in his new book, *Hostage to History: Cyprus from the Ottomans to Kissinger*, the old thug was directly responsible for the island's partition. On 13 August 1974, he declared that the Turkish community needed 'a greater degree of autonomy'. Like the Indonesian government a year later, the Turks recognized a green light when they saw one; the very next morning their army set about occupying the whole of northern Cyprus – creating the pariah state that is now best known as Asil Nadir's bolthole. Since Kissinger's betrayal of Cyprus was aided and abetted by a Labour government in London, Blair would probably wish to forget the whole business.

Angola, Chile, Bangladesh? No, no, no: Kissinger brought death and destruction in all these places. I hope Blair kept well away from China, too, where Kissinger displayed his own commitment to the 'protection and promotion of human rights' by defending the Tiananmen Square massacre in 1989 while modestly forbearing to declare his own financial interest. As Walter Isaacson points out: 'Kissinger's relationship with the Deng regime was such that he could bring clients and guests to China and be met by the top leadership, a highly marketable asset.' Quite so: why let morality stand in the way of the all-conquering market? And now that Kissinger can be met by the 'top leadership' in London, he becomes more marketable than ever.

Let us be charitable. Tony Blair may be an innocent who paid no attention to world affairs throughout the 1960s and 1970s – though you'd think someone in Downing Street would vaguely remember Kissinger's name and sound the alarm. Or Blair may believe that the deadly Doctor has mellowed with age and become a benign international statesman: New Labour, New Kissinger.

It won't work. You can put a great white shark into a goldfish pond, but it remains a shark for all that. I'm reminded of the wise remark from an American politician when Kissinger's old chum Tricky Dicky was attempting, yet again, to relaunch himself as the New Nixon: 'There is no new Nixon. Only the old Nixon, a little older.'

(*Guardian*, 10 December 1997)

Index